The Swift Path

The Wisdom Culture Series

The *Wisdom Culture Series* is published by Wisdom Publications in association with the Foundation for the Preservation of the Mahayana Tradition (FPMT). Under the guidance of Lama Zopa Rinpoche, the series provides English-language readers with key works for the study and cultivation of the Mahayana Buddhist path, especially works of masters within the lineage of Lama Tsongkhapa and the Geluk school of Tibetan Buddhism. "Wisdom culture," an expression frequently used by Lama Yeshe, is a Dharma culture rooted in wisdom and compassion. The *Wisdom Culture Series* is intended to support this vision by transmitting the timeless wisdom of the Dharma through authoritative and accessible publications.

Volumes:

The Middle-Length Treatise on the Stages of the Path to Enlightenment, Tsongkhapa

The Power of Mantra, Lama Zopa Rinpoche

The Swift Path, Paṇchen Losang Yeshé

More volumes to come!

• THE WISDOM CULTURE SERIES •

THE SWIFT PATH

A Meditation Manual on the Stages of the Path to Enlightenment

Paṇchen Losang Yeshé

Translated by Szegee Toh

Foreword by Lama Zopa Rinpoche

Wisdom

Wisdom Publications, Inc.
199 Elm Street
Somerville, MA 02144 USA
wisdomexperience.org

Library of Congress Cataloging-in-Publication Data
Names: Blo-bzang-ye-shes, Panchen Lama II, 1663–1737, author. | Toh, Szegee, translator.
Title: The swift path: a meditation manual on the stages of the path to enlightenment / Paṇchen Losang Yeshé; translated by Szegee Toh.
Description: First edition. | Somerville: Wisdom Publications, 2023. | Series: Wisdom culture series | Includes bibliographical references and index.
Identifiers: LCCN 2022025026 (print) | LCCN 2022025027 (ebook) | ISBN 9781614298250 (hardcover) | ISBN 9781614298502 (ebook)
Subjects: LCSH: Meditation—Buddhism. | Lam-rim. | Dge-lugs-pa (Sect)—Doctrines. | Spiritual life—Buddhism.
Classification: LCC BQ5612 .B58 2023 (print) | LCC BQ5612 (ebook) | DDC 294.3/4435—dc23/eng/20220723
LC record available at https://lccn.loc.gov/2022025026
LC ebook record available at https://lccn.loc.gov/2022025027

ISBN 978-1-61429-825-0 ebook ISBN 978-1-61429-850-2

27 26 25 24 23
5 4 3 2 1

Cover design by Jess Morphew. Interior design by Gopa & Ted 2.

Printed on acid-free paper that meets the guidelines for permanence and durability of the Production Guidelines for Book Longevity of the Council on Library Resources.

Printed in the United States of America.

Contents

THE STAGES OF THE PATH OF PERSONS WITH GREAT CAPACITY

EPILOGUE

APPENDIXES

Foreword

WHAT IS THE IMPORTANCE of this text, the *Swift Path* by Paṇchen Losang Yeshé? To talk straight, millions and millions of people have depression. Why is that? I believe that the fundamental reason is because they lack an understanding of the meaning of life. In most cases, they haven't met the Dharma, the path to enlightenment, so they don't know the happiness that comes from practicing it. There are also people who have met the graduated path to enlightenment, the *lamrim*, but because they do not really practice it, the lamrim remains on paper; it does not go into their heart. And when, due to past karma, a problem involving an attachment to the happiness of this life arises, say their wife leaves them for someone else, they cannot bear it. They may even have an intellectual understanding of the lamrim, but without having really practiced it in their heart, they cannot renounce their attachment to their wife when she leaves them, or they become consumed by distress when someone important to them dies. It feels like they are the only person in the world experiencing that kind of suffering; with attachment, it can feel like that. In this state, they are vulnerable because of their past karma, their past harmful actions, and some people may even kill themselves in their extreme state.

Suicides even happened among the residents of the refugee camp in Buxa Duar, India, where, after escaping from Tibet, I lived for eight years and studied a little bit of philosophy. During that time, there was a monk who was a pūjā leader. After an influential person who had helped Tibet passed away, the Tibetans in general and the monks in particular were very upset. It was perhaps after that that he took his own life at a place on the way to Pasangkar, where I went many times along with some other monks to get injections for tuberculosis. On a mountain where there had been a landslide, the pūjā leader hanged himself. His body was found hanging from a high branch with a rope around his neck.

Likewise, when America was fighting in Iraq, every minute of the soldiers' lives was uncertain. They saw many acts of violence. Because of this, when the soldiers who survived returned home to see their families, their minds were totally disturbed. They couldn't see any meaning in life. I met one of these American soldiers at my retreat cave in Lawudo, Nepal. He was a very intelligent, highly trained soldier who found out about Lawudo on the internet, and he happened to be in Lawudo while I was there. I called him to come to my cave so that I could ask him some questions. He was someone who didn't talk much, but he told me that the American government introduced the returned soldiers to mindfulness, which comes from Buddhism, because it makes the mind peaceful. I think the idea behind it was that by not thinking about the past and future, and by keeping the mind still, people feel a little bit better.

When people don't know the meaning of life, and don't know the happiness that comes from practicing the Dharma, they then experience unbelievable problems and unhappiness; they become chronically depressed, unable to recover. I heard once about a man in England who had been sick with depression for twenty-five years. He had been to see many doctors, but nothing helped. However, one day, when he was working in a vegetable garden, he tried to think that he was doing it for others. By this intention to use his life to benefit others, to work for others, to serve others, he was able to change his mind, and only then did his depression go away. Like "An apple a day keeps the doctor away," "A thought to benefit others a day keeps depression away."

What sort of Dharma should you practice? Phabongkha Dechen Nyingpo's *Liberation in the Palm of Your Hand* says:

> The Dharma you practice should be the sublime Mahāyāna, which leads fortunate capable beings to buddhahood. It should be the tradition of the two great charioteers, Nāgārjuna and Asaṅga. It should be the profound instruction drawing out the essence of the thought of the glorious, unequaled Lama Atiśa and the great Lama Tsongkhapa, the Dharma king of the three realms. It should set out all the vital points of the essence of the 84,000 teachings, without anything missing, as stages of practice for one person to achieve enlightenment.

Therefore, you should first make sure that the Dharma that you are going to study and practice is the main path traveled by all the buddhas of the three times—past, present, and future. The very heart of the 84,000 teachings taught by the Buddha, when condensed, is the holy Dharma that is the lamrim, the graduated path, which includes both the profound and vast stages. The five great treatises (on Prajñāpāramitā, Madhyamaka, Abhidharma, Pramāṇa, and Vinaya) that form the core curriculum of Geluk monasteries are elaborations of this holy Dharma. If you follow this path, like the buddhas of the three times, you will also be able to achieve buddhahood, the total cessation of obscurations and the completion of realizations.

If, instead, you follow a path that the holy beings of the past did not practice, you risk reaching a very strange place. You might experience the sufferings of the lower realms and the general sufferings of saṃsāra for eons, with no chance for enlightenment. Therefore, before you rush to devour the Dharma that you intend to practice, like a dog rushes to food, you should thoroughly examine it. For, as Jamgön Sakya Paṇḍita said:

> However much this life goes wrong,
> there is neither harm nor benefit to your next life.
> But if you meet a wrong Dharma,
> all your future lives will go wrong.

If something else in your life goes wrong, even if you die and your consciousness is separated from your body, your consciousness will not necessarily go to the lower realms, where you would suffer for eons and eons; you might still go to a pure land or take a higher rebirth. But if you meet and practice a wrong Dharma and follow a wrong path, this could destroy your future lives for eons upon eons because of the negative imprints and habits it creates. You would not meet the Dharma and would not meet a virtuous friend for many lifetimes; you would instead experience great suffering. Do not be like many who, in my experience, practice whatever sounds good and makes them happy right now, never examining the nature of the teachings they are going to practice and where those teachings will lead them.

The instructions that you follow should be complete, with nothing missing, and unmistaken, and you should also be able to endure hardships to practice them. Otherwise, your effort will be mostly useless, in that you will not gain realizations, such as renunciation of the attachment to this life, and you will be unable to achieve enlightenment. As Milarepa said:

> Without meditating on the meaning of the instructions of the oral lineage,
> even if you cling to a retreat place, you will only torture yourself.

Milarepa was a lay person who achieved enlightenment in his lifetime during these degenerate times. After his father died, his aunt and uncle mistreated his family, causing his mother to advise Milarepa to learn black magic. He did so, and later, when the aunt and uncle were hosting a wedding at their house, Milarepa caused rocks from the mountain to crash down upon the house, utterly destroying it. The wedding guests upstairs and the animals downstairs were all killed.

Seeing what he had done, Milarepa felt great sadness and went to see his black magic teacher, who suggested that if he wanted to practice the Dharma, he should go to Lama Marpa. Upon finding him, Milarepa offered his body, speech, and mind. However, Marpa did not give him teachings for many years. Instead, he advised Milarepa to build a nine-story tower by himself (without any help from coolies!). After he built the tower, Marpa had him take it down and put all the stones back where he had found them, and this whole process was repeated two more times. After the third time, Marpa's wife insisted that Marpa now give teachings to Milarepa. From Marpa's side, he wanted Milarepa to bear hardships for even longer so that Milarepa would become enlightened much faster. But because his wife pushed him so much, Marpa, himself an enlightened being, manifested the maṇḍala of the deity and gave Milarepa initiation and teachings. Marpa then sent Milarepa to the mountains to do retreat. Bearing much hardship, Milarepa followed his guru's instructions exactly, while subsisting on only nettles—without even any chili or salt! As a result, Milarepa became enlightened in that very life.

Just as the source of a river is traced back to a snow mountain, the source of the Dharma that you practice should trace back to Guru Śākyamuni Buddha, the founder of unmistaken teachings. Without an authentic source for the Dharma, even if you practice for a thousand years, you will not generate even one valid realization. It would be like wishing for butter by churning water. Thus the Dharma that you practice should have all three of these qualities: it should have been taught by the Buddha, the Omniscient One; it should have been examined well with quotations and logic and verified by the ārya paṇḍitas of India; and it should have been actualized by yogis.

Many people in this world think that they are Buddhists when they don't even have refuge in the Buddha, Dharma, and Saṅgha. The definition of a Buddhist is someone who has taken refuge from their heart by totally relying on the Buddha, Dharma, and Saṅgha, but these people don't even recite a refuge prayer before they meditate. They don't even have a statue of the Buddha in their house. When they meditate on emptiness, their meditation falls into either eternalism or nihilism, as it's not the emptiness of the Middle Way. With nihilism, they think that nothing exists: there is no I, there is no action, there is no object, there is no saṃsāra, there is no nirvāṇa.

One time when I was in Taiwan, I met a young man whose guru accepted only one disciple, who was him. He was trying hard to meditate, but his meditation on emptiness was contemplating that nothing exists. To tease him, I asked him, "Why do you go to the bathroom if nothing exists?" If nothing exists it means that there is no person who needs to urinate or defecate, no food or drink that was consumed, no urine or feces to expel, and no toilet in which to expel them. In the same way, there is no Buddha, Dharma, and Saṅgha. There is no Buddha to guide you to liberation from saṃsāra. There is no Dharma to practice. There is no Saṅgha to help you practice. It all becomes very funny. You don't exist and nor do your parents, brothers and sisters, husband, or wife. None of them exists.

In a sūtra, the Buddha instructed Ārya Kātyāyana, saying:

> Kātyāyana, why do most people in this world strongly cling to existence or nonexistence—that is, to eternalism or nihilism? Clinging like that, they are not free from birth, old age, sickness, death, depression, lamenting, suffering, mental unhappiness, and fighting.

In short, they cannot completely abandon the root of the oceans of suffering of saṃsāra, the ignorance that holds the I and the aggregates to be truly existent. They then cannot be liberated from saṃsāra. For eons upon eons, they must experience countless sufferings in the lower realms.

Therefore, if you contemplate extensively, you will see that having an opportunity to listen to, reflect on, and meditate on the complete and unmistaken teachings, which are like refined gold, of Guru Śākyamuni Buddha, Nāgārjuna, Candrakīrti, and Lama Tsongkhapa is unbelievably fortunate. It is more precious than the whole sky filled with wish-granting jewels.

For this reason, for your whole life—however many years, months, weeks, days, minutes, and seconds you have left to live—you should generate great happiness and rejoice in your good fortune. You are like a blind man who has found in the garbage a wish-granting jewel. If you do not meet the teachings of the graduated path to enlightenment, the heart of the whole entire Buddhadharma, which is like an ocean, you will never achieve liberation from saṃsāra, and you will never achieve enlightenment. As it says in Phabongkha Dechen Nyingpo's *Opening the Door to the Excellent Path*:

> This is because with renunciation, every action you do with your body, speech, or mind becomes a cause of liberation; with bodhicitta, every action you do becomes a cause of enlightenment; and with right view, every action you do becomes a remedy to saṃsāra. If your actions of body, speech, and mind are not conjoined with these three principal aspects of the path to enlightenment, even if you meditate on the cakras, winds, and drops; on *mahāmudrā*, the great seal; on *dzokchen*, the great completion; or on the generation and completion stages of tantra, they all become a cause of saṃsāra. None of them becomes the slightest cause of liberation and enlightenment.
>
> Kadampa Geshé Phuchungwa said to Kadampa Geshé Chen Ngawa, "Which would you choose? To be expert in the five great knowledges, achieve stable concentration, have the five clairvoyances, and achieve the eight siddhis? Or, on the other hand, to have a stable understanding of Lama Atiśa's instructions, such that no one can change your mind, even though you have not exactly actualized them in your heart?"
>
> Kadampa Geshé Chen Ngawa answered, "Master, leaving aside generating the lamrim realizations in my heart, I would choose just facing toward the lamrim, wondering what it is. I have been expert in the five great knowledges, been able to concentrate for eons without distraction, had the five clairvoyances, and achieved the eight siddhis numberless times in the past, but I have not yet passed beyond saṃsāra. If I find definite understanding of Lama Atiśa's graduated path to enlightenment, I will definitely turn away from saṃsāra."

Phabongkha Dechen Nyingpo's *Liberation in the Palm of Your Hand* says:

> When you examine it, you will find there is no holy Dharma that is more sublime than this graduated path to enlightenment. Even the profound qualities of Secret Mantra Vajrayāna depend on the graduated path to enlightenment. Without generating the three principal aspects of the path to enlightenment in your mind, you cannot achieve enlightenment in one life by practicing the tantric path. I myself have indeed heard of many supposedly profound pure visions, Dharma treasures, and so forth from the past, but although there appear to be many wonderful collections of tantric activities and so forth, there do not seem to be any that are a way to bring forth experience of the three principal aspects of the path or that are an instruction that in essence has special qualities.
>
> What is called the *lamrim* is not made up by Lama Tsongkhapa, Lama Atiśa, and so forth. It has been transmitted from the fully enlightened Buddha alone. If you understand that, whether it has the name *lamrim* in the title or not, you will see that all the teachings of the Buddha are the lamrim.

And in relation to Tsongkhapa's *Great Treatise on the Stages of the Path to Enlightenment*, Phabongkha Dechen Nyingpo explained:

> Lama Tsongkhapa composed the requesting prayer [to the lineage gurus of the lamrim] *Opening the Door to the Supreme Path* at the base of a lion-like rockface at Radreng to the north [of Lhasa]. Whenever he invoked and made requests to an image of Lama Atiśa with the holy head tilted to the side, he had a vision of all the gurus of the lamrim lineage discussing Dharma with each other. In particular, for a month Lama Tsongkhapa had visions of Lama Atiśa and [the Kadampa geshés] Dromtönpa, Potowa, and Sharawa. In the end, the other three absorbed into Lama Atiśa, who put his hand on Lama Tsongkhapa's crown and said, "Work for the teachings of the Buddha, and I will help you." That means Atiśa was the one who persuaded Lama Tsongkhapa to write his *Great Treatise on the Stages of the Path*

> *to Enlightenment*. Lama Tsongkhapa then composed the *Great Treatise* up to and including the section on calm abiding. Later, having been persuaded by Mañjuśrī, he composed the section on great insight. Therefore, leaving aside other considerations, know that in dependence on those who persuaded Lama Tsongkhapa to write it, the *Great Treatise* is a treasury of blessings.

The meaning of the lamrim was elaborated on by Guru Śākyamuni Buddha, the paṇḍitas of India, and the great enlightened beings of Tibet, including Lama Tsongkhapa. Because the basis of the lamrim tradition is Lama Atiśa's *Lamp for the Path to Enlightenment*, in *Liberation in the Palm of Your Hand* Phabongkha Dechen Nyingpo set out the elaborate life story of Lama Atiśa. After that, he continued by explaining that this teaching, the graduated path to enlightenment, has four great qualities and three special qualities, making it much more special than other teachings. The explanation that follows comes from Phabongkha Rinpoché.

The first great quality is that it allows you to realize that all the teachings of the Buddha are without contradiction. If taken literally, the Lesser Vehicle, the Great Vehicle, the Vinaya, and the Secret Mantra Vehicle may appear to contradict each other, but because they are all in reality only methods for one person to achieve enlightenment, they are without contradiction. It is like a sick person who goes to the doctor with a high fever. The doctor may give one set of advice initially, but later, when the symptoms change, may advise just the opposite. Although the two sets of advice do indeed appear to be contradictory, both are necessary for the one sick person to recover. Like this, all the subjects of the graduated path are practices for one person to achieve enlightenment.

The second great quality of the lamrim is that it allows every single teaching of the Buddha to appear as an instruction for practice. If you do not meet something like this graduated path to enlightenment, then some of the teachings of the Buddha and the commentaries on them will appear as practical while others will not. Moreover, regarding the gurus who revealed the instructions for practice in this world, there is none higher than Śākyamuni Buddha, and the highest instructions for practice are the supreme teachings of the Buddha. As Maitreya's *Sublime Continuum* says:

> Therefore, in the world, there is no one wiser than the Buddha.
> Only the Omniscient One knows every single sublime reality just as it is; others do not.
> Therefore, do not mess with whatever sūtras were laid out by the Sage himself,
> because that would destroy the Buddha's teachings and harm the holy Dharma.

So, if not all of the teachings of the Buddha and their commentaries appear to you as instructions for practice, it is because you have not understood the meaning of the graduated path to enlightenment. But by understanding the meaning of the graduated path, you will know that all the great scriptures, the Buddha's teachings and the commentaries, are included in the lamrim, and that they are to be integrated into your practice.

The third great quality of the lamrim is that it allows you to easily discern the view of the Buddha. The Buddha's teachings and their commentaries are sublime instructions for practice. Their subject matter is the ultimate view of the Buddha. However, without depending on the guru's instructions, such as those on the graduated path to enlightenment, you will not find the ultimate view of the Buddha by depending on those great scriptures. Even if you are able to find it, it will take a long time and you will undergo extremely great hardships to do so. By depending on this lamrim, without any hardship you will easily find the view of the Buddha that is taught in those great scriptures.

If you ask what that view of the Buddha is, Dakpo Jampal Lhundrup (1845–1919) said it should be taken in general to be the paths of beings of the three capabilities and, in particular, the three principal aspects of the path to enlightenment. That is definite. Lama Tsongkhapa clearly explained the view of the Prāsaṅgika Madhyamaka school as the ultimate view of the Buddha. In *Three Principal Aspects of the Path*, he said:

> As long as these two understandings are seen as separate—
> of *appearance*, unbetraying dependent relation,
> and *emptiness*, the absence of all positions—
> then you have not realized the Buddha's intent.

This directly says that if you do not realize the right view, the Prāsaṅgika Madhyamaka view, you will not realize the view of the Buddha. It implies that if you do realize it, you will find the view of the Buddha. For example, the great scriptures are like an ocean. The view of the Buddha, such as the three principal aspects of the path to enlightenment, is like a jewel in that ocean. The lamrim is like a ship. The guru who reveals it is like a captain. Even though there are jewels in the ocean, if you enter it without depending on a ship, besides not obtaining any jewels, there is the danger that you will lose your life. Similarly, without depending on the lamrim, even if you study the great scriptures, it will be difficult for you to find the view of the Buddha. But if, by depending on a guru who is like a skilled captain, you board the ship of the lamrim, you will easily find the jewel that is the ultimate view of the Buddha in the great ocean of the extensive scriptures.

The fourth great quality of the lamrim is that it allows you to naturally cease the great vice of abandoning the Dharma. If you do not find definite understanding of the previous three great qualities, you will discriminate among the teachings of the Buddha, seeing some as higher and some as lower, some as philosophy and some as practices, and so forth, and then have greater or lesser devotion to them. By maintaining such discrimination, you continuously create the very heavy karma of abandoning the holy Dharma, for which the karmic obscurations are extremely heavy. In the *Sūtra Gathering All Fragments*, the Buddha said:

> Mañjuśrī, the karmic obscurations of abandoning the holy Dharma easily happen. Mañjuśrī, discriminating some of the teachings taught by the Buddha as good and some as bad is abandoning the holy Dharma. Whoever abandons the holy Dharma criticizes the Tathāgata. They talk badly about the Saṅgha. If you say, "This [teaching] is right" and "This is not right," you abandon the holy Dharma. If you say, "This is taught for bodhisattvas" and "This is taught for hearers," you abandon the holy Dharma. If you say, "This is taught for solitary realizers," you abandon the holy Dharma. If you say, "This is not a training for bodhisattvas," you abandon the holy Dharma.

As the *King of Meditative Stabilizations Sūtra* says:

The negative karma of abandoning
the holy Dharma is far greater
than that of destroying all the holy objects
of offering in this Jambūdvīpa.

The negative karma of abandoning
the holy Dharma is far greater
than that of killing as many arhats
as there are sand grains in the Ganges.

By understanding the lamrim, you naturally stop committing the great vice of abandoning the holy Dharma.

This lamrim also has three special qualities. First, it is complete with nothing missing. The lamrim obviously cannot include all the words of the teachings of the Buddha and their commentaries, so when it says that nothing is missing, this means that all the vital points of the meaning are condensed and presented within it, leaving nothing out. That is why Lama Tsongkhapa explained in his *Song of Spiritual Experience*:

Each time you explain or listen to the lamrim,
the condensed essence of all the scriptures,
you collect the benefits of explaining and listening to the holy Dharma.
So, since it condenses the extensive teachings, contemplate its meaning.

The second special quality is that it is easy to practice. Each of us has experienced the various sufferings in this saṃsāra, and each of us can achieve the everlasting happiness of liberation from saṃsāra and of enlightenment. The creator of all these is the mind. And there is nothing better for subduing that mind than the lamrim. Since it was mainly taught as a method for subduing the mind, it is easy to put into practice.

Finally, the lamrim is more special than other traditions. Since the lamrim is adorned with the instructions of Guru Vidyākokila, learned in the tradition of Nāgārjuna, and the instructions of Guru Serlingpa (Suvarṇadvīpa), learned in the tradition of Asaṅga, it is a particularly precious tradition. As Lama Tsongkhapa also said in his *Song of Spiritual Experience*:

> That which is well transmitted respectively from Nāgārjuna and
> Asaṅga—
> crown ornaments of the learned ones of the world,
> banners of renown resplendent among beings—
> is the graduated path to enlightenment.

Not even Maitreya's *Ornament for Clear Realizations* or the king of tantras, the glorious *Guhyasamāja*, has these three special qualities. The entire subject matter of sūtra and tantra is not contained in either of these two, nor do they mainly explain the steps for subduing the mind.

Therefore, while you have this fortunate opportunity to study, reflect, and meditate on such a graduated path to enlightenment, which is extremely special in terms of its four great qualities and three special qualities, do not remain satisfied with a misguided and partial instruction for practice. It is extremely important that you engage with great effort in studying, reflecting, and meditating on this path. In short, no matter how busy you are, reading the lamrim regularly, even just a few pages a day, brings the mind directly into the graduated path to enlightenment and the three principal aspects of the path to enlightenment. Just imagine the benefit of doing that!

I am very pleased that this translation of the meditation instructions of Paṇchen Losang Yeshé is now available to English-speaking students of the Dharma. I have often recommended this text, including to my student Diana, who sponsored the excellent and careful translation here by Szegee. I rejoice in the merit of everyone involved in its creation and publication.

Thank you very much!

Lama Zopa Rinpoche
Kopan Monastery, Nepal

Preface

In the September of 2017, Kyabje Lama Zopa Rinpoche, spiritual director of the Foundation for the Preservation of the Mahayana Tradition (FPMT), led the fifth of a series of teaching retreats known as *Light of the Path* in North Carolina, United States. During that retreat Rinpoche recommended a text entitled *Swift Path* to a student by the name of Diana Carroll. Composed by Losang Yeshé around the turn of the seventeenth century, this text is a meditation manual on the *lamrim*, or "stages of the path to enlightenment." The author, commonly referred to as either the Fifth or Second Paṇchen Lama, depending on the convention for enumeration, formulated it as a supplement to the *Easy Path* (*Delam*) written by his immediate predecessor, Losang Chökyi Gyaltsen, who was tutor to the Fifth Dalai Lama. Carrying great significance in the genre of lamrim literature, it came to be recognized as part of a collection of texts known as the *eight great lamrims*. Advised by Kyabje Lama Zopa Rinpoche to base her lamrim study and practice on the *Swift Path*, Diana contacted the FPMT and offered to sponsor the translation of the text with funds that were available due to the kindness and generosity of her late father, George Carroll. Soon after, I was approached by FPMT Education Services with a proposal to translate the text as a publication project. This development forged a new link in a long chain of causes and conditions that culminated in this translation of the *Swift Path*.

I first took serious interest in the lamrim when Venerable Sangye Khadro (Kathleen McDonald) taught an extensive lamrim course at Amitabha Buddhist Centre, Singapore, in the 1990s. Based upon an impressive dictionary-like book by Phabongkha Rinpoche entitled *Liberation in the Palm of Your Hand*, Venerable Khadro's clear and detailed explanations were a pleasure to hear, and they nurtured my growing appreciation of the lamrim. I recall with fondness the exams the students took periodically as a means to foster learning. Venerable Khadro curated these assessments in such a skillful way that in addition to covering comprehensively the material tested, they served as wonderful sources of encouragement. To the delight of the students, a very heartening, if not perfect score was achievable when they were sufficiently conscientious in their studies. I must admit sheepishly though that this aspect of her wise and compassionate skill did not rub off on me, as she discovered with disappointment in 2008 when she joined the second FPMT Masters Program at Istituto Lama Tsong Khapa in Italy and sat for the exams that I had helped design as teaching assistant!

Over the years I have had the good fortune to receive commentaries on various lamrim texts, one of which is directly related to this *Swift Path* project. When I enrolled in the first Masters Program in 1998, the students were encouraged to attend the monthly weekend courses on the *Easy Path* in order to complement their technical studies on philosophy that were conducted on weekdays. The teacher for all of these lessons was the late Geshe Jampa Gyatso (1932–2007), a classmate and good friend of Lama Thubten Yeshe, who founded FPMT with Lama Zopa Rinpoche. Geshe-la left Tibet in 1959, continued his studies in India, and received his Lharampa degree in 1972. At the request of Lama Yeshe, he first went to Kopan Monastery and later Italy, and in 1983 he implemented a geshe studies program that would become the precursor of the present-day Masters Program, covering subjects such as Maitreya's *Ornament for Clear Realizations*, Candrakīrti's *Entering the Middle Way*, and Vasubandhu's *Treasury of Knowledge*.

During the classes on the *Easy Path*, Geshe-la would read a passage from the *Easy Path* in Tibetan, followed by the corresponding passage of Joshua Cutler's unpublished English translation, before giving his own commentary in English. As the course was open to the general public, all the explanations were translated serially into Italian too. It took many weekends spanning several years for him to complete the course. Till this day I have kept my copy of the English translation peppered with scribbled notes and the Tibetan text that I read along as I tried to hone my language skills. Who would have guessed that those resources would come in handy more than twenty years later in the preparation of this book?

Beyond imparting knowledge as a scholar, Geshe Jampa Gyatso embodied the lamrim as a living tradition. To give an example, we frequently encounter exhortations to develop altruism akin to "the lovingkindness of a mother for her only child," to the extent that the description has almost degenerated into a cliché, but Geshe-la was a precise living example of such lovingkindness. Apart from being an educator in the Dharma, he tirelessly offered advice and guidance to everyone who needed help with any kind of difficulty under the sun. I suspect that a good number of those who went to consult Geshe-la would not even consider confiding their problems to their mothers in real life, much less expect solutions from them! Even after he was diagnosed with lung cancer in 2000, he continued to teach and support the students. I am humbled to have been a fortunate recipient of Geshe-la's boundless kindness. To him I owe a huge portion of my conviction in the efficacy of the mind-training instructions found in the lamrim.

I am also deeply grateful to Geshe Jampa Gelek, current Masters Program instructor and resident teacher at Istituto Lama Tsong Khapa, and Geshe Ngawang Sangye, incumbent Lama Umzé at Gyümé Tantric College, India, for elucidating obscure points in the Tibetan text. Venerable Tenzin Gache of Sera Jey Monastic University checked the contents of appendix 2 as part of another translation project related to Maitreya's *Ornament for Clear Realizations*.

My old friend Nicholas Gallagher kindly accepted the unenviable task of editing my messy first draft when it was completed at the end of 2019. With his superb linguistic skills and immense patience, he cleaned up incomprehensible renderings and greatly improved the flow of the entire manuscript. Diana Carroll read through an early version of the translation and offered useful suggestions and edits. Shenghai Li rendered invaluable assistance with the finer points of the Sanskrit language. I added many notes at the suggestion of Ann Yoshinaga, who meticulously highlighted terminology and concepts in relation to which she felt readers might appreciate clarification. Don Handrick and Venerable Thubten Pema checked the proofs. Venerable Ailsa Cameron and Venerable Joan Nicell edited an early version of the foreword. I also wish to acknowledge the opportunity to view pre-publication Thupten Jinpa's translation of the *Easy Path* in *Stages of the Path and the Oral Transmission: Selected Teachings of the Geluk School* in the Library of Tibetan Classics series. My heartfelt thanks go to François Lecointre, Tom Truty, and Joona Repo of FPMT Education Services for coordinating this project and handling its administrative matters. I also wish to express my sincere gratitude to David Kittelstrom, senior editor at Wisdom Publications, for his remarkable expertise shepherding this translation to its publication. I bear total responsibility for any imperfections in the work.

In addition, Chiara Luce Edizioni, Italy, kindly granted FPMT permission to publish modified versions of their image of the merit field. For detailed instructions on how to visualize the refuge objects and merit field in this system of the *Swift Path*, readers may refer to Gyumed Khensur Lobsang Jampa's explanations in *The Easy Path*, pages 33–46.

Even though I am not able to specify names here, I am indebted to the innumerable teachers and translators who have made the precious lamrim instructions available, whether in written form or as oral teachings, over the past decades and centuries. I also take this opportunity to pay tribute to all who have generously shared resources online for the purpose of furthering knowledge and facilitating research. Some of these resources include the Buddhist Digital Resource Center (BDRC), the Resources for Kanjur & Tanjur Studies (rKTs), the Göttingen Register of Electronic Texts in Indian Languages (GRETIL), the Buddhist Canons Research Database, 84000: Translating the Words of the Buddha, and the Tibetan-English dictionary app developed by Christian Steinert.

The contents of a meditation manual are meant for repeated contemplation and meditation. I have tried my best to make the text accessible to a wider audience and to facilitate understanding and readability by using simple terminology where no change in meaning occurs and reducing the use of emphatic words and adverbials (well, very, properly, and so on) where intrusive to the flow. I have also expanded certain expressions for clarity, such as rendering *stobs bzhi* ("the four powers") as "the four powers of purification," and *tshogs gnyis* ("the two collections") as "the two collections of merit and wisdom."

To maintain consistency, I use a single translation term for the same Tibetan word, but there are occasions where a term has been variously translated according to its contexts. For example, *bla ma* is rendered as "guru" (e.g., Guru Vajradhara), "lama" (e.g., Lama Chöpa), "teacher" (e.g., the teachers with whom I have a direct Dharma connection), "master" (e.g., lineage masters), and "spiritual guide" (e.g., respect him as your spiritual guide).

In addition, for the readers' convenience, I have filled in the intended text when it is clearly implied in the original. An example of this is the outline "Actual," which appears repeatedly to refer to the actual meditation on the respective topic under discussion, and so for instance, I have rendered the outline "Actual" in chapter 3 as "The actual meditation on relying on a spiritual guide," and in chapter 4 as "The actual meditation on extracting the essence of a physical basis endowed with the freedoms and privileges," without setting off the interpolations in square brackets.

Bullet points have been used on several occasions for ease of identification of salient points. Italics is applied to highlight new content in a recurring formulation or to help readers follow the main progression in long descriptions (e.g., Pay *physical* homage by . . . Pay *verbal* homage by . . . Pay *mental* homage by . . .). Non-indented text indicates instructions (e.g., Meditate on immeasurable equanimity as follows), while indented text indicates citations or the actual material that one verbalizes, visualizes, or contemplates (e.g., In the space before me stands a vast and extensive throne).

Within the text itself, the headings in small caps are translations of formal outlines that are spelled out in the Tibetan text (e.g., THE ACTUAL MEDITATION ON THE SEVENFOLD CAUSE-AND-EFFECT INSTRUCTION), while the headings in italics have been added by me to guide the readers (e.g., *Recognizing all sentient beings as having been your mother*). To situate the former in the wider scheme, please refer to appendix 1. I have also added chapter titles to facilitate easy navigation of the material.

Verses are identified by chapter and verse numbers, whenever relevant. For example, "Nāgārjuna, *Precious Garland*, 1.99" refers to chapter 1, verse 99, of Nāgārjuna's *Precious Garland* in accordance with the numbering provided in Michael Hahn, ed., *Nāgārjuna's Ratnāvalī, Vol. 1: The Basic Texts (Sanskrit, Tibetan, Chinese)* (Bonn: Indica et Tibetica Verlag, 1983).

Szegee Toh

Translator's Introduction

What is the lamrim?

Everything we do, all day and night, is for the sake of finding happiness and avoiding suffering. Even when we voluntarily subject ourselves to pain and discomfort, deep in our hearts we harbor the belief that doing so may lead us to happiness. Ancient philosophies, world religions, new-age methods, and self-help industries offer a plethora of solutions to our problems and unhappiness.

While acknowledging that physical health and material comfort are important elements contributing to our sense of well-being, Buddhism teaches that the causes of long-lasting contentment lie within our own minds. For this reason we find a wide range of Buddhist techniques employed for training the mind. Among these is the lamrim, which suggests we will achieve true well-being through strengthening positive states of mind and eliminating disturbing emotions in a graduated manner.

Lamrim, the stages of the path to enlightenment, is the name given to a genre of exposition and system of practice that is associated with the *Lamp for the Path to Enlightenment*, a text composed by the Indian master Atiśa in the eleventh century. Consisting of sixty-eight verses, this text is an explanation that distills and arranges the essential points of the Buddha's vast and profound teachings in the form of instructions for practice by persons with small, medium, and great capacities. It illuminates how the entire corpus of the Buddha's teachings fits harmoniously into the framework of a single person's path to enlightenment. Akin to a tested recipe that has been passed down through generations, the lamrim has been transmitted from Dromtönpa, the foremost Tibetan disciple of Atiśa, through an unbroken lineage of accomplished Tibetan masters to the present day.

In Tibetan, *lam* means "path" and *rim* means "stages." Laying out the *stages* of the entire *path* to enlightenment, the lamrim offers a systematic pathway for transforming our perspectives and attitudes so that we can maximize our potential to achieve full enlightenment, a state of profound peace and stable wellness that is totally free from any trace of suffering or confusion.

What is the point of the lamrim?

Since the lamrim is basically an arrangement of the Buddha's teachings, would it not make better sense to just study and practice the Buddha's teachings themselves, which are already available in the form of sūtras and the great Indian treatises that are commentaries on them?

As spiritual aspirants, we encounter scores of practices—ethics, lovingkindness, compassion, contemplation of suffering, generosity, realization of emptiness, meditative concentration, and so on. How are we supposed to approach them all? For example, perhaps one day, I feel inspired to radiate lovingkindness to all living beings as taught in the *Metta Sutta*, or if I am feeling agitated, I decide to watch my inhalations and exhalations and count my breaths. And yet, on another occasion, I feel like meditating on the emptiness expounded in the *Heart Sūtra*. The contemplation of suffering in the four noble truths probably gets shelved as my mind is far more inclined to dwell in pleasing thoughts than reflection on sickness and death! Two questions arise: Will I make reasonable progress on the spiritual path by cherry-picking several practices that appeal while leaving the rest aside? Or if I am interested in many practices, can I engage in these practices in any random order?

As in the case of a sophisticated dish that calls for a variety of ingredients to be combined in a specific manner, the lamrim proposes an orderly cultivation of our minds so that we can achieve not just a temporary sense of well-being but the everlasting state of perfect enlightenment that is the culmination of our potential. Thus, according to this schema, neither implementing a single isolated practice nor combining many practices haphazardly will bring maximal benefit.

Sequence does make a difference in spiritual development. Certain practices are more complex and require a particular foundation before they can be actualized most effectively. For example, we may be inspired by the idea of generating universal love and cannot wait to encompass all living beings with our compassion, but if we neglect cultivating genuine love and compassion for ourselves first, then whatever love and compassion we generate for all living beings will be flimsy, and our enthusiasm may turn into compassion fatigue before long. For this reason, the meditation on altruism is preceded by the contemplation of the dissatisfactory nature of our present existence, in which we develop the fervent wish to be completely free from our own sufferings of saṃsāra, coarse and subtle. It is an acute awareness of our own state that propels us to do everything we can to free others from suffering. Without this foundation, we might even become jealous of those who possess beauty, wealth, and renown. Compassion for them would be the last thing on our minds!

In general, we can certainly embark on whatever practice we feel drawn to, but we may not derive the benefit that we would gain if we were to instead train our mind methodically with an appreciation of the big picture. Using a framework like the lamrim can help us avoid the pitfall of not seeing the forest for the trees in our practice. For instance, we may contemplate suffering, the first of the four noble truths, as a stand-alone practice, but without being preceded by the reflection on our precious human rebirth and without being succeeded by the reflection of the possibility of the total cessation of suffering and the existence of the path leading to liberation, we risk feeling pessimistic and falling into hopelessness. The topics of the lamrim are masterfully curated so that we are guided to a holistic transformation without falling into mental and emotional imbalance.

What is the precise source of these techniques?

Practicing an errant path is a waste of time and effort; it can even be harmful. How can we be confident that the contents of the lamrim are authentic and can lead us to enlightenment?

Even though *lamrim* is a Tibetan term, its contents were not invented by the Tibetans. At the beginning of what is one of the most influential lamrims ever composed, Tsongkhapa, the founder of the Geluk school of Tibetan Buddhism, explains:

> In general, these instructions are the instructions found in the *Ornament for Clear Realizations* composed by Maitreya. Specifically, the [root] text for this [exposition] is the *Lamp for the Path to Enlightenment* . . .[1]

In 1042, Atiśa traveled to Tibet at the invitation of the king Lha Lama Yeshé Ö to revitalize Buddhism. This master hailing from Vikramaśīla, one of the great centers of learning in northeastern India, spent the last twelve years of his life in Tibet and wrote the *Lamp for the Path to Enlightenment*. From a certain point of view, this composition may be considered the beginning of the lamrim tradition, but if we trace the source of its contents, we discover that the instructions already existed centuries before, albeit in a different format.

What is the *Ornament for Clear Realizations* mentioned in the citation above? Called *Abhisamayālaṃkāra* in Sanskrit, it is a complex text composed of 273 verses by Maitreya. It reveals the hidden meaning of the Perfection of Wisdom sūtras through a framework of eight categories consisting of a total of seventy topics. While the Perfection of Wisdom sūtras explicitly teach emptiness, concealed within them is a presentation of the paths and grounds, the six perfections, and other elements that are central to the Mahāyāna path. In a teaching given in Dharamsala, India, in 1988, His Holiness the Fourteenth Dalai Lama explained:

> The root text of the Lamrim is regarded as being Maitreya's *Abhisamyalankara*, especially the section dealing with what is known as the "serial training" in the sixth chapter of the text. This work categorizes all the various stages of the spiritual journey to full enlightenment by a prospective bodhisattva into four trainings. These four are: (1) training in the complete aspects; (2) peak training; (3) serial training; and (4) momentary training. Basically, the summary verses at the end of the *Abhisamyalankara*, where the entire text is summarized into three divisions—the three objects of meditation, the four trainings, and the resultant *kayas* of buddhahood—are taken as the source of Lamrim meditations. There are specific verses also in the fourth chapter of that text where conviction and faith in the spiritual master are emphasized along with conviction in the law of causality. That section also outlines the process of cultivating the altruistic attitude, bodhicitta, and then engaging in the actual deeds, the practices of the six perfections—thus the entire practice of Lamrim.[2]

Therefore the ultimate source of the lamrim can be said to be the collection of Mahāyāna scriptures known as the Perfection of Wisdom sūtras, which the Buddha taught on Vulture Peak when turning the Dharma wheel of absence of characteristics.[3] In fact, an important feature of the lamrim is that it contains the instructions of the two lineages of profound view and vast deeds that have arisen, respectively, from the explicit and hidden meanings of the Perfection of Wisdom sūtras. Having been transmitted through Nāgārjuna and Maitreya as well as other Indian lineage masters to Atiśa, the instructions were passed to his main disciple Dromtönpa, who founded the Kadam tradition. The Tibetan name pronounced *kadam* is composed of two parts—*bka'*, which refers to the Buddha's speech, and *gdams*, instructions. It implies that the whole of the Buddha's speech should be taken as instructions for practice with attention to each and every syllable. Transmitted through the Kadam lineage masters to Tsongkhapa and his disciples, they are available to us in their complete form.

What benefits can we gain from studying and practicing the lamrim?

One of the benefits of practicing the lamrim is the realization that all of the Buddha's teachings—the Hīnayāna and Mahāyāna and, within the Mahāyāna, the Pāramitāyāna and Vajrayāna—are free of contradiction. The lamrim synthesizes all the essential points of sūtra and tantra so that we can appreciate that they constitute a path for an individual to attain full enlightenment. Even though certain practices may seem incongruent when placed side by side, we can understand that they play their distinctive roles at different stages of a person's spiritual development.

<table>
<tr><th colspan="2">Vehicle</th><th>Goal</th></tr>
<tr><td rowspan="2">Hīnayāna</td><td>Śrāvakayāna (Hearers' Vehicle)</td><td rowspan="2">Individual liberation</td></tr>
<tr><td>Pratyekabuddhayāna (Solitary Realizers' Vehicle)</td></tr>
<tr><td rowspan="2">Mahāyāna</td><td>Pāramitāyāna (Perfection Vehicle)</td><td rowspan="2">Omniscience</td></tr>
<tr><td>Vajrayāna (Vajra Vehicle)</td></tr>
</table>

By studying and practicing the lamrim, we come to appreciate all Buddhist scriptures as instructions for practice. Lamrim explanations enable us to see that what is taught in the sūtras, tantras, and the great commentaries is precisely what we ought to practice. There is no separate set of instructions beyond the scriptures.

Anyone interested in learning about Buddhism can of course study the Buddha's own words. However, those who attempt to explore the hundreds of volumes of scriptures may find themselves bewildered by the plenitude of instructions given to audiences with diverse dispositions and faculties at different times and places. It is no easy task to wade through those hundreds of volumes and, on top of that, to make coherent sense of them in a way that they can be integrated into spiritual endeavor. This is why a presentation of the teachings like the lamrim can help us to easily understand the Buddha's intent.

Not only is this approach not meant to discourage the scholarship of the sūtras, tantras, and great Indian treatises, the lamrim provides a framework that can facilitate the acquisition of new information gleaned from studying canonical literature. By relying on the lamrim, we can avoid feeling adrift in a sea of seemingly scattered and irrelevant details upon perusing the original sources.

Once we realize that the Buddha's teachings are free of contradiction and we appreciate all the scriptures as instructions for our practice, we naturally cease mistakenly rejecting certain elements of the Buddha's teachings due to misconstruing their significance.

Is the Lamrim a Relic of the Past?

What does it take for us to be genuinely happy? Is the cause of true happiness today different from what it was centuries ago? Is the lamrim—whose primary message is to discard the causes of suffering and adopt the causes of happiness—still relevant in our times?

We all want inner peace and do not want to experience unease in any form. These innate desires are present in each and every one of us, past, present, and future. And though humans have made tremendous advancements in science and technology, the eradication of unhappiness is still a distant dream. Even with our fancy gadgets and luxury goods, we modern people are still unhappy, plagued by illness, aging, death, unfulfilled longing, mental and emotional stress, and discontent. Even the illusion that modern medicine has brought us closer to eliminating sickness was dispelled on witnessing how COVID-19 brought the world to its knees.

Undeniably, material affluence can bring a sense of security, but the happiness it can bring is limited. According to Buddhism, the true cause of happiness lies within our minds. In our rush to find happiness and avoid suffering, we never pause to look honestly at whether our methods are truly effective. We may have become more materially well off in modern times, but our minds have changed little in that we remain under the sway of the same mental afflictions—hatred, arrogance, jealousy, attachment, ignorance, and selfishness. These afflictions are the force driving misdeeds such as theft, lies, adultery, and murder. Whether it is common theft or a modern-day ransomware attack, the underlying affliction of greed is the same. For this reason, the lamrim that was first taught centuries ago is still relevant today. Perhaps some contexts may seem outdated and culturally distant, but the essence of the teaching is nonetheless timeless. The methods for uprooting the causes of suffering are as pertinent today as they were thousands of years ago. Embedded in lamrim meditation practices are effective tools that can help us navigate the tribulations of contemporary life and beyond.

In fact, many of us have already had a taste of these techniques and have benefited from them. In recent years, the practice of mindfulness, a hallmark of Buddhism, has been widely adopted in secular contexts to reduce stress, depression, anxiety, drug addiction, and other issues, becoming even a multibillion-dollar industry. While the benefits of secular mindfulness are undeniably impressive, mindfulness meditation has even deeper potential. For instance, mindfulness practice in the context of calm abiding combined with the cultivation of wisdom explained in Buddhism leads to the penetration of reality, which is instrumental in securing total liberation from suffering.

Another wellness practice with Buddhist parallels that has become quite popular in recent years is that of keeping a gratitude journal in order to reap the slew of social, psychological, and physical health benefits that ensue from giving thanks. Positive effects such as better sleep, reduced illness, and more well-being among adults and children alike may be life-changing, but they represent only a modicum of the power of gratitude. The lamrim section on cultivating altruism includes a meditation in which we cultivate gratitude toward every single sentient being on the basis that they have all been our kind mother at some point, whether in this life or previous lives. The fruit of cultivating this often challenging mindset is a profound appreciation for all living beings—not just those who have helped us in this life, but all others, including those who have harmed us. This recognition lays the foundation for us to cultivate universal love and compassion, which will steer us to full enlightenment motivated by the wish to benefit all living beings. So if we want to experience the full power of these constructive attributes that we already admire, we should check out the instructions found in the lamrim.

Don't just study! Practice!

"A butter cover cannot be softened by butter; the mind that has gone astray in relation to the Dharma cannot be tamed by the Dharma."[4] This Tibetan proverb underscores the importance of practice, the bedrock of the path. In olden Tibet, the leather used to wrap yak butter stiffened over time, and such leather was resistant to the normally softening effects of butter. Likewise, someone who knows the Dharma but does not practice it runs the risk of becoming impervious to its benefits. Thus, at the conclusion of the section of the path in common with persons with small capacity, the author cautions against being satisfied with a mere intellectual understanding.

Understanding, appreciating, and desiring a particular good quality does not mean we have already generated it or will generate it effortlessly. Similarly, intellectually knowing that something is bad for us does not mean we abstain from it, as any alcoholic or smoker will attest. We know that anger is bad for us and patience and compassion are salutary, but when driving and someone cuts into our lane abruptly, we still flare up in rage. Transformative techniques are required if we are to weaken such negative tendencies and foster patience, compassion, and other virtues. The methods taught in the lamrim do exactly that; they can help our mind become so even-keeled that nothing upsets it.

Training our mind—accustomed as it is to afflictions and self-sabotaging behaviors—requires sustained effort. Simply praying to a higher power and requesting wisdom does not suffice. Nobody gets the benefits of a workout by watching it on YouTube. Likewise, the benefits from the techniques explained here are not gained by only reading about and understanding them. We must immerse ourselves in the instructions and experience profound realizations through their practice. We need both our analytical and contemplative powers to progressively weed out unskillful thought patterns, the cause of suffering, and we need meditation as well to replace these with constructive habits, the cause of happiness.

Treading the path takes humility and self-awareness. What may appear to be assiduous spiritual practice can sometimes, instead of diminishing and eliminating afflictions, leave the afflictions untouched or even fortified. How is this possible? Contemporary teachers have coined terms such as *spiritual materialism* and *spiritual bypass* to caution against spiritual self-deception. People may have the trappings of a spiritual practitioner—wearing prayer beads, chanting mantras, quoting scripture, and spinning prayer wheels—but if they fail to acknowledge their mental flaws and sincerely work on their own mind, they are not true spiritual practitioners. Dharma practice is not for show. Even the best medicine becomes poison if misused.

Who is the Author of This Lamrim?

The author of the *Swift Path* is Paṇchen Losang Yeshé. The title Paṇchen is an abbreviation of the Sanskrit term *paṇḍita*, which means "learned person," and the Tibetan *chen po*, which means "great." This important lama lineage in Tibet started when Ngawang Losang Gyatso, the Fifth Dalai lama, announced that one of his teachers, Losang Chökyi Gyaltsen, who was also the abbot of Tashi Lhunpo Monastery in Shigatsé, would reappear after his death. In 1668, the Fifth Dalai Lama recognized the four-year-old reincarnation of Losang Chökyi Gyaltsen and enthroned him at Tashi Lhunpo.

According to the Ganden Phodrang's way of enumeration,[5] Losang Chökyi Gyaltsen is considered the First Paṇchen, his reincarnation Losang Yeshé the Second Paṇchen, and so on. However, according to a more common convention, Paṇchen Losang Chökyi Gyaltsen is considered the Fourth Paṇchen, his reincarnation Losang Yeshé the Fifth Paṇchen, and so on. This latter Tashi Lhunpo system counts three lamas—Khedrup Jé Gelek Palsang, Sönam Chökyi Langpo, and Ensapa Losang Döndrup—as the First, Second, and Third Paṇchens, respectively. These three figures came to be given the title of Paṇchen Lama posthumously by virtue of being considered preincarnations of Paṇchen Losang Chökyi Gyaltsen.

Enumeration according to the Tashi Lhunpo system[6]	*Name and dates of the lamas*	*Enumeration according to the Ganden Phodrang system*
First Paṇchen Lama	Khedrup Gelek Palsang (Mkhas grub Dge legs dpal bzang) 1385–1438	—
Second Paṇchen Lama	Sönam Choklang (Bsod nams phyogs glang) 1439–1505	—
Third Paṇchen Lama	Ensapa Losang Döndrup (Dben sa pa Blo bzang don grub) 1505–1566	—
Fourth Paṇchen Lama	Losang Chökyi Gyaltsen (Blo bzang chos kyi rgyal mtshan) 1570–1662	First Paṇchen Lama
Fifth Paṇchen Lama	Losang Yeshé (Blo bzang ye shes) 1663–1737	Second Paṇchen Lama

When the reincarnation of Paṇchen Losang Chökyi Gyaltsen visited the Fifth Dalai Lama at the Potala Palace in Lhasa at the age of eight, he was conferred the vows of a novice monk and given the name Losang Yeshé. At the age of twenty-two, he took full ordination from Könchok Gyaltsen, the abbot of Tashi Lhunpo's tantric college.[7] In 1695, he served as one of the official preceptors who conferred vows on the Sixth Dalai Lama. The Qing dynasty emperor Kangxi bestowed upon him the title Erdeni, a Mongolian term meaning "treasure," in 1713. Losang Yeshé, at the age of fifty-five, bestowed novice vows on the Seventh Dalai Lama and, ten years later, gave him full ordination. By the time he passed away in 1737 at the age of about seventy-four, he had written biographies, poetry, lamrim explanations, tantric commentaries, and supplication prayers, all of which are available in his collected works.

How did the *Swift Path* come about?

On the basis of the "prototype" *Lamp for the Path to Enlightenment*, many Tibetan teachers composed lamrim explanations in various formats and lengths. Some of these stick closely to the schema of the paths of persons with the three levels of spiritual capacities, while others do not, using other methods of organizing the Buddha's teachings instead. The latter category of texts came to be known as *tenrim* (*bstan rim*), where the *stages* (*rim pa*) of the Mahāyāna *teachings* (*bstan pa*) are elucidated.[8] In the colophon of his *Great Treatise*, Tsongkhapa counted tenrim compositions among the influences of his own composition. Thus we may distinguish within the lamrim genre two broad subgenres, lamrim proper and tenrim. Among the texts expounding the lamrim proper composed by Geluk masters are a collection called *the eight great lamrims*. The *Swift Path* translated in this book is one of these.

Title	*Author*
Great Exposition on the Stages of the Path to Enlightenment (*Lam rim chen mo*)	Tsongkhapa (Tsong kha pa), 1357–1419
Middle-Length Exposition on the Stages of the Path to Enlightenment (*Lam rim 'bring po*)	Tsongkhapa
Concise Exposition on the Stages of the Path to Enlightenment (*Lam rim bsdus don*) a.k.a. *Song of Spiritual Experience* (*Nyams mgur*)	Tsongkhapa
Essence of Excellent Discourses (*Legs gsung nying khu*)[9]	Dakpo Gomchen Ngawang Drakpa (Dwags po sgom chen Ngag dbang grags pa), b. fifteenth century
Essence of Refined Gold (*Gser gyi yang zhun*)[10]	Sönam Gyatso, the Third Dalai Lama (Bsod nams rgya mtsho), 1543–88
Easy Path (*Bde lam*)[11]	Paṇchen Losang Chökyi Gyaltsen (Paṇ chen Blo bzang chos kyi rgyal mtshan), 1570–1662

Title	*Author*
Words of Mañjuśrī (*'Jam dpal zhal lung*)[12]	Ngawang Losang Gyatso, the Fifth Dalai Lama (Ngag dbang blo bzang rgya mtsho), 1617–82
Swift Path (*Myur lam*)	Paṇchen Losang Yeshé (Paṇ chen Blo bzang ye she), 1663–1737

In the colophon to the *Swift Path*, Losang Yeshé explains that, in response to requests for a prose commentary that is more extensive than the *Easy Path*, he wrote the *Swift Path* as a supplement to the *Easy Path* composed by his immediate predecessor, Losang Chökyi Gyaltsen. Indeed, beyond fleshing out the brief instructions provided in the *Easy Path*, he also added copious citations from sūtras, Indian treatises, and Tibetan works that provide rich fodder for contemplation and meditation. Losang Yeshé explains:

> Moreover, observing the declining mental capacities of trainees, Tsongkhapa made the following proposition in the *Great Exposition*: "However, those who know how to bring all these explanations into practice seem barely to exist at all, and therefore you should formulate a separate concise presentation of what should be constantly maintained in meditation." Taking this advice to heart, Paṇchen Tamché Khyenpa [Losang Chökyi Gyaltsen] composed the *Easy Path to Omniscience: An Explicit Instruction on the Stages of the Path* . . .

Thus the *Easy Path* is by design a concise meditation manual that guides one to engage in repeated practice and integration. This *Swift Path* is also a meditation manual, albeit a more elaborate one, almost triple the length of *Easy Path*. At one point Paṇchen Losang Yeshé directs the readers to Tsongkhapa's great and small lamrims for the traditional presentations of the greatness of the author, the greatness of the teaching, and so forth. It is obvious that the *Swift Path*, which is about one-sixth the length of Tsongkhapa's *Great Exposition* and two-fifths that of his *Middle-Length Exposition*, was never intended to be an encyclopedic presentation of the lamrim. Since it does not contain many details seen in those longer texts, practitioners wishing to study the lamrim in depth should rely on the more elaborate expositions found elsewhere. However, a reader who is interested in the lamrim but feels intimidated by an extensive exposition like the *Greater Exposition* may wish to first study a shorter presentation such as the *Swift Path* to survey the full range of lamrim meditation topics in preparation for the study of more extensive presentations.

Just in case the adjectives *easy* and *swift* give you the impression that you will accomplish the path quickly and effortlessly in an absolute sense, you need to temper your expectations. The Fourteenth Dalai Lama pointed out that, of the eight great lamrims, only the *Easy Path* and the *Swift Path* incorporate practice elements associated with tantra.[13] Because of combining tantric techniques—such as the visualization of nectar descending and cleansing oneself of misdeeds and obstructions—in its instructions, a path becomes relatively easy and swift in comparison with the sūtra path, which purportedly takes three countless eons to complete. Hence, the onus is on the trainees to equip themselves with the necessary foundation so that they may traverse such a profound and sophisticated path easily and swiftly. At the conclusion of the text, the author urges the meditator to enter the Vajrayāna, but readers need to receive instructions elsewhere, as the subject of tantra is not treated in this text.

How is the explanation structured?

Atiśa divided the stages of the paths into those of persons with the three levels of spiritual capacities, the three scopes. This ingenious approach enables us to grasp the intents of the wide-ranging Indian scriptures and apply the wealth of information found within them. At the most basic level, practitioners are aiming for a good rebirth after this life ends and are called *persons with small capacity*. At the intermediate level, practitioners are more far-sighted; they understand that even a good rebirth is transitory and therefore want to attain total liberation from saṃsāra; they are called *persons with medium capacity*. At the highest level, not satisfied with freeing themselves alone, *persons with great capacity* wish to lead all sentient beings to freedom from suffering and thus aim for the omniscient state of buddhahood to equip themselves with the perfect skills to guide others.

Path	*Destination*
Path of persons with small capacity	High rebirth
Path of persons with medium capacity	Liberation
Path of persons with great capacity	Omniscience

Each of these three divisions contains a number of meditation topics, and the three scopes themselves are preceded by several meditation topics that lay the foundation for traversing the paths. These paths are graduated in the sense that a higher path requires the lower path as foundation. If you lack the wish to attain liberation from saṃsāra for yourself, it is impossible that you will wish the same for all living beings, let alone strive to attain buddhahood in order to help them to attain liberation. Similarly, without aspiring to be free from the suffering of the lower realms, it is impossible that you will aspire to be free from the entirety of saṃsāra with all its allures.

Hence, the lamrim is like a map to three destinations, such that one has to pass through the first in order to arrive at the second, and through the second in order to arrive at the third. And so, for someone aiming for the furthest destination, the first two are transit points rather than final goals. Someone seeking the Mahāyāna ideal of full enlightenment must first pass through the paths *in common with* those of persons with small or medium capacity, rather than *actual* paths of persons with small or medium capacity. From this point of view, the goals of high rebirth and liberation from suffering may be understood as stepping stones to the ultimate destination of buddhahood.

Where we eventually end up depends on where we intend to go in the first place. Three people who step into the same elevator will arrive at different destinations based on the floor to which they intend to go. Just so, the individuals with the three capacities will obtain different fruits corresponding to their motivations. To illustrate the crucial role of motivation in attaining the various goals, suppose three persons are cultivating mindfulness of impermanence. The first wants to attain a good rebirth in the next life, the second liberation from saṃsāra, and the third buddhahood in order to benefit all livings beings. Even though they are all cultivating the mindfulness of impermanence, the first person is practicing a path of persons with small capacity, the second a path of persons with medium capacity *that is in com-*

mon with that of persons with small capacity, and the third a path of persons with great capacity *that is in common with that of persons with small capacity*. Corresponding to their motivations, the meditation on impermanence becomes the cause of a good rebirth, liberation, or buddhahood.

Lamrim practice is structured around various topics that we are to familiarize ourselves with over multiple sessions and during the in-between periods. It has the following basic structure:

1. What to do during the session
   a. Preparation
   b. The actual meditation
   c. Conclusion
2. What to do between the sessions

Each topic is meditated upon during the component of actual meditation, which is sandwiched between a preparation and a conclusion that are very similar for all topics.

The *preparation* consists of six practices to prepare the mind for the subsequent meditation proper, and it ends in a visualization of light rays and nectar descending into us in order to remove obstacles and receive blessings for generating realizations of that particular topic. During the *meditation* proper, we analyze and meditate on the topic for that session—the precious human rebirth, say, or death and impermanence. A visualization of descending light rays and nectar, similar to that in the preparation, occurs at the end of the actual meditation. The *conclusion* consists of another visualization of removing obstacles and receiving blessings and culminates when we arise as a buddha to enact the welfare of sentient beings.

Having concluded the session, we perform other activities such as eating, sleeping, and so forth according to the practice instructions and read supplementary material related to the topic at hand.

Replicating the structure of the *Easy Path*, the *Swift Path* presents a total of nine meditation sessions covering the following subjects: (1) relying on a spiritual guide; (2) the precious human rebirth; (3) impermanence in the form of death, the suffering of lower rebirths, going for refuge, and the principles of karma; (4) aspiring for liberation; (5) the path to liberation; (6) the sevenfold cause-and-effect instruction; (7) training in the bodhisattvas' deeds; (8) calm abiding; and (9) special insight. All four topics subsumed under the path in common with that of persons with small capacity are meditated upon in session 3; for ease of comprehension I have separated these into four different chapters. I have also divided the content covered under the subject of the sevenfold cause-and-effect instruction into three chapters, so that the technique of equalizing and exchanging self and others as well as the rite of committing to bodhicitta are presented in distinct sections. In summary, the actual meditation topics are found in chapters 3 to 16 among the eighteen chapters of this book.

The stages of the path of persons with great capacity	16. Special Insight 15. Calm Abiding 14. Training in the Bodhisattvas' Deeds 13. Committing to Bodhicitta 12. Equalizing and Exchanging Self and Others 11. The Sevenfold Cause-and-Effect Instruction
The path in common with that of persons with medium capacity	10. The Path to Liberation 9. Aspiring for Liberation
The path in common with that of persons with small capacity	8. The Principles of Karma 7. Going for Refuge 6. The Suffering of The Lower Rebirths 5. Impermanence in the Form of Death
Foundation	4. The Precious Human Rebirth 3. Relying on a Spiritual Guide

Synopsis

THE MEDITATION MANUAL entitled *Swift Path* may be conveniently conceptualized as consisting of eighteen chapters that are encompassed by five sections: (1) groundwork, (2) the path in common with that of persons with small capacity, (3) the path in common with that of persons with medium capacity, (4) the stages of the path of persons with great capacity, and (5) epilogue.

GROUNDWORK (CHAPTERS 1–4)

Chapters 1–4 set the stage for the presentation of the actual paths of persons with the three capacities.

Chapter 1. Overview

The author provides a historical background to the lamrim tradition that began with Atiśa, whose *Lamp for the Path to Enlightenment* inspired subsequent lamrim texts. Atiśa received both the vast and profound lineages of the Buddha's teaching from the Indian lineage masters. These instructions were transmitted through a series of Tibetan masters to Tsongkhapa, the founder of the Geluk tradition, who expounded the lamrim in a number of renowned compositions. The tradition continued through a series of Tibetan masters before reaching our author, Paṇchen Losang Yeshé. Having established that the explanation originates from an authentic lineage of eminent masters so that the readers may generate conviction in the narrative, the author addresses the significance of structuring the presentation in terms of the paths of persons with small, medium, and great capacities.

Chapter 2. General Preparatory Practices

To prepare the mind for the actual meditation session, a meditator performs the six preparatory practices at the beginning of every session, or at least the first session of the day. These are: (1) cleaning the room and arranging representations of the enlightened body, speech, and mind; (2) laying out offerings that have been obtained rightfully without deceit and displaying them beautifully; (3) sitting upon a comfortable seat in the eightfold posture or any convenient posture and cultivating refuge, bodhicitta, and the four immeasurables; (4) visualizing the merit field; (5) offering the seven-limbed practice—which distills the essentials of accruing the collections of merit and wisdom and purifying misdeeds—and a maṇḍala; and (6) imbuing the mind with the supplication according to the oral instructions.

These preliminary practices bearing devotional and ritualistic flavors will not feel like a chore if we understand the purpose for doing them. They prepare the mind so that we will have the conditions most conducive to gaining insight into the topic during the actual meditation.

Chapter 3. Relying on a Spiritual Guide

How do we begin our spiritual path? To learn a worldly skill, such as driving a car, we need a qualified teacher to guide us. Similarly, our first step on the spiritual path is to rely on a teacher—not just any teacher, but a well-qualified teacher. Though not addressed here, the qualities of a qualified Mahāyāna teacher should be understood from presentations found in more extensive expositions.[14] In order to appreciate what is at stake when we take someone as a spiritual guide, we begin by reflecting on the advantages of correctly relying on a qualified spiritual guide and the disadvantages of failing to do so. Consequently, we come to realize the gravity of this first step and take care not to mistakenly associate with an unqualified or untrustworthy individual. Having carefully examined the credentials and eventually settled upon a teacher, we reflect on the qualities and kindness of the teacher. This has the effect of engendering humility and helps us to be open to the teacher—prerequisites for receiving guidance. In addition to relying on the teacher through faith and respect, one also relies on them through action, by making material offerings, giving service, and practicing their instructions.

It is prudent for us to recognize from the outset that the teacher-student relationship is inevitably framed within a power dynamic. A relation in which the disciple unquestionably surrenders to the will of the guru, who is worshipped as a god who can do no wrong, can set the stage for abuse and result in unspeakable harm. If a teacher instructs a student to do what is not in accord with the Dharma, the student should refuse.[15]

Chapter 4. The Precious Human Rebirth

Do you feel there is something special about your human existence? Reflecting on our human rebirth and fortunate circumstances helps us to develop self-confidence based neither on others' affirmation nor on superficial attributes such as physical attractiveness or wealth. Healthy self-esteem is necessary for us to embark on the path, persevere in the face of difficulties, and achieve highest enlightenment. A man unaware that the dusty painting hanging in his kitchen is a rare Renaissance masterpiece worth millions cannot benefit from its great value. Similarly, even though we have this magnificent gift, our precious human rebirth, if we are not aware of its value and fail to appreciate it, our good fortune will be squandered. Here we reflect on the eight ways in which we are free from unfavorable conditions and the ten ways in which we enjoy favorable conditions for developing our potential. Realizing the boundless opportunities afforded by our human rebirth, both rare and meaningful, fills us with gratitude, positivity, and enthusiasm.

The Path in Common with That of Persons with Small Capacity (Chapters 5–8)

What do we do after we realize that we have a wonderful precious human rebirth? The following set of meditations is done out of concern for our well-being in future lives. We aim to avoid a bad rebirth and be reborn in the human or god realm. By setting our sights on our happiness beyond this life, our mind becomes more spacious and our obsession with the affairs of this life diminishes. Thus we become more relaxed and develop a sense of calm whether things go well or badly. In other words, we understand that there is no need to sweat the small stuff and realize the futility of undue worry about mundane concerns. We will see the pointlessness of agonizing over trivial matters that will be of no importance in the long term. This series of contemplations releases us from preoccupation with short-term distractions so that we may refocus our attention on more worthy concerns.

Chapter 5. Impermanence in the Form of Death

Will I be alive tomorrow? This question can make us feel uneasy, for we all know intellectually that death can strike any time, but that does not stop us from assuming we will still be around tomorrow, next week, or next year. Science has made great strides in reducing the causes of death and prolonging life, but the stark reality is, no matter how much biohacking we attempt, we cannot escape death. And when we do die, will we depart with regrets?

In this chapter we reflect on the certainty of death, the uncertainty of the time of death, and the fact that when death comes, only spiritual practice helps. Through contemplating these points, we cultivate a mindfulness that our existence in this life is limited, strive to overcome procrastination, and reset our priorities. The mindfulness of death, rather than something unpleasant and frightening, becomes liberating and even joyous as we let go of petty concerns and find the mental space to consider goals beyond this life.

Chapter 6. The Suffering of the Lower Rebirths

What are the consequences of acting unskillfully or causing harm to others? This chapter describes the various sufferings of the hell beings, hungry ghosts, and animals. While we are not naturally drawn to contemplating suffering, this practice leads us away from the unrealistic expectation that we are entitled to a life free from suffering and warns us about the causes of lower rebirth that we should assiduously avoid. The descriptions of the miseries and their causes are provided to empower us, for somebody who anticipates problems is in a far better position to deal with them. Awareness of potential suffering induces heedfulness in our own actions and helps us to generate compassion for those who create the causes of suffering.

Chapter 7. Going for Refuge

Is there a truly reliable protection from unhappiness and suffering? Buddhism does not propound salvation by way of an omnipotent being. It emphasizes self-reliance, one of the hallmarks of Dharma practice. Even while we receive help and guidance from the Buddha and others, we have to do the work of liberating ourselves by modifying our thoughts and behavior.

The Three Jewels to which we go for refuge are the Buddha, the Dharma, and the Saṅgha Jewels. The actual object of refuge is the Dharma, because we become liberated from the mire of suffering only by producing in our own mindstream the path leading to the end of suffering and the cessation in which suffering is irreversibly eliminated. The teacher who provided the Dharma instructions, the Buddha, and those who serve as companions on the path, the Saṅgha, are also objects of refuge. In expanded forms of the refuge practice, we include all buddhas within the Buddha Jewel and also go for refuge to our spiritual guides, who embody the Three Jewels.

Having gone for refuge, we need to learn about the characteristics of the Three Jewels and observe the individual and common refuge guidelines, such as avoiding harmful company and refraining from harming others. It is only by taking this proactive approach that we are able to fully reap the benefits of refuge and one day become objects of refuge for others.

Chapter 8. The Principles of Karma

Do our actions really matter? When frustrated and discouraged, we tend to feel that our happiness and suffering are thrust on us by external agents and events beyond our control. However, our experiences are not random occurrences. They are ultimately determined by our actions, possibly even actions created in other lifetimes of which we have no recollection. Since we all want happiness and do not want suffering, we need to safeguard the causes of happiness we have created in the past and create new ones. At the same time, we need to cleanse ourselves of the causes of suffering we have created in the past and abstain from creating new ones.

We learn about the ten most serious nonvirtues and the factors that determine the gravity of karma, as well as the eight desirable qualities of a human rebirth, such as physical attractiveness and good repute, and their causes. It may come as a surprise to see instructions encouraging us to achieve these seemingly mundane attributes, but remember that whether an action is Dharma or not depends on our motivation. Striving for fame in order to bolster our ego is not Dharma, but doing so for the purpose of benefiting others is. And it is important to remember that if we do something unskillful, we are not forever doomed. Instead of wallowing in self-defeating guilt, we open up to the Three Jewels and squarely acknowledge our imperfections. By implementing the four powers of purification sincerely, we can purify ourselves of our negative karma.

Understanding the workings of karma empowers us to chart the kind of future we envision, so that we truly become masters of our own destinies.

The Path in Common with That of Persons with Medium Capacity (Chapters 9–10)

Are we safe once we obtain a good rebirth? The following meditations are done to cultivate the spiritual maturity and farsightedness that view any pleasure in saṃsāra as fleeting and unreliable. By recognizing the possibility of stable lasting happiness, we are no longer captivated by the transitory splendors within the deluded existences of saṃsāra.

Chapter 9. Aspiring for Liberation

Is there anything wrong with our recurring lives in saṃsāra? In the previous meditations belonging to the path in common with that of persons with small capacity, we reflected on the sufferings of the three lower realms and generated the wish to attain a rebirth in the upper realms. However, the upper realms are not free of suffering. To attain irreversible liberation from suffering, we first need the wish to be free of it. Reflection on the general and specific drawbacks of saṃsāra induces an aspiration in us to get off the ferris wheel of suffering for good.

Chapter 10. The Path to Liberation

Does an everlasting solution to dissatisfaction and unhappiness exist? Suffering originates from karma, which in turn arises from afflictions. Afflictions themselves are rooted in the misconception of inherent existence. Since the root of saṃsāra involves an ignorance of how things really exist, to counteract it we have to cultivate the wisdom that understands reality. The foundation of this profound realization is meditative concentration, which provides the focus we need to penetrate subtle reality. Meditative concentration, in which mental obstacles such as laxity and excitement are overcome, must be supported in turn by ethics, in which coarse misconduct is reined in. In brief, the powerful combination of the three trainings in ethics, meditative concentration, and wisdom shatters the fetters binding us to saṃsāra.

The Stages of the Path of Persons with Great Capacity (Chapters 11–16)

Will we be satisfied with attaining the state of individual liberation? What if we could develop the potential to benefit others infinitely? The aim of the following meditations is to develop altruism and equip ourselves with the skills to help all sentient beings find happiness.

Chapter 11. The Sevenfold Cause-and-Effect Instruction

Why should we help others? Do we not already struggle enough to cope with our own problems? What is the point of concern for those around us?

Even if we profess to be the personification of self-centeredness, it is likely that we do care about some other people, such as our parents, family members, and good friends, who have benefited and supported us in our lives. As we are closely related to them, their well-being or lack thereof affects us.

Now what if everyone out there were closely related to you? What if everyone were as closely related to you as your mother of this life? In this sevenfold cause-and-effect instruction, we rely on the Buddhist concept of infinite past lives to arrive at the conclusion that we are intimately connected to all sentient beings, even those who are total strangers in this life. The notion that all sentient beings have been our kind mother uncountable times during our beginningless existences within saṃsāra induces the motivation to benefit all sentient beings without exception.

Beyond wishing others happiness, what can we do in practice to alleviate their pain and bring about their happiness? Are we ready to take on as Herculean a task as this? Someone with perfect wisdom, compassion, and power is best able to provide the highest benefit to all sentient beings. And Buddhism affirms such a potential in each and every living being. Before we even begin to work on attaining this state of highest enlightenment, we must be convinced of the marvelous benefits of undertaking this enormous project and generate the unflinching intention to do so. Thus we first have to cultivate the altruistic wish for buddhahood, called *bodhicitta* in Sanskrit, until it becomes uncontrived and spontaneous.

The sevenfold cause-and-effect instruction is the first of two well-known methods employed to develop the wish to attain enlightenment for the benefit of others, the ultimate good heart. Prior to the actual steps of this instruction, akin to a farmer ploughing and leveling the land in preparation for planting seeds, we need to cultivate an equanimity that is impartial toward *all* sentient beings. Since the purpose of such cultivation is to prepare the mind for the generation of nondiscriminatory love and compassion embracing all living beings, we need to be aware that the last thing we want to promote is an icy attitude of indifference toward others. We develop equanimity in the following sequence toward different subjects:

- neutral person
- friend
- foe
- friend and foe
- all living beings

After developing impartiality toward others, we now have the foundation to meditate on the sevenfold cause-and-effect instruction, which consists of six causes and one result. (1) Over countless lives, everyone, at some point, has been our mother. (2) A mother's care for her offspring is the epitome of kindness. Even if we have a poor relationship with our mother in this life, our mother's thankless act of carrying us in her womb for months and then giving birth to us is an act of incredible kindness. She was instrumental in giving us our precious human existence, which grants us infinite possibilities for inner development and creation of benefit. (3) Since her kindness is immense, it is only natural that we wish to repay her kindness so that she can be well and happy in every way.

As with the cultivation of equanimity above, to cultivate (4) love and (5) compassion, we need to be quite specific and not simply meditate on a generic "all sentient beings." Therefore, when meditating on love wishing happiness on others, our text suggests the following sequence:

- mother
- father
- neutral sentient beings
- foes
- all living beings

When meditating on compassion wishing others to be free from suffering, the following order is suggested:

- sentient beings in despair
- evil-doing sentient beings
- kin
- neutral sentient beings
- foes
- all living beings

(6) As a result of the steps above, we generate the determination to take the responsibility to eliminate the suffering of sentient beings and lead them to happiness. After producing such an exceptional resolve, the thought arises: But who has such ability? Do I? (7) Realizing that only a fully enlightened being has the ability to do so, we aspire to do whatever it takes to attain full enlightenment for their benefit.

We finish this meditation with the visualization that we have attained full enlightenment and then benefit beings everywhere in need. This skillful technique lends valuable impetus to our progress toward buddhahood.

Chapter 12. Equalizing and Exchanging Self and Others

Have you ever experienced the nagging fear that by caring about others you may end up sacrificing your own happiness?

Years ago I lived near my school in a rented room. One night I was woken by a loud rhythmic noise. As soon as I realized that it was the sound of someone snoring, my mind was filled with joy. Why? My landlady was suffering from insomnia and would often get up in the morning feeling exhausted and miserable after a restless night of turning and tossing. Her snoring meant that she was able to get some much-needed repose. In that moment I felt so glad for her, that in no time I drifted blissfully back to sleep. Now, if I had been preoccupied with myself, I would have become annoyed and even angry at her for having interrupted my slumber. Not only would that reaction have upset my mind and prevented me from falling back asleep, it would have soured my relationship with her. Instead, because of my concern for her well-being, my mind remained unperturbed. This simple incident illustrates how caring about others results in win-win situations. Ultimately there is no conflict between our own well-being and that of others. As radical as it sounds, Mahāyāna Buddhism teaches that the only way we will attain the highest happiness for ourselves is by being concerned about others and benefiting them.

The method of equalizing and exchanging self and others confronts the insecurities of the self-centered mind, which holds our well-being as more important than that of others. Nervous and miserable, a narcissistic person is tormented by jealousy when encountering those who are superior, competitiveness encountering those who are equal, and pride encountering those who are inferior. Self-centeredness prevents us from finding happiness and being at peace with ourselves.

By the time we reach this second well-known method for developing bodhicitta, we should already have established the three qualities developed as a result of meditating on the previous method: equanimity that is impartial toward all sentient beings, recognition that all sentient beings have been our mother, and recollection of their kindness.

Here unbiased concern for all living beings is deepened by reflecting on equanimity from an angle different from that of the context of the sevenfold cause-and-effect instruction. We think about how, just as we want happiness and do not want suffering, the same is true for all others. Based on recognizing this sameness of oneself and others, our habitual self-centeredness that prioritizes ourselves over infinite others becomes suspect. Rejecting selfishness and respecting others' right to happiness, we contemplate the disadvantages of narcissism and the advantages of altruism. It is taught in the more extensive explanations that, after equalizing and exchanging self and others in this manner, we engage in the visualization practice of taking and giving (*tonglen*), in which we imagine taking suffering from others out of compassion and giving them happiness out of love. We conclude the meditation by generating the exceptional resolve and the mind of enlightenment, steps 6 and 7 of the previous method of the sevenfold cause-and-effect instruction.

Chapter 13. Committing to Bodhicitta

To formalize our commitment to achieving enlightenment to benefit others, we take bodhisattva vows through a ritual and promise to engage in deeds that will unswervingly propel us toward buddhahood. In addition to contemplating the benefits of bodhicitta, we learn how to avoid the causes of degenerating bodhicitta and how to adopt the causes of increasing bodhicitta.

Chapter 14. Training in the Bodhisattvas' Deeds

What can we actually do to benefit others? The simple wish to go to a particular destination will not take us there; we have to actually embark on the journey. Therefore, after having generated the wish and conviction to attain enlightenment for the benefit of all sentient beings, we train in generosity and other practices so that we can complete the collections of merit and wisdom required for attaining buddhahood. By engaging in the practice of the six perfections—of generosity, ethics, patience, joyous effort, meditative concentration, and wisdom—we bring our own minds to maturation. By undertaking the four means of gathering disciples—giving, agreeable speech, helpful activity, and consistent conduct—we mature the minds of others. Through cultivating such means, we will attain full enlightenment, the dual accomplishments of completely fulfilling our potential and perfectly benefiting others.

Chapter 15. Calm Abiding

How can we unleash the latent capacity of a focused mind? The fifth of the six perfections is discussed in detail in this chapter. Achieved by the application of the eight antidotes to the five faults, calm abiding is meditative stabilization endowed with the bliss of physical and mental pliancy. Turbocharged by concentration, any virtue we create becomes far more powerful than what we create with a scattered mind.

While calm abiding is a remarkable achievement in itself and serves as the basis for attaining clairvoyance and other feats, it is through being unified with the wisdom penetrating ultimate reality, the subject of the next chapter, that it reaches the pinnacle of its capability.

Chapter 16. Special Insight

Do things exist the way they appear to us? In this chapter devoted to the cultivation of the perfection of wisdom, we probe a specific kind of special insight, one that realizes how things really exist and serves as the key to liberation and full enlightenment. Contrary to doctrines that propound the existence of a permanent independent *ātman* or soul, Buddhism teaches that there is no truly existent self and that the realization of such an emptiness or selflessness is indispensable for eliminating the obstructions that prevent liberation and full enlightenment.

Since there is a real danger of misunderstanding this extraordinary idea of emptiness and falling into nihilism, we must bear in mind from the outset that the emptiness explained in Buddhism is not nothingness. Rather, it is a negation of a *particular mode* of existence—true existence from the side of the object. Our fundamental misconception of reality unconsciously assents to the mistaken appearance of such a mode of existence.

To render this discussion less abstract, first take a good look at the object below:

+

Now, what do you see?

Perhaps you see a plus sign. Some of us may identify it as a cross. Others may recognize the Chinese character for "ten."

Given these subjective perceptions, can we say the object is inherently the plus sign? Is it inherently a cross? Is it inherently the Chinese character for "ten"? Is it inherently all of them? Or is it inherently none of them? Or perhaps some of us simply see two short perpendicularly intersecting lines with no particular symbolism.

Regardless of what we think it is, we all see something existing *out there*. For instance, those of us who see a plus sign will likely feel that "+" *is* the plus sign right there, existing from its own side, independent of the perceiver. However, if we were to analyze objectively what we see, we would have to admit that it is more accurate to say that we see *that which we have labeled as* the plus sign. If it were inherently the plus sign, anyone, such as a toddler or a cat, would see it as the plus sign. This little example illustrates how our minds, often unconsciously and automatically, project identities and affix labels to objects that appear to our senses.

According to the Buddhist Middle Way view, we are caught up in a similar but subtler process of perceiving mistaken appearances of reified existence and assenting to those appearances. The mechanism is analogous to the process of a child seeing a mirage and mistakenly believing that there is water. The pervasive reification of things carries far more serious ramifications though, coloring everything we see, hear, smell, and so on. Not only do we conceive forms, sounds, odors, and so on as inherently existent, we also grasp to an inherently existent I. When we sense that this I is threatened, we react with attachment, jealousy, pride, anger, and other emotions founded on a distortion. Under the influence of these afflictive emotions, we create unskillful actions such as stealing and lying, which cause us to take rebirth again and again. Existing since beginningless time, the innate mistaken reification of things is the root of our contaminated existence in saṃsāra. This ignorance must be eradicated for us to free ourselves completely from the web of suffering. It may be difficult for us to accept that we have been wrong in such a prolonged and fundamental manner about how things exist, but without acknowledging this serious error, we will continue to live in its shadow, oblivious to the fact that it is behind all harm and havoc.

To get a feel for the menace of self-grasping, imagine you have just left the supermarket and are pushing a cart full of groceries to the parking lot. As you approach your car, you notice something that causes you to stop in your tracks. Even in the dim evening light, you can make out the distinct outline of a huge dent in the hood of your new car. Dismay and outrage wash over you as you stare in disbelief. What happened? Who did it? Is the engine damaged? How am I going home with all my perishables? How much will it cost to fix? Will insurance cover it? How long will it be in the repair shop? How will I get to work? Dizzied by the tsunami of panicky reactions, you take a deep breath and try to steady your nerves. Taking another look, you realize that the number on the license plate is not familiar. Your focus on that car relaxes, your field of vision opens up, and you spot, three spaces away, a similar car without the dent and with a familiar license plate. The tightness in your chest evaporates instantaneously, and you are flooded with relief. Turning your attention back to the previous car, you cannot help but burst out laughing!

Now, imagining that you are the protagonist in the above scenario, analyze the panic that was felt by reflecting on its causes along these lines:

- Was my panic caused by the dent in the car?
- Was my panic caused by *me seeing* the dent in the car?
- Was my panic caused by me seeing the dent in the car *that was mine*?
- Was my panic caused by me seeing the dent in the car that *I thought* was mine?

> Well, my panic was not caused by the dent in the car, because the dent was already there even before I saw it and I was not panicking then. Perhaps that was because I hadn't seen it yet. My

> panic was not caused by *me seeing* the dent in the car, because I was laughing in relief when I saw it afterward. Perhaps that was because that car wasn't mine. My panic was not caused by me seeing the dent in the car *that was mine*, because that car was never mine at any point in time. So, my panic was caused by me seeing the dent in the car that *I thought* was mine.

Nothing had the power to make you upset—as long as no palpable sense of the I was involved. Your alarm was triggered when you conceived the car as yours and perceived harm to your sense of a self and its belongings, even though no harm was inflicted in reality. The culprit behind your turmoil did not lie outside; nothing really changed externally while your emotional drama played out. What tripped you up was your own inner self-grasping.

In general, the stronger our self-grasping, the more neurotic we become. In such moments, we find a strong grasping to a concrete independent self. Such a self is utterly nonexistent, like the water a child believes he sees when looking at a mirage. Known as the *object of negation*,[16] that appearance of intrinsic identity is recognized through personal experience and refuted through reasoned analysis. The mind grasping to such a self will be refuted once we realize its nonexistence, just as the mind believing that there is water in the mirage is refuted once the child discovers that there is no water there. Note that we are not denying our conventional self-identity, as when we casually think "I wake up at six every morning. I brush my teeth twice a day. I eat breakfast at seven o'clock."

To understand the difference between the conventionally existent self and the nonexistent self that is the object of negation, consider another scenario. You are fumbling about for your car keys in your bag when your hand feels a piece of paper. It turns out to be the lottery ticket you bought a week ago. Taking a closer look, you note to yourself, "I bought the number 97531." Since the winning number should already have been announced three days ago, you take out your phone and look up the results. The webpage starts to load, and the winning number unfolds. Your eyes widen as you realize that the number that has won 10 million dollars is 97531. "I bought the number 97531," your mind screams in shock, as euphoria sweeps over you.

Compare your sense of the I in the two instances when you generated the thought "I bought the number 97531." In the later instance, the sense of the I is likely much more vivid; that I appears to exist inherently, from its own side, independent of anything else. This reified I is the object of negation, for an inherently existent I is impossible. Nothing whatsoever can exist inherently. And the mind apprehending a reified I is a wrong consciousness, like the mind apprehending water when there is none.

The technical name for this mind involved in the reification of identity is the *conception of self*, of which there are two kinds: the conception of self of *persons* and the conception of self of *phenomena*. These two kinds of conceptions are distinguished by their objects, whether persons (such as a human being, an animal, or any other type of living being with a mind) or entities other than persons (such as a vase or a pillar).

How do we rid ourselves of these erroneous conceptions? Mere knowledge that they are erroneous is not sufficient to eradicate them, as these innate forms of ignorance have been deeply ingrained in our mental continuum since beginningless time. Reasoned analysis and repeated meditation are the methods recommended by the lamrim. We first correctly identify the object of negation, the reified existence—also called inherent existence, true existence, independent existence, or existence by way of its own character—that appears vividly to us, especially when we are experiencing strong emotions such as anxiety or elation. Like the water that appears to a child looking at a mirage, inherent existence appears but does not exist in reality. We can easily refute the existence of water in the above physical example by approaching the mirage and so confirming its nonexistence, whereas in the case of refuting inherent existence, we draw close by applying the logic that proves that things do not exist inherently despite appearing to do so.

Many logical reasonings can be employed to prove that persons and other phenomena do not exist inherently. The reasoning called *absence of being one or many* is employed in the *Swift Path* to prove that the object of negation does not exist. This approach may seem unnatural initially, but it is a rigorous and thorough method whose power will become apparent with repeated application. The main steps of the reasoning process are summarized under the four essential points: (1) ascertaining how the object of negation appears, (2) ascertaining the entailment exhaustively, (3) ascertaining the absence of being truly one, and (4) ascertaining the absence of being truly many.

Once we develop a clear idea of what a truly existent person would be like were it to exist, we consider that if such a truly existent person did exist, it would have to be either truly singular or truly plural; there is no third possibility. Having determined such an entailment, we proceed to explore the feasibility of each of those two alternatives. If, upon thorough examination, we discover that it can be neither, then we must conclude that the person is not truly existent.

The inference process is straightforward, but at first glance it may seem abstract, so let us illustrate it using an analogy. Say you are scrolling through Instagram and you come across a stunning photograph of a salad that looks absolutely delectable. Following the five-star recipe accompanying the photo, you begin to assemble the list of ingredients, and your culinary venture is progressing nicely until you arrive at the last item, a fresh herb called chervil. Your mother happens to be an avid gardener and grows many varieties of herbs in both her garden beds. If there is fresh chervil at home, it has to be in one of these two garden beds. However, if you cannot find it after looking thoroughly through the herbs in both beds, then you have to conclude that you do not have fresh chervil at home and you are missing that ingredient. We follow a similar logical procedure when proving that there is no inherent self by the reasoning called *absence of being one or many*. The understanding that "If there is fresh chervil at home, it must be in one or the other garden bed" illustrates the second essential point, ascertaining the entailment exhaustively. Looking for the herb in the two beds and not finding it in either bed illustrates the third and fourth essential points.

The first essential point is actually the most crucial and challenging step. In the analogy, suppose you have no recollection of ever encountering this herb chervil and have not the slightest idea what it looks, smells, or tastes like. How then can you determine whether it is in the garden beds?

So, in the proof that true existence does not exist, you need first and foremost to identify how something, say a person, would exist if it were truly existent. Simply knowing that the object of negation is called *true existence* or *inherent existence* does not cut it, just as knowing that the herb is called *chervil* is insufficient for you to identify it among the herbs in the garden beds.

The importance of identifying the object of negation correctly cannot be overemphasized. What are the chances of you hitting a target when you do not really know what the target is? Great meditators have explained that once you have correctly identified the object of negation—in a way that is neither overly narrow nor overly broad—then you are not far from realizing emptiness. Do not underestimate what it takes to nail this step. On the one hand, you have to take every precaution to prevent yourself from falling into the extreme of utter nonexistence due to negating too much and denying even conventional existence. On the other hand, you have to guard against falling into the extreme of inherent existence due to negating too little and assenting to false appearances. It is imperative that you put effort into the first essential point and develop a clear idea of what a truly existent person would be like if it existed, before plunging into the remaining steps to refute true existence.

In the second essential point of ascertaining the entailment exhaustively, we consider that if such a truly existent person were to exist, it would have to be either *one* or *more than one* in terms of quantity. There is no other possibility.

Conventionally speaking, for example, an egg is just one in quantity, whereas a dozen eggs are many in quantity. However, to claim that something is truly one is to assert that it is a singular entity in an absolute sense. This is tantamount to saying that it has no divisions whatsoever from any point of view. While it is perfectly fine for one egg to exist, an egg that is *truly* one is infeasible, for an egg that is *truly* one cannot contain parts—such as the egg white and yolk. In the case of a human, the parts are the body and mind, or more technically, the five aggregates, as Buddhism defines the constituents of body and mind as forms, feelings, discriminations, compositional factors, and consciousnesses. Since everything has parts, nothing can be truly one. And if truly existent singularity is impossible, then truly existent plurality—composed of multiple singularities—is impossible too. In this way, we ascertain that a truly existent person is neither truly one nor truly many, thus fulfilling the third and fourth essential points.

Through this reasoning process, we eventually arrive at the conclusion that the person is not truly existent. It is important to bear in mind that this means that the *truly existent* person does not exist; it does *not* mean that the person does not exist. We do exist—conventionally!

Once we understand the reality that nothing exists truly, we become like a person who wakes up from a nightmare, realizing that all our sufferings have been unnecessary.

Chapter 17. Concluding Advice

Here the author shares nuggets of advice on what to do when we run into roadblocks on our path. The exhortation to practice made at the end of the section on the path of persons with small capacity is reiterated here. In addition, he warns of the pitfall of trying to practice without studying. Theory and practice must always go hand in hand.

Chapter 18. Colophon

The author explains that his composition *Swift Path* is a supplement to the *Easy Path* composed by his predecessor.

The Swift Path to Omniscience

An Explicit Instruction on
the Stages of the Path to Enlightenment

༄། །བྱང་ཆུབ་ལམ་གྱི་རིམ་པའི་དམར་ཁྲིད་
ཐམས་ཅད་མཁྱེན་པར་བགྲོད་པའི་མྱུར་ལམ།།

Paṇchen Losang Yeshé
(1663–1737)

Groundwork

1 | Overview

Namo guru munīndraya.[17]

With your wondrous courage and hook of compassion,
you guide beings, unruly and incorrigible,
who cannot be freed by other sugatas;[18]
to you, the supreme guide, preeminent among the Śākyas,[19] reverently
I pay homage.

Ajitanātha,[20] lord of the vast deeds,
Mañjughoṣa, bestower of the profound view,[21]
Nāgārjuna and Asaṅga, who beautify Jambūdvīpa,[22]
until I reach the essence of enlightenment,[23] to you I go for refuge.

Atiśa, the supreme master of instructions on exposition and practice,
foremost Dromtönpa, the forefather of Kadam teachings,
the four yogis,[24] three brothers,[25]
and the rest of the Kadam masters, from my heart I bow down to you.

From the ocean of your good understanding (*losang*) of the Muni's
complete teachings,
you stir up the mighty waves of compositions, explanations, and debates,
scattering in the ten directions sea sprays of pristine repute (*drak*);
to you, glorious Losang Drakpa, with my crown I bow down.[26]

Supremely intelligent one (*losang*) who upholds the banner of Dharma
(*chökyi gyaltsen*)[27]
and the lord of speech (*ngagi wangchuk*), an ocean of intelligence
(*losang gyatso*),[28]

kind teachers who reveal the unmistaken path, to you reverently
I bow down;
please hold me with your hook of compassion!

HERE, FOR FORTUNATE trainees who are not merely enthralled by words, but who truly seek omniscience,[29] the instructions on the stages of the path to enlightenment that lead to buddhahood are presented in two parts: an explanation of how to develop conviction in the enumeration and sequence of the paths through an account of the lineage masters who are their sources[30] and an actual explanation of how to train your mind in the stages of the paths after having developed conviction in their enumeration and sequence.[31]

An Explanation of How to Develop Conviction in the Enumeration and Sequence of the Paths through an Account of the Lineage Masters Who Are Their Sources

Just as the source of a river must be traceable to snow [in the mountains], the transmission of the excellent Dharma must be traceable to the perfect complete Buddha, who is the principal of the teachings. The stages of the paths of persons with the three capacities may be considered from the point of view of the stages of the *vast path* and the stages of the *profound path*.

Transmission through the Indian lineage masters

The stages of the *vast path* were transmitted from the perfect complete Buddha to Venerable Maitreya, then to Asaṅga, his brother [Vasubandhu], and so on. The stages of the *profound path* were transmitted from the perfect complete Buddha to Venerable Mañjuśrī, then to the glorious protector Ārya Nāgārjuna, and so on. The glorious Dīpaṃkara [Atiśa][32] received both these transmissions. In brief, as the glorious protector Ārya Nāgārjuna was renowned as the second Teacher [Buddha] in relation to these teachings, and there was nothing known by him that was not known by Jowo [Atiśa][33] concerning the Dharma, you should generate conviction in Atiśa as the principal of the teachings.

Transmission through the Kadam lineage masters

The great Atiśa gave this lamrim instruction as a hidden teaching to Geshé Tönpa.[34] When Geshé Dromtönpa asked Atiśa why he conferred the lamrim instruction on him and tantric instructions on others, Atiśa replied that he could not find any other suitable candidate for the lamrim instruction. Therefore Atiśa gave this oral instruction to Geshé Dromtönpa and blessed him as the principal of this teaching, thus initiating an auspicious chain of events that culminated in Geshé Dromtönpa's vast activities.

The great Geshé Dromtönpa taught it to the Naljor Wangchuk Gönpawa,[35] who in turn taught it to Neusurwa, who taught it to Thakmapa, who taught it to Gyerchenpo. Geshé Dromtönpa also taught it to Chen Ngar Tsultrim Bar,[36] who taught it to Jayulwa. These were the two lamrim [lineages] that were transmitted through the Kadam followers of quintessential instructions.[37] The great venerable Dharma king, Tsongkhapa, received them from Lhodrak Drupchen Lekyi Dorjé.[38]

Geshé Dromtönpa also taught it to Geshé Potowa, who taught it to Geshé Dölpa and Sharawa. This was the lamrim that was transmitted through the Kadam followers of texts.[39] Tsongkhapa received it from Drakor Khenchen Chökyab Sangpo.[40]

The stages in which these lineages were subsequently transmitted to later masters are as they have been clearly stated in the *Lamrim Supplication Prayer*.[41]

Transmission through the Geluk lineage masters

In the beginning the Foremost Great Being[42] mainly trained his mind in the three—renunciation, bodhicitta, and the correct view—that were taught by Venerable Mañjuśrī. Later, he brought the image of Atiśa renowned as the Tilted Head[43] to the Radreng Gyalwa Hermitage.[44] By making heartfelt supplications over a long period of time, he saw all the lineage masters—ranging from the perfect complete Buddha to Lhodrak Drupchen Namkha Gyaltsen, and in particular Atiśa, Dromtönpa, Potowa, and Sharawa—for a month. After bestowing many instructions and teachings upon him, finally the three—Potowa and so forth—absorbed into Atiśa. Placing his hand on Tsongkhapa's crown, Atiśa told him to perform extensive deeds for the sake of the Buddha's teachings and assured Tsongkhapa that he would assist him

Lamrim Transmission Lineage

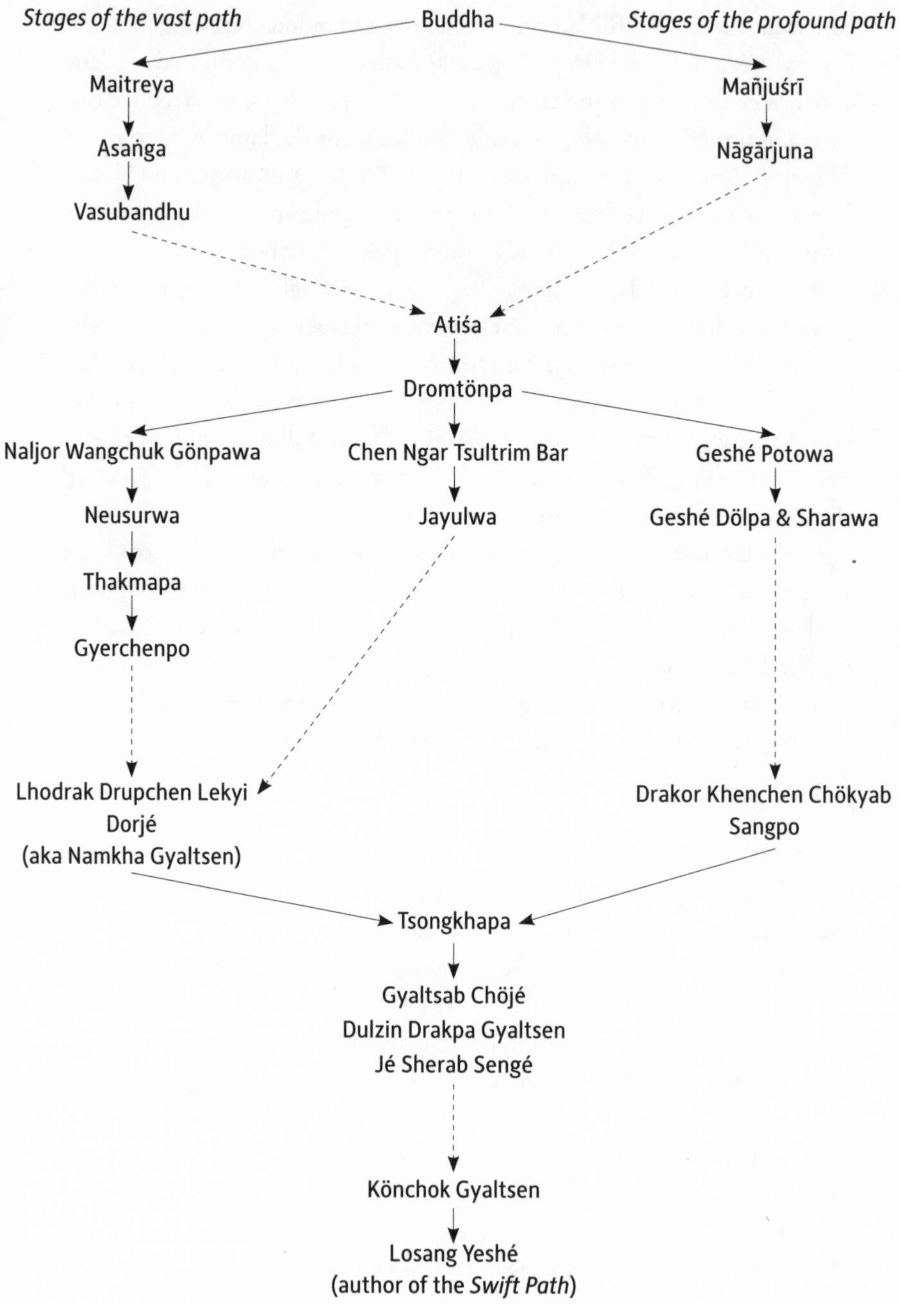

Note that a dotted arrow signifies the presence of other lineage masters whose names are not explicitly spelt out.

to achieve his own enlightenment and enact the welfare of sentient beings. After that he vanished. Such wondrous events occurred frequently.

During this period, at the urgings of Khenchen Surphuwa Könchok Palsangpo, Lochen Kyabchok Palsangpo, and others, Tsongkhapa composed the *Great Exposition on the Stages of the Path to Enlightenment*.[45] Venerable Mañjuśrī asked him, "Did you not include within it the path taught by me, the one that guides trainees by means of renunciation, bodhicitta, and the correct view?"

Tsongkhapa replied, "I did not incur the fault of omitting that. I took those three principal aspects as the lifeblood of the text, supplemented them with passages from the *Lamp for the Path to Enlightenment* and other texts, and connected them to the stages of the paths of persons with the three capacities."[46]

Such inconceivable secret exchanges between the two took place, and therefore these essential points of the stages of the path may be taken as having been transmitted from Venerable Mañjuśrī himself to Jé Rinpoché.

Many disciples of Tsongkhapa received the transmission of the instructions, so the modes of the lamrim's transmissions are as numerous as them. The lineage that Gyalwa Ensapa and his spiritual son[47] received had been transmitted from one master to the next in the following sequence:

- Tsongkhapa
- Gyaltsab Chöjé[48]
- Dulzin Drakpa Gyaltsen[49]
- Khedrup Chöjé[50]
- Jé Sherab Sengé[51]
- Dulzin Lodrö Bepa
- Paṇchen Chökyi Gyaltsen[52]
- Jé Kyabchok Palsang
- Jé Drupai Wangchuk Losang Döndrup[53]
- Jé Sangyé Yeshé
- Paṇchen Tamché Khyenpa Losang Chökyi Gyaltsen[54]
- Dorjé Dzinpa Könchok Gyaltsen Palsangpo[55]

It is through the kindness of Dorjé Dzinpa Könchok Gyaltsen Palsangpo that I received this Dharma. Alternatively, the lineage was transmitted as follows:

- Tsongkhapa
- Jé Sherab Sengé
- Dulzin Lodrö Bepa
- And the rest are as listed previously [Paṇchen Baso Chökyi Gyaltsen, etc.]

Or else:

- Tsongkhapa
- Dulzin Drakpa Gyaltsen
- Jé Sherab Sengé
- And the rest are as listed previously [Dulzin Lodrö Bepa, etc.]

Tsongkhapa's great and small lamrims

Having thus composed the *Great Exposition*, Tsongkhapa composed a smaller lamrim that excellently summarized all the essential points without omission.[56] This was achieved by dispensing with citations, refutations [of incorrect positions], and proofs [of correct positions] that were provided in the *Great Exposition.*

Moreover, observing the declining mental capacities of trainees, Tsongkhapa made the following proposition in the *Great Exposition*:

> However, those who know how to bring all these explanations into practice seem barely to exist at all, and therefore you should formulate a separate concise presentation of what should be constantly maintained in meditation.[57]

Taking this advice to heart, Paṇchen Tamché Khyenpa[58] composed the *Easy Path to Omniscience: An Explicit Instruction on the Stages of the Path*, and Gyalwang Tamché Khyenpa Chenpo[59] composed the *Words of Mañjuśrī*,[60] which are both of intermediate length and governed by scripture and reasoning.

There is nothing lacking in these treatises if you have the ability to meditate on them. However, at the insistence of others, and reflecting, if I, who am wanting in merit and intellect, were to develop a deep understanding of these stages of the path, it would contribute significantly to my own inquiry about advanced achievements, I shall, in accordance with my own understanding, write about their enumeration, sequence, and individual natures. You should understand from the greater and smaller *Expositions on the Stages of the Path to Enlightenment* the points regarding the greatness of the author, the greatness of the Dharma, and how to listen to and explain the Dharma.[61]

Atiśa

It is stated [in the *Great Exposition on the Stages of the Path to Enlightenment*] that "The author of that is also the author of this."[62] Some may claim that this means Atiśa and Tsongkhapa are of one mental continuum. Even though the two of them are indeed of one mental continuum, since Tsongkhapa is very unassuming, how could he openly profess that he is of one mental continuum with Atiśa? Rather, this statement means that the *Lamp for the Path to Enlightenment* is the root text that serves as the subject of explanation of the *Stages of the Path*,[63] *Stages of the Teachings*,[64] and *Supreme Path*.[65] Therefore it is stated that "[The author of that] is also the author of this," and the author in this context is taken to be also the author of the *Lamp for the Path to Enlightenment*—namely, Atiśa. Doing so can be likened to bringing forward the statement of authorship, normally found in the colophon at the end of the great commentaries, to the beginning of the text.

While it is stated in certain lamrim writings that Atiśa lived in Tibet for only thirteen years, the explanation given by Tsongkhapa that Atiśa lived in Tibet for seventeen years is accurate. Indeed, the source for Atiśa's biography can be traced to Naktso Lotsāwa, and it is stated in the *Praise of Atiśa in Eighty Verses* composed by Naktso himself that Naktso relied on Atiśa for nineteen years, of which two years were spent in India and seventeen in Tibet.[66] The *Praise of Atiśa in Eighty Verses* says:

> Even though I relied upon you and accompanied you for
>   nineteen years,
> I never saw any flaws
> in your body, speech, and mind.[67]

And:

When you were in Somapuri teaching the *Blaze of Reasoning*[68]
you said, "I will pass away
in twenty years."
Then, two years later,
when setting off for Tibet,
at Vikramaśīla,[69]
you said, "Passing away
in eighteen years,
I will leave this body behind in Tibet."
It happened exactly as you declared—
how amazing![70]

QUESTION: It is explained that when one relies on the *Lamp for the Path to Enlightenment* or the *Stages of the Path*, all teachings will be realized to be free from contradictions, and all scriptures without exception will dawn as instructions.[71] (1) Why then is it that all the paths that are the subject matter of the scriptures are subsumed within the stages of the paths of those with the three capacities? (2) Why must one first traverse the path in common with that of persons with medium capacity in order to produce the path of those with great capacity in one's mindstream? Why is it that the path in common with that of persons with small capacity must first be produced in one's mindstream in order for the path in common with that of persons with medium capacity to be produced in one's mindstream?

ANSWER: (1) Initially the Buddha generated bodhicitta. Then he accrued the collections of merit and wisdom. Finally he displayed the deed of attaining complete buddhahood. Since these were all done for the sake of sentient beings, the Dharma he taught was only ever for the sake of accomplishing their welfare. Their welfare consists of high rebirths,[72] which are temporary, and beatitude, which is final. *Beatitude* refers to liberation and omniscience.[73]

Every kind of Dharma taught for the purpose of accomplishing high rebirths is either directly subsumed under the actual Dharma of those with *small* capacity or under the Dharma in common with that of persons with small capacity. Every Dharma taught for the purpose of accomplishing liberation is subsumed under the Dharma in common with that of persons with *medium* capacity.[74] Every kind of Dharma taught for the purpose of accomplishing omniscience is subsumed under the Dharma of those with *great* capacity.

Therefore all the paths that are the subject matter of the scriptures are subsumed within the stages of the paths of persons with the three capacities.

Welfare of sentient beings		*Dharma that is the means of achieving their welfare*
Temporary	High rebirths	Actual dharma of those with small capacity or dharma in common with that of persons with small capacity
Final	Liberation	Actual dharma of those with medium capacity or dharma in common with that of persons with medium capacity
	Omniscience	Dharma of those with great capacity

(2) The two divisions of Mahāyāna are Pāramitāyāna and Vajrayāna.[75] Regardless of which of these two you enter, it is certain that the doorway to the Mahāyāna is bodhicitta.[76] In order to produce bodhicitta in your mindstream, you must possess the compassion that cannot bear the thought of all sentient beings being pained by suffering. In order to produce such great compassion, generate a mindset consisting of two components—fear of the sufferings of saṃsāra and specifically those of the lower rebirths,[77] and conviction that the Three Jewels are able to protect from the sufferings—explained in the contexts of persons with small and medium capacities. This mindset is essential as, lacking fear of the sufferings of saṃsāra and of specifically the lower rebirths and the fervent desire to become free from them, you will be unable to generate an intense compassion that cannot bear the thought of others being pained by suffering. *Kṣitigarbha's Ten Wheels Sūtra* says:

> If you lack even the strength to drink up a river,
> how can you swallow a great ocean?
> If you lack the ability to familiarize yourself with the two vehicles,[78]
> how can you train in the Mahāyāna?[79]

And the *Stages of the Path* says:

> Imagine a person who reflects on himself wandering in saṃsāra, deprived of happiness and tormented by suffering, and yet still fails to be sufficiently moved that goosebumps appear. Under such circumstances, such a person will never find unbearable the thought of other sentient beings being deprived of happiness and pained by suffering. Accordingly, *Engaging in Bodhisattva Deeds* says:
>
>> If those beings have not
>> previously dreamt of such a mind
>> for their own welfare in their dreams,
>> how can they produce it for the welfare of others?[80]

Therefore guiding a person through the stages of the paths of persons with the three capacities in this context does not refer to guiding them on the *actual* paths of persons with small and medium capacities. Rather, it refers to guiding them through certain paths *that are in common with those* of persons with small and medium capacities, as preliminary branches of the path of persons with great capacity, for the purpose of accruing the collections of merit and wisdom and purifying obstructions.

QUESTION: If the Dharmas of persons with small and medium capacities are branches of the Dharma of persons with great capacity, then one could take them as paths of persons with great capacity. Why is it necessary to use the expression "stages of the paths *that are in common with those* of persons with small and medium capacities?"

ANSWER: Distinguishing persons with the three capacities and then guiding [them accordingly] serves two great purposes: (1) It destroys the pride that believes one is a person with great capacity when one has not even managed to produce the mindsets that are in common with those of persons with small and medium capacities. (2) There is great benefit for those of the three levels of mindsets—the superior, the middling, and the least. Those with greater spiritual intellect—namely, those with great and medium capacities—need to obtain the state of an upper rebirth, the physical basis for practicing the Dharma.[81] Even if a person with minimal capacity sets his sights on entering the path of persons with great capacity, without training in the mindsets of persons with small and medium capacities, he will be unable to produce a higher attitude. Neglecting the two lower stages, such an individual will attain nothing.

Therefore, if you wish to enter the stages of the Mahāyāna path, and specifically highest yoga tantra,[82] it is vital that you pay great attention to the paths that are in common with those of persons with small and medium capacities. Venerable Mañjuśrī taught that initially you should set aside the instructions of tantra and so forth, regardless of how profound they are supposed to be; instead, you must try to elicit the experiential realizations of renunciation and bodhicitta.[83] Once these realizations are produced, all ensuing virtues will automatically become the causes of liberation and omniscience. Anyone who deems as worthless the meditations on [renunciation and bodhicitta] is a person utterly ignorant of the essentials of the path.

2 | General Preparatory Practices

An actual explanation of how to train your mind in the stages of the paths after having developed conviction in their enumeration and sequence

This is explained in two parts: the way of relying on a spiritual guide, the root of the path; and having relied on a spiritual guide, the stages of how to train your mind. The first is explained in two parts: what to do during the session and what to do between the sessions. The first of those has three parts: preparation, the actual meditation on relying on a spiritual guide, and conclusion.

Preparation[84]

This consists of six practices: (1) cleaning the room and arranging representations of the enlightened body, speech, and mind; (2) laying out offerings that have been obtained rightfully without deceit and displaying them beautifully; (3) sitting upon a comfortable seat in the eightfold posture or any convenient posture and cultivating refuge, bodhicitta, and the four immeasurables; (4) visualizing the merit field; (5) offering the seven-limbed practice—which distills the essentials of accruing the collections of merit and wisdom and purifying misdeeds—and a maṇḍala; and (6) imbuing your mind with the supplication according to the oral instructions.[85]

(1) Cleaning the room and arranging representations of the enlightened body, speech, and mind

Regardless of whether your dwelling is a monastery, medicinal grove, mountain hermitage, or any other place, the way to clean your dwelling is the same. If you dwell in a mountain hermitage and the surrounding area is spacious, erect four markers in the four directions of your abode, and after generating the markers into the four great kings,[86] make offerings and offer tormas to them.[87] Then request their assistance to dispel unfavorable conditions and obstacles and create favorable conditions so you may meditate on the instructions of the stages of the path to enlightenment. Sprinkle water[88] and sweep the floor of your dwelling.

Having made your dwelling into a space where you can joyfully abide, next arrange the representations of the enlightened body, speech, and mind. Adhering to the tradition of past Kadampa lamas who would always carry an image of Buddha Śākyamuni inseparably with them, place an image of Buddha Śākyamuni upon a high altar before you. Regard it as the actual Buddha. If you do not have an image of Buddha Śākyamuni, configure a very smooth surface called the *accomplishment maṇḍala*[89] and anoint it with *bachung* and scents.[90] If even that is unavailable, use a flat piece of wood or stone. Place nine heaps of grains such as barley or rice on its surface and visualize them as the actual principal figure Śākyamuni along with his retinue.

Draw a swastika under your seat with white chalk in a Dharma-turning manner.[91] It is necessary to place a soft cushion of *durva* grass above the swastika. Arrange the strands neatly so that the tips point inward and the base points outward. In the past, the perfect complete Buddha accepted grass from the grass-seller boy called Svastika[92] and fashioned it into a cushion by neatly arranging the strands of grass so that the tips pointed inward and the base outward. At the break of dawn on the fifteenth day of the month, he displayed the deed of attaining full enlightenment. As such an auspicious chain of events [ensued from sitting on the cushion of *durva* grass], trainees who try to emulate past deeds of the Teacher's life adopt this practice. If you already have in your dwelling a crafted cushion, you may use that. If not, a soft cushion crafted from *artemisia*[93] or any type of grass may be used. Adjust it so that it is slightly higher at the back and slightly lower in front.

(2) Laying out offerings that have been obtained rightfully without deceit and displaying them beautifully

The best vessels for the offerings are fashioned from gold or silver, and middling ones from copper or brass. If you cannot acquire those, vessels of any material, such as wood, can be used. Present all the offerings—drinking water, water for washing the feet, and so forth—in these vessels. Do not offer them perfunctorily, as if fulfilling a tax obligation, or by blindly following others. Moreover, the offerings should be given without anticipating gain, reputation, fame, and other advantages of this life. Instead, reflect as follows:

> No matter what it takes, I will attain the precious state of full enlightenment swiftly, swiftly for the sake of all mother sentient beings. To that end, I offer these to the Three Jewels.

When the offerings are presented with such an attitude, the person making the offerings derives benefit and those offerings become meaningful. Therefore perform your offerings in like manner.

(3) Sitting upon a comfortable seat in the eightfold posture or any convenient posture and cultivating refuge, bodhicitta, and the four immeasurables

Sit upon a comfortable seat in the eightfold posture or any convenient posture. The eightfold posture is as taught by the great Gyalwa Ensapa:

> The legs, the hands, the midriff are three,
> with the teeth, lips, and tongue combined as the fourth.
> The head, the eyes, the shoulders, and the breath are four.
> These are the eight attributes of Vairocana.

The eight attributes are as follows. (1) Upon the seat prepared above, sit with your legs in the vajra posture,[94] or if that is not possible, sit in the half-vajra posture. To sit in the half-vajra posture, draw your left leg inward, place your right leg outside of that, and—rather than placing the front part of your left foot under your right thigh or at the back of your right knee—place your left heel by your groin. (2) To arrange your hands in the gesture of meditative equipoise, cup your right hand in your left and set them four finger-widths below your navel. Lightly join the tips of your thumbs. This arrangement carries special auspicious implications pertaining to the essential points of your channels.[95] (3) Straighten your midriff. (4) Slightly bow your head.

Leave your teeth and lips in their natural positions. Touch the roof of your mouth lightly behind the teeth with the tip of your tongue. (5) Keep your head straight without tilting to either side. (6) Direct your eyes at the tip of your nose. (7) Level your shoulders. (8) Breathe naturally.

To breathe naturally, avoid breathing in a way that is noisy, forceful, agitated, and the like. You will ready your mind for the cultivation of meditative stabilization if you count twenty-one rounds of gentle inhalation and exhalation before you begin the practice. *Highway of the Conquerors: A Root Text for the Precious Geluk Tradition of Mahāmudrā* says:

> Upon a comfortable seat of meditative stabilization,
> sit in the posture endowed with the seven essentials of the body.[96]
> Expel the stale winds over nine rounds.[97]

Some high Kagyü lamas of the past identified sitting in this physical posture as the first step of meditation, as in the phrase "In the language of India."[98] Yet some high excellent beings assert that faith is the first step of meditation, as in the same phrase "In the language of India." However, in our system the proper examination of the motivation in one's mental continuum is taken to be the first step of meditation. Paṇchen [Losang Chökyi Gyaltsen's] *Melodious Speech of Losang's Assertions: Responses to Sincere Queries* says:

> "The first step of all meditations
> is to examine well one's mental continuum,
> as in the phrase 'In the language of India,'"
> the supreme peerless lama asserts.[99]

Therefore meditate on the instructions on the stages of the path to enlightenment only after properly examining the motivation in your mental continuum. Investigate, "Am I meditating out of the desire for wealth in this life? The desire for fame? Or the eight worldly concerns of gain, honor, reputation, and so forth? Or am I meditating for the sake of my future life?"[100] Any action done out of the desire for wealth or fame in this life, or the worldly concerns of gain, honor, and reputation, will not contribute to the well-being of your next rebirth. The *General Rituals for All Maṇḍalas Tantra* says:

> Do not desire the results of this life.
> By desiring this life,
> the purpose of the life beyond will not be fulfilled.
> Produce the aspiration seeking the life beyond,
> and the results of this life will expand.[101]

And Atiśa taught that if a plant's roots are poisonous, its branches and leaves will also be poisonous, and if a plant's roots are medicinal, its branches and leaves will also be medicinal. Similarly, whatever action motivated at its root by the three—attachment, aversion, and ignorance—can only ever be nonvirtuous.

Geshé Dromtönpa asked Atiśa, "What are the results of actions done out of desire for the pleasure, gain, and honor of this life?" Atiśa answered, "The results will only ever be those." Dromtönpa asked, "What will lie in store in the next life?" Atiśa replied, "Hell, hungry ghost realm, animal realm."

As explained, actions done out of desire for the pleasure, gain, and honor of this life are mostly causes for lower rebirths. Actions done out of desire for human and godly pleasures in future lives are mostly only causes for saṃsāra.[102] Actions created by way of an attitude seeking one's own happiness of pacification alone are the causes for falling into the extreme of pacification.[103]

In general, there are many types of virtuous minds—such as lucid faith in the Three Jewels, faith of conviction in karma and its results,[104] the mind of charity, and the wish to guard one's ethics—but the special virtuous mind in this context refers to bodhicitta. Therefore reflect as follows:

> Just as I am pained by suffering, so are all sentient beings. Moreover, all these sentient beings who are pained by suffering, without exception, have been my kind mother. Not a single sentient being has not. Each has been my mother countless times. And in each and every one of those instances, they tenderly nurtured me as my mother in this life has. Their kindness is boundless.

Reflect further:

> Now, who should be responsible for freeing all sentient beings from suffering? I should. However, though that responsibility

> is mine, at present I do not have the ability to fulfill the welfare of even one, let alone the welfare of all sentient beings. Even if I were to attain the state of the two types of arhats,[105] apart from benefiting sentient beings in limited ways, I would lack the ability to guide all sentient beings to the fully enlightened state of buddhahood. Who has that ability? Only a perfect complete buddha. Therefore, no matter what it takes, I will attain the precious state of a perfect complete buddha for the sake of all mother sentient beings.

Meditate earnestly in this way until you elicit the experiential realization of bodhicitta.[106]

While conjoined with bodhicitta, go for refuge as follows. First visualize the following:

> In the space before me is a high and vast throne made of precious stones and supported by eight great lions. Above it is a seat consisting of a multicolored lotus, moon disc, and sun disc. Upon it sits [the central figure], in nature my kind root teacher, having the aspect of Conqueror Śākyamuni.[107] His body is the color of refined gold. Endowed with a crown protrusion,[108] he has one face and two arms. His right hand presses the ground, and his left displays the gesture of meditative equipoise while holding an alms bowl filled with nectar.[109] He is clad in orange Dharma robes. Adorned with the signs and exemplifying marks,[110] he has the nature of transparent light. He sits with his legs in the vajra posture amid a profusion of light emanating from his body.
>
> He is surrounded by the direct and lineage masters, deities,[111] buddhas, bodhisattvas, and hosts of heroes, heroines,[112] ḍākas, ḍākinīs,[113] Dharma protectors, and guardians. In front of each is a splendid stand upon which the Dharma teachings given by them take the aspect of volumes of texts having the nature of light. The members of the merit field display their pleasure with me.

From a state of great faith recollecting the excellent qualities and compassion of the merit field, contemplate as follows:

The field of refuge (see description on page 56).

The merit field (see description on pages 67–68).

Nāgārjuna says:

> The amount of milk imbibed by a person exceeds the
> four oceans,[114]
> but know that the wanderer in saṃsāra
> who follows the ways of ordinary beings
> still has far more to drink.[115]

Āryadeva says:

> When this ocean of suffering
> has utterly no limit,
> O fool, you who have sunk into it,
> why are you not afraid?[116]

As said, you have sunk into this ocean of suffering whose breadth and depth are difficult to fathom. Yet you do not experience the slightest unease, dismay, fear, or trepidation that should cause your hair to stand on end. If you are not a fool, what are you then? A wise man? Reflect as follows:

> Since beginningless time till now, I and all mother sentient beings have experienced the various sufferings of saṃsāra, specifically those of the three lower rebirths, and yet it is still difficult for us to comprehend the scope of that suffering.[117] This time I have obtained a special physical basis endowed with the freedoms and privileges, one so hard to find and greatly meaningful when found.[118] I have also encountered the precious teachings of the Buddha, which are difficult to encounter. Should I fail to act and attain now the state of a perfect complete buddha, the supreme liberation in which all sufferings of saṃsāra have been abandoned, I will once again experience the sufferings of saṃsāra and specifically those of the lower rebirths. My teacher and the Three Jewels dwelling before me have the ability to protect me from those sufferings. Hence, I will go for refuge to my teacher and the Three Jewels so that I can attain the state of a perfect complete buddha for the sake of all mother sentient beings.[119]

An extensive way of going for refuge[120]

Having reflected on the above points, imagine yourself and all sentient beings surrounding you slowly reciting "I go for refuge to my teachers." Recite it to the best of your ability, one hundred and eight, twenty-one, or at least three times. As you recite, perform the following visualization:

> Streams of five-colored nectar[121] along with light rays descend from the bodies of Guru Munīndra and the surrounding direct teachers and lineage masters. Permeating my body and mind and also those of all other sentient beings, they cleanse us of all the misdeeds and obstructions we have amassed since beginningless time, and in particular, *those of harming the bodies of our esteemed teachers, disobeying their oral instructions, disturbing their minds, losing faith in them, deriding them, and the like.* All our misdeeds and obstructions created in relation to our teachers are expelled through the orifices of our sense organs and pores as smoke and coal that have taken the form of liquids. Thus we are cleansed.

Consider the analogy of pouring water on red hot ashes lying on a slope and the water washing away all the ashes in its wake, or the alternative analogy of bringing a bright lamp into a dark space and the darkness vanishing without a trace. The great Gyalwa Ensapa asserts that the latter is more powerful [in visualizing the cleansing of all misdeeds and obstructions]. Think:

> We have been cleansed of all our misdeeds and obstructions created in relation to our spiritual guides. Our lifespan, merit, and all excellent qualities of scripture and realization develop and increase. In particular, all the blessings of body, speech, and mind of our esteemed spiritual guides permeate our bodies and minds, and we come under the protection of our esteemed spiritual guides.

Next, recite "I go for refuge to the buddhas" as many times as possible.[122] As you recite, perform the following visualization:

> Streams of five-colored nectar along with light rays descend from the bodies of Conqueror Vajradhara and the surrounding

> buddhas—Guhyasamāja, Heruka, Vajrabhairava, Hevajra, Kālacakra, the thousand buddhas of the good eon,[123] the Thirty-Five Buddhas,[124] and the rest. Permeating my body and mind and also those of all other sentient beings, they cleanse us of all the misdeeds and obstructions we have amassed since beginningless time, and in particular, those of maliciously shedding the blood of a tathāgata,[125] destroying stūpas, which are representations of the exalted mind, and the like. In brief, *we are cleansed of all misdeeds and obstructions resulting from the transgressions of the refuge guidelines that are related to going to the buddhas for refuge.* Our bodies become the nature of transparent light. Our lifespan, merit, and all excellent qualities of scripture and realization develop and increase. In particular, all the blessings of body, speech, and mind of the Buddha Jewel permeate our bodies and minds and we come under the protection of the Buddha Jewel.

Next, recite "I go for refuge to the Dharma" as many times as possible. As you recite, perform the following visualization:

> From the volumes of texts resting in front of the individual objects of refuge, streams of five-colored nectar along with light rays descend. Permeating our bodies and minds, they cleanse us of all the misdeeds and obstructions we have amassed since beginningless time, particularly *those of abandoning the Dharma, selling scriptures, using scriptures as collateral, and placing scriptures directly on the ground.*

Abandoning the Dharma can take various forms—for example, abandoning the Mahāyāna on account of one's belief in the common vehicle [Hīnayāna];[126] abandoning tantra on account of one's belief in the Pāramitāyāna; abandoning the higher classes of tantra on account of one's belief in the lower classes of tantra; abandoning the lower classes of tantra on account of one's belief in the higher classes of tantra; pointlessly prattling about whether a Dharma teacher is charismatic; and by abandoning a teacher, abandoning all the Dharma in that teacher's continuum.

To explain briefly, these misdeeds based upon the Dharma are very subtle. The *King of Meditative Stabilizations Sūtra* says:

Much greater is the misdeed
of one who abandons this sūtra
than of someone who would destroy
all the caityas in this Jambūdvīpa continent.[127]

Much greater is the misdeed
of one who abandons this sūtra
than of someone who would kill as many arhats
as there are grains of sand in the Ganges.[128]

Think:

> We are cleansed of all misdeeds and obstructions created in relation to the Dharma. Our body becomes the nature of transparent light. Our lifespan, merit, and all excellent qualities of scripture and realization develop and increase. In particular, all the blessings of the Dharma Jewel permeate our bodies and minds, and we come under the protection of the Dharma Jewel.

Next, recite "I go for refuge to the Saṅgha" as many times as possible. As you recite, perform the following visualization:

> Streams of five-colored nectar along with light rays descend from the bodies of the Saṅgha Jewel—bodhisattvas, hearers,[129] solitary realizers,[130] heroes, heroines, ḍākas, ḍākinīs, Dharma protectors, guardians, and the rest. Permeating my body and mind and those of all other sentient beings, they cleanse us of all the misdeeds and obstructions we have amassed since beginningless time, particularly *those of deprecating the ārya Saṅgha, causing schism among them, appropriating their possessions, and the like.* We are cleansed of all misdeeds and obstructions created in relation to the Saṅgha. Our body becomes the nature of transparent light. Our lifespan, merit, and all excellent qualities of scripture and realization develop and increase. In particular, all the blessings of the Saṅgha Jewel permeate our bodies and minds, and we come under the protection of the Saṅgha Jewel.

A brief way of going for refuge

The abbreviated refuge is as follows. Recite:

> I go for refuge to the Buddha, the Dharma, and the Supreme Assembly until I attain enlightenment.[131]

Reflect as follows:

> Streams of five-colored nectar along with light rays descend from the bodies of all the members of the merit field. Permeating my body and the bodies of all other sentient beings, they cleanse us of all the misdeeds and obstructions we have amassed since beginningless time, particularly *those created in relation to the Three Jewels.* Our bodies become the nature of transparent light. Our lifespan, merit, and all excellent qualities of scripture and realization develop and increase. In particular, all the blessings of the Three Jewels permeate our bodies and minds, and we come under the protection of the Three Jewels.

Generating bodhicitta

The way to generate bodhicitta is as explained below. Recite:

> By the merit of performing generosity and so forth, may I achieve buddhahood for the benefit of living beings![132]

Generate *wishing bodhicitta* by thinking:

> In dependence on these roots of virtue arisen from generosity, ethics, meditation, and so forth, may I swiftly, swiftly attain the state of a perfect complete buddha for the sake of all sentient beings!

Generate *engaging bodhicitta* by thinking:

> No matter what it takes, I will swiftly, swiftly attain the precious state of a perfect complete buddha for the sake of all mother sentient beings. To that end, I will train assiduously in all the

> bodhisattva deeds—the six perfections of generosity and so on, the four means of gathering disciples, and so forth.[133]

Induced by your supplications, there emerges from Guru Munīndra a second figure of Guru Munīndra, who absorbs into you, whereby your form clearly becomes that of Guru Munīndra.

It is taught that there are special auspicious implications in cultivating divine identity by identifying yourself with this visualized form, thinking "*I* am Guru Munīndra."[134]

It is also taught that if your focus is the cultivation of calm abiding, you can cultivate it [at this point] by taking as the object of meditation the visualization of yourself as Munīndra. There is no need for you to wait for the section of calm abiding in the text to practice the above.[135]

Visualizing yourself as Munīndra, think that light rays radiate from your body and strike all sentient beings who are surrounding you, setting them also in the state of Guru Munīndra.

How to meditate on the four immeasurables[136]

Meditate on immeasurable equanimity as follows:

> All sentient beings have fallen into misery due to attachment and aversion, attached to their own interests and averse to others' welfare. If only all sentient beings could dwell in the equanimity that is free from the bias of attachment and aversion! May they dwell in such equanimity! I will cause them to dwell in such equanimity. Guru-deity, please bless me that I may do so!

Meditate on immeasurable love as follows:

> If only all sentient beings could have happiness and its causes! May they have happiness and its causes! I will cause them to have happiness and its causes. Guru-deity, please bless me that I may do so!

Meditate on immeasurable compassion as follows:

> If only all sentient beings could be free from suffering and its causes! May they be free from suffering and its causes! I will cause them to be free from suffering and its causes. Guru-deity, please bless me that I may do so!

Meditate on immeasurable [joy] as follows:

> If only all sentient beings could be inseparable from the excellent happiness of upper rebirths and liberation! May they be inseparable from such an excellent happiness! I will cause them to be inseparable from such an excellent happiness. Guru-deity, please bless me that I may do so!

Think:

> Due to these requests, streams of five-colored nectar along with light rays descend from the bodies of all the members of the merit field. Permeating my body and mind and also those of all other sentient beings, they cleanse us of all the misdeeds and obstructions we have amassed since beginningless time, and in particular, all sickness, maleficent spirits, misdeeds, and obstructions that hinder us from cultivating the four immeasurables. Our bodies become the nature of transparent light. Our lifespan, merit, and all excellent qualities of scripture and realization develop and increase. In particular, all sentient beings and I dwell in the four immeasurables.

Having gone for refuge, generated bodhicitta, and cultivated the four immeasurables in the above manner, generate an especially strong motivation of compassion that cannot bear the thought of sentient beings being pained by suffering, and recite the following seven or twenty-one times:

> No matter what it takes, I will swiftly, swiftly attain the precious state of a perfect complete buddha for the sake of all mother sentient beings. To that end, I will meditate on the instructions of the stages of the path to enlightenment by means of the profound path of guru-deity yoga.

The great Gyalwa Ensapa asserts that the significance of saying "swiftly" twice is as follows. (1) The first "swiftly" signifies practicing the path by means of meditation on the instructions of the stages of the path to enlightenment, and (2) the second "swiftly" signifies practicing the path by taking guru yoga as the life force of the path.[137] Alternatively, (1) the first "swiftly" signifies attaining buddhahood in the body of this lifetime without having to spend three countless eons accruing the collections of merit and wisdom,[138] and (2) the second "swiftly" signifies attaining buddhahood in a single short lifetime of the degenerate age.[139]

By practicing guru yoga as the life force of the path, you will swiftly attain buddhahood. Geshé Dromtönpa declared that the blessing obtained from supplicating Atiśa is greater than the supplication to any other. Tsongkhapa says that at a time when your mind is very weak—such that when you listen you cannot retain the words, when you contemplate you cannot understand the meaning, and when you meditate you cannot produce the realizations in your continuum—what is prescribed in the oral instructions is reliance on the power of the field [with special qualities].[140] Tilopa said to Nāropa:

> The supreme among effective means is the guru, O yogi!

Mokchokpa said:[141]

> It is doubtful whether you can be liberated through unrelenting meditation.
> There is no doubt that you will be liberated through respectful belief.

He also said:

> When the One with Great Compassion is white, *he* is also white. When the Venerable Lady is red, *he* is also red. When Hevajra is blue, *he* is also blue. I have never been parted from the appearance of my teacher regardless of where I am. It seems like the attainment of buddhahood in this life is coming closer and closer now.

(4) Visualizing the merit field

You may visualize the merit field using either of the two methods: the way of visualizing the merit field according to the system of the *Lama Chöpa*[142] and the way of visualizing the merit field according to the system of this explicit instruction.[143]

The way of visualizing the merit field according to the system of the Lama Chöpa

Reflect as follows:

> In the space before me stands a vast and extensive wish-fulfilling tree beautified by leaves, flowers, and fruits. In its center is a high and vast throne made of precious stones and supported by eight great lions. Above it is an inconceivable multicolored lotus. Its bottom petals slightly cover the lion throne. The higher petals become progressively narrower.
>
> In the center [of this multicolored lotus] is a four-petal lotus. At its center is a seat consisting of another multicolored lotus, moon disc, and sun disc. Upon it sits my kind root teacher, dressed as a fully ordained monk who is a tantric practitioner endowed with the three principles.[144] His body radiates the hue of saffron. His right hand displays the gesture of explaining the Dharma, and his left displays the gesture of meditative equipoise while holding an alms bowl filled with nectar. He is clad in orange Dharma robes and wears a yellow pandit's hat on his head. Adorned with the signs and exemplifying marks,[145] he has the nature of transparent light. He sits with his legs in the vajra posture amid a profusion of light emanating from his body. At his heart is Conqueror Śākyamuni, and at Conqueror Śākyamuni's heart is Conqueror Vajradhara. He is surrounded by:
>
> - The assembly of deities of Vajrabhairava dwelling upon the petal to his right
> - The assembly of deities of Cakrasaṃvara dwelling upon the petal to his left

- The assembly of deities of Guhyasamāja dwelling upon the petal to his front
- The assembly of deities of Hevajra dwelling upon the petal to his back

They are in turn progressively encircled by:

- Other assemblies of *deities of highest yoga tantra*, such as Kālacakra, Kṛṣṇayamāri, Raktayamāri, who dwell upon the lotus petals below [the deities mentioned above]
- The assemblies of *deities of yoga tantra*, such as Sarvavid Vairocana, who dwell below them
- The assemblies of *deities of performance tantra*, such as Vairocanābhisaṃbodhi, who dwell below them
- The assemblies of *deities of action tantra*, such as Trisamayavyūhamuni, who dwell below them
- The thousand *buddhas* of the good eon, the Thirty-Five Buddhas, and so forth, who dwell below them
- *Bodhisattvas*, such as the eight great close spiritual sons,[146] who dwell below them
- The twelve *solitary realizers* and the rest, who dwell below them;
- The great *hearers*, such as the sixteen elders,[147] who dwell below them
- *Dharma protectors and guardians*, who dwell below them[148]

In the four directions beyond them, dwelling in the manner of guarding against hindrances are:

- Dhṛtarāṣṭra surrounded by hosts of gandharvas[149]
- Virūḍhaka surrounded by hosts of kumbhāṇḍas[150]
- The nāga king Virūpākṣa surrounded by hosts of nāgas[151]
- The yakṣa king Vaiśravaṇa surrounded by hosts of yakṣas[152]

From the heart of Guru Munīndra, light rays equaling the number of masters [of the blessed practice lineage] radiate upward. At their tips are seats, each consisting of a multicolored lotus, moon disc, and sun disc, upon which dwell Conqueror Vajradhara surrounded by the masters of the *blessed practice lineage*—Tilopa, Nāropa, the glorious supreme Ḍombhipa, and so forth.

Light rays radiate to the right [of Guru Munīndra]. At their tips are seats, each consisting of a multicolored lotus and moon disc, upon which dwell Venerable Maitreya surrounded by the masters of the *vast conduct lineage*—Ārya Asaṅga and so forth.

Light rays radiate to the left [of Guru Munīndra]. At their tips are seats, each consisting of a multicolored lotus and moon disc, upon which dwell Venerable Mañjuśrī surrounded by the masters of the *profound view lineage*—Ārya Nāgārjuna and so forth.

My kind root teacher dwells in front [of Guru Munīndra], surrounded by the teachers with whom I have a direct Dharma connection.

In front of each figure is a splendid stand upon which the Dharma teachings given by them take the aspect of volumes of texts having the nature of light. Beyond them, inconceivable arrays of emanations radiate to the ten directions, guiding trainees according to their needs.

The way of visualizing the merit field according to the explicit instructions of this system

[Reflect as follows:]

In the space before me is a high and vast throne made of precious stones and supported by eight great lions. Above it, slightly toward the back, is a small throne made of precious stones and supported by eight great lions, above which is a seat consisting of a multicolored lotus, moon disc, and sun disc. Upon it sits [the central figure], in nature my kind root teacher, having the aspect of Conqueror Śākyamuni. His body is the color of refined gold. Endowed with a crown protrusion, he has one face and two arms. His right hand displays the gesture of explaining the Dharma,[153] and his left displays the gesture of meditative equipoise while holding an alms bowl filled with nectar. He is immaculately clad in orange Dharma robes. Adorned with the signs and exemplifying marks, he has the nature of transparent light. He sits with his legs in the vajra posture amid a profusion of light emanating from his body.

- From the heart of Guru Munīndra, light rays equaling the number of masters radiate upward. At their tips are seats, each consisting of a lion throne, moon disc, and sun disc, upon which dwell Conqueror Vajradhara surrounded by the masters of the blessed practice lineage.[154]
- Light rays radiate to the right [of Guru Munīndra]. At their tips are seats, each consisting of a lotus and moon disc, upon which dwell Venerable Maitreya surrounded by the masters of the vast deeds lineage.[155]
- Light rays radiate to the left [of Guru Munīndra]. At their tips are seats, each consisting of a lotus and moon disc, upon which dwell Venerable Mañjuśrī surrounded by the masters of the profound view lineage.[156]
- Light rays radiate to the front [of Guru Munīndra]. At their tips are seats, each consisting of a lion throne, lotus, and moon disc, upon which dwell my kind root teacher surrounded by the teachers with whom I have a direct Dharma connection.

They are surrounded by deities, buddhas, bodhisattvas, and hosts of heroes, heroines, and Dharma protectors who are wisdom beings.[157] In front of each is a splendid stand upon which the Dharma teachings given by them take the aspect of volumes of texts having the nature of light. Beyond them, inconceivable arrays of emanations radiate to the ten directions, guiding trainees according to their needs.

The principal figure and the members of his retinue are each marked clearly by a white *oṃ* at their crown, a red *āḥ* at their throat, and a blue *hūṃ* at their heart. Light rays radiate from the *hūṃ* at the heart of Guru Munīndra, whereby wisdom beings who look identical to the ones visualized are invited from their natural abodes.[158]

Recite verses such as the following:

You who became the protector of all sentient beings without
exception,

> deity who destroys the intractable legions of māras along with their
> armies,
> you who came to perfectly know all realities without exception,
> O Bhagavān, please come to this place along with your retinue!
>
> O Bhagavān, out of lovingkindness for migratory beings,
> you trained in compassion for many eons . . .[159]

They absorb into the respective commitment beings. Next, visualize bathing chambers and request them to wash their bodies and so on.[160]

(5) Offering the seven-limbed practice—which distills the essentials of accruing the collections of merit and wisdom and purifying misdeeds—and a maṇḍala

The limb of paying homage

Pay *physical* homage by emanating as many of your bodies as the number of atoms of the buddha lands[161] and then performing prostrations. Pay *verbal* homage by emanating countless heads on each body, countless mouths in each head, and countless tongues in each mouth, and then expressing melodious praises with pleasing tunes. Pay *mental* homage by regarding the members of the merit field as having extinguished all faults and possessing all excellent qualities, and then paying respect mentally. Pay *physical, verbal, and mental* homage by reciting the following verses:

> Your body was produced by ten million splendid virtues and
> excellences,
> your speech fulfills the hopes of infinite beings,
> and your mind sees all existents exactly as they are—
> to the chief of the Śākyas, I pay homage!
>
> Maitreya, Asaṅga, Vasubandhu, Vimuktisena,
> Paramasena, Vinītasena, Kīrtisena,[162]
> Haribhadra, the two Kuśalīs, and Suvarṇadvīpa—
> to the vast deeds lineage, I pay homage!

Mañjuśrī and the Ārya father and his spiritual sons, who safeguarded
the Buddha's intent,
Nāgārjuna, who destroyed the extremes of existence and
nonexistence,
along with Candrakīrti, Vidyākokila the Elder, and the rest—
to the profound view lineage, I pay homage![163]

Sugata Vajradhara endowed with great compassion,
the supreme seers Tilopa and Nāropa,
and the glorious supreme Ḍombhipa and Atiśa—
to the blessed practice lineage, I pay homage!

Avalokiteśvara, great treasure of nonobjectifying compassion,
Mañjuśrī, lord of stainless wisdom,
Tsongkhapa, crown ornament of the scholars of the Land of
Snows,[164]
Losang Drakpa, at your feet I pay homage![165]

You attained dominion over the glory of the oceans of sūtra and
tantra
by accomplishing the instructions of Venerable Mañjuśrī;
to you, a beautiful ornament dwelling before Losang's teachings,
Jampal Gyatso, at your feet I pay homage!

Pristine virtue and goodness (*gelek*), you attained the supreme state
of the glorious (*pal*) four buddha bodies
through the force of familiarizing with the two collections of merit
and wisdom.
Even so, through your good (*sang*) deeds you do not desert your
disciples;
to you, esteemed teacher, at your feet I pay homage![166]

Amid many who are skilled in discerning the intended meaning of
the boundless Dharma,
you are beautiful like the crowning top of a victory banner (*gyaltsen*);

to you, the second glorious Nāgārjuna, lord of the Dharma (*chökyi*),
one who has a fine name, at your feet I pay homage![167]

You found the vajra (*dorjé*) body in a single life
through the force of practice by gathering the essence
of the Dharma (*chökyi*) taught by all the conquerors;
to you, supreme immortal yogi, I pay homage![168]

To you, esteemed teacher who bestows upon everyone
all the attainments of great bliss, good-minded vajra holder,
venerable emanation body encompassing all three objects of refuge,
Losang Döndrup, at your feet I pay homage![169]

To you, who uphold the essence of Losang's teachings in the present,
through the force of fulfilling the prayers of generating bodhicitta
made in the past,
yogi who is free from denial and affirmation, rejection and adoption,
Sangyé Yeshé, at your feet I pay homage!

To you, the source of all excellent qualities of virtue and goodness
without exception,
magnificent one who upholds the victory banner of Dharma (*chökyi gyaltsen*)
at the peak of the mansion of Losang's stainless teachings,
esteemed teacher, at your feet I pay homage![170]

To you, supreme one who upholds the victory banner (*gyaltsen*) of
exposition and practice
of the second conqueror's scriptural and realizational Dharma,
who embodies the wisdom and compassion of the Three Jewels
(*könchok*),
excellent tutor, at your feet I pay homage![171]

To you, Guru Vajradhara encompassing all three objects of refuge,
who takes the form of a spiritual mentor guiding trainees according
to their needs

and bestows supreme and common attainments,
kind guru, I pay homage!

To the peerless teacher, the precious Buddha,
the peerless refuge, the precious excellent Dharma,
the peerless guide, the precious Saṅgha,
the peerless Three Jewels, I pay homage!

To all those worthy of homage,
with as many bodies as the atoms of the realms,
bowing down with supreme faith in every way,
I pay homage!

When performing the practice in accordance with the *King of Prayers of Excellent Deeds*,[172] the *homage combining the three doors* is expressed in one verse:

However many there are in the worlds of the ten directions—
those lions among humanity of the three times—
I bow to them all without exception in a state of lucid faith
with body, speech, and mind.

Focusing your attention on all the conquerors of all ten directions and all three times,[173] not just the buddhas of the world systems of certain directions or one time, respectfully pay homage with your three doors from the bottom of your heart.

As for the prostrations of the individual three doors, *physical homage* is expressed in one verse:

By the power of prayers of excellent deeds
I bow down to all the conquerors
with as many bodies as the atoms of the pure lands,
perceiving all the conquerors as manifest objects of my mind.

Focus your attention on all the conquerors included within the ten directions and three times as if they are manifest objects directly perceived by your mind. Having emanated as many of your bodies as the number of atoms of the buddha lands, offer prostrations to them. Also, having generated the power of faith in the excellent deeds of these conquerors, make prostrations motivated by such faith.

Mental homage is expressed in one verse:

> Upon each atom, as many buddhas as there are atoms
> dwell amid the buddhas' sons.
> I generate belief that all dharma spheres everywhere
> are thus filled with conquerors.

Upon each atom dwell buddhas equaling the number of all atoms, each surrounded by bodhisattvas. Generate the belief that recollects their excellent qualities.

Verbal homage is expressed in one verse:

> I proclaim oceans of inexhaustible laudations
> of the excellent qualities of all the conquerors and
> praise all these sugatas
> with all sounds from the oceans of branches of melodies.

Pay verbal homage by emanating countless heads on each body, countless mouths in each head, and countless tongues in each mouth, and then proclaiming inexhaustible laudations of the conquerors' excellent qualities with pleasant melodies. The "melodies" in this verse are the praises. Its "branches" are its causes—the tongues. "Ocean" conveys plenitude.

The limb of making offerings

The series of offerings, whether extensive or brief, consists of surpassable and unsurpassable offerings. *Surpassable offerings* are expressed by two verses:

> With excellent flowers and excellent garlands,
> the finest music, ointments, and parasols,
> the finest butter lamps and excellent incense,
> I make offerings to these conquerors.

With excellent garments and the finest fragrances,
and with heaps of powder as large as Mount Meru,
all in the finest arrays,
I make offerings to these conquerors.

"Excellent flowers" are the splendid loose flowers of humans and gods. "Garlands" are various flowers strung together. Both come in real and fabricated forms. "Music" refers to music from string instruments such as the *vīṇā*, wind instruments such as the conch and the flute, instruments involving beating such as the clay drum and the gong, and instruments involving ringing such as little cymbals.[174] "Ointments" refers to fragrant creams. "Finest parasols" are the finest of parasols. "Butter lamps" refers to the clear light [emitted by lamps] of fragrant scented butters and so forth, and to the clear light of precious gems so [bright] that one cannot tell night from day. "Incense" refers to crafted incense that is known nowadays as "stiffened incense"[175] and single ingredients such as *akaru* or *duruka*.[176] "Excellent garments" are the finest clothing. "Finest fragrances" are liquids infused with scents that permeate the billionfold world systems.[177] "Heaps of powder" are heaps as large as Mount Meru alternating layers of sprinkled aromatic incense powder, incense pouches, or colored powders for drawing maṇḍalas.[178] "Arrays," signifying abundance, quality, and variety, applies to all the above offering substances.

Unsurpassable offerings are expressed by one verse:

I also visualize those extensive unexcelled offerings
[presented] to all the conquerors.
By the power of faith in excellent deeds,
I pay homage and present offerings to all the conquerors.

[The previous] surpassable offerings are mundane offerings, whereas the unsurpassable offerings here are all kinds of exquisite offerings emanated through the bodhisattvas' great powers and the like.

The last two lines of this verse are to be applied to all offerings, not just the offerings expressed in its first two lines. They indicate homage, the offerings, the motivation, and the recipients of the offerings.

The limb of confession of misdeeds[179]

Generate again and again the mind of regret for the misdeeds you have committed in the past as if you have ingested poison, and generate the mind of restraint resolving not to repeat them even at the cost of your life. When you find time, perform the confession [of transgressions] of the three types of vows individually.[180] Do this by trying your best to perform confession and restraint from time to time through the four powers of purification,[181] using practices such as the *General Confession*[182] and the *Confession of Bodhisattva Downfalls.*[183]

If you do not sincerely confess your past misdeeds by feeling regret for them and generating the intention to refrain from committing them in the future, then excellent qualities that have not yet been produced in your continuum will not be produced, and those that have been produced will decline. If, instead, you sincerely regret the misdeeds you have committed in the past as if you have ingested poison, and produce the mind of restraint that resolves not to repeat them again even at the cost of your life, then excellent qualities that have not yet been produced in your continuum will be produced, and those that have been produced will increase.

Therefore holy beings of the past have regarded the confession of misdeeds and downfalls as of utmost importance. During his journey to Tibet, whenever the tiniest of misdeeds occurred, Atiśa would immediately assemble the leaders of the caravan, offer a maṇḍala, and perform confession. "Should I die before confessing it, I will be reborn in the lower rebirths," he would say. Accordingly, he would carry a wooden stūpa with him wherever he went and would perform confession and restraint right there and then [whenever a misdeed occurred]. This was done so that he would "not be accompanied by misdeeds or downfalls for longer than a day." Upon arriving at the Chölung Monastery,[184] Tsongkhapa was highly inspired and strove assiduously in the accruing of the collections of merit and wisdom and the purification of misdeeds. He first perceived Nāgeśvararāja[185] and later the Thirty-Five Buddhas and so on. We must emulate these holy beings of the past and train accordingly.

Confession, when performed as it is presented in the *King of Prayers of Excellent Deeds*, is expressed by one verse [in the *King of Prayers of Excellent Deeds*]:

Whatever misdeeds I have committed
through the force of attachment, aversion, and confusion,
and through body, speech, and likewise with mind,
I individually confess them all.

[Misdeeds committed] in dependence on the causal three poisons through the three bases of body and so forth[186] are such that one (1) commits the misdeed—actually performs it oneself—(2) instigates others to do it, or (3) rejoices in that committed by others. All three are encompassed generally under the phrase "Whatever misdeeds I have committed."

If you are able to bring to mind the drawbacks of these misdeeds and confess them wholeheartedly by means of regret for past misdeeds and by means of the mind of restraint regarding future misdeeds, then the increase of past misdeeds will be halted and the tendencies for future misdeeds will be cut off. If you lack a strong mind of restraint that turns away from misdeeds, then even though you proclaim, "I shall not conceal them; I shall not hide them; henceforth, I shall put a stop to them and refrain from them,"[187] on top of not having eliminated your past misdeeds, you will now have committed the additional misdeed of lying. This has been explained in the extensive commentaries on the Vinaya. Therefore it is taught that it is important to frequently generate the mind of restraint—thinking, "I shall give up for a long time misconduct that is easy to give up" and "I will give up if only for a day misconduct that is difficult to give up." By doing so, you will fulfill the power of not repeating misdeeds.

The limb of rejoicing

If, without pride or conceit, you cultivate joy from the bottom of your heart regarding the virtues of the three times created by yourself and others—including all ordinary beings and āryas—then all your past virtues will increase. It has been taught in the *Vinaya Scripture* that when King Prasenajit venerated the Buddha and his retinue, a beggar rejoiced and obtained greater virtue than the king.[188] It is with this characteristic in mind that Tsongkhapa described rejoicing as creating "powerful [merit] with little effort . . ."[189]

If you were to develop pride or conceit in relation to a virtue that you have created, not only will that virtue not increase, it will dissipate. The chapter on guarding virtues in the *Compendium of Trainings in Verse* says:

By giving up craving for the fruitional results of your own purpose,
you will always guard your virtues.
Do not regret your virtues and
do not boast about what you have done.[190]

In brief, recite the verse [in the *King of Prayers of Excellent Deeds*]:

I rejoice in the merit of
the conquerors of the ten directions,
bodhisattvas and solitary realizers,
as well as those still in training, those of no more learning, and all living beings.

Cultivate joy by recalling the benefits of the virtues of these five types of persons.[191]

The limb of request to turn the wheel of Dharma

This is expressed by one verse [in the *King of Prayers of Excellent Deeds*]:

I request all the protectors,
lamps for the world of the ten directions
who have found the unattached state of buddhahood in the stages of enlightenment,
to turn the unexcelled wheel.

Emanating as many of your bodies as the atoms of the buddha lands, offer a thousand-spoke golden wheel to each of those in the world systems who have just attained the full enlightenment of buddhahood but dwell in complete silence without turning the wheel of Dharma.[192] Request them to turn the wheel of Dharma for the purpose of creating benefit and happiness for all living beings. In return, think that they accept your request and turn the wheel of Dharma. This practice is as described in the following request:

Then the gods came before the Teacher and said,
"From inviting all living beings as guests to unsurpassed bliss,
you have now gained enlightenment.
This act of passivity is unreasonable.

Blind living beings who have fallen into ravines
have no other refuge or protector.
O great treasury of compassion, swiftly rise
and turn the excellent wheel of Dharma!" [193]

By making the request to turn the wheel of Dharma in this manner, you are cleansed of the karma to be deprived of the Dharma, of your misdeeds creating obstacles for others in relation to the Dharma, and the like.

The limb of supplication to not pass into nirvāṇa

This is expressed by one verse:

I beseech with joined palms those wishing
to display passing into nirvāṇa:
May you remain for as many eons as the atoms in the universe
to bring benefit and happiness to all beings.

Emanating as many of your bodies as the atoms of the buddha lands, request those who display passing into nirvāṇa in the buddha lands of the ten directions to remain for an eon or even longer for the purpose of bringing happiness and benefit to all living beings. Reflecting thus, recite the above verse. In addition, if you repeatedly offer long-life pujas to teachers who have the ability to personally instruct you well in the Dharma, this is the supreme long-life practice for yourself.

The limb of dedication

This is expressed by one verse:

Whatever slight virtue I have created from paying homage,
making offerings, confession, rejoicing,
requesting, and supplication,
I dedicate it all to enlightenment.

Sharing with all sentient beings all virtues, as illustrated by the virtues of the previous six limbs, dedicate them with intense aspiration as the causes of full enlightenment. Recite the above verse as you reflect thus. When you dedicate the roots of virtue as the cause of unsurpassed full enlightenment for the sake of all sentient beings, even if the roots of virtue allocated to each sentient being are no greater than the tip of a needle, due to the enormous power of the [dedicated] roots of virtue, they will not dissipate before you attain enlightenment. The *Teaching of Akṣayamati Sūtra* says:[194]

> Just as a drop of water poured into the great ocean
> is not spent before the ocean dries up,
> so too virtue dedicated to enlightenment
> is not spent before buddhahood is achieved.[195]

It is like, for example, the contents of a great ocean that are not spent no matter how it is used.

Maṇḍala offering

For the purpose of achieving the desired goals that will be presented below, offer the maṇḍala. When you ask an important person for a great favor, first you offer gifts, and then you make your request, saying, "I would like to ask a favor." Offering the maṇḍala is like that.

The best maṇḍala set is fashioned from gold or silver, middling ones from copper or brass. If you cannot acquire any of those materials, then an alternative such as wood can be used. Anoint it with *bachung*[196] and scented water. Apply scented water to the offering grains too. If your mind is capable, clearly visualize the billionfold world systems, even though neither the maṇḍala expands nor the billionfold world systems contract. If you cannot manage that, then clearly visualize all bodies and enjoyments, along with the roots of virtue, of yourself and others, as well as the four continents and Mount Meru. Then offer the maṇḍala from the bottom of your heart and request the three great purposes sincerely and single-pointedly:

> Please grant your blessings that (1) all erroneous minds, from disrespect for the spiritual guide to grasping at signs of the two selves,[197] cease; (2) all unerring minds, respect for the spiritual guide and so forth, easily arise; and (3) all outer and inner hindrances are pacified.

(6) Imbuing your mind with the supplication according to the oral instructions

Focusing on your kind root teacher dwelling before you,[198] make the following request, ensuring that your mind is imbued with the supplication according to the oral instructions:

> O glorious and precious root teacher,
> seated on a lotus and moon disc, please reside above my crown.
> Out of your great kindness, please protect me and
> bestow the attainments of body, speech, and mind.

Reflect:

> Light rays radiate from the heart of Guru Munīndra, striking all the infinite peaceful and wrathful figures surrounding him. They dissolve into light from the outer edges inward and absorb into the lineage masters of vast conduct and the profound view.
>
> These masters melt into light from the bottom upward in stages, with the masters of the vast conduct lineage absorbing into Maitreya and the masters of the profound view lineage into Mañjuśrī.
>
> The masters of the blessed practice lineage absorb into Vajradhara.
>
> The teachers with whom I have a direct Dharma connection absorb into my kind root teacher.

Pause for a while and elicit clear appearances with respect to the above five figures.[199]

> Next, Maitreya and Mañjuśrī absorb into Munīndra, and their seats, each consisting of a lotus and moon disc, absorb into Munīndra's lion throne.
>
> Then my kind root teacher melts into light and absorbs into the heart of Munīndra.
>
> Vajradhara enters Guru Munīndra through his crown and dwells at his heart in the manner of a wisdom being.[200]

Such a figure is called Munīndra Vajradhara.[201]

> Next, the two seats [of my kind root teacher and Vajradhara], each consisting of a lion throne, lotus, and moon disc, also absorb into Munīndra's lion throne, lotus, and moon.

Again, pause for a while and elicit clear appearance with respect to Munīndra Vajradhara. Reflect as follows:

> Then Munīndra absorbs into my kind root teacher above my crown. Upon the seat consisting of a lion throne, lotus, moon disc, and sun disc on my crown sits [the figure], in nature my kind root teacher, having the aspect of Conqueror Śākyamuni. His body is the color of refined gold. Endowed with a crown protrusion, he has one face and two arms. His right hand presses the ground, and his left displays the gesture of meditative equipoise while holding an alms bowl filled with nectar. He is immaculately clad in the three orange Dharma robes. Adorned with the signs and exemplifying marks, he has the nature of transparent light. He sits with his legs in the vajra posture amid a profusion of light emanating from his body.

With this visualization in mind, make a brief offering of the seven-limbed practice along with a maṇḍala and then make requests. Pay homage by reciting the verse below:

> I pay homage to the foremost of the Śākyas,
> whose body was produced by ten million excellent virtues,
> whose speech fulfills the hopes of limitless beings,
> and whose mind sees all things exactly as they are.

Next:

> I make offerings of every type, both actual and emanated by my mind.
> I confess all misdeeds and transgressions amassed since beginningless time.

I rejoice in the virtues of ordinary beings and āryas.
I beseech you to remain until saṃsāra ends,
turning the wheel of Dharma for sentient beings.
I dedicate my own virtues and those of others to great enlightenment.

Offer a maṇḍala:

I offer to the gurus, deities, and the Three Jewels,
a maṇḍala of precious stones including Mount Meru, the four continents, the sun and moon,
and the seven precious objects, together with a mass of excellent offerings.
Out of compassion, please accept them and bestow your blessings upon me.

[Make supplication:]

O guru, extraordinary deity, who is the essence of the four buddha bodies,[202]
Munīndra Vajradhara, to you I make supplication!

O guru-deity, the essence of the dharma body free of obstruction,
Munīndra Vajradhara, to you I make supplication!

O guru-deity, the essence of the enjoyment body of great bliss,
Munīndra Vajradhara, to you I make supplication!

O guru-deity, the essence of multifarious emanation bodies,
Munīndra Vajradhara, to you I make supplication!

O guru, extraordinary deity, who encompasses all the gurus,
Munīndra Vajradhara, to you I make supplication!

O guru, extraordinary deity, who encompasses all the deities,
Munīndra Vajradhara, to you I make supplication!

O guru, extraordinary deity, who encompasses all the buddhas,
Munīndra Vajradhara, to you I make supplication!

O guru, extraordinary deity, who encompasses all the excellent Dharma,
Munīndra Vajradhara, to you I make supplication!

O guru, extraordinary deity, who encompasses all the Saṅgha,
Munīndra Vajradhara, to you I make supplication!

O guru, extraordinary deity, who encompasses all the ḍākas and ḍākinīs,
Munīndra Vajradhara, to you I make supplication!

O guru, extraordinary deity, who encompasses all the Dharma protectors,
Munīndra Vajradhara, to you I make supplication!

O guru, extraordinary deity, who encompasses all the objects of refuge,
Munīndra Vajradhara, to you I make supplication!

Reflect as follows:

> Having continuously taken birth in saṃsāra, I and all mother sentient beings have experienced a variety of prolonged and intense sufferings. This plight is owing to our failure to rely correctly upon the spiritual guide through thought and action. Guru-deity, please bless me and all mother sentient beings that we may now *rely correctly upon the spiritual guide through thought and action*!

Think:

> From having made supplications in this manner, streams of five-colored nectar along with light rays descend from the body of the guru-deity above my crown. Permeating my body and mind

and also those of all other sentient beings, they cleanse us of all the misdeeds and obstructions amassed since beginningless time, and in particular those misdeeds and obstructions along with sickness and maleficent spirits that prevent us from *relying correctly upon the spiritual guide*. Our bodies become the nature of transparent light. Our lifespan, merit, and all excellent qualities of scripture and realization develop and increase. The special realization of being able *to rely upon the spiritual guide through thought and action* is now produced in our continua.[203]

3 | Relying on a Spiritual Guide

The actual meditation on relying on a spiritual guide

This is explained in four parts: the benefits of relying on a spiritual guide, the drawbacks of not relying on a spiritual guide, the way to rely on the spiritual guide through thought, and the way to rely on the spiritual guide through action.

The benefits of relying on a spiritual guide

Visualize that the teachers with whom you have a direct Dharma relationship are emanated from the heart of Guru Munīndra and they dwell in the space before you. Reflect on the benefits of relying on the spiritual guide as follows:

> (1) I will become closer to buddhahood by relying on my spiritual guide. (2) I will please the conquerors. (3) I will not be deprived of spiritual guides. (4) It will be difficult for bad karma and afflictions to overcome me. (5) Being mindful of the bodhisattva deeds and acting accordingly, my stores of excellent qualities will expand continuously. (6) It is taught that I will achieve all short-term and ultimate aims. (7) I will not fall into lower rebirths. By devoting myself to my spiritual guide, my karma occasioning lower rebirths will be experienced as a slight physical or mental discomfort, or in a dream. And so, it will ripen and be exhausted.[204] (8) Also, it has been taught that the roots of virtue arising from relying on the spiritual guide surpass those of making offerings to countless buddhas and the like. Relying on my spiritual guide brings infinite benefits.

(1) You will become closer to buddhahood by properly relying on your spiritual guide through thought and action. Accordingly, the protector Nāgārjuna says in the *Five Stages*:

> Giving up all [other types of] offerings,
> correctly make offerings to your teachers.
> By pleasing them,
> you will obtain the supreme wisdom of omniscience.[205]

(2) Should you make offerings to the buddhas and bodhisattvas while neglecting to properly protect your vows and pledges, though some meager benefit of just making the offerings might occur, you will not receive the benefits of the buddhas and bodhisattvas accepting the offerings with delight. However, when making offerings to a single teacher through properly relying on him as your spiritual guide, all the buddhas and bodhisattvas, uninvited, will come and enter the body of the teacher and gladly accept the offerings. In this way you will please the conquerors. Accordingly, the *Oral Teaching Called Meditation on the Reality of the Two Stages* says:[206]

> Dwelling in the body of a person
> in relation to whom doing so is meaningful,
> I will accept the offerings practitioners make.
> Having pleased me, they will cleanse
> their minds of karmic obstructions.[207]

(3) You will not be deprived of spiritual guides, because Potowa's *Blue Manual* says:

> Therefore, as long as you have not forged a Dharma relationship [with a teacher], there are not many [commitments to observe].
> Once you have forged one, show respect [to the teacher] as your spiritual guide.
> It is the nature of things that in the future you will have access to spiritual guides,
> because karma does not dissipate.[208]

(4) It will be hard for karma and afflictions to overcome you.

(5) Being mindful of the bodhisattva deeds and acting accordingly, your stores of excellent qualities will expand continuously. Venerable Sakya Paṇḍita said:

> The stores [of excellent qualities accrued] from giving away your
> head, arms, legs, and possessions
> as practiced in the Pāramitā system for thousands of eons
> are encompassed by a single instant [of practice] through this path of
> the spiritual guide.
> Revere him and cultivate joy![209]

(6) It is taught that you will achieve all short-term and ultimate aims.

(7) Furthermore, by devoting yourself to your spiritual guide, the karma inducing lower rebirths will be experienced as a slight discomfort in body or mind, or in a dream, and so it will manifest and be exhausted. The *Stem Array* says:

> Child of the lineage, a bodhisattva who is thoroughly cared for by a spiritual guide will not fall into a lower rebirth. It will be difficult for karma and afflictions to overcome a bodhisattva who is perfectly cared for by a spiritual guide.[210]

(8) It has also been taught that the roots of virtue arising from relying on your spiritual guide surpass those of making offerings to countless buddhas and the like. Relying on your spiritual guide brings about such infinite benefits. The *Saṃpuṭa Tantra* says:

> Why? Compared to the merit of
> buddhas and bodhisattvas of the ten directions,
> that of a single pore of the teacher is superior.
> Therefore the buddhas and bodhisattvas recognize
> that one should make offerings to the teacher.[211]

The drawbacks of not relying on a spiritual guide

Reflect as follows:

> If, having taken someone as a spiritual guide, I err in relying on him, I will be troubled by frequent sickness and malicious spirits in this life, and in future lives I will experience countless sufferings in lower rebirths.

Accordingly, *Fifty Verses on the Spiritual Guide* says:

> Having consciously taken such a protector [as your spiritual guide]
> and become his student, if you deride him,
> you deride all the buddhas.
> Thus you will experience constant suffering.[212]

A citation in the *Commentary on the Difficult Points of the Kṛṣṇayamāri Tantra* says:

> If you do not hold as your spiritual guide
> someone from whom you have heard a single verse,
> you will take birth a hundred times as a dog
> and then be born in the lowest caste.[213]

Furthermore, the *Vajrapāṇi Initiation Tantra* says:

> [Vajrapāṇi asks,] "Bhagavān, what is the fruitional result of deriding the teacher?"
>
> The Bhagavān replies, "Vajrapāṇi, do not ask! The world along with its gods would be aghast. However, O Lord of Secrets,[214] this much I will say. Gather your courage and listen:
>
> > The terrible hells of immediate retribution and so forth
> > I have explained
> > are said to be their abodes.
> > There they will dwell for infinite eons.
> > Therefore do not deride the teacher
> > in any way at any time."[215]

The *Ornament of Vajra Essence Tantra* says:[216]

> Do not see those who deride their teacher
> even in dreams.[217]

Tsongkhapa says that those who claim to strive in listening, contemplation, and meditation but do not shy away from actions such as deriding the teacher open the door to lower rebirths,[218] as the *Ornament of Vajra Essence Tantra* says:

> He who derides the teacher,
> even though he practices intensely for a thousand eons
> the supreme practices of all tantras,
> giving up sleep and avoiding hustle,
> will achieve the hells and the like.[219]

Furthermore, even if you have committed the actions of immediate retribution,[220] abandoned the Dharma,[221] incurred the four prātimokṣa defeats,[222] and created other grave misdeeds, you can still achieve the supreme attainment in the Vajrayāna. However, should you truly despise your teacher, you will never achieve it even if you practice for thousands of eons. Even those who keep company with you will not achieve it. Accordingly, the *Guhyasamāja Tantra* says:

> Even if one has committed the actions of immediate retribution
> and grave misdeeds,
> one can achieve the result in this supreme vehicle,
> the great ocean of Vajrayāna.
> However, should one truly despise one's teacher,
> one will never achieve the result even if one were to practice.[223]

The *Kālacakra Root Tantra* says:

> One destroys virtues accrued over as many eons
> as the instants of anger directed at one's spiritual guide,
> and one will experience excruciating pain
> in the hells and the like for as many eons.[224]

Therefore, if you generate a single instant of anger at your spiritual guide, you destroy the roots of virtue accrued in an eon and have to dwell in Unrelenting Torment for the same.[225] Just imagine the consequences of a hundred [such instants]!

In addition, excellent qualities that have not been produced will not be produced, and those that have been produced will degenerate, and they will degenerate continuously with every passing year, month, and day, and even within a single day or night.

QUESTION: Well then, how should a student regard his teacher?

ANSWER: The *Vajrapāṇi Initiation Tantra* says:

> O Lord of Secrets, if you were to ask, "How should a student regard his teacher?" I would say that he should regard his teacher as he would the Buddha Bhagavān.[226]

Were you to rely on immoral spiritual guides and bad companions, your good qualities would diminish and faults increase, whereupon undesirable consequences would ensue. So avoid them at all costs.

QUESTION: Well then, who are bad companions?

ANSWER: Know that bad companions are those who, through your association with them, cause your practice of the three trainings inspired by bodhicitta and the activities of hearing, contemplation, and meditation to deteriorate.[227] The *Blue Manual* says:

> Places where the three trainings inspired by bodhicitta increase are good places.
> Companions whose company increases [the three trainings inspired by bodhicitta] are good companions.
> Those contrary are bad places and bad companions.[228]

The precious child of the conquerors says:[229]

> The practice of bodhisattvas is to abandon bad companions who, when associated with,
> cause afflictions to increase,

> the activities of hearing, contemplation, and meditation to
> degenerate,
> and love and compassion to vanish.

Holy beings of the past have cautioned that bad companions do not declare that they are bad companions; they do not come dressed roughly in yak-hair garments. Rather, they come in sweet affectionate forms, doing you various favors and pouring you cups of tea, and cause you to become distant from your spiritual guides. When they intensify your obsession with this life—even if they are your parents—they are still māras.[230] You must turn your back on them. The *Foundations of Mindfulness* says:

> Serving as the bases for all attachment, hatred, and ignorance,
> bad companions are like a poisonous tree.[231]

The *Passing into Nirvāṇa Sūtra* says:

> Bodhisattvas do not fear drunk elephants and the like in the same way they fear bad companions, as drunk elephants and the like only threaten the body, whereas bad companions threaten both virtue and the pure mind.[232]

The *Collection of Aphorisms* says:

> They lack faith, are stingy,
> tell lies, and are jealous.
> Wise ones do not befriend them.
> Do not keep company with bad people.
>
> If one who does no evil whatsoever
> keeps close to those who do evil,
> he will be suspected of doing evil and
> given a bad name.[233]

Geshé Dromtönpa says that if someone of bad character associates with a good companion, he will turn out no better than mediocre, but someone of good character associating with a bad character will easily become of bad character.

The way to rely on the spiritual guide through thought

This is explained in two parts: training in the root, faith, and recollecting the great kindness of the spiritual guide.

Training in the root, faith

Clearly visualize your spiritual guides dwelling before you and reflect as follows:

> My spiritual guides are actual buddhas. The perfect complete buddhas taught in the precious tantras that Conqueror Vajradhara will display himself during the degenerate age as spiritual guides and enact the welfare of sentient beings. Therefore my spiritual guides are actual buddhas.

QUESTION: Well then, how is it taught in the tantras that during the degenerate age Conqueror Vajradhara will display himself as spiritual guides and enact the welfare of sentient beings?

ANSWER: The *Hevajra Tantra* says:

> In the future,
> I will manifest in the form of a teacher.[234]

The *Vajra Tent Tantra* says:

> He who is called Vajrasattva
> will take the form of a teacher.
> Attending to the benefit of sentient beings,
> he will dwell in ordinary forms.[235]

And:

> Furthermore, in the last five hundred years,[236]
> I will take the form of a teacher.
> Thinking that he is me,
> generate respect for him at that time.[237]

And:

> In the future, at the end of time,
> I will display the form of a childish being
> and forms that are various means [of guiding sentient beings].[238]

And:

> Do not discriminate between
> the teacher and Vajradhara.[239]

Regard your teacher and Vajradhara as inseparable. A person who claims that there is a Vajradhara superior to his teacher will not achieve any attainments in his continuum. This is because the lamrim transmitted through Jayulwa says:[240]

> Should a person assert that there is a separate Vajradhara or deity who is better than his teacher, he will achieve no attainments in his mindstream.

Once, Marpa was sleeping in front of Nāropa. Having emanated in the sky the deity Hevajra along with the supporting and supported maṇḍalas[241] at the break of dawn, Paṇchen Nāropa called out to Marpa, "Son, Martön Chökyi Lodrö,[242] wake up, do not sleep! Your deity Hevajra has come along with his supporting and supported maṇḍalas in the sky! Will you prostrate to me or to your deity?" Marpa prostrated to the deity Hevajra along with his supporting and supported maṇḍalas. Nāropa then said:

> Prior to the spiritual guide,
> the name "buddha" does not even exist.
> Even the buddhas of a thousand eons

arise in dependence on teachers.
The deity is the emanation of the spiritual guide.

Having said that, he absorbed the maṇḍala back into his heart. He proclaimed, "By the dependent chain of events, your family line will not last long.[243] That dependent chain of events is the lot of sentient beings."

Furthermore, buddhas display various forms in accordance with the fortunes of individuals. The *Meeting of Father and Son Sūtra* says:

The buddhas appear as Indra, Brahmā,
and sometimes māras
to enact the welfare of sentient beings.
Worldly beings cannot comprehend this phenomenon.
They appear as women and perform activities.
They are also present in animal rebirths.

Even though they are unattached, they display attachment.
Even though they are fearless, they display fear.
Even though they are lucid, they display confusion.
Even though they are sane, they display madness.
Even though they are able-bodied, they display disabilities.
By means of various emanations,
they guide sentient beings.[244]

Reflect as follows:

Guru-deity, please bless me and all mother sentient beings to perceive these spiritual guides as actual Munīndra Vajradharas.

Think:

From having made supplications in this manner, streams of five-colored nectar along with light rays descend from the body of the guru-deity above my crown. Permeating my body and mind and also those of all other sentient beings, they cleanse us of all the misdeeds and obstructions amassed since beginningless time, and in particular those misdeeds and obstructions that prevent us from

> perceiving these spiritual guides as actual Munīndra Vajradhara. Our bodies become the nature of transparent light. Our lifespan, merit, and all excellent qualities of scripture and realization develop and increase. The special realization of *perceiving these spiritual guides as actual Munīndra Vajradhara* is produced in our minds.

OBJECTION: A buddha has extinguished all faults and possesses all excellent qualities. However, my spiritual guide has various faults motivated by the three poisons. He is not really a buddha.

REPLY: That perception occurs through the force of your own impure appearances. In the past, Sunakṣatra saw all the deeds of our Teacher, the Buddha, as a sham through the force of his own impure appearances.[245] Asaṅga saw Venerable Maitreya as a female dog.[246] Maitrīpa saw the lord of yogis, Śavaripa, committing unbecoming actions such as slaughtering pigs. Nāropa saw Tilopa engaging in crazy behavior, such as roasting live fish.[247] The novice monk called Tailor saw Vajravārāhī as a leper woman.[248] Ācārya Vajraghaṇṭapa saw Vajravārāhī as a swineherd.[249] Ācārya Buddhajñānapāda saw Ācārya Mañjuśrīmitra as a monastic householder, with a Dharma robe wrapped around his head while ploughing the fields.

At the advice of the sage Jayoṣmāyatana, youthful Sudhana, the merchant's son, went to request instructions from King Anala on the bodhisattva deeds. The king happened to be carrying out his judicial duties and was seated upon a huge throne ornamented by precious stones. Ten thousand ministers and executioners who were as terrifying as hell guardians were meting out punishments such as gouging out eyes and cutting off arms and legs. Upon witnessing that, Sudhana thought, "This King Anala is devoid of spiritual virtue; he creates nothing but misdeeds. How can he have the instructions on the bodhisattva deeds?" When he gave rise to that doubt, the gods in the sky spoke, "Do you not remember the instructions of the sage Jayoṣmāyatana?" Sudhana then circumambulated the king three times, and the king led him into the palace. The king explained, "I have attained the bodhisattva's play of illusory liberation. Since most of the people residing in my country engage in various nonvirtues, by displaying emanated executioners who kill emanated victims, these residents will come to fear misdeeds and feel remorse."[250]

It is taught in Ārya Asaṅga's *Bodhisattvas' Grounds* that bodhisattvas overthrow wicked kings and then rule according to the Dharma.[251]

Two novice monks in Khotan meditated on Venerable Mañjuśrī for twelve years but failed to receive a vision of him. They lamented, "Ārya [Mañjuśrī]'s compassion is too feeble," whereupon Venerable Mañjuśrī appeared in space and informed them that they had no karmic connection with him. He told them that Avalokiteśvara was residing in the Land of Snows, where he had taken birth as Songtsen Gampo,[252] and advised them to go there. When they arrived in Tibet, they saw heads, arms, and legs that had been chopped off lying in the lower valley of Tölung as a result of punishments dealt out by the king,[253] and also walls of heads, heaps of eyeballs, and torture chambers of arms and legs within the tents in Denbak.[254] They thought, "That Mañjuśrī [who appeared to us] must be a māra. What is he an emanation of? This king is a murderer."

Thinking that, they prepared to leave. The king summoned them before him, removed his headdress to reveal Amitābha, and spoke, "I am the Avalokiteśvara of Tibet.[255] You do not have to be afraid."

They asked, "Well, is the killer of all of these living beings Avalokiteśvara, the Great Compassionate One?"

He replied, "Since coming to power, I have not caused even the slightest harm to living beings. Since these trainees of mine cannot be guided by peaceful means, I display emanated instruments that punish emanated victims. What do the two of you want?"

They replied, "We just want to go home."

He said, "Well then, fill your bags with sand and lie on them." They did as they were told and found themselves at the opening of a rock cave in Khotan. At sunrise, the sand turned into gold. If the two novice monks had not developed misconceptions toward the king in the beginning, they would have attained the supreme attainment of *mahāmudrā*, yet they achieved nothing in their lifetime apart from that attainment [of the sand turning into gold]. However, it is said that they attained the state of unadorned arhats in their next birth.[256]

For the purpose of cleansing Jetsun Milarepa of his obstructions, Marpa made him build a nine-story tower by himself. Sores formed on Milarepa's back as a result, exposing his spine. When Marpa was conferring initiations on others, he would eject Milarepa from the rows of initiates. On those occasions, Milarepa became so overwhelmed with despair that he thought, "May the ground open up and swallow me!" However, Marpa's only wish was to cleanse Milarepa of his karmic obstructions, and he did not harbor the slightest selfish desire. Reflect as follows:

> In a similar manner, I do not know the motives behind the various actions of my spiritual guides. Guru-deity, please bless me and all sentient beings so that we do not produce even an instant of critical attitude toward these spiritual guides and so that we easily generate in our minds the great faith that sees whatever they do as excellent qualities!

Think:

> From having made supplications in this manner, streams of five-colored nectar along with light rays descend from the body of the guru-deity above my crown. Permeating my body and mind and also those of all other sentient beings, they cleanse us of all the misdeeds and obstructions amassed since beginningless time, and in particular those misdeeds and obstructions along with sicknesses and maleficent spirits that prevent great faith that sees whatever spiritual guides do as excellent qualities. The special realization of *great faith that sees whatever spiritual guides do as excellent qualities* is produced in our mental continua.

The conditions that hinder such faith are the notions that certain teachers are bad-tempered, prejudiced, stingy, negligent in their precepts, or lacking in knowledge. Single out each of the teachers in whom you lack faith and analyze in detail the meaning of the scriptural citations from the sūtras and tantras presented above. Meditate until you put an end to critical minds and can produce vivid faith. This is taught to be a salient point.

Recollecting the Great Kindness of the Spiritual Guide

Visualize your spiritual guides in front of you and reflect as follows:

> My spiritual guides are very kind because it is through the kindness of these spiritual guides that I will realize the profound path

> that easily bestows the precious state of complete buddhahood, the supreme liberation in which all the sufferings of saṃsāra and specifically those of the lower rebirths have been abandoned.

In the past, for the sake of a single verse, or even just half a verse of Dharma, the Buddha drove a thousand iron spikes into his body and inserted a thousand lamps,[257] and for the sake of Dharma, he fed his lovely queen and beloved child to a ferocious yakṣa.[258]

For the sake of hearing instructions on bodhicitta from Guru Suvarṇadvīpa, glorious Atiśa sailed for thirteen months on the ocean.[259]

Past translators, disregarding their bodies and lives, crossed vast plains to travel to India on a journey fraught with peril, during which they frequently encountered terrifying wild animals and poisonous snakes. The hardships they endured are as taught:

> The jungles were so dense; it seemed like we would never emerge from them.
> The mountain passes were so high; it seemed like we would never cross them.
> The wild beasts, narrow paths, and rivers seemed never-ending.
> The tree trunks were stiff like human corpses.
> It makes me shudder even now to recall
> all the heat and cold experienced during that journey as I speak about them.

Without your having to undergo such hardship, your spiritual guides confer instructions on you the way a father teaches his son without withholding anything. Thus they are exceedingly kind. Atiśa said, "You obtain the profound Dharma without any austerity. Bear in mind its great meaning!"

Consider the example of a man who has consumed food and poison and is on the verge of death. A skillful doctor makes him throw up the poison he has consumed, transforms the food he has consumed into medicine, and transforms the medicine he has consumed into the nectar of immortality. For the patient there is nothing more significant [than this development of events] and no one kinder than the doctor.

Similarly, a qualified teacher causes a qualified student to confess by means of the four powers of purification the karmas the student has amassed that will occasion birth in the lower rebirths and to refrain from committing them again. He causes the roots of virtue that the student has created for the sake of this life to transform into those that will bring about the aims of the next life. Also, he causes the virtues that the student has created for the sake of a god or human rebirth in the next life to be dedicated as causes of liberation and omniscience. For the student there is nothing more significant [than this development of events] and no one kinder than the teacher.

Your spiritual guides, like providers of food and caregivers for a wretched person on the verge of starvation, teach the methods of engaging in hearing, contemplation, and meditation to those who were not able to be directly taught the Dharma by earlier buddhas and bodhisattvas and help them to realize the essential points of the profound path. Therefore they are exceedingly kind. With this meaning in mind, the protector Nāgārjuna says in his *Five Stages*:

> He is the self-arisen Bhagavān.
> He alone is the special deity.
> Because of bestowing instructions,
> the vajra ācārya is superior.[260]

If you fail to generate the respect that recollects his great kindness and do not feel grateful, then even if Mañjuśrī and Avalokiteśvara actually come and teach you the Dharma, no excellent quality whatsoever would be produced in your mind. Potowa's *Blue Manual* says:

> Whether the blessings of the teacher are great or small
> does not depend on whether he is an actual buddha but on you.
> If you are ungrateful and lack belief,
> even if Mañjuśrī and Avalokiteśvara actually come,
> it would be utterly pointless.
> Have belief, respect, and gratitude!
> Even if he is not a teacher with complete excellent qualities,
> you will receive his blessings.
> Belief and gratitude are more important.[261]

And:

> If you lack respect for your teachers,
> you would not benefit even from relying on the Buddha himself.[262]

And:

> Therefore it is taught that it is vital
> that you avoid conceit and respect your teacher.[263]

Reflect as follows:

> Guru-deity, please bless me and all sentient beings so that the great respect that recollects the kindness of our spiritual guides is easily produced in our continua!

Think:

> From having made supplications in this manner, streams of five-colored nectar along with light rays descend from the body of the guru-deity above my crown. Permeating my body and mind and also those of all other sentient beings, they cleanse us of all the misdeeds and obstructions we have amassed since beginningless time, and in particular those misdeeds and obstructions that prevent the great respect that recollects the kindness of our spiritual guides. The special realization of *great respect that recollects the kindness of our spiritual guides* is produced in our mental continua.

In this context, recollect the kindness of the teacher by reflecting in the following manner:

> When my teacher bestows a Dharma teaching upon me, this and that fault are eliminated; I turn away from this and that misbehavior; this and that excellent quality, such as faith, arise; I hear for the first time this Dharma teaching that I have not heard before; and I realize this meaning that I have not realized before.

> Out of compassion he provides for my various needs: food, clothing, a dwelling, and bedding;[264] and he affectionately and unreservedly teaches me short-term and long-term guidelines.

Reflecting, "How very kind he is," count on your rosary the instances of his kindness, and recollect his kindness.

If you do not generate the respect that recollects such kindness when it has been shown to you, your behavior is poor, improper, and vulgar. The *Verses of the Nāga King Bherī* says:

> Mountains, lands, and
> oceans are not burdens;
> any ingratitude
> is my heavy burden.[265]

And Venerable Sakya Paṇḍita says:

> Repaying goodness is good.
> Not repaying kindness is bad.

The way to rely on the spiritual guide through action

While visualizing your spiritual guides in front of you, reflect on the way to rely on the spiritual guide through action. There are three ways to rely on the spiritual guide through action: (1) making material offerings to the teacher, (2) physically offering service, and (3) pleasing him by offering practice according to his instructions.

Making material offerings to the teacher

Offer the best to your teachers. If you offer poor-quality possessions while you have others of better quality, you risk incurring the fault of degenerate pledges. However, if you only have possessions of poor quality or your teachers are pleased with them, then there is no fault in offering those.

Physically offering service

Recollect that you will obtain countless excellent qualities through the practice of offering service to your teachers in the form of therapeutic massage, nursing them when they are sick, and so forth. Sakya Paṇḍita says:

> When I was young, I cultivated guru yoga in order to achieve [the state of a guru-deity]. Jetsun Drakpa Gyaltsen turned down my request for a guru-yoga practice, saying, "You do not recognize me as a buddha. Rather, you see me as an uncle. You are not able to endure hardships for your teacher by means of your body and possessions." Later, I received the signs of death and became physically unwell. At that time, my teacher also became unwell for several days. Disregarding sleep and food, I nursed him continuously, day and night. It seemed like I purified heavy misdeeds by doing so. After that, he conferred the primordial guru yoga upon me. The recognition of the teacher as actual buddha was produced, and I directly perceived the nature of all buddhas as Ārya Mañjuśrī. As a result, I became free from the signs of death and fully regained my health. Since then, I have grasped unerringly all the essential points of scripture and reasoning, such as grammar, epistemology, prosody, Vinaya, and Abhidharma. I attained the confidence of fearlessness regarding the three scriptural baskets.[266] All gods, spirits, and humans behave lovingly toward me. All haughty beings such as Chinese emperors requested the Dharma and showed great appreciation. Perfect realizations were born within me. My teacher's illness at that time was a display to benefit me. Those who follow my example will acquire complete extensive stores [of excellent qualities].[267]

The great pandit Nāropa also disregarded his body and life and underwent countless hardships before achieving his goals. After Nāropa passed away, Jé Marpa Lotsāwa searched for his teacher with strong faith and was eventually able to meet him.

Jetsun Milarepa single-handedly built a nine-story tower for Marpa, and at night he dutifully attended Marpa's wife, Dakmema, carrying water, grinding parched grain, kindling fire, and sweeping ashes, even acting as a stool while she milked the cattle. He thereby achieved all his goals.

When Dromtönpa met Atiśa, he asked, "Have my previous activities been Dharma or not?" Atiśa replied, "Only your service to your teacher Setsun qualified as a spiritual path; the rest have not."[268]

Also, someone remarked to Atiśa, "There are many teachers in Tibet who have meditated and practiced, yet none have gained special qualities." Atiśa replied, "All excellent qualities of the Mahāyāna, large or small, are produced in dependence on the teacher. In Tibet, you see your teachers as mere ordinary beings, so how can you produce special qualities?"

As verbal devotion to your teacher, proclaim his excellent qualities out loud in the cardinal and intermediate directions and make requests to him with melodious praises. Even if he teaches no more than a single verse, offer your compliments; it goes without saying that you should do likewise when he teaches the Dharma extensively.

Pleasing him by offering practice according to his instructions

This is to practice as you have been taught. Reflect as follows:

> For the sake of these spiritual guides who are actual buddhas, I will give up my body, life, and possessions without regard for them and, in particular, please these spiritual guides by offering my practice according to their instructions. Guru-deity, please bless me and all sentient beings that we may do so!

Think:

> From having made supplications in this manner, streams of five-colored nectar along with light rays descend from the body of the guru-deity above my crown. Permeating my body and mind and those of all other sentient beings, they cleanse us of all the misdeeds and obstructions we have amassed since beginningless time, and in particular those misdeeds and obstructions that prevent the special realization that enables us to offer up our body, life, possessions, and the like without regard for them and also please these spiritual guides by offering practice according to their instructions. The special realization *that enables us to offer up our body, life, and possessions without regard for them and, in particular, please these spiritual guides by offering our*

practice according to their instructions is produced in our mental continua.[269]

During the actual session, train your mind in this way. Between sessions, do your best to immediately implement whichever aspects you are capable of practicing.

Conclusion

Turning your attention to Guru Munīndra above your crown, recite the following as many times as possible:

> To Guru Conqueror Śākyamuni, I pay homage, make offerings, and go for refuge.

Think:

> Induced by my supplications, there emerges from Guru Munīndra a second figure of Guru Munīndra, who absorbs into me, whereby my form clearly becomes that of Guru Munīndra. Radiating from the *hūṃ* at my heart, light rays strike all sentient beings surrounding me and place them in the state of Guru Munīndra. I and all sentient beings, each visualized as Munīndra, have at the heart a moon disc, upon which is a white *a* marked with a yellow *hūṃ*. It is encircled by the mantra *Oṃ mune mune mahāmunaye svāhā*.

Focusing your attention on the mantra, recite it as many times as you can. To conclude the session, recite dedication verses such as:

> By this virtue, may I quickly
> achieve the state of Guru Buddha and
> place all sentient beings without exception
> in that state.

With the strong aspiration to fulfill your and others' short-term and ultimate wishes, dedicate the virtues arisen from your practice. If you can, perform prayers such as the *King of Prayers of Excellent Deeds.*[270]

What to do between the sessions

Between sessions, read the scriptures and commentaries that teach how to rely on a spiritual guide, such as how Sadāprarudita relied on Dharmodgata, Nāropa on Tilopa, Marpa on Nāropa, Milarepa on Marpa, and Dromtönpa on Lama Setsun and Atiśa. Do not read many other texts. Endowed with mindfulness and introspection, restrain the doors of your sense faculties. Consume food in appropriate quantities. Strive in yoga without lying down, and when you do lie down, practice accordingly. Strive in the yogas of washing and of eating.[271]

4 The Precious Human Rebirth

Having relied on a spiritual guide, the stages of how to train your mind

This is explained in two parts: exhortation to extract the essence of a physical basis endowed with the freedoms and privileges and how to extract such an essence. The first is explained in two parts: what to do during the session and what to do between the sessions. The first of those has three parts: preparation, the actual meditation on extracting the essence of a physical basis endowed with the freedoms and privileges, and conclusion.

Preparation

Carry out the preparatory practices up to the following lines:[272]

> O guru, extraordinary deity, who encompasses all the objects of
> refuge,
> Munīndra Vajradhara, to you I make supplication!

Reflect as follows:

> Having continuously taken birth in saṃsāra, I and all mother sentient beings have experienced a variety of prolonged and intense sufferings. This plight is owing to our failure to realize how a physical basis endowed with the freedoms and privileges is greatly meaningful and difficult to find. So guru-deity, please bless me and all mother sentient beings that we may generate the special realization of how a physical basis endowed with the freedoms and privileges is greatly meaningful and difficult to find!

Think:

> From having made supplications in this manner, streams of five-colored nectar along with light rays descend from the body of the guru-deity above my crown. Permeating my body and mind and also those of all other sentient beings, they cleanse us of all the misdeeds and obstructions amassed since beginningless time, and in particular those misdeeds and obstructions that prevent the special realization of how a physical basis endowed with the freedoms and privileges is greatly meaningful and difficult to find. Our bodies become the nature of transparent light. Our lifespan, merit, and all excellent qualities of scripture and realization develop and increase. The special realization of *how a physical basis endowed with the freedoms and privileges is greatly meaningful and difficult to find* is produced in our mental continua.

The actual meditation on extracting the essence of a physical basis endowed with the freedoms and privileges

This is explained in two parts: reflecting on how a physical basis endowed with the freedoms and privileges is greatly meaningful and reflecting on how a physical basis endowed with the freedoms and privileges is difficult to find. The first is explained in two parts: reflecting on the eight freedoms and reflecting on the ten privileges.

Reflecting on the eight freedoms

While meditating on the guru-deity above your crown, reflect as follows:

> *Freedom* here refers to having the liberty to practice the excellent Dharma and to being spared the eight states deprived of liberty. The eight states deprived of liberty are explained in the *Verse Summary on the Perfection of Wisdom*:
>
> > Through ethics, [a bodhisattva] eliminates many
> > circumstances of rebirths as an animal and

> the eight states deprived of liberty. Through ethics,
> he always obtains freedom.[273]

The *Letter to a Friend* says:

> To be born holding wrong views,
> as an animal, hungry ghost, or hell being,
> deprived of the Conqueror's teachings, and
> as a barbarian in a border region, a fool,
> or a long-lived god
> are the eight faulty states lacking liberty.
> Having gained the states of liberty free from those,
> strive for the sake of overcoming rebirth.[274]

These eight states deprived of liberty consist of four human states lacking liberty and four nonhuman states lacking liberty.

The four human states lacking liberty are: (1) [living] in a border region, which is a place where the four types of Buddhist followers are inactive;[275] (2) lacking complete faculties so that one is mentally disadvantaged or has a disability in terms of major and minor limbs[276] or hearing; (3) holding wrong views, in which one denies past and future lives, karma and its results, the Three Jewels, and so forth; and (4) being deprived of the Conqueror's teachings in a situation where a buddha has not appeared. And the four nonhuman states lacking liberty are: (5–7) the three lower rebirths and (8) rebirth as a long-lived god.

Regarding the long-lived gods, the *Extensive Explanation of the Letter to a Friend* explains that there are two types, those without discrimination and those belonging to the formless realms.[277] The former are ordinary beings who have been born in a region of Great Fruit, an abode of the fourth *dhyāna*,[278] which is akin to a secluded location set away from the city. The latter are ordinary beings who have been born in the formless realm. The *Discussion of the Eight States Deprived of Liberty* explains that long-lived gods are desire-realm gods who are constantly distracted by their indulgence in activities of desire.[279]

Reflecting on the ten privileges

Reflect as follows:

> There are five privileges related to self and five to others. The first five related to self are:
>
> > Being human, being born in a central region, having
> > complete faculties,
> > not having committed extreme actions, and having
> > faith in the source.[280]

As said, [the five privileges related to self are]: (1) being human, (2) being born in a central region, (3) having complete faculties including intellectual ability, (4) not having committed extreme actions—that is, actions of immediate retribution—and (5) having faith in the source, that is, faith in the subduing Dharma.[281] Reflect as follows:

> The five privileges related to others are:
>
> > The Buddha has come, he taught the Dharma,
> > the teachings remain, there are followers,
> > and [there are those who act out of] lovingkindness
> > for others.[282]

As said, the second set of five related to others is: (1) the Buddha has come to the world system, (2) he taught the Dharma, (3) the Dharma taught by him remains, (4) there are people following those Dharma teachings, and (5) there are donors and sponsors who give Dharma robes and the like, teachers who explain the Dharma to others with lovingkindness, and so on.

And if, especially, the favorable factors are complete—rarely falling sick, conducive conditions coming together, having the great wisdom of hearing and contemplation, not falling prey to immoral spiritual guides and bad companions, meeting a virtuous spiritual guide, striving in practice and understanding the essential points of practice, all the scriptures appearing to one as instructions, and staying at a pleasant place of practice—this is like possessing a vast collection of jewels indispensable for the practice of Dharma.

A person who has all the eight freedoms does not necessarily have all the ten privileges, but a person who has all the ten privileges necessarily has all the eight freedoms. The eight freedoms are posited from the point of view of being parted [from unfavorable conditions], whereas the ten privileges are posited from the point of view of being endowed [with favorable conditions]. Therefore, regarding this physical basis endowed with the complete freedoms and privileges, difficult to find and greatly meaningful when found, that you have obtained, *freedoms* refers to having the liberty to practice the excellent Dharma, and *privileges* refers to having the complete outer and inner conditions for practicing the Dharma.

This physical basis of freedoms and privileges that you have obtained is immensely meaningful, because in dependence on it, you can accomplish generosity, ethics, patience, joyous effort, and the like, which are the causes of the excellent body, resources, and retinue of an upper rebirth. In addition, you are able to accomplish stronger practice by virtue of the (1) field, (2) thought, (3) item, (4) basis, and (5) time.

The ability to accomplish stronger practice by virtue of the field[283]

Suppose all sentient beings of the ten directions have their eyeballs gouged out and are imprisoned. Compared to freeing them, restoring their sight, and setting them in Brahmā's bliss,[284] there is greater benefit in gazing at a single bodhisattva with lucid faith. Compared to making offerings to all bodhisattvas, there is greater benefit in making offerings to a single pore of a buddha. Compared to making offerings to all buddhas, there is greater benefit in making offerings to a single pore of one's teacher. You can achieve these great benefits with your present physical basis [endowed with the freedoms and privileges].

The ability to accomplish stronger practice by virtue of the thought

By giving a morsel of food to an animal motivated by the thought "I shall achieve complete enlightenment for the sake of all sentient beings," you will create enormously powerful roots of virtue. Since your beneficiaries are countless sentient beings and your goal is endowed with the inconceivable excellent qualities of complete enlightenment, you will be able to achieve enormously powerful roots of virtue. You can achieve that with your present physical basis [endowed with the freedoms and privileges].

The ability to accomplish stronger practice by virtue of the item[285]

Compared to a householder who performs charity with innumerable material gifts, a monastic who gives a verse of Dharma creates far greater merit. Those of you who are renunciates can achieve that now.

The ability to accomplish stronger practice by virtue of the basis[286]

Compared to a householder bodhisattva offering a lamp by inserting a wick the size of Mount Meru into an ocean of grain oil, there is greater benefit in a monastic bodhisattva offering a lamp by inserting a wick the size of the tip of a needle into a drop of grain oil. Even though there is no difference in them being bodhisattvas, there is greater strength [in the latter offering] by virtue of the basis [of a practitioner holding a greater number of vows]. Those who presently have the basis of a fully ordained bodhisattva can achieve that.

The ability to accomplish stronger practice by virtue of time

Compared to practicing ethics for an eon in the northeastern land of Buddha Īśvararāja, there is greater benefit in practicing a single type of ethics in this world system of endurance.[287] Compared to practicing ethics for an extended period during the time when the Buddha's teachings have not entered decline, there is greater benefit practicing ethics for a single morning now, when the teachings are close to destruction. Furthermore, the *Saṃvarodaya Tantra* says:

> The humans of the three continents[288]
> live with abundant resources.
> They lack analytical powers and intelligence.
> Foolish and confused, they are not discerning.
>
> Those born in Jambūdvīpa
> are known as inhabitants of the land of karma.[289]

Since the people of Jambūdvīpa are inhabitants of the land of karma,[290] the karmas they create early on in life can subsequently come to fruition later in life. Thus the inhabitants of Jambūdvīpa are praised as having the supreme basis for attaining enlightenment in a single short lifetime of the degenerate age. They are praised because even bodhisattvas who have been born in Sukhāvatī make prayers [to be reborn in Jambūdvīpa]: "The special physical basis for attaining enlightenment in a single short lifetime in the degenerate age is obtainable in the world system of endurance that lies east of here. May I too be reborn there!"[291]

In brief, you can produce all three types of vows[292] upon this physical basis and easily achieve buddhahood in a single short lifetime of the degenerate age. Reflect as follows:

> I will not allow this precious opportunity, obtained just this once, to pass me by. I will extract the essence of this physical basis endowed with the complete freedoms and privileges, difficult to find and greatly meaningful when found. Guru-deity, please bless me that I may do so!

Think:

> From having made supplications in this manner, streams of five-colored nectar along with light rays descend from the body of the guru-deity above my crown. Permeating my body and mind and also those of all other sentient beings, they cleanse us of all the misdeeds and obstructions we have amassed since beginningless time, and in particular those misdeeds and obstructions that prevent the special realization of how a life endowed with the freedoms and privileges is greatly meaningful. Our bodies become the nature of transparent light. Our lifespan, merit, and all excellent qualities of scripture and realization develop and increase. The special realization of *how a life endowed with the freedoms and privileges is greatly meaningful* is produced in our mental continua.

Reflecting on how a physical basis endowed with the freedoms and privileges is difficult to find

While meditating on the guru-deity above your crown, reflect as follows:

> Not only is the attainment of a physical basis endowed with the freedoms and privileges greatly meaningful, such a life is also exceedingly difficult to find.

How a physical basis endowed with the freedoms and privileges is difficult to find from the point of view of causes

The *Chapters on Vinaya* says that those who die and transfer from either an upper or lower rebirth to a lower rebirth are as numerous as the atoms of the great ground, whereas those who transfer to an upper rebirth are like the atoms clinging to the tip of the Buddha's fingernail.[293] The *Four Hundred Verses* says:

> Most human beings
> adhere to wrong positions.
> Therefore, most ordinary beings
> will surely go to lower rebirths.[294]

As said, most humans and other living beings frequently commit the ten nonvirtues and other misdeeds. These misdeeds hinder the attainment of freedoms and privileges. Specifically, to attain a pure physical basis endowed with the complete freedoms and privileges, one needs to take pure ethics as foundation, supplement ethics with practices such as generosity, and transition to the new rebirth with stainless prayers. Since it seems very few beings accomplish such causes, the attainment of the resultant physical basis endowed with the complete freedoms and privileges is extremely rare.

Moreover, compared to upper rebirths of a similar type, the attainment of this physical basis endowed with the complete freedoms and privileges is exceedingly rare; even among hundreds and hundreds of human beings, such a rebirth is as rare as [seeing] a star during daytime.

How a life endowed with the freedoms and privileges is difficult to find from the point of view of examples

To explain how a life endowed with the freedoms and privileges is difficult to find by means of examples, the *Teaching to Venerable Nanda on Entry into the Womb* teaches that it is more difficult to be reborn from a lower rebirth into an upper rebirth than for a mustard seed to cling to the tip of a needle or a pea to cling to a glass surface when thrown at it.[295]

The *Connected Discourses* gives the following example.[296] Suppose this great earth becomes a great ocean. Upon it floats a yoke with a hole, blown in all directions by the winds of the four directions. Moreover, within that ocean dwells a blind turtle that surfaces once every hundred years. It is much more difficult for a person to be reborn from a lower rebirth into an upper rebirth than for that turtle to insert its neck into the hole of that yoke.[297]

Also, for example, compared to redirecting the waters of the present Nyang River to the height of a mountain peak, it is more difficult for a person to be reborn from a lower rebirth into an upper rebirth.[298] The reason is that once someone is born in the lower rebirths, it is difficult to produce a virtuous mind, and misdeeds are committed soon after. Therefore it is exceedingly difficult for a person to be reborn from a lower rebirth into an upper rebirth.

How a life endowed with the freedoms and privileges is difficult to find from the point of view of numbers

It is said that among the three lower rebirths, animals are the least in number, hungry ghosts are more numerous than animals, and hell beings outnumber hungry ghosts. There are [uncountable] animals living in the depths of the oceans, and some are dispersed in the realms of gods and humans. The number of bees swarming around a thicket during summer exceeds all the humans in Jambūdvīpa. Reflect as follows:

> I have obtained just this once a physical basis endowed with the complete freedoms and privileges, difficult to find and greatly meaningful when found. Therefore I will not allow it to pass me by. To extract its essence, I will rely inseparably on the guru-buddha, practice his essential Mahāyāna instructions, and attain buddhahood easily in this very life. Guru-deity, please bless me that I may do so!

Think:

> From having made supplications in this manner, streams of five-colored nectar along with light rays descend from the body of the guru-deity above my crown. Permeating my body and mind and also those of all other sentient beings, they cleanse us of all the misdeeds and obstructions we have amassed since beginningless time, and in particular those misdeeds and obstructions that prevent the special realization of how a physical basis endowed with the freedoms and privileges is difficult to find. Our bodies

become the nature of transparent light. Our lifespan, merit, and all excellent qualities of scripture and realization develop and increase. The special realization of *how a physical basis endowed with the freedoms and privileges is difficult to find* is produced in our mental continua.

Conclusion

Turning your attention to Guru Munīndra above your crown, recite the following as many times as possible:

> To Guru Conqueror Śākyamuni, I pay homage, make offerings, and go for refuge.

Think:

> Induced by my supplications, there emerges from Guru Munīndra a second figure of Guru Munīndra, who absorbs into me, whereby my form clearly becomes that of Guru Munīndra. Radiating from the *hūṃ* at my heart, light rays strike all sentient beings surrounding me and place them in the state of Guru Munīndra. I and all sentient beings, each visualized as Munīndra, have at the heart a moon disc, upon which is a white *a* marked with a yellow *hūṃ*. It is encircled by the mantra *Oṃ mune mune mahāmunaye svāhā.*

Focusing your attention on the mantra, recite it as many times as you can. To conclude the session, recite dedication verses such as:

> By this virtue, may I quickly
> achieve the state of Guru Buddha and
> place all sentient beings without exception
> in that state.

With the strong aspiration to fulfill your and others' short-term and ultimate wishes, dedicate the virtues arisen from your practice. If you can, perform prayers such as the *King of Prayers of Excellent Deeds.*

What to do between the sessions

Between the sessions, read the scriptures and commentaries that teach about *a physical basis endowed with the freedoms and privileges*, and perform other activities explained above [in the section on how to rely on a spiritual guide].[299]

The Path in Common with That of Persons with Small Capacity

5 Impermanence in the Form of Death

How to extract such an essence

This is explained in three parts: how to train your mind in the path in common with that of persons with small capacity, how to train your mind in the path in common with that of persons with medium capacity, and how to train your mind in the stages of the path of persons with great capacity. The first is explained in two parts: what to do during the session and what to do between the sessions. The first of those has three parts: preparation, the actual meditation on the path in common with that of persons with small capacity, and conclusion.

Preparation

Carry out the preparatory practices up to the following lines:[300]

> O guru, extraordinary deity, who encompasses all the objects of refuge,
> Munīndra Vajradhara, to you I make supplication!

Reflect as follows:

> Having continuously taken birth in saṃsāra, I and all mother sentient beings have experienced a variety of prolonged and intense sufferings. This plight is owing to our failure to:
>
> - Contemplate impermanence in the form of death
> - Recollect the suffering of lower rebirths and produce the fervent wish to be freed from it

- Wholeheartedly go to the Three Jewels for refuge out of fear of the suffering of lower rebirths
- Produce the faith of conviction in karma and its results

So, I and all mother sentient beings have to:

- Be mindful of impermanence in the form of death
- Recollect the suffering of lower rebirths and produce the fervent wish to be freed from it
- Wholeheartedly go to the Three Jewels for refuge out of fear of the suffering of lower rebirths
- Produce the faith of conviction in karma and its results

By generating these special realizations in our minds, we will give up misdeeds and practice virtue correctly. Guru-deity, please bless us that we may do so!

Think:

From having made supplications in this manner, streams of five-colored nectar along with light rays descend from the body of the guru-deity above my crown. Permeating my body and mind and also those of the other sentient beings, they cleanse us of all the misdeeds and obstructions we have amassed since beginningless time, and in particular those misdeeds and obstructions that prevent the special realizations of the path in common with that of persons with small capacity. Our bodies become the nature of transparent light. Our lifespan, merit, and all excellent qualities of scripture and realization develop and increase. The special realizations of *the path in common with that of persons with small capacity* are produced in our mental continua.

The Actual Meditation on the Path in Common with That of Persons with Small Capacity

This is explained in four parts: reflecting on impermanence in the form of death, reflecting on the suffering of lower rebirths, training in going to the Three Jewels for refuge, and generating the faith of conviction in karma and its results.

Reflecting on impermanence in the form of death

While meditating on the guru-deity above your crown, reflect on the following points.[301]

Death is definite

[Reflect as follows:]

> (1) This physical basis endowed with the complete freedoms and privileges, difficult to find and greatly meaningful when found, decays quickly. The lord of death will definitely come.

No matter what kind of body you have taken, it cannot circumvent death. The chapter on impermanence in the *Collection of Aphorisms* says:

> If the buddhas, the solitary realizers,
> and the buddha's hearers
> must cast off their physical bodies,
> what need be said of ordinary beings?[302]

As said, if even the tathāgatas, who have attained the vajra body,[303] depart for other worlds for the sake of trainees, there is no need to speak of ordinary beings like ourselves. No matter where you dwell, you will not be able to circumvent death. The *Collection of Aphorisms* says:

> A location where you can circumvent death
> does not exist anywhere,
> not in the sky, not in the ocean,
> and not in the mountains.[304]

Death cannot be averted by swiftly fleeing, or by strength, wealth, substance, mantra, medicine, or anything else. There is no safe haven to which you can quickly escape. Aśvaghoṣa's *Dispelling Sorrow* says:[305]

> Although a great sage with the five supernatural powers
> can fly far into the sky,

he cannot reach a place
where he will not experience death.[306]

Death cannot be averted by strength, wealth, substance, mantra, medicine, or anything else. By no outer or inner circumstance can it be averted.

Next, reflect as follows:

(2) My lifespan cannot be lengthened, and it decreases continuously.

In a context where the average lifespan is sixty years, for those who have reached that age, death will happen before long—perhaps this year, today, or tomorrow. For those who have reached the age of fifty, there will be no more than ten years remaining. Similarly, some have two-thirds of their life left; some have just half left. Moreover, whatever remains of your lifespan slips away. A year goes by with each passing month; a month goes by with each passing day; a day goes by with each passing daytime and nighttime; the daytime goes by with each passing morning and afternoon; a morning goes by with each passing instant. Accordingly, *Engaging in Bodhisattva Deeds* says:

Without remaining day or night,
this life is always slipping away
and never lengthening.
If that is the case, why would death not come to one like me?[307]

Reflect as follows:

(3) Death will definitely come even if I do not find time for spiritual practice while alive.

It is said in the *Teaching to Venerable Nanda on Entry into the Womb* that during the [first] ten years when one is a child, one does not produce the thought of spiritual practice. At the end, during the [last] twenty years when one is aged, one does not have the circumstances for spiritual practice. Between those periods, half the time is spent asleep, and a great deal of time is consumed by sickness and the like. So there is hardly any occasion for spiritual practice.[308]

The time of death is uncertain

Reflect as follows:

(1) Not only will I die, the time of my death is uncertain.

In general, the lifespan of inhabitants of Kuru is fixed at a thousand years.[309] Even though how long those of other continents can live is not certain, most have a fixed lifespan.[310] However, the lifespan of the inhabitants of Jambūdvīpa is very uncertain. In the beginning they live for an uncountable number of years, but in time their maximum lifespan is no more than ten years.[311] Their time of death is uncertain, regardless of whether they are old, young, or middle-aged. The *Treasury of Knowledge* says:

> Here it is indefinite: in the end ten years
> and in the beginning uncountable.[312]

The *Collection of Aphorisms* says:

> Many people are seen in the morning,
> but some of them will not be seen in the evening.
> Many people are seen in the evening,
> but some of them will not be seen in the morning.
>
> If many men and women,
> and even those in the prime of their youth, die,
> how can you, saying, "Oh, he's young,"
> be so sure that this person will still be alive?
>
> Some die in the womb;
> some as soon as they are born;
> some as soon as they are able to crawl;
> some as soon as they are able to run;
> some when old; some when young;
> some in their prime.
> In stages, they move on,
> like a ripe fruit falling.[313]

> I cannot tell which will come first,
> tomorrow or my next life.
> So instead of putting effort into tomorrow,
> I should put effort into my next life.[314]

Reflect as follows:

> (2) The conditions leading to death are many, while those for staying alive are few.

The *Precious Garland* says:

> The causes of death are many,
> while those of staying alive are few.[315]

External circumstances can arise where a person is slain by arms, poison, yakṣas, rulers, *tsen* spirits,[316] *mātṛ* spirits,[317] and so forth. There are other unforeseen circumstances that can cause death, such as an imbalance among the four elements,[318] incompatible food, drug allergies, a fall from a cliff, a collapsing house, a shipwreck, a capsizing boat, or a stroke—all can happen without warning. Understand that the nature of your existence is the same as illustrated in these examples.

Reflect as follows:

> (3) My body is as fragile as a water bubble.

Thus the time of your death is uncertain. The *Letter to a Friend* says:

> If even the ground, Mount Meru, and the oceans
> will burn up through the blazing of seven suns[319]
> so that not even their ashes will remain,
> what need be said of these extremely frail embodied beings?[320]

The *Precious Garland* says:

> For you live amid the causes of death
> like a lamp standing in a draft.[321]

As taught, reflect as follows:

> I may die suddenly, even from a thorn puncturing my skin.

Nothing but spiritual practice helps

[Reflect:]

> (1) Apart from spiritual practice, nothing can help me at the time of death. (2) No matter how fond I am of my friends and relatives, I will not be able to take with me even a single one of these people surrounding me. No matter how many heaps of alluring jewels I may have, I will not be able to take even a speck with me. (3) If I have to part from even this body with which I was born, of what use is my attachment to the splendors of this life? Death, the enemy, will inevitably come, yet it is uncertain when. Since I may die even today, I must ensure that I am prepared. The way to prepare for death is to let go of the pleasures of this life and engage in pure spiritual practice now. Guru-deity, please bless me that I may do so!

Think:

> From having made supplications in this manner, streams of five-colored nectar along with light rays descend from the body of the guru-deity above my crown. Permeating my body and mind and also those of the other sentient beings, they cleanse us of all the misdeeds and obstructions we have amassed since beginningless time, in particular those misdeeds and obstructions that prevent us from letting go of the pleasures of this life and engaging in pure spiritual practice now. The special realizations of *letting go of the pleasures of this life and engaging in pure spiritual practice now* are produced in our mental continua.

6 The Suffering of Lower Rebirths

Reflecting on the suffering of lower rebirths

While meditating on the guru-deity above your crown, reflect as follows:

> This human basis complete with the freedoms and privileges, difficult to find and greatly meaningful when found, quickly decays. After death I will not simply go out of existence. I will have to take rebirth, and where I am reborn can only be either an upper rebirth or a lower rebirth. If I am reborn in a lower rebirth, inconceivable sufferings will lie in store for me: in the *hell* realms are sufferings such as heat and cold; in the *hungry ghost* realms are sufferings such as hunger and thirst; and in the *animal* realms are the sufferings of foolishness, ignorance, and being preyed on by other animals.

The suffering of the hells

When contemplating the suffering of the hells, reflect on the four types of hells: (1) the great hells of sentient beings, (2) the surrounding hells, (3) the cold hells, and (4) the partial hells.

The great hells of sentient beings

The Revival Hell lies 32,000 yojanas[322] below the surface of the earth. Located below it are seven other hells, each separated from the hell above it by four thousand yojanas.

1) In the Revival Hell, sentient beings are gathered, and they attack each other with weapons that have arisen through the force of their karma. After they faint and fall to the ground, a voice from the sky declares, "May you

be revived!" Standing up, they attack each other as before. As a result, they experience unending suffering.

2) In the Black Line Hell, the hell guardians draw squares and other shapes with black lines on sentient beings and then chop along those lines with implements. As a result, the denizens of this hell experience untold suffering.

3) In the Crushing Hell, sentient beings are herded into a single location and then crushed between mountains that resemble the faces of goats, sheep, and so forth.[323] As a result, they experience suffering without end.

4) In the Wailing Hell, sentient beings are consumed by blazing fire within an iron chamber.

5) In the Great Wailing Hell, sentient beings are consumed by blazing fire within a double-layered iron chamber.

6) In the Hot Hell, sentient beings are incinerated within an iron cauldron many yojanas wide. They are impaled on iron poles, whose spikes emerge from their crowns. Fire blazes from all their sense doors and burns them.

7) In the Very Hot Hell, sentient beings are impaled on tridents whose spikes emerge from their crown and two shoulders. Their bodies are wrapped in sheets of burning iron, and they are laid out on their backs upon the iron ground. Their mouths held open by iron instruments, they are fed blazing iron pellets and boiling molten iron. As a result, the iron burns their mouth, throat, and intestines and then emerges from the lower orifices.

8) In the Hell of Unrelenting Torment, sentient beings are trapped within an iron chamber blazing with fire. The fire is fanned by ferocious winds whipping from the four directions, burning the bodies of the hell beings such that they become indistinguishable from fire.

Comparing the hotness of hell fire and human fire

It is taught that the fire in the eon of destruction[324] is seven times hotter than the fire in the human realm. The fire in the hell realms is seven times hotter than that. Compared to the fire in the hell realms, the fire in the human realm is cool like snow. Just as any part of the body burned by fire of the human realm feels cooled and relieved when coming in contact with the cool waters of *gośīrṣa* sandalwood,[325] any part of the body burned by the fire of hell feels cooled and relieved when coming in contact with the fire of the human realm.

The lifespan of hell beings

It is as said in the *Letter to a Friend*:

> In this way, the sufferings are unbearable.
> Even if they have been experienced for a billion years,
> until their nonvirtues have been exhausted,
> beings do not die.[326]

Alternatively, it is said that the lifespan of a being in the Revival Hell is 1.62 trillion human years.[327] The lifespan of each lower level is twice that of the one above it.

The surrounding hells

Having been freed from the suffering of the great hells, the being arrives at the Pit of Embers, where just by stepping into it, their leg sinks into it and all the flesh is consumed. Next, they arrive at the Swamp of Corpses, where they sink into it up to their neck, and worms called *sharp-lipped* bore [through their flesh] until reaching their bones and marrow. Then they arrive at the Path of Sharp Knives, where their flesh and skin are sliced open as they walk along. When they arrive at the Sword-Leafed Forest, swords slice off their major limbs and minor limbs.[328] When climbing up and down the trees in the Silk-Cotton Forest,[329] their flesh and skin are torn open by thorns. Crows with iron beaks perch on their shoulders or head and peck out their eyeballs. Located close by is the River with No Ford, which is filled with caustic water. Falling headlong into it, they sink and are burned by it.

The cold hells

The cold hells are located 10,000 yojanas beyond the hot hells. At the location of the Blistering Hell, 32,000 yojanas below the surface of the earth, the ground is completely frozen. Vicious winds lash above the ground, causing blisters to erupt on the body. The Hell of Bursting Blisters is even colder, causing the blisters to burst. In the Achu Hell and Kyihu Hell, while sentient beings are unable to let out loud moans, sounds such as *kyihu* are produced from deep down in their throats. In the Clenched-Teeth Hell, they cannot emit any sound whatsoever. In the Splitting-Like-an-Utpala Hell, the body turns blue from exposure to the savage winds. In the Splitting-Like-a-Lotus Hell, the blue color fades, and the body, turning red, splits into ten or more "petals." In the Great Splitting-Like-a-Lotus Hell, the body splits into a hundred, a thousand, or more "petals."

The partial hells

The partial hells are places located in the vicinity of the hot hells and cold hells, and the *Grounds of Yogic Practitioners* teaches that some of them also exist within the human realms.[330] Since these are explained in the biographies of Śroṇa Koṭikarṇa[331] and Saṅgharakṣita,[332] you should refer to them.

The causes of hell rebirth

The general causes for being born in the hells are taught to be the ten great nonvirtues. In particular, it is also taught that committing the five actions of immediate retribution, engendering wrong views, incurring the four defeats, and disregarding the prātimokṣa infractions are causes of rebirth in the Revival Hell, and disdaining the prātimokṣa individual confessions is a cause of rebirth in the Black Line Hell.[333] It is said in *Engaging in Bodhisattva Deeds* that you will be reborn in the hells for as many eons as the instants you incur a bodhisattvas' root downfall and for as many eons as the instants of anger you direct at a bodhisattva.[334] The tantras state that you must stay in the Hell of Unrelenting Torment for as many eons as the instants you incur a tantric root downfall before restoring it. It is taught in the *Kālacakra Root Tantra* that you destroy all the roots of virtue accrued over as many eons as the instants of anger toward your spiritual guide and you have to stay in the hells for as many eons. Reflect as follows:

> I have amassed in my mindstream inconceivably powerful karmic potentials that will issue forth hell sufferings, and I have not yet purified them. Judging from my current capacity, I know that I am unable to purify all these karmas before death strikes. If I die suddenly, today or tomorrow, still bearing these karmas, I will surely be destined to a rebirth in the hells. And if I am reborn there, will I be able to endure those sufferings?

Meditate in this way until you are shaken by palpable trepidation. When uncontrived angst and fear is produced, immediately put aside all mundane activities—apart from procuring the food and clothes essential to spiritual practice—and strive day and night in confession and restraint through the four powers of purification, the excellent method for purifying those misdeeds and downfalls.[335]

The suffering of hungry ghosts

Hungry ghosts are tormented by inconceivable hunger and thirst as well as other kinds of miseries. The *Letter to a Friend* says:

> Among the hungry ghosts, there is continuous pain
> caused by unfulfilled desires.
> Know that they are confronted with horrific miseries of
> hunger, thirst, cold, heat, fatigue, and fear.[336]

Imagine how hideous, wretched, and frightened you would be as a hungry ghost.

Hungry ghosts with *external obstructions* cannot find anything to eat, drink, or use. If perchance they see something and approach it, they discover that the river or fruit tree is watched over by guards wielding various weapons, it appears as bloody pus, or it simply vanishes, and so they suffer deprivation.

Those with *inner obstructions* have mouths the size of a needle's eye, throats as fine as a strand of hair on a horse's tail, and limbs that resemble stalks of straw. Even if they look for food, drinks, or other sustenance, they cannot find it; if perchance they manage to find food or drink, it does not fit in their mouth; if perchance it fits in their mouth, they cannot swallow it; and if perchance they can swallow it, it does not fill their stomach. In such ways they suffer.

Those with *obstructions to food and drinks* are of various types. The hungry ghosts called Having Rows of Flames are such that everything they eat or drink bursts into flames and burns them. Those called Filth Eaters eat feces and drink urine; they eat and drink only that which is unclean, foul-smelling, harmful, and detestable. Some cut off their own flesh and eat it; they cannot consume food and drink that are clean and wholesome. Some are afflicted by heat due to moonlight during the summer and by cold due to sunlight during the winter. Some are such that their limbs cannot support their trunk, and so they suffer exhaustion wandering everywhere in search of food and drink. The more powerful hungry ghosts attack the weaker ones. Hungry ghosts also suffer fear and terror due to humans, dogs, and so forth.

The lifespan of hungry ghosts

Regarding their lifespan, the *Treasury of Knowledge* says:

> A month being a day, it is five hundred.[337]

As explained, the life of a hungry ghost lasts five hundred years, where a day is equivalent to one month in the human realm.[338]

The *Foundations of Mindfulness* says that they live for five hundred years, where a day[339] is equivalent to ten human years. Thus the lifespan of a hungry ghost is equivalent to 1.8 million human years.[340]

The causes of hungry ghost rebirth

The causes for being born as a hungry ghost are attachment, miserliness, covetousness, taking what is not given, and so forth. If you do not wish for these sufferings, strive to purify the causes of such a rebirth that you have amassed in the past and refrain from committing them in the future.

The suffering of animals

Animals are tormented by the inconceivable sufferings of foolishness and ignorance and of being preyed on by other animals. The main abodes of water animals are the waters of the great oceans, which are extremely dark at their depths. There are creatures of various sizes, colors, and shapes packed together like piles of grains. Imagine how it would be like for you to be born into such circumstances. Smaller organisms are devoured whole by the larger ones. A multitude of smaller ones gather to feed on a larger one, boring into its body. It is so dark that you would not even see yourself bending or stretching your arm. Smaller creatures are oppressed by the larger ones, so there is the suffering of suffocating anxiety.

Animals belonging to the class of nāgas experience the terror of garuḍas in the sky[341] and are tormented daily by the difficulties caused by sandstorms and the like. Wild animals flee from pursuing hunters and packs of dogs and are killed when they cannot escape. They are consumed by ferocious predators and become carrion for birds.

Domestic horses, buffaloes, donkeys, pigs, and other animals encounter countless sufferings, as they are worked, exploited, overburdened with loads, hit, beaten, made to plough, milked, sheared, slaughtered, and so forth.

The lifespan of animals

Their lifespans are as taught in the *Treasury of Knowledge*:

> Animals with the longest lifespan live for an eon.[342]

Those with a long lifespan can live up to an eon, while those with shorter lives have indefinite lifespans.

The causes of animal rebirth

The causes for being reborn as an animal are abandoning the Dharma, disrespecting the Dharma and its teachers, and criticizing fellow Dharma practitioners. Reflect as follows:

> Such sufferings of lower rebirths will be hard for me to endure. At this time, having obtained a human basis endowed with the complete freedoms and privileges, difficult to find and greatly meaningful when found, I will attain the state of a guru-buddha in which all sufferings of lower rebirths have been abandoned. Guru-deity, please bless me that I may do so!

Think:

> From having made supplications in this manner, streams of five-colored nectar along with light rays descend from the body of the guru-deity above my crown. Permeating my body and mind and also those of all other sentient beings, they cleanse us of those misdeeds and obstructions that prevent us from attaining the state of a guru-buddha in which all sufferings of lower rebirths have been abandoned. The special realization of *attaining the state of a guru-buddha in which all sufferings of lower rebirths have been abandoned* is produced in our mental continua.

7 | Going for Refuge

Training in going to the Three Jewels for refuge

I WILL NOW EXPAND slightly on the steps of the refuge practice presented in the *Easy Path*.[343]

The causes of refuge

The main causes of going for refuge are twofold: (1) our fear of the sufferings of saṃsāra, particularly those of lower rebirths, and (2) our understanding that the Three Jewels can protect us from those sufferings. Accordingly, the *Melodious Speech of Losang's Assertions: A Response to the Pure-Minded Queries* says:

> The essence of refuge is
> going for refuge on account of our fears and
> knowing that the Three Jewels have the power to protect us,
> O you who knows all asserts![344]

In dependence on those causes, the objects in which we seek refuge

Regarding the objects of refuge, [the Buddha] himself has been freed from all fears, he is skilled in the methods for freeing others from their fears, he engages all living beings with impartial great compassion, and he enacts the welfare of every living being regardless of whether that individual has benefited him.

Only perfect complete buddhas possess all those excellent qualities. If great gods such as Rudra and Viṣṇu lack those excellent qualities, what need is there to mention nāgas, hungry ghosts viewed as local spirits, and the like? Therefore, presented with the Three Jewels or non-Buddhist teachers, the Three Jewels alone are worthy of being held as a refuge. *Seventy Verses on Refuge* says:

The Buddha, Dharma, and Saṅgha
are the refuge for those who desire liberation.[345]

Reflecting on the excellent qualities of the Three Jewels

The Buddha's *body* is ornamented by the thirty-two excellent signs and eighty excellent exemplifying marks.[346] The excellent qualities of his *speech* are such that a single melodious verbal expression can reveal the Dharma to all sentient beings in their respective languages by way of possessing the sixty-four branches.[347] His excellent qualities of *mind* are wisdom and lovingkindness. His wisdom realizes directly and simultaneously all things and how they really exist, while his lovingkindness is such that he engages all sentient beings impartially with great compassion, like the lovingkindness of a mother for her only child, ever ready to guide them whenever appropriate. Without any exertion, his *activities* occur spontaneously and continuously.

Think that this Buddha,[348] who possesses infinite excellent qualities, arose as a result of actualizing and cultivating the scriptural and realizational Dharmas. These Dharmas have the nature of the true cessation [of suffering] and the true path [leading to the cessation of suffering], in which faults have been abandoned and excellent qualities accomplished.

The Saṅgha mainly refers to ārya persons. Think of the Saṅgha as those who keep in mind the excellent qualities of the Dharma and properly practice it.

Understanding the distinguishing features of the Three Jewels

1) Regarding the distinguishing features based on their *defining characteristics*, the Buddha Jewel has the characteristic of manifest full enlightenment, the Dharma Jewel has the characteristic of being the result of that [manifest full enlightenment], and the Saṅgha Jewel has the characteristic of correct practice guided by others' instructions.

2) Regarding the distinguishing features based on their *activities*, the Buddha Jewel bestows teachings, the Dharma Jewel focuses on abandoning the objects of abandonment, and the Saṅgha Jewel enthuses [over practice of the Dharma and sharing of knowledge].[349]

3) Regarding the distinguishing features based on [trainees'] *belief*, the Buddha Jewel is adhered to as an object to be venerated and honored, the Dharma Jewel as that which is to be actualized, and the Saṅgha Jewel as the companions who accord with the Dharma.

4) Regarding the distinguishing features based on *practice*, one practices by means of performing acts of offering and reverence in relation to the Buddha Jewel, by means of familiarizing with yogic applications in relation to the Dharma Jewel, and by means of sharing the Dharma and material resources in relation to the Saṅgha Jewel.

5) Regarding the distinguishing features based on *how they are recollected*, recollect their individual excellent qualities as stated:

> Thus the Buddha, Bhagavān . . .[350]

6) Regarding the distinguishing features based on the *increase of merit*, the differences [among the Three Jewels] stem from the increase of merit in terms of persons and the Dharma.[351]

Going for refuge with commitment

This means to hold the Buddha as the teacher of refuge, the Dharma as the actual refuge, and the Saṅgha as the companions who assist in accomplishing refuge.

Going for refuge that disavows other refuges

This is going for refuge aware of the differences between Buddhist and non-Buddhist teachers and their teachings.

The brief way of going for refuge

According to the brief instructions stated in the *Easy Path*, clearly visualize as follows:

> Gurus, deities, the Three Jewels, and hosts of heroes, heroines, protectors, and guardians are emanated from the body of the guru-deity above my crown, filling the space above. These objects of refuge surround the guru-deity above my crown.

Recollecting the excellent qualities of their body, speech, mind, and activities, visualize the sufferings of the lower rebirths that have been explained above. Shaken by palpable angst and fear, request:

> Please protect me and all mother sentient beings now from the fears of saṃsāra and specifically those of the lower rebirths!

Retaining that sense of longing [for their protection], recite the following refuge formula a hundred, a thousand, ten thousand, a hundred thousand, or more times:

> I go for refuge to the guru-deity and the Three Jewels.

Train properly in the refuge guidelines with the awareness of the short-term and ultimate benefits of seeking refuge in the Three Jewels.

The benefits of going for refuge

The benefits of going for refuge in the Three Jewels are: (1) you enter the ranks of Buddhists, (2) you become the support of all vows,[352] (3) karma and obstructions amassed in the past diminish and become extinguished, (4) you create extensive merit, (5) you do not fall into the lower rebirths, (6) you are protected from the fears of this life, (7) you fulfill all your wishes, and (8) you quickly attain buddhahood.

To illustrate the benefit of not falling into the lower rebirths, a son of the gods who was due to be reborn as a pig went for refuge to the Buddha. He became freed from the fears of the lower rebirth and was even reborn in a god realm higher than his previous one.[353]

As for the benefit of being protected from the fears of this life, Pūrṇa's elder brother Dārukarṇin[354] and his companions were sailing on the ocean in a ship filled with sandalwood when yakṣas conjured a storm. At the point when the ship was about to sink, [Dārukarṇin and his companions] went for refuge to Pūrṇa, and they were freed from their fears.[355] If going for refuge to a hearer arhat delivers such benefits, what need is there to mention going for refuge to a buddha?

Refuge guidelines

Refuge guidelines are of two types, individual guidelines and common guidelines.

Individual guidelines can be divided into proscriptive guidelines and prescriptive guidelines. In terms of proscriptive guidelines, having gone for refuge to the Buddha, do not pay homage and make offerings to other gods; having gone for refuge to the Dharma, give up harming sentient beings; and having gone for refuge to the Saṅgha, do not keep company with tīrthikas.[356] In terms of prescriptive guidelines, do not disparage images of tathāgatas and so forth.[357]

Train in the *common guidelines* as follows. By recollecting the distinguishing features and excellent qualities of the Three Jewels, go for refuge to them again and again. By recollecting their great kindness, strive to always make offerings, and [in particular] offer the first portion of your food and drink to them. Recollecting their great compassion, help other living beings to likewise [go for refuge]. Entrust yourself wholeheartedly to the Three Jewels in every task. Do not abandon the Three Jewels even at the cost of your life or in jest.

8 | The Principles of Karma

Generating the Faith of Conviction in Karma and Its Results

While meditating on the guru-deity above your crown, reflect on the following:

> It is taught in the Conqueror's scriptures that by creating a virtuous cause, only happy results will arise, never suffering; by creating a nonvirtuous cause, only suffering results will arise, never happiness. Even the pleasure that arises when a person troubled by heat is cooled by a gentle breeze stems from virtuous karma created in the past. Even the suffering of a person pricked by a thorn stems from nonvirtuous karma created in the past. Therefore karma is certain.
>
> When I create virtuous or nonvirtuous karma, even if it is a tiny one, as long as it is not impeded, a huge result will ensue. In a past life the novice monk Kyunté[358] said to a fully ordained monk who had an unpleasant voice, "You sound like a barking dog," as a result of which Kyunté was reborn as a dog for five hundred lives.[359] And, to a very agile fully ordained monk, he said, "You are like a monkey," as a result of which he was reborn as a monkey. Such accounts illustrate the great increase of karma.
>
> I will not experience happiness or suffering if I do not create the causes, virtue or misdeed. Therefore I will not encounter karma I have not created.
>
> If I create a causal virtue or misdeed and it is not impeded, that karma will not dissipate. Accordingly, it is said in a sūtra:

> The karmas of embodied beings
> do not dissipate even in a hundred eons.
> When the conditions assemble and the time arrives,
> the results will come to fruition.[360]

Here I will explain a little about the ten karmic paths.

Killing

- The basis of killing is a sentient being with a different mindstream from oneself.
- The thought of killing has three components: (1) the recognition, which refers to the unmistaken identification of the basis, (2) the affliction, which is any of the three poisons, and (3) the motivation, which is the desire to kill.
- The execution entails killing by means of poison, arms, knowledge mantra, and so forth.
- The culmination occurs when that sentient being dies before the perpetrator.

Stealing

- The basis of stealing is another's possession.
- The thought of stealing has three components: (1) the recognition, which refers to the unmistaken identification of the basis, (2) the affliction, which is any of the three poisons, and (3) the motivation, which is the desire to permanently deprive a person of a possession they have not freely offered.
- The execution is taking the possession by force, stealth, or deceit when it has not been given.
- The culmination occurs when the awareness is produced that one has obtained the possession.

Sexual misconduct

- The basis of sexual misconduct is an inappropriate partner such as one's mother; an inappropriate organ such as the mouth or anus; an inappropriate time such as the time of pregnancy or when abiding in one-day vows;[361] or an inappropriate location such as in front of a stūpa or one's guru.

- Regarding [the thought of sexual misconduct, it has three components:] (1) the recognition of the targeted basis; it makes no difference whether it is identified correctly or mistakenly; (2) [the affliction, which is any of the three poisons]; and (3) [the motivation, which is the desire to copulate].[362]
- [The execution][363]
- The culmination occurs when the two [organs] come into contact.

Lying

- The basis of lying is of four types [and their inverse]: what is seen, heard, differentiated, or known, and what is unseen, unheard, undifferentiated, or unknown.
- [The thought of lying has three components:] (1) the recognition, which involves a misrepresentation of the basis, such as misrepresenting what is seen as unseen, (2) the affliction, which is any of the three poisons, and (3) the motivation, which is the desire to communicate the misrepresentation.
- The execution entails communicating the misrepresentation or wittingly keeping silent.
- The culmination occurs when the other person comprehends what is communicated.

Divisive speech

- The basis of divisive speech is people who are either harmonious or disharmonious.
- The thought of divisive speech has three components: (1) the recognition, which refers to the unmistaken identification of the basis, (2) the affliction, which is any of the three poisons, and (3) the motivation, which is the desire to divide those who are harmonious and to prevent those who are disharmonious from reconciling.
- The execution entails speaking [such divisive words] pleasantly or unpleasantly.
- The culmination occurs when they comprehend the divisive words that have been spoken.

Harsh speech

- The basis of harsh speech is a sentient being who serves as the basis for one to produce a hostile mind.

- The thought of harsh speech has three components: (1) the recognition, which refers to the unmistaken identification of the basis, (2) the affliction, which is any of the three poisons, and (3) the motivation, which is the desire to speak harshly.
- The execution entails delivering pleasant or unpleasant content with true or untrue words that are spoken for one's or others' purpose.[364]
- The culmination occurs when the other person comprehends [what has been spoken].

Idle chatter

- The basis of idle chatter is a meaningless subject matter.
- The thought of idle chatter has three components: (1) the recognition, which refers to the unmistaken identification of the basis, (2) the affliction, which is any of the three poisons, and (3) the motivation, which is the desire to say something simply for its own sake.
- The execution entails engaging in idle chatter.
- The culmination occurs when the idle chatter is uttered.

Covetousness

- The basis of covetousness is the wealth and possessions of others.
- The thought of covetousness has three components: (1) the recognition, which refers to the unmistaken identification of the basis, (2) the affliction, which is any of the three poisons, and (3) the motivation, which is the desire to make the targeted basis one's own.
- The execution entails indulging in that thought.
- The culmination occurs when one thinks, "May that wealth or possession become mine!"

Malice

- The basis of malice is as for harsh speech [i.e., a sentient being who serves as the basis for one to produce a hostile mind].
- The thought of malice has three components: (1) the recognition, which refers to the unmistaken identification of the basis, (2) the affliction, which is any of the three poisons, and (3) the motivation, which is the desire to beat up the person and the like.
- The execution entails indulging in that thought.
- The culmination occurs when one decides to kill, tie up, or beat up the person or something similar.

Wrong view

- The basis of wrong view is an existing phenomenon.
- The thought of wrong view has three components: (1) the recognition, which refers to recognizing the meaning derived from having denied [an existing phenomenon] as the truth, (2) the affliction, which is any of the three poisons, and (3) the motivation, which is the desire to deny the targeted basis.
- The execution entails entertaining that thought.
- The culmination occurs when one is certain in one's denial.

The virtuous karmic paths

Using the virtue of abandoning killing as an illustration, the complete karmic path consists of various parts.

- The basis is another living being.
- The thought is the desire to abandon killing [that living being] through seeing its drawbacks.
- The execution entails striving to refrain from killing [that living being].
- The culmination occurs upon [creation of] the physical karma of having completely refrained from killing [that living being].

Understand the other nine virtuous karmic paths accordingly.

Karmas that are powerful from various points of view

From the point of view of the *field*,[365] no matter what harm or benefit is done to the Three Jewels, gurus, parents, and the like, it is powerful. From the point of view of the *thought*, deeds performed by way of strong compassion, strong hatred, and the like are powerful. From the point of view of the *item*, the giving of Dharma and superior material objects is powerful. From the point of view of the *basis*, whatever virtue or misdeed one creates while possessing the three vows and the like is powerful. Reflect as follows:

> By generating the faith of conviction in the explanations above, I will strive to adopt virtue and discard nonvirtue—accomplishing the ten virtues and so forth, even tiny virtues, and maintaining my three doors untainted by the ten nonvirtues and so forth, even tiny nonvirtues. Guru-deity, please bless me that I may do so!

Think:

> From having made supplications in this manner, streams of five-colored nectar along with light rays descend from the body of the guru-deity above my crown. Permeating my body and mind and also those of all other sentient beings, they cleanse us of all the misdeeds and obstructions we have amassed since beginningless time, and in particular those misdeeds and obstructions that prevent us from making effort to adopt virtues and discard nonvirtues, accomplishing the ten virtues and so forth, even tiny virtues, and maintaining our three doors untainted by the ten nonvirtues and so forth, even tiny nonvirtues. These special realizations *of making effort to adopt virtues and discard nonvirtues, accomplishing the ten virtues and so forth, even tiny virtues, and maintaining our three doors untainted by the ten nonvirtues and so forth, even tiny nonvirtues*, are produced in our mental continua.

The eight fruitional qualities

By keeping the ethics of abandoning the ten nonvirtues in this way, you will attain the physical basis of an upper rebirth. However, if you obtain a special basis that possesses the eight fruitional qualities, you will be able to make extraordinary strides in your accomplishment of omniscience.

Identifying the eight fruitional qualities

The eight fruitional qualities are: (1) longevity, (2) attractiveness, (3) excellent lineage, (4) power, (5) honorable speech, (6) reputation, (7) being male,[366] and (8) strength.

The functions of the eight fruitional qualities

(1) Through longevity, you will be able to create virtue for a long time. (2) Through being attractive, trainees will be drawn to you and listen to your words. (3) Through having excellent lineage, having been born into a high class, nobody will defy your orders. (4) Through having power, you will gather many living beings and bring them to maturation. (5) Through having honorable speech, your words will be held as the truth. (6) Through having reputation, others will always promptly obey your instructions. (7)

Through being male, you will have confidence and encounter fewer hindrances. (8) Through having strength, you will be endowed with great enthusiasm in your activities and the causes for rapid supernatural abilities.

The causes of the eight fruitional qualities

(1) The cause of longevity is refraining from harming sentient beings, being committed to the ideal of nonviolence, saving lives, deterring others from harming sentient beings, giving medicine, and serving as nurses and the like. (2) The cause of attractiveness is abandoning anger, providing lamps and flowers, and giving new ornaments and clothes. (3) The cause of excellent lineage is giving up pride. (4) The cause of power is giving food, clothes, and the like to those who beg for them and, even when others do not beg for them, readily giving them in order to benefit others. (5) The cause of honorable speech is giving up faulty forms of speech. (6) The cause of reputation is respecting and honoring the Three Jewels, spiritual guides, preceptors, teachers, parents, and so forth. (7) The cause of being male is viewing the female state as disadvantageous, turning away desire for a female body, and rescuing living beings from castration. (8) The cause of strength is taking upon yourself what others are incapable of accomplishing, helping others, and giving food, drinks, and the like.

Ardently and wholeheartedly practice these eight causes and dedicate your virtues to complete enlightenment. Give up jealousy, competitiveness, and contempt, respectively, in relation to those who are spiritually more advanced than, equal to, or less advanced than you. Rejoice [in their virtues]. Even if you are incapable of practicing certain virtues, investigate every day how you can practice them. Practice in a sustained manner those that you can. Help others to adopt these causes, and praise those who have adopted them. These points are taught in the *Blue Manual*:

> Do not expect thorough fulfillment in this life.
> Engage in practice for your future lives.[367]

Tsongkhapa himself had the same intent when he said:

> Until we have obtained the perfectly qualified physical basis to practice the supreme path,
> there is no way to make great strides,

> so we must train in the indispensable causes of such a physical basis.
> As our three doors are tarnished by misdeeds and downfalls,
> it is crucial that we cleanse ourselves of bad karma and obstructions,
> so we must be dedicated to the continual application of the complete four powers of purification.
> I, a yogi, have practiced in this way;
> you who aspire for liberation, please do likewise.[368]

Immediately put these instructions into practice as best you can. Suppose you strive to give up nonvirtues and accomplish virtues, but your antidotes are weak and your afflictions strong. In that case, strive to engage in confession and restraint through the four powers of purification whenever you are tainted by nonvirtue in any way.

The four powers of purification

The way to perform confession and restraint through the four powers of purification is to first clean your dwelling and then arrange representations of the enlightened body, speech, and mind,[369] regarding them as the actual Three Jewels. Also think that your spiritual guides, deities, buddhas, bodhisattvas, and hosts of heroes, heroines, ḍākas, ḍākinīs, Dharma protectors, and guardians are actually dwelling in the space before you. In their presence, generate regret for the misdeeds and downfalls you have committed in the past, as if you have ingested poison. Wholeheartedly resolve to refrain from nonvirtues by thinking, "From now on I will never commit them even at the cost of my life." When you have time, perform confession and restraint through the four powers of purification as stated in the *Sublime Golden Light Sūtra*, the [*Confession of Downfalls*] based on the Thirty-Five Buddhas, individual confessions of the three vows, the *General Confession*, and so forth. In brief, the *power of support* consists of going for refuge and generating bodhicitta.

The *power of repudiation* refers to generating intense regret for the misdeeds you have committed in the past.

The *power of applying the antidote* involves carrying out any of the following: a practice based on profound sūtras; a practice based on profound emptiness such as that of not observing the three spheres of the misdeed [as inherently existent];[370] the meditation and recitation practice of Vajrasattva including the repetition of the hundred-syllable mantra; construction of buddha images and stūpas; a practice based on making offerings; and articulation of the exceptional names of the buddhas and bodhisattvas.[371]

The *power of turning away from misdeed* entails frequently generating the intent of restraint thinking, "I will not be tainted by misconduct and downfalls, even minute ones."

Conclusion

Turning your attention to Guru Munīndra above your crown, recite the following as many times as possible:

> To Guru Conqueror Śākyamuni, I pay homage, make offerings, and go for refuge.

Think:

> Induced by my supplications, there emerges from Guru Munīndra a second figure of Guru Munīndra, who absorbs into me, whereby my form clearly becomes that of Guru Munīndra. Radiating from the *hūṃ* at my heart, light rays strike all sentient beings surrounding me and place them in the state of Guru Munīndra. I and all sentient beings, each visualized as Munīndra, have at the heart a moon disc, upon which is a white *a* marked with a yellow *hūṃ*. It is encircled by the mantra *Oṃ mune mune mahāmunaye svāhā*.

Focusing your attention on the mantra, recite it as many times as you can. To conclude the session, recite dedication verses such as:

> By this virtue, may I quickly
> achieve the state of Guru Buddha and
> place all sentient beings without exception
> in that state.

With the strong aspiration to fulfill your and others' short-term and ultimate wishes, dedicate the virtues arisen from your practice. If you can, perform prayers such as the *King of Prayers of Excellent Deeds.*

What to do between the sessions

Between the sessions, read the scriptures and commentaries that teach about the series of practices that are in common with those of persons with small capacity and the like, and perform the other activities as explained above [in the section on how to rely on a spiritual guide].

The criterion for having produced the mindset of the stages of the path that is in common with those of persons with small capacity

Having trained in the stages of the path in common with those of persons with small capacity, what is the criterion for having produced the mindset? Your past concern for the affairs of this life, which you held as primary, and that for spiritual practice for the sake of your next life, which you held as ancillary, become reversed. In other words, you now consider the affairs of this life as ancillary and primarily seek the purpose of the next life. This is the criterion.

If, instead, even though you have trained your mind, you do not feel the slightest angst or fear of the possibility of death striking quickly and a rebirth in the lower rebirths experiencing prolonged intense suffering, this indicates that your latencies of the Dharma from previous lives are weak. Or, it is a sign that even if you have been engaging in hearing, contemplation, and meditation in this life, they have not been effective, and your mind has gone astray in relation to the Dharma.[372] This is a serious fault.

> A woman wandering among three men,
> a bird slipping away from the snare,
> a Buddhist monastic gone astray in relation to the Dharma,
> among all kinds of guile, these three are the worst.[373]

Shawo Gangpa says:[374]

> If you neglect to perform inner contemplation, it seems the more words you hear, the more you regress; and the more frequently

> you hear the words, the less frequently you meditate. This is the cause for the mind going astray.

Lamas of the past used to lament, "The phenomenon known as the *outwardly diverted mind* is a bane."[375] It is a greater fault than not ever having engaged in hearing, contemplation, and meditation. Therefore Tsongkhapa's *Stages of the Path* says:

> The purpose of understanding after hearing [about the essential points of what is to be discarded and what is to be adopted] is to act on them. Hence, it is crucial to put into practice the meaning that you have heard as best you can.[376]

And:

> Do not allow yourself to be affected by your friends, body, resources, and the like. Instead, be unstinting in your resolve to practice the Dharma. Therefore, even though this may be difficult, since it is the bedrock of the path, make every effort.[377]

Even if you are not able to produce realizations now by cultivating this series of practices pertaining to the persons of small capacity as taught, make heartfelt requests to your teachers and the Three Jewels that you will produce them in the future. Strive to accrue merit and wisdom, engage in purification, make an even greater effort focusing on the objects of practice, and meditate. Make prayers for these realizations to arise in future lives. Accordingly, Tsongkhapa says:

> The [human existence endowed with] freedoms and privileges that issues from [practicing] the teachings given by [the spiritual guide],
> its great meaning, rarity, and easy disintegration,
> the sufferings of lower rebirths,
> going for refuge that protect from those sufferings, and karma and its results:

by contemplating these points well, gain a stable ascertainment of
them.
May it become the foundation of a true path![378]

Some people meditate on these stages of the path but become listless and place their hopes in secular subjects of knowledge. Having perfunctorily chanted mantras, some hope to attain powers of speech and receive visions of deities. Having cultivated the mental abidings,[379] some check to see if subtle supernatural powers have arisen. Some simply perform recitations.

Regarding such behavior, Phuchungwa asked Chen Ngawa, "From among these—attaining the five supernatural powers,[380] being skilled in the five sciences,[381] attaining the eight great feats,[382] or producing in your mental continuum these stages of the path presented by Atiśa—which would you choose?"

Chen Ngawa replied, "Leaving aside producing these stages of the path in my mental continuum, developing a mere intellectual understanding that discerns 'The stages of the path are such and such' would be an obvious choice over those [mundane attainments]. We have attained the five supernatural powers, been skilled in the five sciences, and attained the eight great feats countless times, but we have neither transcended nor prevailed over saṃsāra. If we gain an ascertainment of the stages of the path, we will be able to turn away from saṃsāra and emerge from it."

Know that [the behavior of those people mentioned above, who meditate on these stages of the path but become listless and place their hopes in secular subjects of knowledge, and others] are signs that they have not realized the essentials of these teachings presented above and have not gained ascertainment of the stages of the path.

The Path in Common with That of Persons with Medium Capacity

9 | Aspiring for Liberation

How to Train Your Mind in the Path in Common with That of Persons with Medium Capacity

This is explained in two parts: generating the mindset that seeks liberation and delineating the nature of the path leading to liberation. The first is explained in two parts: what to do during the session and what to do between the sessions. The first of those has three parts: preparation, the actual meditation on the mindset that seeks liberation, and conclusion.

Preparation

Carry out the preparatory practices up to the following lines:[383]

> O guru, extraordinary deity, who encompasses all the objects of refuge,
> Munīndra Vajradhara, to you I make supplication!

Reflect as follows:

> Having continuously taken birth in saṃsāra, I and all mother sentient beings have experienced a variety of prolonged and intense sufferings. This plight is owing to our failure to understand that the entirety of saṃsāra is suffering in nature and to thus produce the fervent wish to be freed from it. Guru-deity, please bless me and all mother sentient beings to understand that the entirety of saṃsāra is suffering in nature and to thus produce the fervent wish to be liberated from saṃsāra.

Think:

> From having made supplications in this manner, streams of five-colored nectar along with light rays descend from the body of the guru-deity above my crown. Permeating my body and mind and also those of all other sentient beings, they cleanse us of all the misdeeds and obstructions we have amassed since beginningless time, and in particular those misdeeds and obstructions that prevent the special realizations of understanding that the entirety of saṃsāra is suffering in nature and wishing fervently to be freed from it. Our bodies become the nature of transparent light. Our lifespan, merit, and all excellent qualities of scripture and realization develop and increase. The special realizations of *understanding that the entirety of saṃsāra is suffering in nature and wishing fervently to be freed from it* are produced in our mental continua.

The actual meditation on the mindset that seeks liberation

This is explained in two parts: reflecting on the general sufferings of saṃsāra and reflecting on the specific sufferings of saṃsāra.

Reflecting on the general sufferings of saṃsāra

While meditating on the guru-deity above your crown, reflect as follows:

> By training in the ethics of abandoning the ten nonvirtues, I will attain an upper rebirth, free from the suffering of lower rebirths. However, as long as I have not attained a liberation in which suffering has been eradicated from the root, I can never be truly happy. By analogy, say there is a criminal who is to be executed in a month and is tortured daily by having hot tar dripped on him, being beaten with sticks, and so forth. Fortunately, because someone in power intercedes on his behalf, he is spared the pain of daily beatings with sticks. Nonetheless, as the day of execution draws closer and closer, he is never truly at ease. Similarly, as long as I have not attained a liberation in which suffering has been eradicated from the root, no matter what kinds of upper rebirths I may attain, once the projecting results of my previous

good karma are exhausted, I will fall into a lower rebirth and be confronted with countless sufferings.

Furthermore, as long as I am reborn into this saṃsāra through the force of karma and afflictions, my rebirth will not transcend the nature of suffering. Since foes turn into friends and friends into foes, harm and benefit in saṃsāra are unpredictable.

Accordingly, Nāgārjuna says:

> The father turns into the son. The mother turns into the wife.
> The foe turns into the friend.
> Their reverse occurs.
> There is never certainty in saṃsāra.[384]

And:

> He eats the flesh of his father, hits his mother,
> and cradles in his lap his evil-doing enemy.
> The wife gnaws at the bones of her husband.
> The events in saṃsāra are a joke.[385]

As taught, there is never certainty in saṃsāra—your father in a previous life can become your son in this life; your mother in a previous life can become your wife in this life; your friend in a previous life can become your foe in this life; your foe in an earlier part of this life can become your friend in the later part; your friend in an earlier part of this life can become your foe in the later part; and so forth. The *Questions of Subāhu Tantra* says:

> Sometimes foes turn into friends
> and friends into foes.
> Likewise, sometimes friends or foes become strangers.
> Strangers can also turn into foes
> and likewise into friends.
> Intelligent ones should never develop attachment.[386]
> Turn away thoughts taking delight in friends and
> set yourself comfortably in virtue.[387]

Reflect as follows:

> No matter how much I partake of the pleasures of saṃsāra, I will never achieve true satisfaction.

The *Play in Full Sūtra* says:

> Your Majesty, even if a person
> were to obtain all the pleasures of the gods
> and all the exquisite sensual delights of humans,
> he would still not be content and would search for more.[388]

As said, even if a person were to obtain all the sensual delights of gods and humans, he would not attain lasting satisfaction. [The longing for such] lasting satisfaction is the principal malady and anguish, as every satisfaction [derived from sensual delights] is subject to decay. Accordingly, Āryaśūra says:

> Procuring these sensual delights,
> relying on them daily,
> and hoarding them never brings contentment.
> So there is no malady more serious than that.[389]

Reflect as follows:

> No matter how marvelous the bodies I acquire are, I must discard them time and again. Therefore they are not dependable.

Accordingly, the *Letter to a Friend* says:

> Even having become Śakra, worthy of worship by the world,[390]
> you will eventually fall to earth through the force of karma.
> Even having become a wheel-turning king,[391]
> you will eventually become a slave in saṃsāra.[392]

And:

> Having obtained the great pleasures of sensual delights in the god
> realms
> and happiness free from attachment in the Brahmā realms,[393]
> know that you will again find yourself suffering uninterruptedly
> as fuel for the fires of Unrelenting Torment.[394]

Reflect as follows:

> I have been taking rebirth in saṃsāra since beginningless time, so there is no limit to my rebirths.

Accordingly, Nāgārjuna says:

> The amount of milk imbibed by a person exceeds the four
> oceans,[395]
> but know that the wanderer in saṃsāra
> who follows the ways of ordinary beings
> still has far more to drink.[396]

Ordinary beings have been each other's mother, and the breast milk each being has suckled exceeds the amount of water in the oceans. If they still do not strive toward the path, without any foreseeable end to rebirths in saṃsāra, the amount of breast milk each will suckle [in the future] will exceed that already consumed.

Similarly, ordinary beings, having become foes, have decapitated one another. Their heads piled high surpass the Brahmā realms. While others, having become friends, weep over one another's deaths. If these tears of sorrow were collected, they would exceed even the waters of the oceans. [If they still do not strive toward the path], without any foreseeable end to rebirths in saṃsāra, [the tears shed will exceed that already shed]. Accordingly, *Eliminating Sorrow* says:

> The amount of hot molten copper you drank
> when you were in the hell realms
> time and again
> exceeds that of the waters in the oceans.

The mass of filth you ate
when you were a dog or pig
is far greater in size than
Mount Meru, the king of mountains.

The drops of tears you shed,
weeping when you were parted
from your friends in saṃsāra,
cannot be contained even by the oceans.

If your heads chopped off
during disputes
were piled high,
they would reach beyond the Brahmā realms.[397]

Reflect as follows:

No matter how much I partake of the splendors of saṃsāra, in time I must relinquish them. The acquisition of such pleasures is capricious.

Accordingly, a sūtra says:

All that has been accrued will be spent.
That which is high will fall.
Those who have gathered will disperse.
The living will die.[398]

And the *Garland of Birth Stories* says:[399]

Old intimate friends
will be separated by death,
and great sorrow will arise.
This is certain in the world.[400]

Reflect as follows:

> Since I will go to the next life alone, I cannot rely upon companions.

Accordingly, *Engaging in Bodhisattva Deeds* says:

> Although this body arose as a unit,[401]
> the bones and flesh with which it was born
> will break up and separate.
> What need is there to mention friends?
>
> At birth I was born alone,
> and at death I will die alone too.
> If my distress cannot be borne by others,
> of what use are hindering friends?[402]

Reflect as follows:

> At this time of having obtained once this physical human basis endowed with the complete freedoms and privileges, difficult to find and greatly meaningful when found, no matter what it takes I will attain *the precious state of a perfect complete buddha, the supreme liberation in which all the sufferings of saṃsāra have been abandoned*. Guru-deity, please bless me that I may do so![403]

Think:

> From having made supplications in this manner, streams of five-colored nectar along with light rays descend from the body of the guru-deity above my crown. Permeating my body and mind and also those of all other sentient beings, they cleanse us of all the misdeeds and obstructions we have amassed since beginningless time, and in particular those misdeeds and obstructions that prevent the special realization of supreme liberation in which the sufferings of saṃsāra have been abandoned. Our bodies become the nature of transparent light. Our lifespan, merit, and all excellent qualities of scripture and realization develop and increase. The special realization of *the precious state of a perfect complete*

buddha, the supreme liberation in which the sufferings of saṃsāra have been abandoned, is produced in our mental continua.

Reflecting on the specific sufferings of saṃsāra

While meditating on the guru-deity above your crown, think the following:

Once the appropriated aggregates are established,[404] I cannot avoid suffering.

The suffering of human beings

Setting aside the horrors of the three lower rebirths, even by taking rebirth as a human being, I am vulnerable to the hardships of hunger, thirst, and the constant quest to satisfy myriad desires. Throwing caution to the wind, I try to accumulate riches through various means, all while disregarding misdeed, disrepute, and suffering. As soon as I obtain a little wealth, others deprive me of it by imposing exorbitant taxes, borrowing, stealing, or robbing. As a result, I experience great hardship being forced to spend beyond my means. To safeguard my wealth, I grovel to powerful people, exercise extreme caution in what I say, become embroiled in disputes, conduct nighttime surveillance, and the like, so that I lose my appetite by day and suffer sleeplessness at night. Misery is my recompense.

The suffering of being separated from dear friends

When I am separated from my family, relatives, servants, retinue, friends, caring gurus, noble teachers, and benevolent rulers, I am thrown into despair—mentally I am overcome by sadness, verbally I moan and groan, physically I tear my hair out, and so on.

The suffering of encountering hated foes

The world is as if plunged into darkness when I encounter my foes, and I am left pained. However, as soon as the foe departs, light returns like the rising sun. I experience the suffering of being persecuted by foes, fearing their abuse, and so forth.

The suffering of not finding the desired

Not having created merit in previous lives, I suffer deprivation in this life. There are inconceivable sufferings such as lacking food, clothes, a dwelling, bedding, and so forth; sowing crops that do not yield a good harvest; engaging in commerce that does not make a profit; rearing livestock that fail to breed; not finding a lender when in need or, on acquiring a loan, being unable to repay it; and when forced to repay debts, in desperation, becoming an indentured servant to past beneficiaries and inferiors.

The suffering of encountering the undesired

There are the sufferings of being bound and killed by rulers, thieves, thugs, and so forth and the fear of such torment.

The suffering of birth

After conception, I endured nine months and ten days in my mother's unclean womb, as though doubled over in a dirty, fetid, charred pot.[405] Then, at delivery, I experienced sufferings greater than being pulled through a hole of a metal plate for making iron threads or a ripe boil being squeezed. After delivery, during the first week, the 404 diseases afflicted my illusion-like body;[406] during the second week I was afflicted by the 80,000 types of interferers;[407] and during the third week I was afflicted by the 84,000 types of microorganisms.[408] As a result, my body was fragile, hungry, and thirsty, my mind restless, and I became susceptible to disease and spirit harm. Therefore this birth is the vessel of all suffering.

Accordingly, the *Letter to a Friend* says:

Since saṃsāra is like that,
know that birth as a god, human,
hell denizen, hungry ghost, or animal is noxious.
It is the vessel of countless harms.

If your head or clothes were to suddenly catch fire,
you would do everything to extinguish it.

Strive like that to end future existences.
There is no greater purpose than this.[409]

The suffering of aging

My spine has become curved like a bow. My head is as white as edelweiss flowers. My forehead is covered in lines like a chopping board. Because of my diminished strength, I struggle when walking, standing, lying down, or sitting. My eyesight and other sense faculties have deteriorated. I can no longer enjoy sensual pleasures. My life force is on the verge of exhaustion, and death draws nigh. Inconceivable sufferings such as these arise.

The suffering of sickness

My flesh and complexion degenerate, and I feel ill at ease. I am prevented from enjoying my favorite foods and the like. Harsh invasive treatments are required. The idea of death petrifies me.

The suffering of death

At the time of death, I am grieved having to part from my family, body, possessions, retinue, servants, and so forth.

Accordingly, the *Play in Full Sūtra* says:

When the time of passing away arrives,
one is forever separated from one's loved ones.
There will be no returning or meeting again,
just as fruits or leaves carried away by the river never meet the tree again.[410]

The suffering of demigods

Reborn as a demigod,[411] I am mentally tormented by jealousy that cannot abide the glory and wealth of the gods. Consequently, I experience physical suffering [as if] struck by lightning.

The suffering of gods

Reborn as a god of the desire realm, when fighting with the demigods, I experience the pain of my major and minor limbs being hacked off[412] and my body being wounded, torn apart, inflicted with fatal injuries, and the like. Powerless, I must face the five omens of death when they strike. The awareness that I will have to experience the suffering of the lower rebirths after separating from the gods' glory and wealth also fills me with anguish.

Accordingly, the *Letter to a Friend* says:

> Their body complexion turns ugly,
> they no longer delight in their cushions, their flower garlands wilt,
> their clothes become dirty,
> and sweat appears on their bodies for the first time.
>
> The gods living in the divine abodes
> receive the five omens foretelling their death and transference from the upper rebirth,
> like those heralding the death of humans on earth.[413]

And furthermore:

> The anguish from the impending fall into the lower rebirths
> that is intensely felt by the gods
> is not matched even by sixteen times
> the pain of the hells of sentient beings.[414]

Reflect as follows:

> Even if I am reborn in the higher realms,[415] since I have no control over the duration of my time there, once the projecting effects of my past good karma are exhausted, I will plummet into a lower rebirth and experience countless sufferings. In addition, ordinary beings who are reborn in the higher realms dwell for eons in a state where their continuum of analytical wisdom is impeded. When they are later reborn into the desire realm, because of a previous prevalence of stupidity and ignorance, their attainment of liberation is seriously delayed. This is taught in the *Praise of Confession*.[416]

In brief, these appropriated aggregates act as the basis for the birth, aging, sickness, death, and other miseries of this life, and they induce the suffering of suffering and the suffering of change in both this and future lifetimes. This is because as soon as these aggregates are established, I am born under the influence of conditioned factors, and all conditioned factors that are under the influence of previous karma and afflictions are conditioned true sufferings.[417]

Therefore, no matter what it takes, I will attain the precious state of a guru-buddha in which I am freed from saṃsāra having the nature of the appropriated aggregates. Guru-deity, please bless me that I may do so!

Think:

From having made supplications in this manner, streams of five-colored nectar along with light rays descend from the body of the guru-deity above my crown. Permeating my body and mind and also those of all other sentient beings, they cleanse us of all the misdeeds and obstructions we have amassed since beginningless time, and in particular those misdeeds and obstructions that prevent the special realization of the precious state of a guru-buddha in which I am freed from saṃsāra having the nature of the appropriated aggregates. Our bodies become the nature of transparent light. Our lifespan, merit, and all excellent qualities of scripture and realization develop and increase. The special realization of *the precious state of a guru-buddha in which I am freed from saṃsāra having the nature of the appropriated aggregates* is produced in our mental continua.

Conclusion

Turning your attention to Guru Munīndra above your crown, say the following as many times as possible:

To Guru Conqueror Śākyamuni, I pay homage, make offerings, and go for refuge.

Think:

> Induced by my supplications, there emerges from Guru Munīndra a second figure of Guru Munīndra, who absorbs into me, whereby my form clearly becomes that of Guru Munīndra. Radiating from the *hūṃ* at my heart, light rays strike all sentient beings surrounding me and place them in the state of Guru Munīndra. I and all sentient beings, each visualized as Munīndra, have at the heart a moon disc, upon which is a white *a* marked with a yellow *hūṃ*. It is encircled by the mantra *Oṃ mune mune mahāmunaye svāhā*.

Focusing your attention on the mantra, recite it as many times as you can. To conclude the session, recite dedication verses such as:

> By this virtue, may I quickly
> achieve the state of Guru Buddha and
> place all sentient beings without exception
> in that state.

With the strong aspiration to fulfill your and others' short-term and ultimate wishes, dedicate the virtues arisen from your practice. If you can, perform prayers such as the *King of Prayers of Excellent Deeds*.

What to do between the sessions

Between the sessions, read the scriptures and commentaries that explain *how the entirety of saṃsāra is suffering in nature*, and perform the other activities as explained above [in the section on how to rely on a spiritual guide].

10 | The Path to Liberation

Delineating the Nature of the Path Leading to Liberation

This is explained in two parts: what to do during the session and what to do between the sessions. The first of those has three parts: preparation, the actual meditation on the nature of the path leading to liberation, and conclusion.

Preparation

Carry out the preparatory practices up to the following lines:[418]

> O guru, extraordinary deity, who encompasses all the objects of refuge,
> Munīndra Vajradhara, to you I make supplication!

Reflect as follows:

> Having continuously taken birth in saṃsāra, I and all mother sentient beings have experienced a variety of prolonged and intense sufferings. This plight is owing to our failure to generate the mind seeking liberation and train well in the path of the three trainings. Guru-deity, please bless me and all mother sentient beings that we may generate the mind seeking liberation and train well in the path of the three trainings!

Think:

> From having made supplications in this manner, streams of five-colored nectar along with light rays descend from the body of the guru-deity above my crown. Permeating my body and mind and also those of all other sentient beings, they cleanse us of all the misdeeds and obstructions we have amassed since beginningless time, and in particular those misdeeds and obstructions that prevent us from being able to generate the mind seeking liberation and train well in the path of the three trainings. Our bodies become the nature of transparent light. Our lifespan, merit, and all excellent qualities of scripture and realization develop and increase. The special realization of *being able to generate the mind seeking liberation and train well in the path of the three trainings* is produced in our mental continua.[419]

The actual meditation on the nature of the path leading to liberation

Training in wisdom

While meditating on the guru-deity above your crown, reflect as follows:

> Mind itself is neutral.[420] Initially, upon observing the I and mine, the mind apprehends them as existing inherently. In dependence on the mind apprehending the I and mine as a self,[421] distorted mental states such as attachment to self, aversion to others, and pride apprehending myself as superior arise. These distorted mental states in turn trigger doubts and wrong views that deny the Teacher who teaches selflessness as well as his teachings on karma and its results, the four truths, the Three Jewels, and so forth. As a result, other afflictions ferment. Creating karma under their influence, I am compelled to endure the various sufferings of saṃsāra. Therefore the root of all sufferings can be traced back to ignorance.

The *Commentary on Validity* says:

> The root of all faults
> is the view of the transitory collection.[422]

And:

> One who sees the self
> constantly clings to it as I.
> From that clinging comes craving for pleasure.
> Craving obstructs [the seeing of] faults.
>
> By seeing [faults as] good qualities, one's craving becomes absolute,
> and one grasps to "mine" as its fulfillment.
> Thus, as long as one is attached to self,
> one will circle in saṃsāra.
>
> When there is self, one identifies [what is not self as] other.
> On account of self and other, there is grasping and aversion.
> Linked to self and other,
> all faults arise.[423]

Entering the Middle Way says:

> . . .through initially adhering to a self, an "I,"
> and then generating attachment for things, thinking "This is mine."[424]

Reflect as follows:

> Therefore, no matter what it takes, I will attain the precious state of a perfect complete buddha, the supreme liberation in which the sufferings of saṃsāra have been abandoned. To that end, I will train well in the path of the three precious trainings.

Training in ethics

If I guard [ethics], there will be great benefits, and if I do not, there will be grave drawbacks.

What Is Treasured by a Fully Ordained Monk Sūtra says:

The ethics of some is happiness.
The ethics of some is suffering.
Being ethical is happiness.
Being unethical is suffering.[425]

During this period nearing the destruction of the Buddha's teachings, guarding pure ethics for just a single day and night brings greater benefit than practicing generosity with countless material gifts. Accordingly, the *King of Meditative Stabilizations Sūtra* says:

Compared to revering billions of buddhas with lucid faith
through offerings of food, drinks,
parasols, flags, and rows of lamps
for as many eons as there are grains of sand of the Ganges,
he who practices a single type of ethical discipline for a day and night
at a time when the excellent Dharma is in decline
and the Sugata's teachings are coming to an end
creates superior merit.[426]

Failing to guard ethics brings serious ramifications. It is taught that when Buddha Kāśyapa came to the world, a fully ordained monk cut off the branch of a plant out of disdain for a stipulation that had been laid down by Buddha Kāśyapa. As a result, he was reborn as a nāga with an enormous *tala* tree emerging from the center of his brains.[427] To this day he is still experiencing boundless suffering and will continue to do so for a long time to come. A sūtra also says:

Here, some escape punishment
even though they transgress the king's commands several times.
However, if one rashly defies the instructions of the Muni,
one will be born as an animal, as in the case of the nāga Elapatra.[428]

Reflect as follows:

Therefore, even at the cost of my life, I will train well in ethics as I have committed to do so. Since *ignorance* is a door to transgres-

> sions, as its antidote, I will learn about the precepts and master them.[429]

The way to educate yourself on the precepts is to rely on a well-qualified spiritual guide in whom scholarliness does not undermine integrity and integrity does not undermine scholarliness. Ideally he should have completed the stages of the path. If he has not achieved that, he should have understood the general precepts of [bodhisattvas'] deeds. If not that, he should have at least understood the stages of the paths of persons with small and medium capacities.

If you are a novice monk,[430] look at the commentaries on the *Fifty Verses*[431] and the *Three Hundred Verses on the Śrāmaṇera's Precepts*[432] and understand them. If you are a fully ordained monk,[433] learn about the precepts of a fully ordained monk and, at the very least, the condensed precepts within the collected works of Losang Chökyi Gyaltsen.[434] Alternatively inform yourself about the brief presentation of the precepts of a fully ordained monk composed by the Fifth Dalai Lama.[435]

If you have obtained the four initiations of highest yoga tantra in their entirety,[436] make yourself conversant with the bodhisattva precepts and the presentation of the root downfalls and gross infractions[437] from explanations such as *Twenty Verses on the Bodhisattva Vows*.[438] It is indispensable to put these into practice having become informed about them. Reflect as follows:

> Since *disrespect* is a door to transgressions, as its antidote, I should respect the Teacher[439] and the precepts stipulated by him, as well as fellow celibate practitioners who are training well in those precepts.
>
> Since *heedlessness* is a door to transgressions, as its antidote, I should cultivate shame, which is based on reasons pertaining to myself, and embarrassment, which is based on reasons pertaining to others.[440] I should become heedful by generating mindfulness, introspection, shame, and embarrassment.
>
> Since *unchecked afflictions* are a door to transgressions, I should cultivate antidotes to the afflictions by, for example, meditating on ugliness as an antidote to attachment, meditating on love as

an antidote to hatred, and meditating on dependent arising as an antidote to ignorance.

Therefore I will strive to uphold pure ethics untainted by faults. Guru-deity, please bless me that I may do so!

Think:

From having made supplications in this manner, streams of five-colored nectar along with light rays descend from the body of the guru-deity above my crown. Permeating my body and mind and also those of all other sentient beings, they cleanse us of all the misdeeds and obstructions we have amassed since beginningless time, and in particular those misdeeds and obstructions that prevent the special realization of pure ethics untainted by faults. Our bodies become the nature of transparent light. Our lifespan, merit, and all excellent qualities of scripture and realization develop and increase. The special realization of *pure ethics untainted by faults* is produced in our mental continua.

Conclusion

Turning your attention to Guru Munīndra above your crown, say the following as many times as possible:

To Guru Conqueror Śākyamuni, I pay homage, make offerings, and go for refuge.

Think:

Induced by my supplications, there emerges from Guru Munīndra a second figure of Guru Munīndra, who absorbs into me, whereby my form clearly becomes that of Guru Munīndra. Radiating from the *hūṃ* at my heart, light rays strike all sentient beings surrounding me and place them in the state of Guru Munīndra. I and all sentient beings, each visualized as Munīndra, have at the heart a moon disc, upon which is a white *a* marked

> with a yellow *hūṃ*. It is encircled by the mantra *Oṃ mune mune mahāmunaye svāhā*.

Focusing your attention on the mantra, recite it as many times as you can. To conclude the session, recite dedication verses such as:

> By this virtue, may I quickly
> achieve the state of Guru Buddha and
> place all sentient beings without exception
> in that state.

With the strong aspiration to fulfill your and others' short-term and ultimate wishes, dedicate the virtues arisen from your practice. If you can, perform prayers such as the *King of Prayers of Excellent Deeds.*

What to do between the sessions

Between the sessions, read [the scriptures and commentaries that teach about] the *prātimokṣa precepts* as explained,[441] and perform the other activities as explained above [in the section on how to rely on a spiritual guide].

This completes the explanation of how to train your mind in the stages of the path in common with those of persons with medium capacity.

The Stages of the Path of Persons with Great Capacity

11 | The Sevenfold Cause-and-Effect Instruction

How to train your mind in the stages of the path of persons with great capacity

Having thus trained your mind in the paths in common with those of persons with small and medium capacities, you attain the liberation that is freedom from saṃsāra on account of having properly trained in the path of the three trainings. However, as you have not consummated your own purpose, your ability to secure others' welfare will be limited. You will be prompted to enter the Mahāyāna by the buddhas' light rays of compassion. As you must eventually do so, you should ideally enter the Mahāyāna path from the outset; otherwise it is like rolling up your trouser legs twice in order to ford a stream. Accordingly, the *Compendium of Perfections* says:

> They totally bypass the two vehicles
> that are not sufficient to accomplish the welfare of the world.[442]
> Having the nature that is of one taste with benefiting others,
> they enter the teachings on compassion of the Conqueror Muni's vehicle.[443]

And the *Blue Manual* says:

> Without rolling up your trouser legs twice when fording a stream,
> enter the Mahāyāna path from the outset.[444]

Therefore train your mind in the stages of the path of persons with great capacity. This is explained in two parts: how to train in the mind aspiring for enlightenment and how to train in the deeds after having generated the mind aspiring for enlightenment. The first is explained in two parts: the actual way to generate the mind aspiring for enlightenment and how to uphold the mind aspiring for enlightenment through ritual. The first of those has two parts: how to generate the mind aspiring for enlightenment by means of the sevenfold cause-and-effect instruction and how to generate the mind aspiring for enlightenment by means of equalizing and exchanging self and others.

How to generate the mind aspiring for enlightenment by means of the sevenfold cause-and-effect instruction

First achieve impartiality[445] toward all sentient beings and then meditate on [the seven steps]—beginning from recognizing all sentient beings as having been your mother until bodhicitta. This is explained in two parts: what to do during the session and what to do between the sessions. The first of those has three parts: preparation, the actual meditation on the sevenfold cause-and-effect instruction, and conclusion.

Preparation

Carry out the preparatory practices up to the following lines:[446]

> O guru, extraordinary deity, who encompasses all the objects of refuge,
> Munīndra Vajradhara, to you I make supplication!

Reflect as follows:

> Guru-deity, please bless me and all mother sentient beings to be able to generate the special realizations—the impartiality free from the bias of attachment and aversion toward all sentient beings, the recognition that all sentient beings have been our mother, the recollection of their kindness, the wish to repay their kindness, love, compassion, [the exceptional resolve],[447] and bodhicitta.

Think:

> From having made supplications in this manner, streams of five-colored nectar along with light rays descend from the body of the guru-deity above my crown. Permeating my body and mind and also those of all other sentient beings, they cleanse us of all the misdeeds and obstructions we have amassed since beginningless time, and in particular those misdeeds and obstructions that prevent the special realizations of the impartiality free from the bias of attachment and aversion toward all sentient beings, the recognition that all sentient beings have been our mother, the recollection of their kindness, the wish to repay their kindness, love, compassion, [the exceptional resolve], and bodhicitta. Our bodies become the nature of transparent light. Our lifespan, merit, and all excellent qualities of scripture and realization develop and increase. The special realizations of *the impartiality free from the bias of attachment and aversion toward all sentient beings, the recognition that all sentient beings have been our mother, the recollection of their kindness, the wish to repay their kindness, love, compassion, [the exceptional resolve], and bodhicitta* are produced in our mental continua.

The actual meditation on the sevenfold cause-and-effect instruction

When meditating on the sevenfold cause-and-effect instruction, you must first achieve impartiality toward all sentient beings. If you neglect to do so, any love and compassion you generate will only be partial—and partial love and compassion is *not* great love and compassion. This is because great love or great compassion must encompass *all* sentient beings. It is said:

> The supreme fruit of the complete tree of bodhicitta
> arises from the unbroken seed of compassion
> that is moistened by the water of love [in] the ground of equanimity;
> O omniscient one, at your feet I make request![448]

Therefore, while meditating on the guru-deity above your crown, clearly visualize in front of you a neutral person who has neither helped nor harmed you and reflect as follows:

> Putting myself in their shoes, I can understand that they want to be happy and do not want to suffer. Therefore, instead of benefiting them sometimes by holding them close and harming them sometimes by holding them distant, I will develop the impartiality that is free from the bias of attachment and aversion toward them. Guru-deity, please bless me that I may do so!

Think:

> From having made supplications in this manner, streams of five-colored nectar along with light rays descend from the body of the guru-deity above my crown. Permeating my body and mind and also those of all other sentient beings, they cleanse us of all the misdeeds and obstructions we have amassed since beginningless time, and in particular those misdeeds and obstructions that prevent the special realization of the impartiality free from the bias of attachment and aversion. Our bodies become the nature of transparent light. Our lifespan, merit, and all excellent qualities of scripture and realization develop and increase. The special realization of *impartiality that is free from the bias of attachment and aversion* is produced in our mental continua.

Now, if you are a hermit, visualize your neighbor living to the right of your dwelling and cultivate impartiality toward him. When you have succeeded in doing so, do the same with your neighbor to the left. Next, meditate by visualizing both together. In turn, meditate on others.

When your mind has become impartial [toward neutral persons], meditate by visualizing a person whom you regard as pleasing. The *Prophecy Concerning the Girl Candrottarā Sūtra* says:

> In the past, I killed all of you.
> Likewise, you previously hacked me to pieces and slayed me.
> We are all enemies and kill one another.
> Why do you also engender attachment?[449]

Reflect as follows:

> My partial mind [toward this pleasing person] occurs through the force of attachment. By craving for what is pleasing, I have been taking rebirth in saṃsāra since beginningless time.

Your family, relatives, servants, retinue, friends, and so forth are just like people who have come together in a bazaar to conduct dealings and have become acquainted for several days before parting ways. Therefore do not develop attachment to anyone. *Engaging in Bodhisattva Deeds* says:

> Leaving all behind, I must depart alone.[450]
> Not understanding this,
> I committed all manner of misdeeds
> for the sake of friends and foes.
>
> Even my foes will become nothing.
> My friends will also become nothing.
> I too will become nothing.
> Likewise all will become nothing.[451]

And the lamrim text *Countering the Four Attitudes* says:[452]

> All of one's parents, children, nephews, nieces,
> friends, and helpers:
> take them as unrelated to each other,
> like travelers gathered at a destination![453]

When you have cultivated impartiality toward [the person whom you regard as pleasing], clearly visualize in front of you a sentient being you have labeled as unpleasant and cultivate impartiality toward them by reflecting as follows:

> The reason why I am not impartial toward them is that my mind apprehends them as absolutely disagreeable, whereby aversion is produced. As long as my mind is partial toward them, there is no way I can generate bodhicitta.

Engaging in Bodhisattva Deeds says:

> Whatever wholesome deeds
> such as generosity and making offerings to the sugatas
> that have been amassed over a thousand eons
> will all be destroyed by an instant of anger.[454]

And the glorious Candrakīrti says:

> One instant of anger at a bodhisattva destroys
> the virtues arising from giving and ethics
> accrued over a hundred eons.
> Thus there can be no worse failing than impatience.[455]

Reflect on the drawbacks of hatred and anger as taught and put a stop to them. Moreover, as was stated in the passage from the *Questions of Subāhu Tantra* cited under the topic of uncertainty in the section on persons with medium capacity, foes, friends, and strangers are never certain.[456] Therefore, pondering "Why do I hate them?" put a stop to hatred and cultivate impartiality.

When you have produced impartiality with respect to [the disagreeable person], clearly visualize in front of you two figures—a mother-like sentient being who is greatly pleasing and a foe-like sentient being who is greatly displeasing—and reflect as follows:

> Putting myself in their shoes, I can understand that they are similar in wanting to be happy and not wanting to suffer. This person I now hold as my friend has acted as my main foe countless times, since beginningless saṃsāra; and this person I now hold as my foe has been my mother and nurtured me with loving-kindness also countless times in beginningless saṃsāra. So, to whom should I be attached? For whom should I have aversion? I will maintain impartiality free from the bias of attachment and aversion. Guru-deity, please bless me that I may do so!

When you have attained impartiality toward [a mother-like sentient being who is greatly pleasing and a foe-like sentient being who is greatly displeasing], meditate on impartiality toward all sentient beings. The way to do so is as follows:

> All sentient beings are similar in desiring happiness and not desiring suffering. Since all sentient beings have been my kin, instead of benefiting some by holding them close and harming others by holding them distant, I will regard them with impartiality free from the bias of attachment and aversion. Guru-deity, please bless me that I may do so!

Think:

> From having made supplications in this manner, streams of five-colored nectar along with light rays descend from the body of the guru-deity above my crown. Permeating my body and mind and also those of all other sentient beings, they cleanse us of all the misdeeds and obstructions we have amassed since beginningless time, and in particular those misdeeds and obstructions that prevent us from impartiality toward all sentient beings. The special realization of *impartiality toward all sentient beings* is produced in our mental continua.

Next, meditate on the points beginning from the recognition that all sentient beings have been your mother until bodhicitta in the following manner.

The recognition that all sentient beings have been your mother

While meditating on the guru-deity above your crown, reflect as follows:

> The *Commentary on Validity* says:
>
> > When taking rebirth,
> > the respiration, sense powers, and minds
> > do not arise from the body alone
> > without relying on their similar types.[457]

Consider the syllogism "Regarding the subject—the consciousness of a being who has just been reborn in the womb—it is preceded by a prior consciousness that serves as its substantial cause, because it is a consciousness, as in the case of the present consciousness."[458] In dependence on the reasoning above proving consciousness is beginningless, one proves that saṃsāra has no beginning. With that as the basis, you should meditate, thinking, "All sentient beings—without exception—have been my mother." Accordingly, Paṇchen [Losang Chökyi Gyaltsen's] *Melodious Speech of Losang's Assertions: Responses to Sincere Queries* says:

> Regarding how to meditate on the recognition that all sentient beings have been one's mother,
> you explained that one meditates with the magical skillful means of
> scripture and reasoning that proves
> that consciousness has no beginning,
> such as "When taking rebirth . . ." in the *Commentary on Validity*.[459]

QUALM: Well then, why has every sentient being been my kin?
REPLY: Reflect as follows:

> Since saṃsāra is beginningless, there is no beginning to my rebirths. As I pass from one rebirth to another, there is not a single place where I have never been reborn; my rebirths are countless. There is not a single type of body I have never taken; the types of bodies I have taken are countless. There is not a single sentient being who has not been my mother; each has been my mother countless times. And there is not a single sentient being who has not been my mother in a human rebirth; each has been my mother in a human rebirth countless times and each will be again. Therefore each and every sentient being—without exception—has been my mother who nurtured me with kindness.

OBJECTION: Since there are countless sentient beings, not all sentient beings have been my mother.

REPLY: When such a thought arises, reflect as follows:

> Just because there are countless sentient beings does not mean that all sentient beings have not been my mother. Just as sentient beings are countless, my rebirths are countless too. Therefore each and every sentient being, without exception, has been my mother.

OBJECTION: Since I and all sentient beings do not recognize each other, they cannot have been my mother.

REPLY: When such a thought crosses your mind, reflect as follows:

> It is not the case that, since I and all sentient beings do not recognize each other, they have not been my mother. There are many cases of mother and child not recognizing each other even in the same lifetime. For example, the fully ordained nun Utpalavarṇā and her son became husband and wife, and she and her daughter become his wives, yet they failed to recognize each other.[460] Furthermore, as cited previously:
>
> > He eats the flesh of his father, hits his mother,
> > and cradles in his lap his evil-doing enemy.
> > The wife gnaws at the bones of her husband.
> > The events in saṃsāra are a joke.[461]
>
> A father dies and is reborn as a fish, whose flesh is eaten by his son. The son's mother dies and is reborn as a female dog, which gnaws at the fish bones. The son's murderer of a previous life is reborn as his child.[462] However, he fails to recognize them.

OBJECTION: All sentient beings may have been my mother in previous lives, but it is incorrect to consider them as such now, as those instances have passed.

REPLY: When such rationalization occurs, reflect as follows:

> [It follows that] my mother of yesterday would not be my mother today, since that instance has passed.[463] Therefore there is no difference between my mother of yesterday and my mother of today

in their being my mother. There is also no difference between them in their nurturing me with kindness.

Furthermore, if a ruler spares my life and then, a year later, spares my life again, apart from the mere difference in time, one being earlier and the other later, there is no difference between those two instances in his kindness, one being great and the other small. Similarly, there is no difference between my mother of a previous life and my mother of this life in their being my mother. There is no difference in their nurturing me with kindness.

Therefore all sentient beings, without exception, have been my mother.

The recollection of the kindness of all sentient beings

Having recognized all sentient beings as having been your mother, while meditating on the guru-deity above your crown, reflect on their kindness:

> Not only has my mother been my mother in this life, she has been my mother countless times before, since beginningless lifetimes. In this life she first took care of me with lovingkindness in her womb. When I was born, she placed me on a soft mattress, held me up on the tips of her ten fingers and softly rocked me, pressed me against her warm body, welcomed me with a loving smile, looked upon me with joyful eyes, wiped the mucus from my nose with her mouth, and cleaned away my feces with her hands. When I suffered a slight sickness, she endured greater hardship than if her own life had been threatened. If there had been a way to take on my pain, she would have done so unhesitatingly, sacrificing her life for mine.
>
> Disregarding misdeed, suffering, disrepute, and her own life, she compassionately supplied all my food and resources, which she toiled hard to procure. For either a son's marriage or monastic education, or a daughter's dowry, with no sense of loss, she was able to give everything, saving for them the best of food, drinks, and clothes that she could afford.
>
> In short, my mother has endlessly ensured my happiness and well-being, protecting me from countless harms and suffering as best she could. She is so kind.

Meditate by visualizing each of these illustrations. Visualizing an abstraction cannot yield a realization and is thus a pitfall. Since these points are the mother-like basis,[464] it is fundamental to meditate on them until you have elicited heartfelt experiential realizations. Do not be concerned if this takes some time.

When the kindness of your mother comes to mind vividly, transfer [your experience] to your father of this life and meditate. It is important to transfer the experience based on one person to the next and meditate on them one by one in a similar way.

Next, meditate on neutral sentient beings. Visualize them clearly in front of you and think [with respect to one neutral sentient being]:

> Even though this person and I seem to be totally unrelated, they have been my mother countless times before, since beginningless lifetimes. Every time they were my mother, they nurtured me with kindness in the same way my mother of this life nurtured me with kindness. They are so kind.

When you have elicited the experiential realization [with respect to neutral sentient beings], meditate on foes in the following way by visualizing them clearly in front of you. Think [with respect to one foe]:

> Why do I now hold this person as my foe? They have been my mother countless times before, since beginningless lifetimes. Every time they were my mother, they endlessly ensured my happiness and well-being, protecting me from countless harms and suffering. Whenever they were absent, I felt ill at ease. Similarly, whenever I was absent, they too felt ill at ease. There are uncountable instances of such mutual affinity. The current state of our relationship is due to bad karma. Were it not for this, they would be only my mother who nurtured me with kindness.

When you have elicited the experiential realization [in kindness] with respect to foes, reflect on the kindness of all sentient beings.

The wish to repay the kindness of all sentient beings

Having reflected on their kindness in this way, meditate on [wishing to] repay their kindness. Visualize the guru-deity above your crown and reflect as follows:

> My mothers, who have cared for me with kindness since beginningless time, are mentally disturbed by the demons of afflictions and have become insane, their minds out of control. They lack the eye that sets its sights on the paths of high rebirths and beatitude. They are deprived of a virtuous spiritual guide who serves as a guide for those who are blind. Teetering from being tossed by their turbulent desires inducing misconduct in every single moment, they wander at the edge of the terrifying abyss of saṃsāra, especially the lower rebirths.
>
> It would be contemptible were I to ignore these mothers. Therefore, to repay their kindness, I will free them from the suffering of saṃsāra and set them in the happiness of liberation. Guru-deity, please bless me that I may do so!

Think:

> From having made supplications in this manner, streams of five-colored nectar along with light rays descend from the body of the guru-deity above my crown. Permeating my body and mind and also those of all other sentient beings, they cleanse us of all the misdeeds and obstructions we have amassed since beginningless time, and in particular those misdeeds and obstructions that prevent us from realizing the wish to repay the kindness of our mother. The special realization of *wishing to repay the kindness of our mother* is produced in our mental continua.

The cultivation of love

Next, visualize a pleasing person, such as your mother, and reflect as follows:

> How could she experience uncontaminated happiness when she does not even get to experience contaminated happiness?[465]

> All that she now clings to as happiness is turning into suffering. Although she yearns for happiness and earnestly strives for it, her efforts create causes for suffering in the lower rebirths. Even in this life, apart from creating misery by making her weary and exhausted, her efforts never result in true happiness.
>
> If only she could have happiness and the causes of happiness! May she have happiness and the causes of happiness! I will see to it that she has happiness and the causes of happiness! Guru-deity, please bless me that I may do so!

Think:

> From having made supplications in this manner, streams of five-colored nectar along with light rays descend from the body of the guru-deity above my crown. Permeating my body and mind and also those of all other sentient beings, they cleanse us of the misdeeds and obstructions we have amassed since beginningless time, and in particular those misdeeds and obstructions that prevent us from developing love. The special realization of *love* is produced in our mental continua.

When you have elicited the experiential realization in love with respect to her, meditate as before on kin such as your father followed by neutral sentient beings, then foes, and finally all sentient beings.

The benefits of meditating on love

It is taught that if you meditate on love in relation to just Jambūdvīpa in this life, you will become a wheel-turning king ruling over Jambūdvīpa; if you produce love in relation to two continents, you will become a copper-wheel-turning king ruling over those two continents;[466] if you produce love in relation to three continents, you will become a silver-wheel-turning king ruling over those three continents; if you produce love in relation to four continents, you will become a gold-wheel-turning king ruling over those four continents; if you produce love in relation to the billionfold world systems, you will become Brahmā, the lord of gods; if you produce love in relation to the millionfold or thousandfold world systems, you will become the lord ruling over those world systems; and if you produce love for all sentient beings pervading the limits of space, the result will be none other than complete buddhahood.

In general, our karma is something that can only be created by ourselves. However, as the power of love is extraordinary, it is said that if it is genuinely produced, it will benefit others, as in the case of King Maitrībala,[467] and even if it is produced just superficially, it also serves as the best protection. The Bhagavān tamed billions of māras with his meditative stabilization on love. Chen Ngawa told Nyuk Rumpa, "Seriously, there is no way to conquer others except through love."[468] He taught that love thus functions in a way that a person is inspired simply by hearing its name. It is said:

> Its merit is not matched by that of
> constantly giving
> inestimable offerings of every type
> to supreme beings in billions of lands.[469]

And the protector Nāgārjuna also said:

> Even if one does not become freed [from saṃsāra],
> one will be endowed with the eight excellent qualities of love:
> [gods and humans will be friendly,
> even nonhumans will protect you,]
> one will attain mental bliss and many kinds of happiness,
> one will be invulnerable to poison and weapons,
> one will achieve one's goals effortlessly, and
> one will be reborn in a Brahmā world.[470]

And:

> The merit of giving food in three hundred clay vessels
> thrice daily
> cannot match that of
> cultivating love for a brief moment.[471]

The cultivation of compassion

While meditating on the guru-deity above your crown, begin by visualizing migrating beings in despair, such as sheep under the butcher's knife. Clearly visualize them in this aspect in front of you and reflect as follows:

> With their limbs bound, their chests are slit open. They are fully conscious of the butcher's hand thrust in and their life force being severed. Staring at the butcher's face with glassy eyes, despair washes over them.
>
> If only they could be freed from all suffering and the causes of suffering! May they be freed from all suffering and the causes of suffering! I will see to it that they are freed from all suffering and the causes of suffering! Guru-deity, please bless me that I may do so!

Think:

> From having made supplications in this manner, streams of five-colored nectar along with light rays descend from the body of the guru-deity above my crown. Permeating my body and mind and also those of all other sentient beings, they cleanse us of the misdeeds and obstructions we have amassed since beginningless time, and in particular those misdeeds and obstructions that prevent us from developing compassion. The special realization of *compassion for sentient beings in despair* is produced in our mental continua.

When you have elicited the experiential realization [of compassion toward *sentient beings in despair*], clearly visualize before you those who carelessly use the Saṅgha's possessions, have corrupt ethics, abandon the Dharma, hold wrong views, harm sentient beings, and readily commit various misdeeds and nonvirtues, and reflect as follows:

> By behaving in this way, they cannot experience happiness in this life. They will inevitably be reborn in the lower rebirths immediately after death. Once born there, they will have to experience all manner of prolonged and intense suffering.

If only they could be freed from all suffering and the causes of suffering! May they be freed from all suffering and the causes of suffering! I will see to it that they are freed from all suffering and the causes of suffering! Guru-deity, please bless me that I may do so!

Think:

From having made supplications in this manner, streams of five-colored nectar along with light rays descend from the body of the guru-deity above my crown. Permeating my body and mind and also those of all other sentient beings, they cleanse us of the misdeeds and obstructions we have amassed since beginningless time, and in particular those misdeeds and obstructions that prevent us from developing compassion. The special realization of *compassion for evil-doing sentient beings* is produced in our mental continua.

When you have elicited the experiential realization in compassion [toward evil-doing sentient beings], clearly visualize in front of you kin, such as your mother, and reflect as follows:

Toiling all her life managing affairs of the livelihoods of friends and foes, she is tormented by the suffering of suffering and the suffering of change and is deprived of even the slightest mental peace. Ensnared in negative actions, she has failed to produce any mind of virtue in this life, so it is inevitable that she will immediately plummet into the lower rebirths upon death. Once reborn there, she will have to experience all manner of prolonged and intense suffering.

If only she could be freed from suffering and the causes of suffering! May she be freed from suffering and the causes of suffering! I will see to it that she is freed from suffering and the causes of suffering. Guru-deity, please bless me that I may do so.

Think:

> From having made supplications in this manner, streams of five-colored nectar along with light rays descend from the body of the guru-deity above my crown. Permeating my body and mind and also those of all other sentient beings, they cleanse us of the misdeeds and obstructions we have amassed since beginningless time, and in particular those misdeeds and obstructions that prevent the realization of compassion. The special realization of *compassion for kin* is produced in our mental continua.

Once you have elicited the experiential realization in compassion toward [kin such as] your mother, meditate as before on neutral sentient beings, then foes, and finally all sentient beings.

Meditation on the exceptional resolve

When you have elicited the transformative experiential realizations in love and compassion, meditate on the exceptional resolve. While meditating on the guru-deity above your crown, reflect as follows:

> I myself will see to it that all sentient beings who are pained by suffering and deprived of happiness are freed from suffering and the causes of suffering. I will see to it that they enjoy happiness and the causes of happiness. In particular, I will ensure that, no matter what it takes, all mother sentient beings attain the precious state of a perfect complete buddha, the supreme liberation in which the two obstructions along with their latencies have been abandoned. Guru-deity, please bless me that I may do so!

Think:

> From having made supplications in this manner, streams of five-colored nectar along with light rays descend from the body of the guru-deity above my crown. Permeating my body and mind and also those of all other sentient beings, they cleanse us of the misdeeds and obstructions we have amassed since beginningless time, and in particular those misdeeds and obstructions that prevent the special realization of exceptional resolve. Our bodies

become the nature of transparent light. Our lifespan, merit, and all excellent qualities of scripture and realization develop and increase. The special realization of *exceptional resolve* is produced in our mental continua.

Generating bodhicitta

While meditating on the guru-deity above your crown, ask yourself, "Well then, can I set all sentient beings in the state of perfect complete buddhahood?" Reflect as follows:

No, at present I cannot set even one sentient being in the state of perfect complete buddhahood. Moreover, even those who have attained the state of either of the two types of arhats, except for benefiting sentient beings in limited ways, cannot set all sentient beings in the state of perfect complete buddhahood. Then, who has this ability? A perfect complete buddha has it.

The excellent qualities of a buddha's *body* are such that his body is ornamented by the clear and complete signs and exemplifying marks. The excellent qualities of his *speech* are such that each instant of his melodious speech possessing the sixty branches is able to effortlessly reveal the Dharma to all sentient beings in their respective languages. His excellent qualities of *mind* are his [wisdom] directly realizing all things and how they really exist—simultaneously—and his great compassion that impartially engages all sentient beings, like the lovingkindness of a mother for her only child, ever ready to guide them whenever it is time to do so. His *activities* occur effortlessly and spontaneously. For instance, each emanated light ray of his body, speech, and mind is able to set countless sentient beings in the state of omniscience.

In brief, only a buddha can be endowed with every kind of excellent quality and be free from every kind of fault.

Reflect as follows:

If I am to bring about both my own and others' purpose, I must attain buddhahood. Therefore, no matter what it takes, I will attain this precious state of a complete buddha for the sake of all

> mother sentient beings. Guru-deity, please bless me that I may do so!

Think:

> Induced by my supplications, there emerges from the guru-deity dwelling above my crown a second figure of the guru-deity, like one flame of a butter lamp separating from another. He absorbs into me, whereby my form clearly becomes that of Conqueror Śākyamuni, seated upon a multicolored lotus, moon disc, and sun disc set above a high and vast throne made of precious stones and supported by eight great lions. My body is the color of refined gold. Endowed with a crown protrusion, I have one face and two arms. My right hand presses the ground, and my left displays the gesture of meditative equipoise while holding an alms bowl filled with nectar. I am immaculately clad in orange Dharma robes. Adorned with the signs and exemplifying marks, I have the nature of transparent light. I sit with my legs in the vajra posture.

Having visualized the above, cultivate strong joy and divine identity while thinking:

> In accordance with my previous intention, I have attained the state of a buddha for the sake of all sentient beings.

It is taught that there are special auspicious implications in cultivating this thought. While visualizing yourself as Munīndra, imagine the following:

> Countless light rays, resembling streams of cool water, emanate from Munīndra's body and strike all sentient beings in the *hot hells* as well as their abodes. All sufferings from the heat are pacified, and their abodes transform into a special pure environment.
>
> Countless light rays, resembling fire or sunlight, emanate from Munīndra's body and strike all sentient beings in the *cold hells* as well as their abodes. All sufferings from the cold are pacified, and the faults of the environment are eliminated.

> Countless light rays radiate from Munīndra's body and strike the *hungry ghosts* as well as their abodes. All sufferings of hunger, thirst, cold, heat, and exhaustion, as well as miserliness, the karmic obstructions created by miserliness, and the faults of the environment are eliminated.[472]
>
> Countless light rays radiate and strike *humans* as well as the faults of their environment such as ravines. All sufferings of humans, such as birth, aging, sickness, death, and the constant quest to satisfy myriad desires, are eliminated, as are karmic obstructions. The environment becomes a pure land.
>
> Again countless light rays radiate, eliminating the *demigods'* battles, hatred, and jealousy, as well as the *gods'* deaths, fall to lower rebirths, and pervasive conditioned suffering.

It is taught that such visualizations carry special auspicious implications for the purification of the land where you will become enlightened.

To perform these briefly in accordance with the instructions in the *Easy Path*, while visualizing yourself as Munīndra, imagine that you radiate your body, resources, and roots of virtue in the aspect of nectar and five-colored light rays and offer them to sentient beings. Thus all sentient beings attain the perfect happiness of high rebirths and beatitude.

Conclusion

Turning your attention to Guru Munīndra above your crown, say the following as many times as possible:

> To Guru Conqueror Śākyamuni, I pay homage, make offerings, and go for refuge.

Think:

> Induced by my supplications, there emerges from Guru Munīndra a second figure of Guru Munīndra, who absorbs into me, whereby my form clearly becomes that of Guru Munīndra. Radiating from the *hūṃ* at my heart, light rays strike all sentient beings surrounding me and place them in the state of Guru

> Munīndra. I and all sentient beings, each visualized as Munīndra, have at the heart a moon disc, upon which is a white *a* marked with a yellow *hūṃ*. It is encircled by the mantra *Oṃ mune mune mahāmunaye svāhā*.

Focusing your attention on the mantra, recite it as many times as you can. To conclude the session, recite dedication verses such as:

> By this virtue, may I quickly
> achieve the state of Guru Buddha and
> place all sentient beings without exception
> in that state.

With the strong aspiration to fulfill your and others' short-term and ultimate wishes, dedicate the virtues arisen from your practice. If you can, perform prayers such as the *King of Prayers of Excellent Deeds.*

What to do between the sessions

Between sessions, read the scriptures and commentaries that present *love, compassion, and bodhicitta* and perform the other activities as explained above [in the section on how to rely on a spiritual guide].

12 | Equalizing and Exchanging Self and Others

How to generate the mind aspiring for enlightenment by means of equalizing and exchanging self and others

The meditation on the three points—equanimity that is impartial toward all sentient beings, recognizing them as having been one's mother, and recollecting their kindness—have already been explained above in the context of the sevenfold cause-and-effect instruction. Meditate on each of them as explained until you elicit experiential realizations of them. After that, while clearly visualizing all sentient beings surrounding you, engage in equalizing self and others. Śāntideva says:

> Whoever wishes to quickly protect
> himself and others
> should practice the sublime secret—
> exchanging self for others.[473]

Exchanging self and others does not mean meditating on oneself as others and others as oneself. Rather, exchange the two minds—the mind preoccupied with yourself and the mind neglecting others—so that you stop obsessing over yourself and develop concern for others. Ask yourself, "Who, in my heart, is more important? Self or others? Who is less important?" Through such investigation, the mind preoccupied with oneself and the mind neglecting others will manifest spontaneously. At that time, reflect as follows:

> Due to my self-centeredness, I have neglected others. This is inappropriate as both I and others are the same in desiring happiness and not desiring suffering. Therefore, I must cherish others in the

way I cherish myself, for just as I like it when others cherish me, others will like it when I cherish them.

Out of the desire to achieve the very best for myself, I have been self-absorbed since beginningless saṃsāra. Not only have I failed to achieve my purpose or that of others, I have also been the recipient of untold sufferings.

Accordingly, *Engaging in Bodhisattva Deeds* says:

> Whatever happiness there is in this world
> all comes from desiring others' happiness,
> and whatever suffering there is in this world
> all comes from desiring happiness for myself.
>
> Is there any need to say more?
> The childish work for their own purpose,
> while the Muni works for others'.
> Look at the difference between these two!
>
> If I do not exchange my happiness
> for the sufferings of others,
> I will not accomplish the state of buddhahood,
> and even in saṃsāra I will have no happiness.[474]

As said, self-centeredness is the source of all troubles, such as the sufferings of saṃsāra and specifically those of the lower rebirths. Reflect as follows:

> I must deter future self-centeredness and eradicate my existing self-centeredness. Cherishing others is the source of all excellent qualities, so I will generate the mind cherishing others not yet produced and increase that already arisen. Guru-deity, please bless me that I may do so!

Think:

> From having made supplications in this manner, streams of five-colored nectar along with light rays descend from the body of

> the guru-deity above my crown. Permeating my body and mind and also those of all other sentient beings, they cleanse us of all the misdeeds and obstructions we have amassed since beginningless time, and in particular those misdeeds and obstructions that prevent the special realization of equalizing and exchanging self and others. Our bodies become the nature of transparent light. Our lifespan, merit, and all excellent qualities of scripture and realization develop and increase. The special realization of *equalizing and exchanging self and others* is produced in our mental continua.

In brief, Munīndra, rejecting self-centeredness and embracing concern for others, enacted only others' purpose, whereby he attained manifest complete buddhahood. If you had done the same, you would have attained enlightenment long ago. Because you have failed to do so, you are still wandering in saṃsāra.

In a previous life, our teacher was a householder by the name of Maitrakanyaka.[475] Due to the fruitional result of kicking his mother in the head, he found himself in a partial hell. Upon his arrival, a spinning iron wheel descended on his head. When this occurred, he thought, "Many people have kicked their mother in the head, as I have done. May the suffering of all these people come to fruition upon me!" As soon as he gave rise to that thought, the wheel ascended into the sky.

Even in today's world, the words of altruistic leaders who act principally to further good and look after their subjects are taken as authoritative. Fair-minded people applaud them and rejoice in their virtues but cringe at those who are self-serving. Reflect as follows:

> As long as self-centeredness has a place in me, the mind cherishing others will not be newly produced, and even that existing will not be able to continue. Therefore, instead of putting myself before others, I will put others first. Taking upon myself others' suffering and misdeeds and giving them all my happiness and virtues, I will ensure that all sentient beings are freed from suffering and are endowed with perfect happiness.
>
> Presently I am unable to do so. Who has that ability? Only a perfect complete buddha has it. No matter what it takes, I will

> attain the precious state of a perfect complete buddha for the sake of all mother sentient beings. Guru-deity, please bless me that I may do so!

Think:

> From having made supplications in this manner, streams of five-colored nectar along with light rays descend from the body of the guru-deity above my crown. Permeating my body and mind and also those of all other sentient beings, they cleanse us of all the misdeeds and obstructions we have amassed since beginningless time, and in particular those misdeeds and obstructions that are preventing the special realization of bodhicitta. Our bodies become the nature of transparent light. Our lifespan, merit, and all excellent qualities of scripture and realization develop and increase. The special realization of *bodhicitta* is produced in our mental continua.

13 | Committing to Bodhicitta

How to uphold the mind aspiring for enlightenment through ritual

This is explained in two parts: how to obtain the vows that have not been obtained and how to guard against degeneration the vows that have been obtained.

How to obtain the vows that have not been obtained

Even though you can commit to the wishing and engaging minds through the sequential rituals in the *Stages of the Path*,[476] it is more expedient for you to make commitments to the two minds together in accordance with Śāntideva's system as follows. After you have integrated and sustained the general preliminary practices and the specific practices of the actual meditation topics beginning from relying on a spiritual guide up through bodhicitta, meditate on the guru-deity above your crown and reflect as follows:

> For the sake of all sentient beings, I will swiftly attain the precious state of a perfect complete buddha. To that end, from this moment until I reach the essence of enlightenment, I will uphold the bodhisattva vows, train in the powerful deeds of bodhisattvas, and attain enlightenment for the sake of all sentient beings.

Thinking, "I will uphold this mind until I achieve buddhahood," visualize that Guru Munīndra pronounces the following lines and that you repeat after him for a total of three recitations:

> O all buddhas and bodhisattvas,
> please pay attention to me!

Just as the sugatas of the past
generated bodhicitta
and dwelled in the bodhisattva trainings
in stages,
I too, for the benefit of migrating beings,
shall generate bodhicitta and
train in the bodhisattva trainings
in stages.[477]

Simultaneous with the completion of the third recitation, generate the conviction that you have obtained the bodhisattva vows.

Next, generate enthusiasm while reciting:

Now my life is fruitful.
I have attained a good human existence.
Today I have been born in the buddha lineage.
I have become a child of the Buddha.

Now, no matter whatever happens,
I will conduct myself in accord with this lineage.
I will not sully
this flawless, holy lineage.[478]

How to guard against degeneration the vows that have been obtained

While meditating on the guru-deity above your crown, reflect as follows:

> No matter what it takes, I will swiftly attain the precious state of a perfect complete buddha for the sake of all mother sentient beings. To that end, I will contemplate the benefits of bodhicitta and uphold the mind of bodhicitta three times in the day and three times at night. Regardless of how sentient beings behave, I will not forsake even one. In order to increase my bodhicitta, I will strive to accrue the two collections of merit and wisdom through making offerings to the Three Jewels and engaging in other practices.

The benefits of bodhicitta

A person endowed with bodhicitta in his mindstream comes under the protection of twice as many guardians as those protecting a wheel-turning king. Even if maleficent nonhumans try to harm them, they will find no opportunity. Such a person will quickly accomplish knowledge mantras that others cannot accomplish. Calamities such as epidemics and famines will not occur where such an individual is present and will quickly pass if perchance they occur. A person endowed with bodhicitta is a focal point of homage and offerings for the world along with the gods, for *Engaging in Bodhisattva Deeds* says:

> When bodhicitta is generated, in that moment
> a wretched one fettered in the jail of saṃsāra
> will be called *child of the sugatas*
> and be revered by humans and gods.[479]

Abandon the causes for degenerating bodhicitta, such as the practice of the four black dharmas: (1) deceiving gurus and individuals of similar stature with lies for the sake of amusement, (2) causing others to regret having created virtue, (3) speaking offensively with hatred to bodhisattvas, those who have entered the Mahāyāna, and (4) acting deceitfully in the absence of an altruistic attitude. Train in the causes of increasing bodhicitta, such as the practice of the four white dharmas.[480] Reflect as follows:

> In brief, until I reach the essence of enlightenment, I will guard the pure bodhisattva vows, never tainted by the faults of the eighteen root downfalls and forty-six infractions, even at the cost of my own life. Guru-deity, please bless me that I may do so!

Think:

> From having made supplications in this manner, streams of five-colored nectar along with light rays descend from the body of the guru-deity above my crown. Permeating my body and mind and also those of all other sentient beings, they cleanse us of all the misdeeds and obstructions we have amassed since beginningless time, and in particular those misdeeds and obstructions that

prevent the special realization of being able to guard the pure bodhisattva vows. Our bodies become the nature of transparent light. Our lifespan, merit, and all excellent qualities of scripture and realization develop and increase. The special realization of *being able to guard the pure bodhisattva vows* is produced in our mental continua.

14 | Training in the Bodhisattvas' Deeds

How to train in the deeds after having generated the mind aspiring for enlightenment

This is explained in two parts: how to train in the bodhisattvas' deeds in general and how to train in the deeds of the last two perfections in particular. The first is explained in two parts: what to do during the session and what to do between the sessions. The first of those has three parts: preparation, the actual meditation on the bodhisattvas' deeds in general, and conclusion.

Preparation

Carry out the preparatory practices up to the following lines:[481]

> O guru, extraordinary deity, who encompasses all the objects of refuge,
> Munīndra Vajradhara, to you I make supplication!

Reflect as follows:

> Guru-deity, please bless me and all mother sentient beings to be able to train properly in the powerful vast and profound bodhisattvas' deeds.

Think:

> From having made supplications in this manner, streams of five-colored nectar along with light rays descend from the body of

> the guru-deity above my crown. Permeating my body and mind and also those of all other sentient beings, they cleanse us of all the misdeeds and obstructions we have amassed since beginningless time, and in particular those misdeeds and obstructions that prevent the special realization of being able to train properly in the powerful vast and profound bodhisattvas' deeds. Our bodies become the nature of transparent light. Our lifespan, merit, and all excellent qualities of scripture and realization develop and increase. The special realization of *being able to train properly in the powerful vast and profound bodhisattvas' deeds* is produced in our mental continua.

The actual meditation on the bodhisattvas' deeds in general

This is explained in two parts: the practice of the six perfections, which brings one's own mind to maturation, and the practice of the four means of gathering disciples, which brings the minds of others to maturation.

The practice of the six perfections, which brings one's own mind to maturation

The practice of generosity

While meditating on the guru-deity above your crown, reflect as follows:

> No matter what it takes, I will swiftly, swiftly attain the precious state of a perfect complete buddha for the sake of all mother sentient beings. To that end, I will practice the *generosity of Dharma* without expecting gain, honor, or reputation, by teaching the excellent Dharma as best I can to those deprived of it.[482]

Even when you have not been delegated the task of teaching the Dharma, when others solicit answers to their questions regarding words and meanings in the scriptures, benevolently explain the words and reveal the meanings in their entirety. When you recognize others as suitable receptacles for the Dharma, help them through casual conversation and discussion to generate the wisdoms of hearing, contemplation, and meditation. As much wisdom as you generate in others, that much wisdom you will attain in your future rebirths. Since wisdom is the principal cause of a buddha's dharma body, Ārya Nāgārjuna says:

> The principal of the two is wisdom.[483]

Therefore, from among the three types of generosity, monastics should mainly perform the generosity of Dharma. Their practice of generosity should not transpire through neglecting their practice of hearing, contemplation, meditation, and ethics, nor through channeling wealth gained through deceit and dishonesty. For *A Bodhisattva's Accomplishment of the Four Prātimokṣa Qualities Sūtra* says:

> Śāriputra, the Tathāgata does not allow monastics to perform material giving.[484]

And Sharawa says:

> I do not preach the benefits of giving. Rather, I preach the drawbacks of withholding.

However, if you inadvertently gain wealth, it would be advantageous to make offerings to the Three Jewels, give alms to the poor and wretched, and materially support virtuous companions—all while not damaging your practice of hearing, contemplation, and meditation as well as ethics. In this way, favorable conditions for spiritual practice in future lives—such as food, clothes, a dwelling, and bedding—will arise effortlessly without toil. Therefore strive to practice generosity through understanding the prohibitions and purposes of doing so.[485] Reflect as follows:

> I will practice the *generosity of fearlessness*, protecting living beings from fears of humans such as rulers, robbers, and thieves; from fears of wild animals such as tigers, lions, poisonous snakes, and carnivorous birds; and from harm by the elements such as fire and water.

The generosity of fearlessness can be as little as deftly rescuing ants from being swept away by water or protecting insects from being burned by the sun or fire. Reflect as follows:

> I will practice *material generosity*, by abandoning miserliness and giving appropriate donations to poor destitute sentient beings without expectation of recompense or fruitional results.

OBJECTION: If I were to give away my resources, I would become poor, so I cannot give.

REPLY: When such a thought crosses your mind, give while thinking:

> My body, life force, and resources are as transient as a water bubble. If I do not give them away now, I will still have to leave them all behind eventually. However, if I practice generosity now with what must inevitably be given up, no matter how small a thing I give, I will in future lives obtain wealth a hundredfold over and will not be poor and destitute.

Accordingly, *Engaging in Bodhisattva Deeds* says:

> All will be given away similarly.
> It is best that I give to all sentient beings.[486]

And the *Garland of Birth Stories* says:

> It is taught that you extract the essence of your wealth by means of generosity.[487]

Furthermore, Atiśa says:

> Since the future is longer than this life, as provision for your future life, bury your wealth as a hidden treasure.[488]

And Phadampa says:[489]

> Most of your friends have passed on to their future abodes.
> Do you have companions and provisions, O people of Dingri?[490]

As taught, strive to practice generosity—in the best way, conjoined with bodhicitta; in the middling way, conjoined with the renunciation disillusioned with saṃsāra as a whole; and at the very least, conjoined with the wish to not be deprived of the resources of a high rebirth. In brief, reflect as follows:

> No matter what it takes, I will swiftly attain the precious state of a perfect complete buddha for the sake of all mother sentient beings. To that end, without any sense of loss, I will practice giving by mentally emanating my body, resources, and roots of virtue as whatever is wished for—food for those who wish for food, clothes for those who wish for clothes, drinks for those who wish for drinks, dwellings, bedding, mounts, boats, bridges, gold, silver, wish-fulfilling gems, and so forth. Guru-deity, please bless me that I may do so!

Think:

> From having made supplications in this manner, streams of five-colored nectar along with light rays descend from the body of the guru-deity above my crown. Permeating my body and mind and also those of all other sentient beings, they cleanse us of all the misdeeds and obstructions we have amassed since beginningless time, and in particular those misdeeds and obstructions that prevent the special realization of the perfection of generosity. Our bodies become the nature of transparent light. Our lifespan, merit, and all excellent qualities of scripture and realization develop and increase. The special realization of *the perfection of generosity* is produced in our mental continua.

The practice of generosity entails intensifying the intention to give. Accordingly, the *Great Exposition of the Stages of the Path* says:

> The practice of the perfection of generosity is generating the intention to give in all contexts—even when you have nothing material to offer—and gradually giving more and more.[491]

The practice of ethics

While meditating on the guru-deity above your crown, think:

> No matter what it takes, I will swiftly attain the precious state of a perfect complete buddha for the sake of all mother sentient beings. To that end, I will abandon any misconduct that contravenes my commitment to refrain from the ten nonvirtues and other misdeeds, and I will dwell in the ten virtues, thus practicing the main form of the ethics of restraint.[492]

Accordingly, the *Classifications of Vinaya* says:

> Guard your speech and exercise mental restraint.
> Do not commit nonvirtues with your body.
> If you train in these three types of karmic paths,
> you will attain the path taught by the Sage.[493]

Reflect as follows:

> Furthermore, I will generate in my mindstream the six perfections of generosity and so forth, and the pure virtues of ethics and so forth, that have not yet arisen and increase those that have. I will also acquaint all sentient beings with the pure virtues of ethics and so forth and guide them to the maturing and liberating paths. Guru-deity, please bless me that I may do so!

Think:

> From having made supplications in this manner, streams of five-colored nectar along with light rays descend from the body of the guru-deity above my crown. Permeating my body and mind and also those of all other sentient beings, they cleanse us of all the

misdeeds and obstructions we have amassed since beginningless time, and in particular those misdeeds and obstructions that prevent the special realization of the perfection of ethics. Our bodies become the nature of transparent light. Our lifespan, merit, and all excellent qualities of scripture and realization develop and increase. The special realization of *the perfection of ethics* is produced in our mental continua.

The practice of patience

While meditating on the guru-deity above your crown, reflect as follows:

> No matter what it takes, I will swiftly attain the precious state of a perfect complete buddha for the sake of all mother sentient beings. To that end, even if all sentient beings become my enemies, I will seek their well-being in return for their harm, without countenancing anger for an instant.[494] I will realize completely the qualities of a buddha, such as the perfection of patience, in myself and others.

Furthermore, *Engaging in Bodhisattva Deeds* says:

> Is it not wonderful if a man condemned to death
> is released having his hand cut off instead?
> Is it not wonderful if I am spared hell
> by way of human suffering?[495]

And:

> Furthermore, suffering has good qualities:
> when disheartened, arrogance is dispelled,
> compassion arises for those in saṃsāra,
> negativities are shunned, and joy is found in virtue.[496]

As said, when unwished-for suffering—such as illness or the lack of food, wealth, a dwelling, bedding, and the like—transpires, [remind yourself that] such an experience is the result of having created negative karma in the past.

Undergoing suffering exhausts plenty of negative karma; therefore it is not undesirable at all. In particular, generating patience toward suffering that occurs in the course of spiritual practice draws you closer to the path of omniscience. Reflect as follows:

> Therefore, accepting suffering when it occurs, I will sever the stream of suffering of saṃsāra, especially the lower rebirths, my own and those of others. Moreover, the results will be remarkable when I generate conviction in the following truths: the fruitional results of black and white karma, the causes to be discarded and to be adopted; the blessings of the Three Jewels, the objects of faith; the inconceivable power of the great beings, the buddhas and bodhisattvas; unsurpassed enlightenment, the object to be actualized; true cessation and true path; the two types of selflessness; the twelve branches of scripture,[497] the objects of hearing and contemplation; and the essential points of the bodhisattvas' trainings. Having generated belief in them, I will train well, for the sake of attaining unsurpassed enlightenment, in the essential points of the bodhisattvas' precepts, the meanings revealed by the twelve branches of scripture. Guru-deity, please bless me that I may do so!

Think:

> From having made supplications in this manner, streams of five-colored nectar along with light rays descend from the body of the guru-deity above my crown. Permeating my body and mind and also those of all other sentient beings, they cleanse us of all the misdeeds and obstructions we have amassed since beginningless time, and in particular those misdeeds and obstructions that prevent the special realization of the perfection of patience. Our bodies become the nature of transparent light. Our lifespan, merit, and all excellent qualities of scripture and realization develop and increase. The special realization of *the perfection of patience* is produced in our mental continua.

The practice of joyous effort

While meditating on the guru-deity above your crown, reflect as follows:

> No matter what it takes, I will swiftly attain the precious state of a perfect complete buddha for the sake of all mother sentient beings. For that purpose, I will achieve every quality of a buddha, such as the signs and exemplifying marks, and accomplish every quality of a bodhisattva, such as generosity. To that end, even if I must achieve buddhahood by dwelling in Unrelenting Torment for a hundred thousand countless great eons—in which a day is made up of a thousand great eons, where a great eon consists of eighty intermediate eons, a month made up of thirty such days, and a year made up of twelve such months—I will strive unfalteringly and generate enthusiasm.[498]

OBJECTION: I cannot sustain armor-like joyous effort for that long.
REPLY: When such a thought crosses your mind, reflect as follows:

> If I ardently train in the stages of the paths of persons with the three capacities and likewise master the technique of exchanging self and others, I will be free from physical discomfort as a result of having abandoned the causal ten nonvirtues, and I will be free from mental discomfort as a result of having become skilled in the meaning of all phenomena being devoid of inherent existence. My body and mind enhanced by joy and happiness will sustain me, and I will never be discouraged or indolent even if dwelling in saṃsāra for ages.

Accordingly, *Engaging in Bodhisattva Deeds* says:

> From having abandoned misdeeds, there is no suffering,
> and owing to skill, there is no unhappiness.[499]

And:

> Having mounted the horse of bodhicitta
> that dispels all disheartenment and weariness,

proceeding from happiness to happiness,
what sensible person would lapse into despondency?[500]

If you sincerely dedicate all your roots of virtue, big and small, to the goal of accomplishing the short-term and ultimate benefit and happiness of all sentient beings, you will obtain merit commensurate with that number of sentient beings. In addition, by the blessings of the buddhas and bodhisattvas, your two collections of merit and wisdom will increase limitlessly and be easily completed. Therefore there is never a need to feel disheartened. The *Precious Garland* says:

> If the merit of the practices that have been spoken about
> had form, it could never fit
> into the realms of worlds as numerous
> as the sand grains of the Ganges.
>
> The Bhagavān said so,
> and the reason is this:
> [the infinitude of the merit of] wishing to help the infinite realms of sentient beings
> is the same [as the infinitude of those beings themselves].[501]

Reflect as follows:

> By integrating all the virtuous vast and profound qualities into my mind and guiding others to the path of virtue too, I will attain unsurpassed enlightenment. Guru-deity, please bless me that I may do so!

Think:

> From having made supplications in this manner, streams of five-colored nectar along with light rays descend from the body of the guru-deity above my crown. Permeating my body and mind and also those of all other sentient beings, they cleanse us of all the misdeeds and obstructions we have amassed since beginning-

less time, and in particular those misdeeds and obstructions that prevent the special realization of the perfection of joyous effort. Our bodies become the nature of transparent light. Our lifespan, merit, and all excellent qualities of scripture and realization develop and increase. The special realization of *the perfection of joyous effort* is produced in our mental continua.

The practice of meditative concentration[502]

While meditating on the guru-deity above your crown, reflect as follows:

> No matter what it takes, I will swiftly attain the precious state of a perfect complete buddha for the sake of all mother sentient beings. To that end, I will train in all types of bodhisattvas' meditative concentrations: (1) from the point of view of nature, mundane and supramundane concentrations; (2) from the point of view of class, meditative concentrations that are calm abiding, special insight, and a union of calm abiding and special insight; and (3) from the point of view of function, meditative concentrations in which the body and mind abide blissfully in this life, meditative concentrations that act as the support for excellent qualities, and meditative concentrations that enact the welfare of sentient beings. Guru-deity, please bless me that I may do so!

Think:

> From having made supplications in this manner, streams of five-colored nectar along with light rays descend from the body of the guru-deity above my crown. Permeating my body and mind and also those of all other sentient beings, they cleanse us of all the misdeeds and obstructions we have amassed since beginningless time, and in particular those misdeeds and obstructions that prevent the special realization of the perfection of meditative concentration. Our bodies become the nature of transparent light. Our lifespan, merit, and all excellent qualities of scripture and realization develop and increase. The special realization of *the perfection of meditative concentration* is produced in our mental continua.

The practice of wisdom[503]

While meditating on the guru-deity above your crown, reflect as follows:

> No matter what it takes, I will swiftly attain the precious state of a perfect complete buddha for the sake of all mother sentient beings. To that end, I will train in all types of bodhisattvas' wisdoms: (1) the wisdom realizing the ultimate knowledge of the way things exist,[504] (2) the wisdom realizing the conventional knowledge of the five sciences, and (3) the wisdom realizing how to enact the welfare of sentient beings. Guru-deity, please bless me that I may do so!

Think:

> From having made supplications in this manner, streams of five-colored nectar along with light rays descend from the body of the guru-deity above my crown. Permeating my body and mind and also those of all other sentient beings, they cleanse us of all the misdeeds and obstructions we have amassed since beginningless time, and in particular those misdeeds and obstructions that prevent the special realization of the perfection of wisdom. Our bodies become the nature of transparent light. Our lifespan, merit, and all excellent qualities of scripture and realization develop and increase. The special realization of *the perfection of wisdom* is produced in our mental continua.

The practice of the four means of gathering disciples, which brings the minds of others to maturation

While meditating on the guru-deity above your crown, reflect as follows:

> No matter what it takes, I will swiftly attain the precious state of a perfect complete buddha for the sake of all mother sentient beings. To that end, I will place all sentient beings in the maturing and liberating paths in dependence on the following methods

for enacting others' welfare, as taught in the *Ornament for the Mahāyāna Sūtras*:

> *Giving* is the same [as above]; teaching, causing
> adoption,
> and oneself engaging are asserted to be
> *agreeable speech*, *helpful activity*,
> and *consistent conduct*.[505]

Thus I will (1) take trainees under my wing through providing for their needs, (2) speak agreeably by refuting with scripture and reasoning those who propound falsehoods and taking care of them, (3) act helpfully by [causing others to] practice the meaning presented in the Dharma, and (4) engage in consistent conduct by practicing the way I have taught others to do.[506] Guru-deity, please bless me that I may do so!

Think:

> From having made supplications in this manner, streams of five-colored nectar along with light rays descend from the body of the guru-deity above my crown. Permeating my body and mind and also those of all other sentient beings, they cleanse us of all the misdeeds and obstructions we have amassed since beginningless time, and in particular those misdeeds and obstructions that prevent the special realization of the four means of gathering disciples. Our bodies become the nature of transparent light. Our lifespan, merit, and all excellent qualities of scripture and realization develop and increase. The special realization of *the four means of gathering disciples* is produced in our mental continua.

Conclusion

Turning your attention to Guru Munīndra above your crown, say the following as many times as possible:

> To Guru Conqueror Śākyamuni, I pay homage, make offerings, and go for refuge.

Think:

> Induced by my supplications, there emerges from Guru Munīndra a second figure of Guru Munīndra, who absorbs into me, whereby my form clearly becomes that of Guru Munīndra. Radiating from the *hūṃ* at my heart, light rays strike all sentient beings surrounding me and place them in the state of Guru Munīndra. I and all sentient beings, each visualized as Munīndra, have at the heart a moon disc, upon which is a white *a* marked with a yellow *hūṃ*. It is encircled by the mantra *Oṃ mune mune mahāmunaye svāhā*.

Focusing your attention on the mantra, recite it as many times as you can. To conclude the session, recite dedication verses such as:

> By this virtue, may I quickly
> achieve the state of Guru Buddha and
> place all sentient beings without exception
> in that state.

With the strong aspiration to fulfill your and others' short-term and ultimate wishes, dedicate the virtues arisen from your practice. If you can, perform prayers such as the *King of Prayers of Excellent Deeds.*

What to do between the sessions

Between the sessions, read the scriptures and commentaries that teach about *the powerful bodhisattva deeds, vast and profound*, and perform the other activities as explained above [in the section on how to rely on a spiritual guide].

15 | Calm Abiding

How to train in the deeds of the last two perfections in particular

This is explained in two parts: how to train in calm abiding, which has the nature of meditative concentration, and how to train in special insight, which has the nature of wisdom. The first is explained in two parts: what to do during the session and what to do between the sessions. The first of those has three parts: preparation, the actual meditation on calm abiding, which has the nature of meditative concentration, and conclusion.

Preparation

The preparation for meditating on calm abiding consists of the general preparatory practices and the specific training in the mindsets of those with small and medium capacities. The *Ornament for the Mahāyāna Sūtras* says:

> The place where an intelligent person practices is
> one that is well obtained, and it has a good location,
> favorable land, excellent companions,
> and the facilities for comfortable yoga.[507]

First you should fulfill the prerequisites for accomplishing calm abiding as follows. At a congenial place—where the land is favorable and there are excellent companions as mentioned in the verse above—dwell in pure ethics, give up excessive socializing with all and sundry, and relinquish coarse conceptualizations that hanker after sensual delights. With contentment and few desires, sit on a comfortable cushion with your midriff erect, legs in the vajra posture, and hands in the gesture of meditative equipoise, breathe naturally, and so on.[508]

The actual meditation on calm abiding, which has the nature of meditative concentration

Although many types of objects of observation for accomplishing calm abiding have been taught, observing a deity's form is excellent, since it serves as the best principal way of recollecting the Buddha and fulfills many purposes such as that of rendering one a suitable receptacle for practicing tantric deity yoga. Thus visualize the Buddha the size of a fava bean dwelling in the space in front of your navel. Imagine him as follows:

> From the heart of the guru-deity above my crown, a light ray, like a strand of spider's silk, radiates outward. On its tip is a multicolored lotus, moon disc, and sun disc. Seated upon it is Conqueror Śākyamuni. His body is the color of refined gold. Endowed with a crown protrusion, he has one face and two arms. His right hand presses the ground, and his left displays the gesture of meditative equipoise while holding an alms bowl filled with nectar. He is immaculately clad in orange Dharma robes. Adorned with the signs and exemplifying marks, he has the nature of transparent light. He sits with his legs in the vajra posture amid a profusion of light emanating from his body.

Focusing your attention on him, meditate single-pointedly. Alternatively, visualize as follows:

> From Guru Munīndra dwelling above my crown emerges a second figure of Guru Munīndra, like one flame of a butter lamp separating from another. He absorbs into me, whereby I clearly transform into the form of Conqueror Śākyamuni seated upon a multicolored lotus, moon disc, and sun disc placed above a high and magnificent throne made of precious stones and supported by eight great lions. My body is the color of refined gold. Endowed with a crown protrusion, I have one face and two arms. My right hand presses the ground, and my left displays the gesture of meditative equipoise while holding an alms bowl filled with nectar. I am immaculately clad in orange Dharma robes. Adorned with the signs and exemplifying marks, I have

> the nature of transparent light. I sit with my legs in the vajra posture. Like a rainbow in the sky, I appear but am devoid of inherent existence.

Focusing your attention on yourself in the form of Conqueror Śākyamuni, meditate single-pointedly.

It may happen during your practice that, while you wish to meditate on the image as gold in color, the image appears red or some other color; while you wish to meditate on the image in the seated aspect, it appears standing; or while you wish to meditate on a single figure, many appear. Do not yield to these appearances; meditate by refocusing on the original object single-pointedly.

In the beginning, even if the object of observation does not arise clearly in the nature of luminous light, meditate by focusing single-pointedly on the clear partial conceptual appearance of the Buddha's form.[509] Ensure that laxity and excitement are totally absent throughout the session. Generate the strong aspiration thinking, "In the event that laxity or excitement arises, I will immediately dispel it," and single-pointedly concentrate on the object without forgetting it. By recollecting the object of observation again and again, sustain the continuum of that awareness. This is an excellent method for beginners to accomplish the mental abidings.[510]

If your mind struggles to hold the appearance of the Tathāgata's body the size of a fava bean, enlarge it so that its height becomes the length of your thumb's first joint. If that is still unmanageable, enlarge it so that its height becomes five finger widths and maintain your concentration on that. Sometimes a partial conceptual appearance of the head, two arms, two legs, or the abdomen may appear. Be content and maintain your concentration on that. When your mind is able to manage that, meditate in increments, occasionally visualizing downward starting from the Buddha's crown protrusion, and occasionally visualizing upward starting from the lotus and moon seat.

It is crucial to optimize the degree of mental tension and set the mind single-pointedly in a state that lucidly[511] ascertains the object of observation. However, some earlier practitioners—based on Saraha's instruction "When a mind that is bound in a tangle is relaxed, without a doubt it is freed"[512]—unwittingly entered into subtle laxity due to the mind being too relaxed. Yet other later practitioners—based on Tsongkhapa's instructions that one should generate an intense[513] mindfulness and a strong mode of apprehension—were unable to achieve stability due to the mind being overly taut. Accordingly, Ācārya Candragomin says:

> When I make effort, excitement is produced.
> When I abandon it, slackness[514] is produced.
> When it is difficult to achieve an appropriate balance between the two,
> what should I do with my disturbed mind?[515]

There are people for whom the object of observation dawns more easily if they observe the mind rather than a deity's form or some other object. The way [to meditate on the mind] is by abandoning all forms of investigation and analysis, such as expectations of good outcomes and fears of bad ones. Without fabricating anything mentally, generate a lucid mindfulness and fix your mind onto your object with the intention thinking, "I will focus my mind on it."

Without newly conceptualizing any object, set your mind lucidly in just the entity of mindfulness itself. If conceptualizations of other objects arise, cut them out entirely. Reinforcing your mindfulness, set your mind on the original object of observation. This is the intent of the following statement:

> Alternatively, like a skillful swordsman,
> cut out entirely any conceptualization that arises.
> After cutting it out, at the time of abiding,
> without losing mindfulness, relax,
> "Tighten it and relax—
> this is where you set the mind."[516]

This is a method for beginners to easily achieve abiding on the mind. It is also a way to introduce the conventional reality of the mind, as opposed to its final reality. In [*Highway of the Conquerors*] it says:

> I, Chökyi Gyaltsen, say that
> this is a marvelous skillful means
> for beginners to achieve abiding on the mind

> and it is the way to introduce the conventional reality of
> the mind.[517]

Therefore meditation taking the mind as the object of observation is also taught in the lamrim.

No matter what type of meditative stabilization you wish to accomplish, skill in relying on mindfulness and introspection is the principal salient point. Accordingly, the *Smaller Exposition on the Stages of the Path to Enlightenment* says:

> If, instead of setting your mind on another object such as a deity's body, you sustain the continuum of the mere nonconceptualizing awareness, then thinking, "I will set my mind without conceptualizing any object," make sure your mind does not wander away and stays undistracted. Also, since the antithesis of distraction is essentially the same as mindfulness that does not forget its object of observation, there is no way to sustain the continuum [of the mere nonconceptualizing mind] apart from sustaining the continuum of mindfulness. Therefore rely on mindfulness in which you elicit the power of the ascertaining consciousness by means of such meditation.[518]

QUESTION: Well then, what is the entity of mindfulness?

ANSWER: It is one's mind familiarizing with or getting at its object of observation without forgetting it. Accordingly, the *Compendium of Knowledge* says:

> What is mindfulness? It is the mind's nonforgetfulness of a familiar object. It has the function of nondistraction.[519]

In brief, when cultivating pure meditative stabilization, rely on the eight antidotes that abandon the five faults. It is said:

> It arises from the cause of cultivating the eight antidotes
> that abandon the five faults.[520]

The five faults are: (1) laziness, (2) forgetting the instructions, (3) laxity and excitement, counted as a single fault, (4) nonapplication of antidotes, and (5) [unnecessary] application of antidotes. Accordingly, *Distinguishing the Middle from the Extremes* says:

> Laziness, forgetting the instructions,
> laxity and excitement,
> nonapplication of antidotes, and application of antidotes—
> these are asserted to be the five faults.[521]

Also, [meditative stabilization] must be achieved by means of relying on the eight antidotes that abandon the five faults.

Five faults	*Eight antidotes*
Laziness	Faith
	Aspiration
	Joyous effort
	Pliancy
Forgetting the instructions	Mindfulness
Laxity and excitement	Introspection
Nonapplication	Application
[Unnecessary] application	Equanimity

1) When practicing meditative stabilization, since laziness is a fault, apply the four antidotes to it: faith that sees the excellent qualities of meditative stabilization; aspiration that seeks meditative stabilization; joyous effort that strives for meditative stabilization; and pliancy, the result of striving.

2) When striving for meditative stabilization, since forgetting the instructions is a fault, apply mindfulness as its antidote. Simply not forgetting the object of observation does not satisfy the requirements of mindfulness; rather, mindfulness is an acute ascertaining consciousness that, within focusing on the object single-pointedly, is endowed with intense awareness.

3) When dwelling in equipoise on meditative stabilization, since laxity and excitement are faults, apply introspection as their antidote. Introspection examines whether laxity or excitement has arisen. The *best* introspection is able to detect the cusp of them arising and prevent them; *middling* introspection is aware of them as soon as they arise and checks them; and even the *least* introspection should notice both soon after they have arisen and abandon them.

QUESTION: How are lethargy, laxity, and excitement different?

ANSWER: *Lethargy*[522] has the aspect of physical and mental heaviness in which the object is unclear. Lethargy necessarily involves ignorance.[523] It is as though the mind has descended into darkness.

Coarse laxity is such that even though the mind does not wander to other objects, mindfulness has weakened such that limpidity and clarity are not present.[524]

Subtle laxity is such that even though limpidity and clear appearance are present, the acute ascertaining consciousness that ascertains the object has slightly weakened.

As antidotes to these, recollect the excellent qualities of the Three Jewels, bring to mind a mark of brightness, and implement the instructions on mixing wind and mind with space.[525]

The instructions on mixing wind and mind with space are as follows. At your navel are the red and white drops, resembling an upright egg.[526] They [rise and] shoot out from your crown to become indivisible with empty space. Single-pointedly set yourself in equipoise on that. This is said to be like mixing awareness with the sphere of door-opening space.[527]

Subtle excitement is such that the mind wanders slightly, not remaining unwaveringly on the object. Its antidote is to meditate by relying on mindfulness and introspection.

Coarse excitement is such that the mind does not remain on its object and wanders to an object of attachment even though one tries to rely on mindfulness and introspection. As its antidote, meditate on impermanence, the sufferings of the three lower rebirths, and the general sufferings of saṃsāra, and implement the instruction that forcefully severs excitement.

The instruction that forcefully severs excitement is the following. Meditate without distraction for five breaths, taking one breath as a single round of exhalation and inhalation. Next, meditate without distraction by incrementally lengthening the duration to ten breaths, then fifteen, and finally twenty-five.

Alternatively, draw in the white upper winds through both nostrils and press them downward,[528] draw up the yellow downward-voiding winds,[529] join them at the navel, and meditate on them in a vase-like manner.[530]

4) Not remedying laxity and excitement when they arise is a fault. So, as its antidote, you should detect laxity and excitement as soon as they arise and eliminate them. When your mind is greatly concentrated on the object, even though there is clarity endowed with intense awareness, since excitement is predominant, it will be difficult to gain stability.[531] And, if you relax your mind slightly without concentrating so strongly, even though there is stability, since laxity is predominant, it will be difficult to gain clarity.

Therefore, evaluating your own experiences, make adjustments as appropriate. If you think "If I were to heighten my mind just this much, excitement will be produced," then relax it slightly; if you think "If I were to relax my mind just this much, laxity will be produced," then heighten it slightly and achieve optimality. At the juncture of the two, shift the mind away from scattering and excitement, and aim for stability. Once stability arises, by being on the alert for laxity, clarity endowed with intense awareness will be produced. Alternating between the two [heightening and relaxing your mind], sustain the continuum of your meditative stabilization to achieve flawless meditative stabilization. Do not be complacent with a mere limpidity in which clarity endowed with an intense mode of apprehension of the ascertaining consciousness is absent.

5) When your mind engages continuously in meditative stabilization due to having eliminated even subtle laxity and excitement, there may be the fault of [unnecessary] application. As its antidote, desist from implementing any remedy and set your mind in a state of relaxed equanimity.

By sustaining the continuum of your awareness well in this manner, you will attain the nine mental abidings[532] in succession and achieve a calm abiding that is accompanied by physical and mental pliancy.

Conclusion

Turning your attention to Guru Munīndra above your crown, recite the following as many times as possible:

> To Guru Conqueror Śākyamuni, I pay homage, make offerings, and go for refuge.

Think:

> Induced by my supplications, there emerges from Guru Munīndra a second figure of Guru Munīndra, who absorbs into me, whereby my form clearly becomes that of Guru Munīndra. Radiating from the *hūṃ* at my heart, light rays strike all sentient beings surrounding me and place them in the state of Guru Munīndra. I and all sentient beings, each visualized as Munīndra, have at the heart a moon disc, upon which is a white *a* marked with a yellow *hūṃ*. It is encircled by the mantra *Oṃ mune mune mahāmunaye svāhā*.

Focusing your attention on the mantra, recite it as many times as you can. To conclude the session, recite dedication verses such as:

> By this virtue, may I quickly
> achieve the state of Guru Buddha and
> place all sentient beings without exception
> in that state.

With the strong aspiration to fulfill your and others' short-term and ultimate wishes, dedicate the virtues arisen from your practice. If you can, perform prayers such as the *King of Prayers of Excellent Deeds*.

What to do between the sessions

Between the sessions, read the scriptures and commentaries that present *calm abiding*, and perform the other activities as explained above [in the section on how to rely on a spiritual guide].

16 | Special Insight

How to train in special insight, which has the nature of wisdom

This is explained in two parts: what to do during the session and what to do between the sessions. The first of those has three parts: preparation, the actual meditation on special insight, which has the nature of wisdom, and conclusion.

Preparation

The preparation for cultivating special insight is like that for calm abiding. What is different in this case is that here you should also fulfill the following conditions: (1) properly rely on a skilled spiritual guide and receive instructions on special insight from them, (2) regard your spiritual guide and your special deity as indivisible and make heartfelt requests to them, and (3) strive in accruing [the collections of merit and wisdom] and purifying [misdeeds and obstructions].

The combination of these three preparatory practices serves as an indispensable preliminary to the realization of the view.

The actual meditation on special insight, which has the nature of wisdom

This is explained in two parts: how to delineate the selflessness of persons and meditate on it and how to delineate the selflessness of phenomena and meditate on it.[533]

How to delineate the selflessness of persons and meditate on it

Many types of reasoning for delineating selflessness have been taught in the scriptures of the Conqueror.[534] However, if you are a beginner, selflessness will dawn more easily to your mind when you delineate it by means of the four essential points.

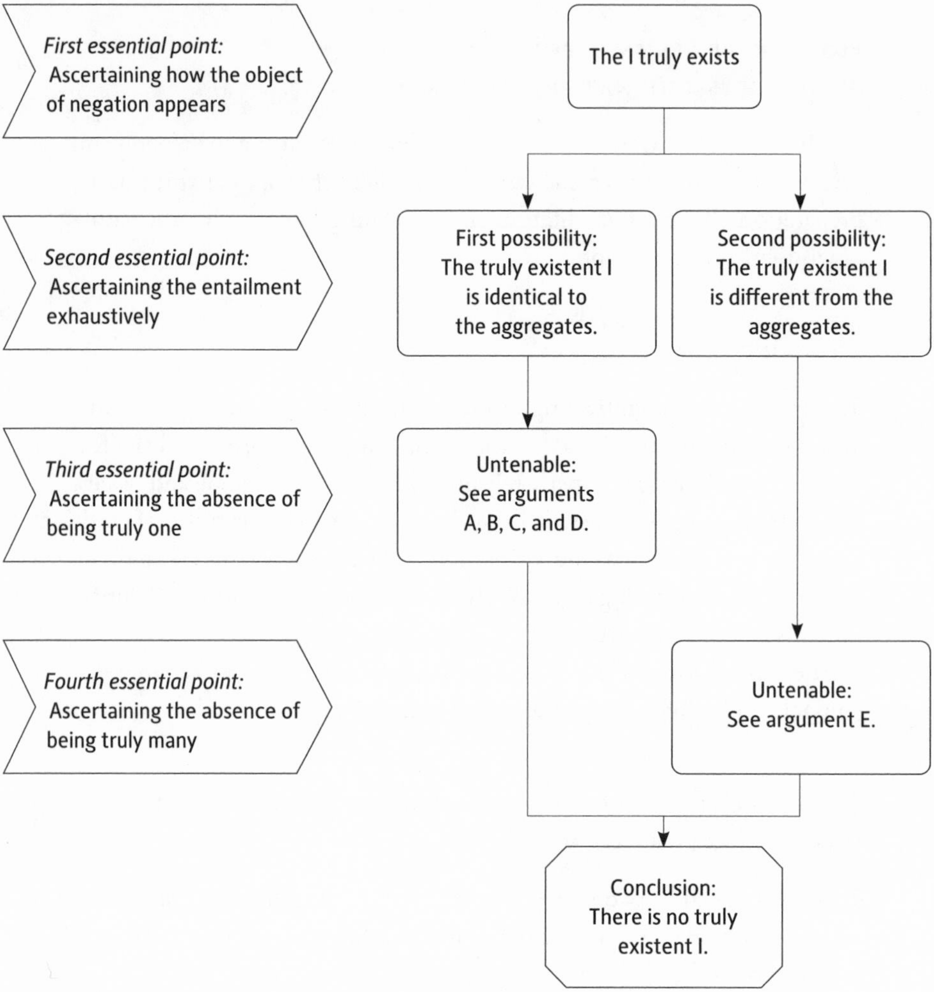
First essential point:
Ascertaining how the object of negation appears
Second essential point:
Ascertaining the entailment exhaustively
Third essential point:
Ascertaining the absence of being truly one
Fourth essential point:
Ascertaining the absence of being truly many
The I truly exists
First possibility: The truly existent I is identical to the aggregates.
Second possibility: The truly existent I is different from the aggregates.
Untenable: See arguments A, B, C, and D.
Untenable: See argument E.
Conclusion: There is no truly existent I.

Charts presenting arguments A–E appear below.

The first essential point: ascertaining how the object of negation appears

At all times, even in deep sleep, your mind holds fast to an I in the core of your heart, thinking, "me, me." This is the innate self-grasping.[535]

Imagine that someone accuses you of misconduct when you are in fact innocent. When he claims "You did it!" you respond, indignant, "I did not do it, yet I am falsely accused!" Your mind tightly apprehends an I in the core of your heart, thinking, "me, me." In that moment, the way the innate self-grasping apprehends the I appears clearly. Just then, with a peripheral part of your consciousness, undertake investigation. What is the I apprehended as? How does the innate self-grasping apprehend it?

If the investigating mind becomes too strong, the previous mind apprehending I will fade, until nothing but blankness remains. Thus, while the general consciousness is continuously generated in the entity of that mind that thinks "I," you must undertake investigation with a peripheral part of the consciousness.

When investigating in this way, you will discover that what the innate self-grasping has apprehended the I as is neither something other than your five aggregates nor something other than your body and mind; it is also not something existing objectively upon each of your five aggregates or upon either your body or your mind.[536] Rather, it is an I that is self-instituting from the beginning,[537] instead of being merely imputed by conception upon the mass that is the mere collection of the five aggregates or the mere collection of body and mind. This is how the innate self-grasping apprehends the I.[538]

Since such an I, which is the object of the mode of apprehension [of such an innate self-grasping],[539] is the object to be negated, you should ascertain it nakedly in relation to your own mind rather than simply having an intellectual idea based upon others' explanations or an abstraction evoked by words. This is the first essential point, that of ascertaining how the object of negation appears.[540]

The second essential point: ascertaining the entailment exhaustively

If the I—as apprehended by the mind thinking "I," which tightly apprehends it at the core of your heart—were to exist objectively upon your five aggregates, then it would exist either as identical to your aggregates or as different from your aggregates. It is utterly impossible that there is a third way of existence apart from those two.[541] Any phenomenon whatsoever must exist as either one or many. You should decide, "It is utterly impossible that there is a third way of existence besides those two."

The third essential point: ascertaining the absence of being truly one[542]

OPINION: The I as apprehended by self-grasping is identical to the five aggregates.

RESPONSE: (A) *Entering the Middle Way* says:

> If the aggregates were the self, then,
> since they are many, the selves would also be many.[543]

Just as a person has five aggregates, the I would also have five different continua.[544] Alternatively, just as there is one I, the five aggregates would be a

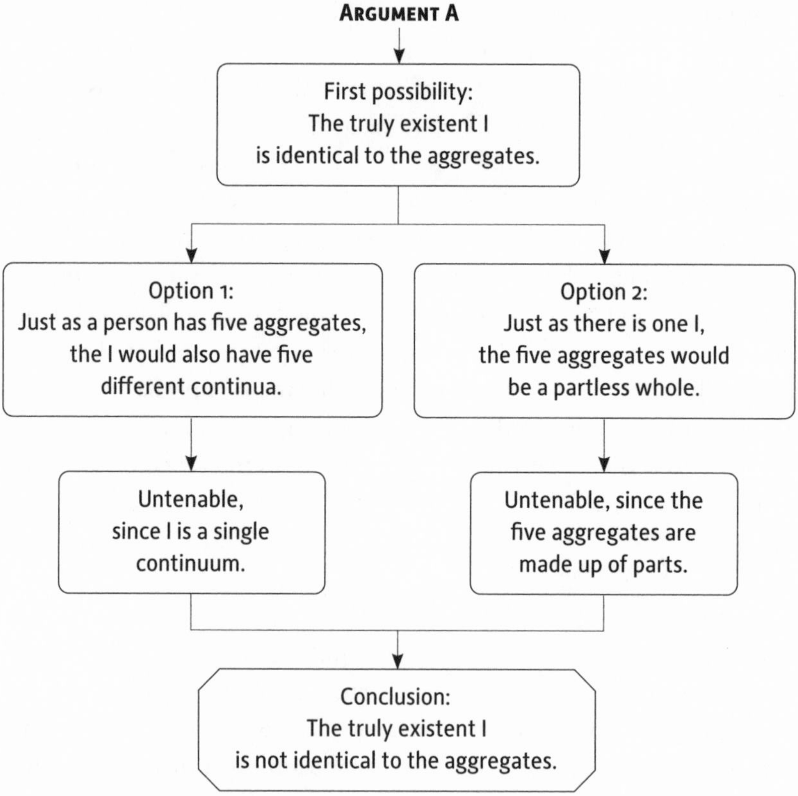
ARGUMENT A
First possibility:
The truly existent I
is identical to the aggregates.
Option 1:
Just as a person has five aggregates,
the I would also have five
different continua.
Option 2:
Just as there is one I,
the five aggregates would
be a partless whole.
Untenable,
since I is a single
continuum.
Untenable, since the
five aggregates are
made up of parts.
Conclusion:
The truly existent I
is not identical to the aggregates.

partless whole. Since there would be many incongruities such as these, you should come to the conclusion, "The I as apprehended by self-grasping is not identical to the aggregates."

(B) Furthermore, if the I as apprehended by self-grasping is established as being identical to the five aggregates, then just as the five aggregates have production and disintegration,[545] the I that exists independently as apprehended by that mind would also have production and disintegration. Accordingly, *Fundamental Verses on the Middle Way* says:

> If the aggregates are the self,
> the self would have production and disintegration.[546]

OPINION: Just as the five aggregates have production and disintegration, the I that exists independently as apprehended by that mind also has production and disintegration.

RESPONSE: Would previous and later instants of the I that has production and disintegration be established as identical or different?

If they were established as identical, then the I of past lives, the I of this life, and the I of future lives would be a partless whole.

If they were established as different, though in general things that are merely different do not have to be different in an unrelated manner, things that are different in an inherently existent way would have to be different in an utterly unrelated manner.[547] Accordingly, *Entering the Middle Way* says:

> It is not feasible for those that are individually established by way of
> their own character
> to be included in a single continuum.[548]

OPINION: The I of past lives, the I of this life, and the I of future lives are [indeed] three different [entities] that are utterly unrelated.[549]

RESPONSE: In that case, one would experience karma one has not created, karma one has created would waste away, and so forth. Since there would be many incongruities such as these, you should come to the conclusion, "The I as apprehended by self-grasping is not established as identical to the five aggregates."

ARGUMENT B

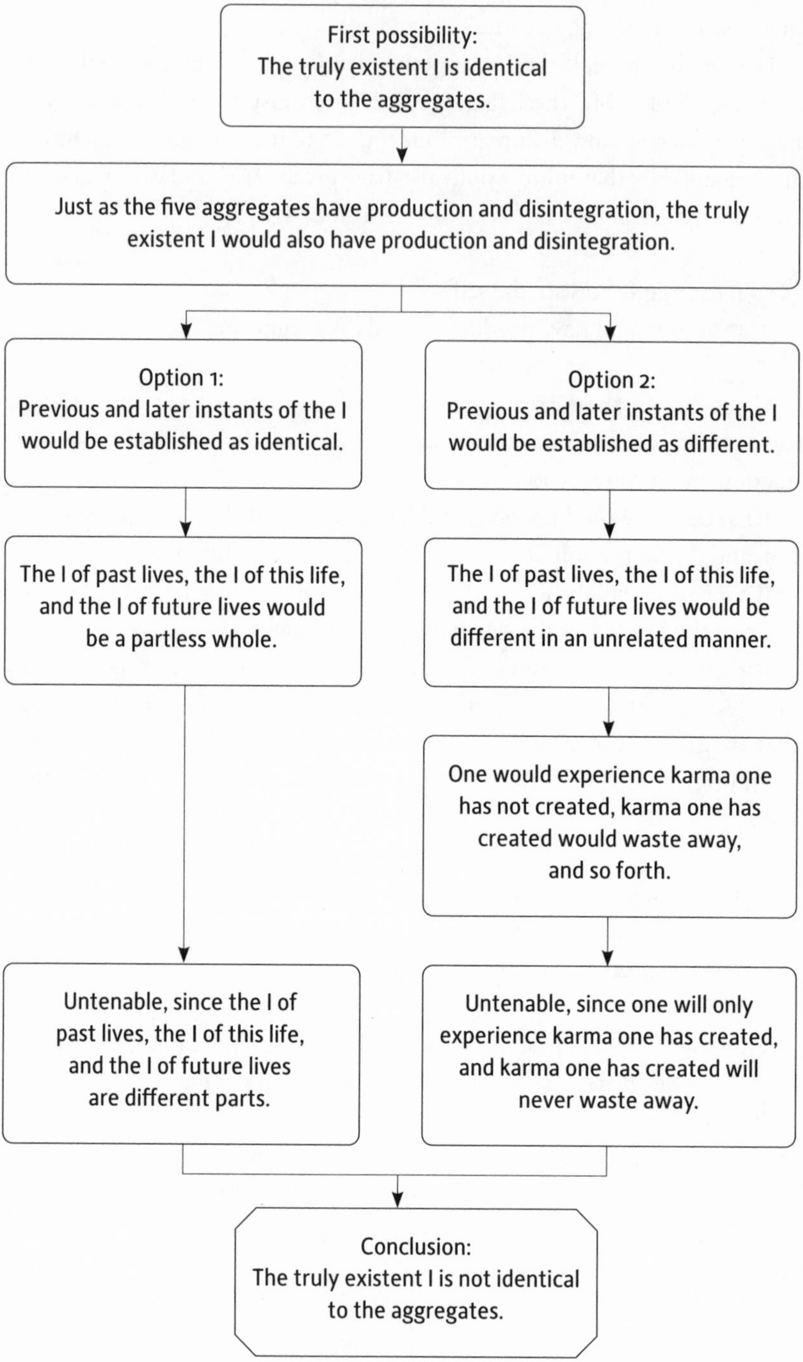
First possibility:
The truly existent I is identical to the aggregates.
Just as the five aggregates have production and disintegration, the truly existent I would also have production and disintegration.
Option 1:
Previous and later instants of the I would be established as identical.
Option 2:
Previous and later instants of the I would be established as different.
The I of past lives, the I of this life, and the I of future lives would be a partless whole.
The I of past lives, the I of this life, and the I of future lives would be different in an unrelated manner.
One would experience karma one has not created, karma one has created would waste away, and so forth.
Untenable, since the I of past lives, the I of this life, and the I of future lives are different parts.
Untenable, since one will only experience karma one has created, and karma one has created will never waste away.
Conclusion:
The truly existent I is not identical to the aggregates.

(C) Furthermore, if the I as apprehended by self-grasping is established as identical to the five aggregates, since the identity here would be an identity that exists truly, the I and the five aggregates would be established as identical in every sense. And if that is the case, then the I or self would not be the appropriator of the five aggregates, and the five aggregates would not be the objects appropriated by the self.[550] There would be many incongruities such as these. Accordingly, *Fundamental Verses on the Middle Way* says:

> If the appropriated were the self,
> your self would be nonexistent.[551]

ARGUMENT C

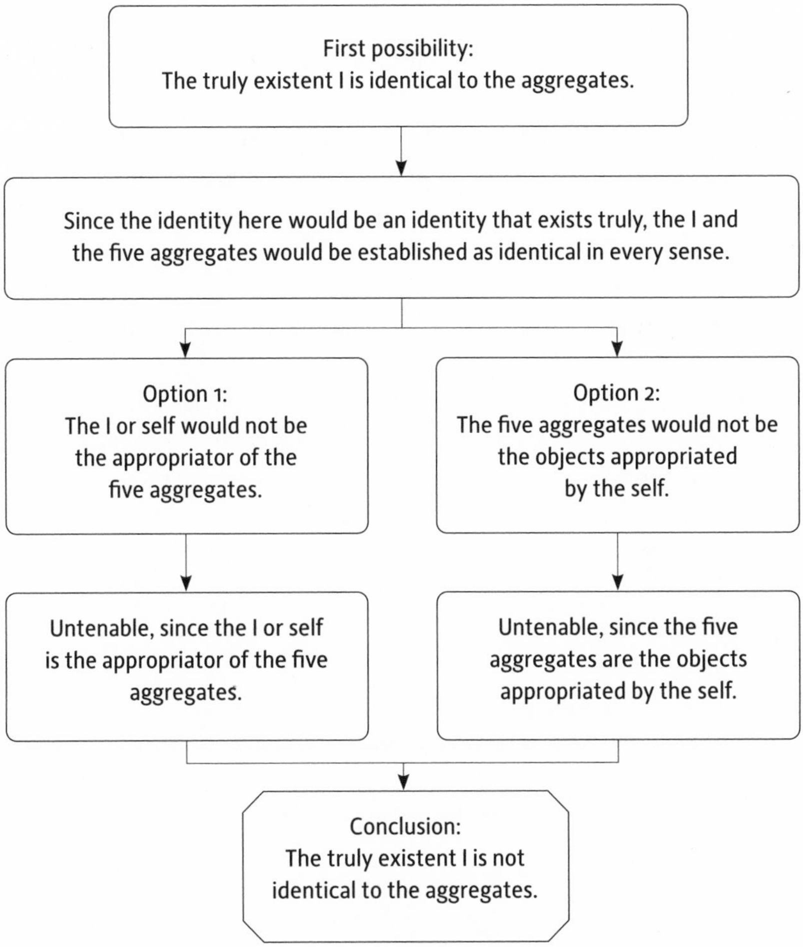
First possibility:
The truly existent I is identical to the aggregates.
Since the identity here would be an identity that exists truly, the I and the five aggregates would be established as identical in every sense.
Option 1:
The I or self would not be the appropriator of the five aggregates.
Option 2:
The five aggregates would not be the objects appropriated by the self.
Untenable, since the I or self is the appropriator of the five aggregates.
Untenable, since the five aggregates are the objects appropriated by the self.
Conclusion:
The truly existent I is not identical to the aggregates.

(D) Moreover, if the self and the aggregates were a partless whole, then a person's body would also be partless. In that case, when the right arm moves, would the left arm move or not?

If their left arm would move, then this position would be refuted by the direct perception that sees that the left arm does not [necessarily] move when the right arm does. If their left arm would not move, then the body would have parts, one that moves and one that does not, [contradicting the position of the body as partless].[552]

Accordingly, the *Commentary on Validity* says:

> If the hand and so forth were to move,
> all would move.
> Since it is inappropriate for contradictory actions to exist in a single body,
> they are, on the contrary, established to be different.[553]

Furthermore, if partless particles were to exist, when a central particle is surrounded at the same time by six particles—above, below, and in the four directions—does the side of the central particle facing the eastern particle face the western particle or not?[554]

If it does not, then the central particle would have two parts, one facing the eastern particle and one not facing the western particle.[555] The position that it is partless would not hold.

If it does, then the positions occupied by those particles would be identical, and so the object resulting from the conglomeration of those particles would be the size of a single particle. In that case, all presentations of mountains, fences, and so forth would be infeasible.[556]

Accordingly, the *Twenty Verses* says:[557]

> When surrounded by six [particles] at the same time,
> a particle has six parts.
> If the six were at a single position,
> the conglomeration would be the size of just a particle.[558]

Argument D

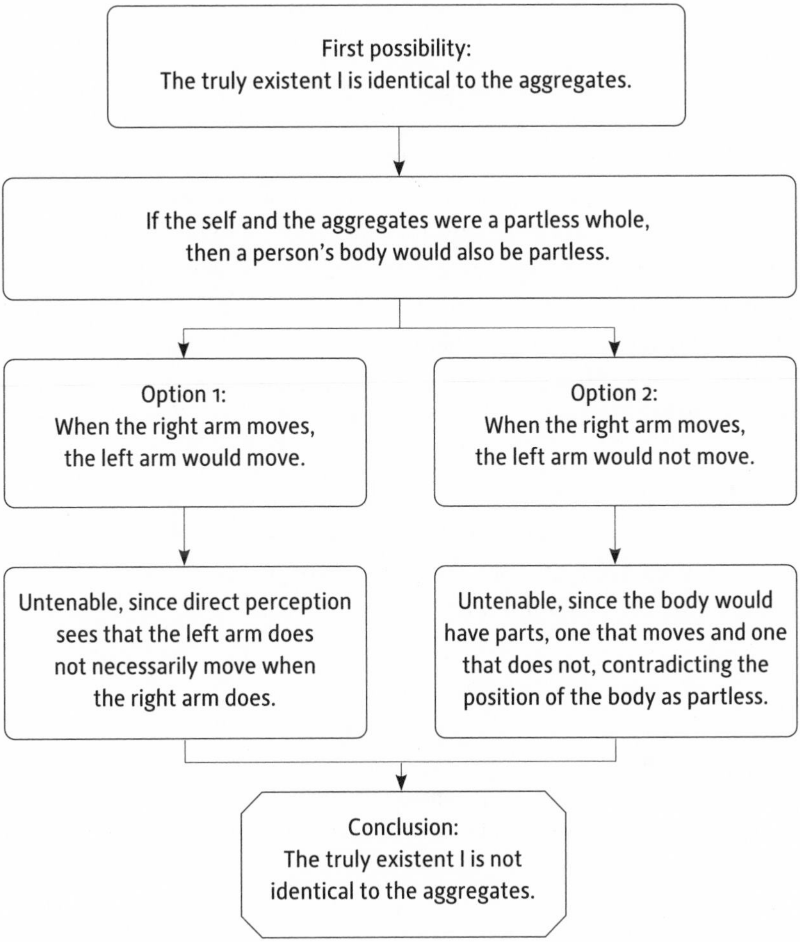

The fourth essential point: ascertaining the absence of being truly many[559]

Opinion: If the I as apprehended by self-grasping is not established as being identical to the five aggregates, it is established as being different from the five aggregates.

Response: (E) [For instance,] after the form aggregate and other [three] aggregates[560] have been eliminated one by one from the five aggregates, there remains something that you can still identify, stating, "*This* is the consciousness aggregate." Similarly, [if the I as apprehended by self-grasping were to exist], after eliminating the form aggregate and the other [four] aggregates one by one, there would have to be something remaining that you could identify as the self, saying, "*This* is the I as apprehended by self-grasping." However, nothing remains.[561] So you should come to the conclusion "The I as apprehended by self-grasping is not established as being different from the five aggregates."

If the I as apprehended by self-grasping were established as being different from the five aggregates, after eliminating the form aggregate and the rest of the aggregates one by one, there would have to be something—the I as apprehended by self-grasping—remaining that you could identify. For example, if there are a horse and a donkey, different unrelated objects, then after driving away the horse, there is something remaining that you can point to, saying, "*This* is the donkey." Accordingly, *Fundamental Verses on the Middle Way* says:

> It is simply inadmissible for the self
> to be different from the appropriated aggregates.
> If it were different, it should be apprehensible
> without them, yet it is not.[562]

Argument E

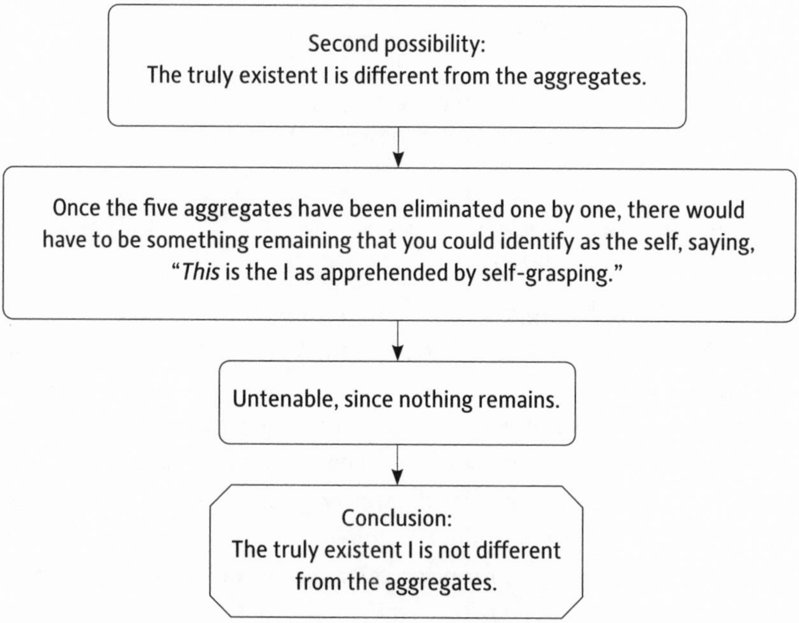

Second possibility:
The truly existent I is different from the aggregates.
Once the five aggregates have been eliminated one by one, there would have to be something remaining that you could identify as the self, saying, "*This* is the I as apprehended by self-grasping."
Untenable, since nothing remains.
Conclusion:
The truly existent I is not different from the aggregates.

In dependence on having thus analyzed by way of the four essential points, when you have ascertained that the I—as apprehended by the innate self-grasping—does not exist, you should single-pointedly sustain the continuum of that very ascertaining consciousness in the absence of laxity and excitement. And if the ascertaining consciousness weakens slightly, beginners should induce the ascertaining consciousness of the absence of true existence through the analysis by way of the four essential points again as before. Those who are advanced can induce the ascertainment of the absence of true existence—similar to what is attained through the analysis by way of the four essential points—by analyzing whether the I exists in the way it appears to the innate self-grasping.

At the end of such analysis, beginners will receive a fright, thinking, "Since the I or self is not established objectively upon the aggregates even in the slightest bit, the I does not exist at all!" This sense of alarm marks what is called "initial gaining of the Middle Way view." When this occurs, single-pointedly sustain the continuum of awareness that is qualified by two attributes—(1) from the perspective of the ascertaining mind, an acute ascertaining consciousness that ascertains the absence of inherent existence, and (2) from the perspective of the appearing object, a voidness that is a mere negation of true existence, the object of negation. This is the way to sustain the continuum of space-like meditative equipoise.[563]

During post-equipoise,[564] meditate on all phenomena, such as the I, as the play of magical illusions. In dependence on having induced the strong ascertaining consciousness of the absence of true existence during meditative equipoise, train during post-equipoise so that whatever appears dawns as the play of a magician's illusion—it appears but is a falsity devoid of true existence.

How to delineate the selflessness of phenomena and meditate on it

This is explained in two parts: how to delineate the emptiness of inherent existence of compounded phenomena and meditate on it, and how to delineate the emptiness of inherent existence of uncompounded phenomena and meditate on it.

Phenomena	Compounded phenomena[565]	Matter e.g., my coarse body
		Consciousness e.g., today's consciousness
		Nonassociated compositional factors e.g., a year
	Uncompounded phenomena[566] e.g., space	

How to delineate the emptiness of inherent existence of compounded phenomena and meditate on it

There are three types of compounded phenomena: matter, consciousness, and nonassociated compositional factors.[567]

Matter

Using my body as an illustration, if my body were established from its own side—without being merely imputed by conception upon this coarse form of flesh and bones that is simply a collection of the five limbs[568]—would it be established as identical to or different from this coarse form?

If my body were established as identical to this coarse form, since this form that is a mere collection of the five limbs is produced from the parents' semen and egg, then even the drop of semen and ovum that serves as the basis of entry for the consciousness would be a coarse form of flesh and bones that is a mere collection of the five limbs too. And just as [the form that is a mere collection of the five limbs] has five limbs, the body would also be five bodies, [each] a collection of the five limbs.

If my body were established as different from this coarse form, then after eliminating the head and the other limbs one by one, there would have to be something remaining that you could point to, saying, "*This* is the body," but nothing remains.

Having induced the ascertaining consciousness thinking, "The body as apprehended by self-grasping *does not exist at all*," sustain the continuum of this awareness as before.

Consciousness

Using today's consciousness as an illustration, if today's consciousness that is established from its own side—without being merely imputed by conception upon today's daytime and nighttime consciousnesses—were to exist,[569] would it be established as identical to or different from today's daytime and nighttime consciousnesses?

If it were established as identical to today's daytime and nighttime consciousnesses, then today's nighttime consciousness would exist upon today's daytime consciousness.[570]

If it were established as different from today's daytime and nighttime consciousnesses, then after eliminating today's daytime and nighttime consciousnesses one by one, there would have to be something remaining that you could point to, saying, "*This* is today's consciousness," but nothing remains.

Having induced the ascertaining consciousness thinking, "The consciousness as apprehended by self-grasping *does not exist at all*," sustain the continuum of this awareness as before.

Nonassociated compositional factors

Using a year as an illustration, if a year that is established from its own side—without being merely imputed by conception upon twelve months, the basis of imputation of a year—were to exist, would it be established as identical to or different from the twelve months?

If it were established as identical to the twelve months, then just as there are twelve months, there would be twelve years too. For, the year would necessarily be identical to each of the twelve months, and just as there are twelve months in a year there would also be twelve years. Recall the statement:[571]

> If the aggregates were the self, then,
> since they are many, the selves would also be many.

It can be neatly modified to read:

> If the *months* were the *year*, then,
> since they are many, the *years* would also be many.

If it were established as different from the twelve months, then after eliminating the twelve months one by one, there should be something remaining that you could point to, saying, "*This* is the year," but nothing remains.

Having induced the ascertaining consciousness thinking, "Such a year *does not exist at all*," sustain the continuum of this awareness as before.

OBJECTION: Well, if after eliminating the twelve months one by one, nothing remains to which you could point stating, "*This* is the year," then the year would not exist at all.

REPLY: That would not be the case, because not finding the imputed object when it is sought means that it does not exist *truly*; it does not mean that it does not exist *at all*.

QUESTION: Well then, how does the year exist?

ANSWER: It exists as a mere designation or convention that is imputed in dependence on the twelve months, and its existing conventionally is enough for it to exist. Even when one seeks the imputed object [with respect to] the designation "year," it cannot be found. Accordingly, the *Precious Garland* says:

> Because forms are merely designations,
> space is also merely a designation.
> Without the elements, how could forms exist?
> Therefore even mere designations do not exist.[572]

HOW TO DELINEATE THE EMPTINESS OF INHERENT EXISTENCE OF UNCOMPOUNDED PHENOMENA AND MEDITATE ON IT

Using space as an illustration, since space has many parts, such as the space in the center and in the cardinal and intermediate directions, if space that is independently existent—without being merely imputed by conception upon those parts—were to exist, it would be established as either identical to or different from those parts.

If it were established as identical to those parts, then since it would be a partless whole that is identical to those parts, space in the eastern direction and space in the western direction would be one. In that case, if it rained in the east, it would also rain in the west. Since there would be many incongruities such as this, space is not established as identical to its parts.

If it were established as different from those parts, then after eliminating those parts of space one by one, there would have to be something remaining that you could point to saying, "*This* is space," but nothing remains.

Therefore, having induced [through the force of] analysis the ascertaining consciousness of the absence of true existence thinking, "Space that is established from its own side *does not exist at all*," sustain the continuum of this awareness.

In brief, the *yoga of space-like meditative equipoise* entails sustaining single-pointedly the continuum of the ascertaining consciousness that ascertains that all phenomena of saṃsāra and nirvāṇa—the I, the aggregates, mountains, fences, houses, neighborhoods, and so forth—have not even an iota of existence from their own side[573] and are devoid of an existence that is not merely imputed by conception; whereas the *yoga of illusion-like post-equipoise* entails understanding all objects that appear during post-equipoise are in the nature of falsities, devoid of true existence, arising in dependence on the aggregation of causes and conditions.

Maintaining the continua of these two yogas, you will produce a meditative equipoise that is conjoined with the bliss of physical and mental pliancy induced by the force of analysis. This very state is posited as full-fledged special insight.[574]

Conclusion

Turning your attention to Guru Munīndra above your crown, recite the following as many times as possible:

> To Guru Conqueror Śākyamuni, I pay homage, make offerings, and go for refuge.

Think:

> Induced by my supplications, there emerges from Guru Munīndra a second figure of Guru Munīndra, who absorbs into me, whereby my form clearly becomes that of Guru Munīndra. Radiating from the *hūṃ* at my heart, light rays strike all sentient beings surrounding me and place them in the state of Guru Munīndra. I and all sentient beings, each visualized as Munīndra,

> have at the heart a moon disc, upon which is a white *a* marked with a yellow *hūṃ*. It is encircled by the mantra *Oṃ mune mune mahāmunaye svāhā.*

Focusing your attention on the mantra, recite it as many times as you can. To conclude the session, recite dedication verses such as:

> By this virtue, may I quickly
> achieve the state of Guru Buddha and
> place all sentient beings without exception
> in that state.

With the strong aspiration to fulfill your and others' short-term and ultimate wishes, dedicate the virtues arisen from your practice. If you can, perform prayers such as the *King of Prayers of Excellent Deeds.*

What to do between the sessions

Between the sessions, read the scriptures and commentaries that present *special insight,* and perform the other activities as explained above [in the section on how to rely on a spiritual guide].

Epilogue

17 | Concluding Advice

I NOW PRESENT a summary of the general path. Your meditation on the lower paths should fuel your desire to attain the higher paths. When you listen to explanations that elucidate the higher paths, your desire to practice the lower paths must be intensified. When meditating on the paths, you must, by eliminating conceptualizations, keep your mind balanced.

Avoiding pitfalls along the journey

When your respect for the spiritual guide leading you on the path seems to wane, since relying on the spiritual guide has been explained as the root of all excellences, you should strive in it.

Similarly, when your enthusiasm for practice dwindles, principally meditate on the topics of the precious human rebirth endowed with the freedoms and privileges.

If you find yourself obsessively caught up with this life, principally meditate on impermanence and the drawbacks of the lower rebirths.

If you seem to neglect the obligations you have pledged to honor, meditate mainly on karma and its results.

If your disillusionment with saṃsāra is feeble, since your striving for liberation has come to nothing but empty talk, reflect on the drawbacks of saṃsāra.

If your desire to enact the welfare of sentient beings is not fervent no matter what you do, since wishing bodhicitta is said to be the root of the Mahāyāna, train in it along with its causes.

If you have taken the bodhisattva vows and yet seem to be tightly fettered by grasping at signs when you train in the bodhisattvas' deeds,[575] destroy such apprehension with the rational consciousness that targets grasping at signs and train in space-like emptiness and illusion-like emptiness.[576]

If your mind cannot rest on the object of observation and seems to fall under the sway of distraction, train mainly in single-pointed stability.

These nuggets of advice have been provided by earlier masters. Based on the above illustrations, you should deduce how to avoid the pitfalls that I have not explicitly addressed.

Striking a balance between learning and meditation

Based on the belief that it is essential to understand the Dharma in order to practice it, you may attempt to dispel your lack of learning by just taking studying as your main goal. However, mere study does not prevent afflictions such as attachment, anger, pride, and jealousy. Through the force of negative karma motivated by those afflictions, you will fall into the lower rebirths. Or, based on the belief that it is essential to tame your mental continuum in order to practice the Dharma, you may attempt to take only meditation as your main practice without paying attention to your lack of learning. However, to do so would be a serious mistake too, for your ignorance of the obligations stipulated by the three vows will lead to your mind being tainted by downfalls. Therefore, in brief, you must render your mind malleable toward all classes of virtue impartially.

When to enter tantra

In this way, having trained well in the common path, you will possess the armor-like joyous effort that endows you with the ability to remain in the hells for eons for the sake of dispelling the suffering of a single sentient being. However, when you bring to mind how sentient beings are pained by suffering, you will think, "If I attain the state of a perfect complete buddha, I will be able to free countless sentient beings from suffering in every instant. If only I could become a buddha now!" When this strong yearning occurs, enter the Vajrayāna. For, in dependence on the Vajrayāna path, you will easily complete the two collections of merit and wisdom without having to spend three countless eons doing so.

How best to extract the essence of your existence

Taking the topics—beginning from how to rely on a spiritual guide until special insight—as experiential instructions,[577] by meditating daily, in four sessions or at least one, elicit transformative experiential realizations in these stages of the path. Doing so is the best method for you to extract the essence of your physical human basis endowed with freedoms.

18 | Colophon

I say:

This explicit instruction on the stages of the path to enlightenment
that subsumes the essential points of all the scriptures
is written at the persistent request of several intelligent individuals
and to refresh my own memory.

For whatever inadequacies there are—
failure to explain what should be explained, wrong exposition, poor composition,
incoherence, excessive clarity, and so forth—
I beg the forgiveness of the root and lineage masters, ḍākas and ḍākinīs, and Dharma protectors.

By whatever merit that has arisen
by striving with my three doors in this endeavor,
may the Kadam teachings that are complete, unerring, and systematic
flourish without limit in all directions!

By the force of this virtue, may all beings
never run the risk of being misled by false paths.
May they instead follow the paths of the great trailblazers and
swiftly attain the state of the omniscient conquerors!

May the power of the gods and humans
who strive to uphold, maintain, continually increase, and guard
the teachings of the Dharma king Tsongkhapa greatly expand,
and may great happiness and excellence prevail in the world!

The *Swift Path to Omniscience: Explicit Instructions on the Stages of the Path* was composed in the Kadam Phodrang by the expounder of the Dharma, Venerable Losang Yeshé—who supplemented the *Easy Path to Omniscience: An Explicit Instruction on the Stages of the Path* with scriptures and reasoning, and ornamented it with oral instructions—at the repeated earnest exhortations of the chant master of Gyalgatsal, Losang Gyaltsen, and others, who reiterated, "We need a very clear and explicit lamrim that is not constrained by poetry's rhyme and meter, one slightly more extensive than the explicit instruction composed by the omniscient Paṇchen." May it be virtuous and auspicious!

Since it seems there were some errors, such as spelling mistakes, when written down, the text was edited in accordance with the *Easy Path to Omniscience*. I myself read the manuscript and corrected it.

Appendix 1: Outline of the *Swift Path*

I. An explanation of how to develop conviction in the enumeration and sequence of the paths through an account of the lineage masters who are their sources

II. An actual explanation of how to train your mind in the stages of the paths after having developed conviction in their enumeration and sequence

- A. The way to rely on a spiritual guide, the root of the path
  - 1. What to do during the session
    - a. Preparation
      - i. Cleaning the room and arranging representations of the enlightened body, speech, and mind
      - ii. Laying out offerings that have been obtained rightfully without deceit and displaying them beautifully
      - iii. Sitting upon a comfortable seat in the eightfold posture or any convenient posture and cultivating refuge, bodhicitta, and the four immeasurables
      - iv. Visualizing the merit field
      - v. Offering the seven-limbed practice—which distills the essentials of accruing the collections of merit and wisdom and purifying misdeeds—and a maṇḍala
      - vi. Imbuing your mind with the supplication according to the oral instructions
    - b. The actual meditation on relying on a spiritual guide
      - i. The benefits of relying on a spiritual guide
      - ii. The drawbacks of not relying on a spiritual guide
      - iii. The way to rely on the spiritual guide through thought
        - a) Training in the root, faith
        - b) Recollecting the great kindness of the spiritual guide
      - iv. The way to rely on the spiritual guide through action
    - c. Conclusion

2. What to do between the sessions

B. Having relied on a spiritual guide, the stages of how to train your mind
  1. Exhortation to extract the essence of a physical basis endowed with the freedoms and privileges
    a. What to do during the session
      i. Preparation
      ii. The actual meditation on extracting the essence of a physical basis endowed with the freedoms and privileges
        a) Reflecting on how a physical basis endowed with the freedoms and privileges is greatly meaningful
          1) Reflecting on the eight freedoms
          2) Reflecting on the ten privileges
        b) Reflecting on how a physical basis endowed with the freedoms and privileges is difficult to find
      iii. Conclusion
    b. What to do between the sessions
  2. How to extract such an essence
    a. How to train your mind in the path in common with that of persons with small capacity
      i. What to do during the session
        a) Preparation
        b) The actual meditation on the path in common with that of persons with small capacity
          1) Reflecting on impermanence in the form of death
          2) Reflecting on the suffering of lower rebirths
          3) Training in going to the Three Jewels for refuge
          4) Generating the faith of conviction in karma and its results
        c) Conclusion
      ii. What to do between the sessions
    b. How to train your mind in the path in common with that of persons with medium capacity
      i. Generating the mindset that seeks liberation
        a) What to do during the session
          1) Preparation
          2) The actual meditation on the mindset that seeks liberation

i) Reflecting on the general sufferings of saṃsāra
ii) Reflecting on the specific sufferings of saṃsāra
3) Conclusion
b) What to do between the sessions
ii. Delineating the nature of the path leading to liberation
a) What to do during the session
1) Preparation
2) The actual meditation on the nature of the path leading to liberation
3) Conclusion
b) What to do between the sessions
c. How to train your mind in the stages of the path of persons with great capacity
i. How to train in the mind aspiring for enlightenment
a) The actual way to generate the mind aspiring for enlightenment
1) How to generate the mind aspiring for enlightenment by means of the sevenfold cause-and-effect instruction
i) What to do during the session
(a) Preparation
(b) The actual meditation on the sevenfold cause-and-effect instruction
(c) Conclusion
ii) What to do between the sessions
2) How to generate the mind aspiring for enlightenment by means of equalizing and exchanging self and others
b) How to uphold the mind aspiring for enlightenment through ritual
1) How to obtain the vows that have not been obtained
2) How to guard against degeneration the vows that have been obtained
ii. How to train in the deeds after having generated the mind aspiring for enlightenment
a) How to train in the bodhisattvas' deeds
1) What to do during the session
i) Preparation

ii) The actual meditation on the bodhisattvas' deeds in general
(a) The practice of the six perfections, which brings one's own mind to maturation
(b) The practice of the four means of gathering disciples, which brings the minds of others to maturation
iii) Conclusion
2) What to do between the sessions
b) How to train in the deeds of the last two perfections in particular
1) How to train in calm abiding, which has the nature of meditative concentration
i) What to do during the session
(a) Preparation
(b) The actual meditation on calm abiding, which has the nature of meditative concentration
(c) Conclusion
ii) What to do between the sessions
2) How to train in special insight, which has the nature of wisdom
i) What to do during the session
(a) Preparation
(b) The actual meditation on special insight, which has the nature of wisdom
(1) How to delineate the selflessness of persons and meditate on it
(2) How to delineate the selflessness of phenomena and meditate on it
(i) How to delineate the emptiness of inherent existence of compounded phenomena and meditate on it
(ii) How to delineate the emptiness of inherent existence of uncompounded phenomena and meditate on it
(c) Conclusion
ii) What to do between the sessions

Appendix 2. The Signs and Exemplifying Marks of the Buddha's Body

The thirty-two signs and eighty exemplifying marks of the Buddha's body are listed in chapter 8 of Maitreya's *Ornament for Clear Realizations*. The following explanation is taken from Gyaltsab's *Ornament of the Essence*,[578] which is an explanation of Haribhadra's *Clear Meaning*,[579] an Indian commentary on Maitreya's *Ornament for Clear Realizations*.

The thirty-two signs of the Buddha's body

1. His hands and feet possess the signs of wheels complete with a thousand spokes, a hub, and a rim, as if they were carved in bone or ivory, because when he was a learner he practiced seeing off and receiving gurus, offering himself as a retinue servant, and so forth.
2. The two soles of his feet, free from depressions, rest evenly on the ground, similar to [the underside of] the tortoise, because he has consummated mental commitment in the perfect adoption of the three vows.
3. The digits of his hands and feet are joined with webs like those of the king of geese because he has consummated activities due to having relied upon the four means of gathering disciples: giving, agreeable speech, and so forth.
4. His hands and feet are smooth and tender because he has offered sublime food, drinks, and the like.
5. He possesses seven elevated areas—since the areas of the backs of the two hands and tops of the two feet, the two regions between the shoulders, and the nape are fleshy and thus elevated—because he has offered creamy delicacies[580] and so forth.
6. The digits of his hands and feet are long because he has consummated the practice of liberating living beings who are to be killed, bound, and so forth.
7. His heels are broad because he has helped to protect others' lives.

8. His body is large and upright, measuring seven cubits tall and free from crookedness, because he has abandoned killing.[581]
9. His kneecaps and anklebones do not protrude outward because he has perfectly adopted the virtuous qualities of generosity and so forth.
10. The hairs of his body point upward individually because he has promoted the perfect adoption of virtue in others.
11. His calves are proportionate, fully developed, rounded, and not debilitated, like the Enaya antelope's, because he has given to others products created through the knowledge of healing, crafts, and so forth.[582]
12. His arms are long and beautiful, with his hands reaching his knees even without him bending the body, because he has not rejected beings who beg for wealth and resources from him.
13. His secret organ is retracted in a sheath like that of the elephant and the wise horse, because he has caused all beings to behave in a chaste manner and safeguarded confidential words to which others are not privy.
14. He has pure and clear skin of golden hue, because he has given sublime mats to others.
15. His skin is smooth like highly refined gold and silver, because he has offered excellences such as fine houses and inestimable mansions.
16. His body hairs curl clockwise individually, without a single pore containing two hairs, because he has completely abandoned bustle, distractions, and so forth.
17. His face is adorned with a treasure hair between his eyebrows—which is smooth, white, soft, three cubits or more in length if extended, curls clockwise if released, with its tip pointing upward, the size of an *āmalaka* fruit, and has the aspect of a silver protrusion—because he has honored all higher beings in accordance with their status as human beings and placed them in positions where they deserve.[583]
18. His torso is broad like the lion's because he has not ridiculed others with haughty words in any way.
19. The tops of his shoulders are rounded, curved, and well connected like the neck of a golden vase, with a network of inconspicuous veins, because he has trained and acted in accordance with others' kind counsel.
20. The region between the tops of his shoulders is broad because he has provided others with medicine, doctors, and the like.

21. He experiences and knows the best of tastes, even with respect to the unpalatable, because he has nursed sick beings, served them, and so forth.
22. His body is well proportioned like the *nyagrodha* tree,[584] the length of the body equaling his arm span, because he has perfectly caused others to construct groves, parks, and so forth.
23. He has a crown protrusion that is round, symmetrical, and curls clockwise, because his offering of temples, fine houses, and so forth has been exceptional.
24. He has a long tongue that is able to touch the opening of his ear and his hairline, and is the color of the red *utpala* flower, because he has spoken soft and pleasant words smoothly over three countless eons.
25. He has the melodious voice of Brahmā that has the five branches—(1) speech that will be known and thoroughly known, (2) speech that is worth listening to and is devoid of discordances, (3) deep and resounding speech, (4) speech that is mesmerizing, not unruly, and is pleasant to the ears, and (5) unconfused and clear speech—because he has caused sentient beings of all the world systems to understand the excellent Dharma in accordance with their own language with a single speech.
26. His cheeks are as round and full as a mirror disc, like the lion's, because he has abandoned senseless talk.
27. His teeth are white because he has honored and praised all beings.
28. His teeth are even, without some being high and others low, because he has pure livelihood in which the five wrong livelihoods have been abandoned.[585]
29. His teeth are well set, with no gaps between them, because he has always used truthful words over three countless eons.
30. He possesses forty teeth, twenty above and twenty below, because he has abandoned divisive words over three countless eons.
31. His eyes are like azure gems, the black and white portions are not mixed, and they are free from red streaks, because he has viewed all sentient beings like an only child.
32. His eyelashes are like the cow's, the upper and lower lashes spread well and are untangled, because he has viewed sentient beings without anger, grasping, confusion, and so forth over a long period.

The eighty exemplifying marks of the Buddha's body

1. His nails are copper-colored because he has consummated the abandonment of attachment to all compounded phenomena.
2. His nails are glossy because he has consummated the extraordinary thought of securing the long-term benefit of all sentient beings.
3. His nails are convex and free of ridges because he has been born in the best of human classes.
4. His digits are rounded because he has consummated all methods of practice without committing any misdeeds.
5. His digits are well developed because he has completed the collection of roots of virtue in the past.
6. His digits are tapered because he has perfected sequential engagement in the classes of realization of the three vehicles.
7. His veins are inconspicuous because he has guarded against the ten nonvirtuous paths of actions of the body and so forth and against wrong livelihood.
8. His veins are free from knots[586] because he has untied the knots of the afflictions and become freed.
9. His smaller ankle bones[587] do not protrude because he possesses intelligence with respect to very hidden phenomena, having realized profound secret essential points.
10. His legs are not unequal in length, because he has liberated beings from all locations difficult to reach.
11. He possesses the gait of a lion because he has been skillful in outshining human beings.
12. He possesses the gait of an elephant because he has been skillful in outshining maleficent nāgas and so forth.
13. He possesses the gait of a swan because he has been skillful in traveling through space like a bird.
14. He possesses the gait of a bull because he has been skillful in leading beings, serving as sentient beings' guide to their desired destinations.
15. He walks to and fro in a clockwise manner because he proceeds in accordance with the path of circumambulation.
16. He walks beautifully because he has been skillful in being pleasant and beautiful to behold when walking.
17. He proceeds without swaying because he is always free of a crooked mind that engages in double-dealing.

18. His body is elegant—well developed and dignified—because he has perfectly expressed others' excellent qualities.
19. His body is as though thoroughly washed, clean and pure, because he has not been defiled by misdeeds of body, speech, and mind.
20. His body is balanced, its height, girth, and other measurements precise and fitting, because he has taught Dharma in accordance with the minds of the trainees.
21. He is clean, with a body that is pure, because his behavior of body, speech, mind, and so forth has been immaculate.
22. His body is soft because his mind has been compassionate.
23. His body is pure because his pure mind has been free from stains.
24. He possesses signs that are complete because he has thoroughly completed all the subduing qualities that destroy the afflictions and conceptualizations in his mind.
25. His body is well built, broad and comely in its features, because he has revealed to others excellent qualities that are vast (due to being extensive) and beautiful (due to being pleasing).
26. His strides are even, with a common span, because he has developed impartiality toward all sentient beings.
27. His two eyes are clear, with no specks and other blemishes, because he has taught pure Dharma that generates only excellent qualities.
28. His body is very youthful-looking because he has taught Dharma using illustrations that are easy to understand.
29. His body is not slack because he has kept his mind dauntless in the face of difficulty.
30. His body is well developed because he has created roots of virtue superior to those of all the worlds.
31. His body is very firm, his flesh not flabby, because he has extinguished the karma for taking rebirth.
32. His primary limbs, such as arms and legs, and his secondary limbs, such as digit joints, are very distinct, their components differentiated, because he has distinctly taught the forward and reverse cause-and-effect processes of dependent arising for the sake of freeing trainees from saṃsāra.
33. His eyesight is without visual aberration of adventitious defilements and is clear, because he has completely taught the meaning of the words based upon very pure high rebirths and beatitude.

34. His waist is circular because he has caused excellent ethics in his students.
35. His waist is appropriately sized because he has not been polluted or defiled by the faults of saṃsāra, having destroyed them with antidotes.
36. His waist is without depressions, not overly long, because he has destroyed the inflatedness of pride.
37. His belly is flat, without highs and lows, because he has turned away from the limited and taught limitlessly the Dharma that is to be known.
38. His navel is deep because he has realized the profound Dharma.
39. The creases of his navel curl clockwise because he has caused his students to uphold the instructions in accordance with his own conduct.
40. He possesses beautiful conduct because he has caused beautiful activity of the three doors in all his retinue.
41. He possesses pure conduct of the three doors because he has developed a mind that, being stainless, is pure.
42. He has no moles or black marks on his body because he does not teach wrong paths or teach the subduing Dharma in an untimely manner, such as subduing trainees at an inopportune time.
43. His hands are smooth like cotton because he has taught the Dharma that serves as the cause for attaining magnificence of the body, speech, and mind.
44. The lines on his hands are radiant because he has attained the state of a great ascetic who is endowed with the radiance of having developed impartiality toward his retinue and others' retinues.
45. The lines on his hands are deep and visible from a long distance because he has abided in the culmination of realizing the profound Dharma.
46. The lines on his hands are long because he has granted short-term happiness and long-term benefit and because he will also perfectly give pure teachings again and again in the future.
47. His face is not overly long because he has taught myriad trainings in accordance with the many levels of the trainees.
48. His lips are as red as the *bimba* fruit in which reflections of forms can appear because he has realized that all worlds of environments and inhabitants are like a reflection.[588]
49. His tongue is supple because he has subdued all trainees with smooth words.
50. His tongue is very slender because he has taught excellent qualities by means of a multitude of logical reasonings.

51. His tongue is red because he has taught a subduing Dharma for destroying afflictions that is difficult to fathom by childish beings who grasp at the I and mine.[589]
52. His voice is thunderous because he has no trepidation, apprehensiveness, or fear that entertains the thought "I will conceal my shortcomings."
53. His voice is pleasant, supple, and smooth, because he has spoken pleasantly through speech that is delightful to the ears.
54. His canine teeth are curved because he has exhaustively restrained the nine entanglements with saṃsāra—attachment and so forth.[590]
55. His canine teeth are sharp because he has tamed strong afflictions in beings who are difficult to tame.
56. His canine teeth are white because he has acted to destroy afflictions with the wholesome subduing Dharma.
57. His canine teeth are even, not differing in length, because he has abided on the ground that realizes the equality of saṃsāra and nirvāṇa.
58. His canine teeth are tapered because he has perfectly taught the serial clear realizations of the three vehicles through their stages.
59. His nose is prominent because he has abided in the supreme wisdom realizing emptiness that is complete in the factor of method.
60. His nose is clean, free of mucus and the like, because his trainees have excellent pure conviction.
61. His eyes are wide because he has taught the vast, boundless Mahāyāna Dharma.
62. His eyelashes are thick because he has led countless multitudes of sentient beings from the abode of saṃsāra.
63. His eyes are such that the white and black parts are defined, unmixed, like the lovely complete petals of a lotus, because he has pleased all young female migrating beings who are difficult to please—gods, demigods, and humans—since he is worthy of praise by them.
64. His eyebrows are long because he has constantly watched migrating beings through checking, "How will they be in the future?"
65. His eyebrows are smooth because he is skilled in the gentle subduing Dharma through subduing with the gentle Dharma that does not rely on the five fires and the like.[591]
66. His eyebrows are glossy because his mental continuum has been thoroughly moistened by virtue.

67. The hairs of his eyebrows are even, not differing in length, because he has seen the faults of afflictions.
68. His arms are long and well developed because he has turned away sentient beings' worst threats—the causes of saṃsāra generally and of bad migrations in particular.
69. His ears are equal, not differing in length or shape, because he has been victorious over attachment and other afflictions, which are difficult to conquer.
70. His ear faculties are unimpaired because he has set all trainees in happiness without their minds degenerating.
71. His forehead is well defined and his hairline stands out well because he has not been influenced by all that is fabricated by views holding to extremes, such as the sixty-two bad views.[592]
72. His forehead is broad because he has defeated all proponents of wrong views.
73. His head is well formed, like a parasol, because he has completed the best of prayers wherein one prays to attain buddhahood for others' welfare.
74. His hair is as black as bees because he has turned away from all craving for objects—forms, sounds, and so forth.
75. His hair is dense without thinning patches because he has exhaustively abandoned the dormant obstructions that are to be abandoned by the path of seeing and the path of meditation.
76. His hair is smooth because he has understood the teachings with a smooth mind that is without the roughness of holding to extremes.
77. His hair is untangled because his mind is not disturbed by attachment and so forth.
78. His hair is not bristly or stiff because he has spoken words that are always free from harshness, having exhaustively abandoned harsh words.
79. His hair is fragrant because he has scattered before the Three Jewels flowers that serve as causes of enlightenment.
80. His hands and feet are adorned with vajra-like *śrīvatsas* on his thumbs and big toes, squarish *svastikas* on the palms of his hands and soles of the feet, and *nandyāvartas* containing seven clockwise-swirling patterns on the rest of his toes and fingers, because his exalted body has been beautiful in all ways.

Appendix 3: Sixty-Four Qualities of the Buddha's Speech

The following explanation is taken from Thokmé Sangpo's commentary on the *Ornament for the Mahāyāna Sūtras*,[593] in which Maitreya mentioned the sixty inconceivable branches of the Buddha's speech. While mostly identical to Vasubandhu's commentary on the same treatise,[594] Thokmé Sangpo's explanation cites four additional qualities to yield a total of sixty-four qualities in accordance with the *Teaching on the Tathāgata's Inconceivable Secrets Sūtra.*

1. The Buddha's speech is soft because it supports the roots of virtue of sentient beings.
2. It is gentle because it gives rise to happiness in this life as soon as it is heard.
3. It is lovely because its meaning is good.
4. It is inviting because its wording is good.
5. It is pure because it is supported on the wisdom that is supreme among all that are supramundane.
6. It is stainless because it has abandoned the causes of mistaken prattle—namely, dormant afflictions and the latencies deposited by them.
7. It is clear because its phrasing is widely understood.
8. It is sonorous because it has the power to destroy the views of the tīrthikas.
9. It is worthy of being heard because one will definitely emerge from saṃsāra by practicing according to what is taught.
10. It is unassailable because it cannot be subjugated by any opponent.
11. It is pleasing because it is delightful to hear.
12. It is taming because it acts as an antidote to afflictions.
13. It is without harshness because it is easy to put into practice and teaches guidelines that bring great benefit.

14. It is kindly because it teaches the method for deliverance from downfalls when one transgresses the precepts.
15. It is subduing because it teaches all three vehicles for the sake of subduing those who hold the three lineages.[595]
16. It is sweet to the ear because one's mind will not be distracted to anything else when one hears it.
17. It brings physical fulfillment because it generates calm abiding.
18. It brings mental fulfillment because it generates the joy of special insight.
19. It gladdens the heart because it severs doubts.
20. It creates joy and happiness because it definitely eliminates that which is wrong.
21. It is not dissatisfying because regret will not arise if one practices according to what is taught.
22. It is to be known because it is the support for the excellent wisdom arisen from hearing.
23. It is to be understood because it is the support for the excellent wisdom arisen from contemplation.
24. It is illuminating because it teaches without avarice.
25. It is gladdening because it gladdens the āryas.
26. It is very gladdening because it gladdens ordinary beings.
27. It is informing because it teaches the inconceivable Dharma regarding reality, the karmas establishing diverse external things, and so forth.
28. It is instructive because it teaches the inconceivable Dharma regarding the aggregates and so forth.
29. It is logical because it does not contradict valid cognition.
30. It is relevant because it teaches Dharma in a manner that is suited to the trainee.
31. It is not redundant because it is not meaningless.
32. It sounds like the roar of a lion because it frightens all tīrthikas.
33. It sounds like the trumpeting of an elephant because it is expansive like the trumpeting of the great celestial elephant called Airāvaṇa,[596] with no sign of scratchiness or hoarseness.
34. It sounds like the roar of a dragon because it is splendid.
35. It sounds like the call of the nāga king because it is worthy of apprehension.
36. It sounds like the song of the gandharvas because it is pleasant.

37. It sounds like the call of the *kalaviṅka* bird because it is piercing and formidable, in that its meaning speaks to oneself and one longs to hear it when it stops.
38. It sounds like the prominent voice of Brahmā because it is audible even across long distances.
39. It sounds like the call of the *jīvañjīva* bird because it accomplishes all aims when heard.
40. It sounds like the voice of the king of gods because it is authoritative.
41. It sounds like the sound of a drum because it heralds victory over all māras and antagonists.
42. It is not conceited because it is free from pride even when praised.
43. It is not self-belittling because it is free from anger even when criticized.
44. It engages all sounds because it predicts all events of the three times.
45. It is uncorrupted because it does not speak out of forgetfulness.
46. It is not incomplete because it speaks to trainees whenever there is a need.
47. It is undaunted because it disregards gain and honor.
48. It is not feeble because it is fearless.
49. It is joyful because it teaches the Dharma tirelessly.
50. It is pervasive because it is expert at all subjects.
51. It is benevolent because it enacts the welfare of those who have not generated roots of virtue.
52. It is continuous because it is uninterrupted.
53. It is related because it manifests in diverse forms.
54. It fulfills all sounds because trainees understand a single teaching in their own languages.
55. It satisfies all faculties because trainees understand the meaning expressed by a single teaching in accordance with their own faculties.
56. It is beyond reproach because it fulfills its promises.
57. It is unwavering because it speaks to trainees in a timely manner.
58. It is unhurried because it does not speak hastily.
59. It resounds to the entire gathering because it is equally heard regardless of whether those gathered are near or far away.
60. It has the best of all aspects because it speaks by using examples that are consistent with the trainees' minds in order that they realize its meaning.

If sixty-four qualities are enumerated, four additional qualities are inserted before the last of the sixty qualities, yielding the following:

60. It pacifies attachment.
61. It calms hatred.
62. It eliminates ignorance.
63. It annihilates māras.
64. It has the best of all aspects.

Notes

1. Tsongkhapa, *Great Exposition*, 2. To view this statement in context, see Tsong-kha-pa, *Great Treatise*, 1:35–36.
2. Tenzin Gyatso, *Path to Bliss*, 25.
3. According to the *Unraveling the Intent Sūtra* (Kangyur D 106), the first Dharma wheel taught at Vārāṇasī, consisting of teachings of the four truths and the like, was given for the sake of Hīnayāna trainees; the second Dharma wheel taught on Vulture Peak, consisting of the Perfection of Wisdom sūtras and the like, was given for the sake of Mahāyāna trainees; and the third Dharma wheel taught at Vaiśālī and other places, which includes *Unraveling the Intent* itself, was given for the sake of both Hīnayāna and Mahāyāna trainees. See English translation at 84000.co (Toh 106), 7.30. For an explanation of the three Dharma wheels, see Sopa and Hopkins, *Cutting Through Appearances*, 171–73.
4. *Mar skogs mar gyis mi thul / chos dred chos kyis mi thul.*
5. The Ganden Phodrang (Dga' ldan pho brang), "Ganden Palace," was the name for the Tibetan government between 1642 and 1959. Named after the residential quarters in Drepung Monastery for the holder of the Dalai Lama lineage, it nowadays refers to the personal office of His Holiness the Fourteenth Dalai Lama.
6. The most recent Paṇchen Lama is enumerated as the eleventh Paṇchen Lama in accordance with the Tashi Lhunpo system.
7. Könchok Gyaltsen (Dkon mchog rgyal mtshan) also served as Losang Yeshé's tutor and transmitted the lineage of the lamrim instructions to him.
8. For a discussion about the place of tenrim literature within the general lamrim genre, see Jackson, "The *bsTan rim* ('Stages of the Doctrine')." For historical background of the tenrim genre, see Jinpa, *Book of Kadam*, 4.
9. Considered a versified abstract of Tsongkhapa's *Middle-Length Exposition*, the *Essence of Excellent Discourses* is also informally known as the *Gomchen Lamrim* after its author, widely known as Dakpo Gomchen (Dwags po sgom chen), "the great meditator of Dakpo," who served as the second abbot of Dakpo Monastery in southeastern Tibet.
10. The *Essence of Refined Gold* is a commentary on Tsongkhapa's *Concise Exposition on the Stages of the Path to Enlightenment*, which is also known as the *Song of Spiritual Experience.*
11. The *Easy Path* was composed in response to Tsongkhapa's observation in *Great Exposition on the Stages of the Path to Enlightenment* that there was a need for "a separate concise presentation of what should be constantly maintained in meditation." See page 44.
12. The *Words of Mañjuśrī* is a commentary on the Third Dalai Lama Sönam Gyatso's *Essence of Refined Gold.*

13. Tenzin Gyatso, *Path to Bliss*, 20.
14. Maitreya's *Ornament for the Mahāyāna Sūtras* mentions ten qualities of a Mahāyāna spiritual guide: (1–3) having accomplished the three trainings of ethics, meditative concentration, and wisdom; (4) being erudite concerning the three scriptural baskets of discipline, discourses, and higher knowledge; (5) knowing reality; (6) possessing qualities surpassing those of the students; (7) being skillful in instructing students; (8) being motivated by pure love and compassion; (9) being enthusiastic about others' welfare; and (10) being tireless. For more details on the defining characteristics of a qualified teacher, see Tsong-kha-pa, *Great Treatise*, 1:70–75. Note that although "him" and "his" are sometimes used in this book when referring to the spiritual teacher, this usage of the male pronoun is for convenience and a spiritual guide can be of any gender.
15. See Tsong-kha-pa, *Great Treatise*, 1:86.
16. *Dgag bya.*
17. In this opening line, homage is paid to Guru Munīndra—one's guru or spiritual guide, who is inseparable in essence from Munīndra. The Sanskrit Munīndra, "Lord of Sages," is a way of referring to Buddhism's founder, Śākyamuni or Gautama Buddha. According to the rules of Sanskrit declension, application of the dative case here yields *gurumunīndrāya* rather than *gurumunīndraya*.
18. *Sugata* (*bde bar bshegs pa*), "well gone," is an epithet of the buddhas. In his commentary on *Amarakoṣa*, the renowned lexicon of Sanskrit composed by Amarasiṃha (ca. fifth century), the Buddhist monk-scholar Subhūticandra explains among many interpretations that buddhas may be considered "well gone" because they realize reality *well* with omniscient wisdom or they *go well* without ever returning to saṃsāra. Subhūticandra, *Wish-Granting Cow*, Tengyur D 4300, *se*, 255b2.
19. This is a verse of homage to Śākyamuni, "Śākya Sage," alluding to the Śākya clan that he was born into.
20. Ajitanātha (Mi pham mgon), "Invincible Protector," refers to Maitreya, who transmitted the Buddha's instructions on vast deeds—that is, the practices of generosity, ethics, and so forth.
21. Mañjughoṣa ('Jam pa'i dbyangs) is another name of Mañjuśrī ('Jam dpal), who transmitted the Buddha's instructions on the profound view—that is, the view of emptiness of true existence. Subsequent occurrences of the name are rendered as Mañjuśrī.
22. According to the cosmology described in the Abhidharma, each world system contains four major human continents. The southern continent Jambūdvīpa is where the human beings of Earth reside.
23. The sūtras, tantras, and Indian treatises are replete with references to persons going to, reaching, and abiding in the essence of enlightenment (*byang chub snying po*). Prior to attaining enlightenment, the Buddha is said to have performed "the deed of going to the essence of enlightenment" (*byang chub snying por gshegs pa'i mdzad pa*). While it is convenient to think of *essence of enlightenment* as a kind of spiritual attainment, its Sanskrit equivalent *bodhimaṇḍa* refers to a physical location according to Edgerton's entry on this term, which states that it is "the *platform* or *terrace* or *seat of enlightenment*, a name given to the spot under the bodhi tree where the Buddha sat when he became enlightened." See Edgerton, *Buddhist Hybrid Sanskrit Grammar and Dictionary*, 402.
24. Jangchup Rinchen (Byang chub rin chen), Wangchuk Gyaltsen (Dbang phyug rgyal mtshan), Sherab Dorjé (Shes rab rdo rje), and Chaktri Chok (Phyag khri mchog) are

the four well-known yogi disciples of Atiśa (*jo wo'i rnal 'byor pa bzhi*). See Ngawang Kunga Sönam, *A Brief and Clear Source of Delight for All*, 2b2.

25. The three spiritual brothers—Phuchungwa Shönu Gyaltsen (Phu chung ba Gzhon nu rgyal mtshan, 1031–1106), Chen Ngawa Tsultrim Bar (Spyan snga ba Tshul khrim 'bar, 1038–1103), and Potowa Rinchen Sal Choklé Namgyal (Po to ba Rin chen gsal Phyogs las rnam rgyal, 1027–1105)—are the three main disciples of Dromtön Gyalwa Jungné ('Brom ston Rgyal ba 'byung gnas, 1005–64). Commonly referred to as Dromtönpa, he is the chief disciple upon whom Atiśa conferred the lamrim instruction.
26. This is a verse of homage to the founder of the Geluk tradition, Tsongkhapa (Tsong kha pa), whose ordination name is Losang Drakpa (Blo bzang grags pa).
27. Losang Chökyi Gyaltsen (Blo bzang chos kyi rgyal mtshan) is the previous incarnation of the author of the *Swift Path*.
28. Ngagi Wangchuk Losang Gyatso (Ngag gi dbang phyug Blo bzang rgya mtsho), or in abbreviated form, Ngawang Losang Gyatso, is the Fifth Dalai Lama, from whom the author of our text received his novice vows.
29. The state of omniscience is the state of buddhahood, or full enlightenment. In addition to having exhaustively abandoned the afflictive obstructions (*kleśāvaraṇam, nyon mongs pa'i sgrib pa*), which prevent liberation from saṃsāra, a buddha has also exhaustively abandoned the obstructions to knowledge (*jñeyāvaraṇam, shes bya'i sgrib pa*). Obstructions to knowledge prevent the knowledge of all phenomena and, in particular, the simultaneous direct realization of the two truths—ultimate truths and conventional truths—with a single mind.
30. This first part is presented in chapter 1 of this book.
31. This second part is covered by the remaining chapters of this book.
32. Dīpaṃkara was Atiśa's ordination name. When King Jangchup Ö—the nephew of Lha Lama Yeshe Ö, who initiated the plan to invite Atiśa to Tibet—realized that his wisdom and compassion surpassed that of other pandits and that he was able to greatly clarify the Buddha's teachings, the king called him Atiśa, which means "preeminent" (*phul du byung ba*). Yangchen Gawai Lodrö, *A Brief Essential Explanation Deciphering the Terms in the Great Exposition of the Stages of the Path to Enlightenment*, 56.
33. The Tibetan expression Jowo Jé (Jo bo rje), "Foremost Lord," is an epithet of Atiśa. Subsequent occurrences of the term in this text are directly rendered as Atiśa.
34. Geshé Tönpa refers to Dromtönpa, the founder of the Kadam tradition who was born into the clan of Drom ('Brom) in central Tibet. The name Tönpa means "teacher." Subsequent occurrences of this name are directly rendered as the more familiar Dromtönpa. Geshé (*dge bshes*), "virtuous friend," is a title given to a spiritual guide in the Kadam tradition. Those who have completed their studies in the Geluk monastic education system also earn this title.
35. The prefix *naljor* (*rnal 'byor*) is an abbreviation of *naljorpa* (*rnal 'byor pa*), which means "yogi." His full name is Gönpawa Wangchuk Gyaltsen (Dgon pa ba Dbang phyug rgyal mtshan), where *gönpawa* means "hermit."
36. Chen Ngar (Spyan sngar 1038–1103), also known as Chen Ngawa (Spyan sngar ba), received ordination at the age of eighteen and was named Tsultrim Bar (Tshul khrims 'bar). The term *spyan snga*, which means "in one's presence," was a title transmitted to successive dignitaries and in fifteenth-century Tibet also came to signify the leader of a monastery. Vetturini, *The bKa' gdams pa School of Tibetan Buddhism*, 8 and 111.
37. *Bka' gdams gdams ngag pa*.

38. Note that Lhodrak Drupchen Lekyi Dorjé (Lho drag grub chen Las kyi rdo rje) is referred to as Lhodrak Drupchen Namkha Gyaltsen (Lho drag grub chen Nam mkha' rgyal mtshan) later in the text. Lhodrak is the name of a place in southern Tibet, while Drupchen means "great adept," and so Lhodrak Drupchen means "the great adept from Lhodrak." This mystic was able to consult Vajrapāṇi on Tsongkhapa's behalf for the purpose of dispelling his lingering doubts about the view of emptiness. See Jinpa, *Tsongkhapa*, 140–42.
39. The texts relied upon by the Kadam followers of texts (*bka' gdams bzhung pa ba*) include the canonical scriptures in general and, in particular, the texts that carry great importance in this tradition: Śāntideva's *Engaging in Bodhisattva Deeds* and *Compendium of Trainings in Verse*, Asaṅga's *Bodhisattvas' Grounds*, Maitreya's *Ornament for the Mahāyāna Sūtras*, Āryaśūra's *Garland of Birth Stories*, and the *Collection of Aphorisms*. Phuchungwa is sometimes described as having received the lineage that is transmitted through the Kadam followers of oral instructions (*bka' gdams man ngag pa*). Some other authors distinguish the following three Kadam lineages: (1) that of the Kadam followers of texts stemming from Potowa, (2) that of the Kadam followers of quintessential instructions (*bka' gdams gdams ngag pa*) stemming from Chen Ngar Tsultrim Bar, and (3) that of the Kadam followers of the stages of the path stemming from Gönpawa. For historical background of the Kadam lineages, see Jinpa, *Book of Kadam*, 8–9.
40. *Drakor* (*grwa skor*) refers to the monastic rounds in which one takes examinations at different centers of learning to prove one's mastery of the various subjects of studies. Khenchen (*mkhan chen*) means "great abbot" or "great preceptor."
41. While staying at Radreng Hermitage, Tsongkhapa composed the supplication prayer to the lamrim lineage masters entitled *Opening the Door to the Supreme Path*. Dakpo Jampal Lhundrup Gyatso composed an expanded version of this prayer entitled *A Necklace for the Fortunate*, which has become the standard procedure for implementing the preparatory practices in the Geluk tradition. For more information on these two texts, see notes 43 and 85.
42. Expressions such as *foremost great being* (*rje bdag nyid chen po*), *foremost precious one* (*rje rin po che*), and *foremost all-knowing one* (*rje thams bcad khyen pa*) have been used to refer to Tsongkhapa in this text. Subsequent occurrences of these epithets are directly rendered as Tsongkhapa.
43. Painted by Dromtönpa himself, this Tilted Head (Dbu yon ma) is a famed scroll painting (*sku thang*) of Atiśa, in which his head is tilted (*dbu yon por mdzas*). Yangchen Gawai Lodrö, *Deciphering the Terms in the Great Exposition*, 46. In the colophon to the *Great Exposition*, Tsongkhapa mentions that he composed the supplication prayer to the lamrim lineage masters entitled *Opening the Door to the Supreme Path* "after having supplicated the image, no different from Atiśa himself, for a long time."
44. Radreng, situated north of the capital Lhasa, was founded by Dromtönpa in 1056 as the primary seat of the Kadam school.
45. Tsongkhapa's most extensive lamrim, the *Great Exposition on the Stages of the Path to Enlightenment* (*Lam rim chen mo*), is arguably his most influential composition. Its formal title is *Greater Exposition on the Stages of the Path to Enlightenment* (*Byang chub lam rim che ba*). This work will simply be referred to as the *Great Exposition* in subsequent notes. For a full English translation, see Tsong-kha-pa, *The Great Treatise on the Stages of the Path to Enlightenment*.
46. This does not imply a one-to-one correlation between the three principal aspects

and the paths of persons with the three capacities. In fact, renunciation is associated with the path of those with medium capacity, bodhicitta with that of those with great capacity, and the correct view with both the paths of those with medium and great capacities. Note that Tsongkhapa composed a separate text of fourteen verses entitled *Three Principal Aspects of the Path* (*Lam gyi gtso bo rnam gsum*).

47. *Gyalwa* (*rgyal ba*) is an epithet meaning "conqueror" or "victorious one." Ensapa (Dben sa pa) was the pre-incarnation of Paṇchen Losang Chökyi Gyaltsen. Born at Ensa (Dben sa) in the Tsang region of Tibet, he began his Dharma studies with the abbot of Ensa Monastery. He became a chief holder of the Ganden Oral Tradition (*dga' ldan snyan rgyud*) in the Geluk school and was interred at Ensa Monastery after his death. His spiritual son refers to Sangyé Yeshé, who later became the teacher of Ensapa's reincarnation, Paṇchen Losang Chökyi Gyaltsen.
48. Gyaltsab refers to Gyaltsab Darma Rinchen (Rgyal tshab Dar ma rin chen), also commonly known as Gyaltsab Jé. One of the two heart disciples of Tsongkhapa, he is usually depicted as seated to the right of Tsongkhapa in paintings of the three figures. Chöjé (*chos rje*) is a title meaning "Dharma master."
49. *Dulzin* (*'dul 'dzin*), "Vinaya holder," is an epithet applied to the name of an esteemed master of the monastic code. Dulzin Drakpa Gyaltsen ('Dul 'dzin Grags pa rgyal mtshan 1374–1434) was known for his writings on the Vinaya and praised by Tsongkhapa for his strict mastery of the monastic codes.
50. Khedrup Chöjé refers to Khedrup Gelek Palsang, also commonly known as Khedrup Jé. One of the two heart disciples of Tsongkhapa, he is usually depicted as seated to the left of Tsongkhapa in paintings of the three figures.
51. *Jé* (*rje*) is an appellation meaning "foremost one."
52. Note that *Paṇchen* ("great learned one") is a title and not part of the actual name. Not to be confused with the Paṇchen Tamché Khyenpa Losang Chökyi Gyaltsen listed later, Paṇchen Chökyi Gyaltsen here refers to Baso Chökyi Gyaltsen (Ba so Chos kyi rgyal mtshan), the younger brother of Khedrup Gelek Palsang. The prefix Baso refers to the monastery of Baso Lhundrup Dechen (Ba so lhun grub bde chen), which he either founded or took over.
53. *Drupai Wangchuk* (*grub pa'i dbang phyugs*) is an epithet meaning "lord of adepts." Losang Döndrup is the ordination name of Ensapa, mentioned above.
54. Note that *Tamché Khyenpa* ("all-knowing one") is a title that is prefixed to the actual name Losang Chökyi Gyaltsen. By no means a unique title, it appears before the names of many eminent masters.
55. *Dorjé Dzinpa* (*rdo rje 'dzin pa*), "vajra holder," is an epithet applied to the name of a respected tantric practitioner.
56. This briefer lamrim mentioned here refers to what is called the *Smaller Exposition on the Stages of the Path to Enlightenment* (*Lam rim chung ba*) or *Small Exposition on the Stages of the Path to Enlightenment* (*Lam rim chung ngu*). This abridgement of the *Great Exposition* is also known in general as the *Middle-Length Exposition on the Stages of the Path to Enlightenment* (*Lam rim 'bring po*). These different titles can be confusing, because in the context of mentioning Tsongkhapa's great, middle-length, and small lamrims, the small lamrim actually refers to the *Concise Exposition on the Stages of the Path to Enlightenment* (*Lam rim bsdus don*), also called the *Song of Spiritual Experience* (*Nyams mgur*).
57. Tsongkhapa, *Great Exposition*, 67. To view this statement in context, see Tsong-kha-pa, *Great Treatise*, 1:116.

58. Paṇchen Tamché Khyenpa, "all-knowing Paṇchen," refers to Paṇchen Losang Chökyi Gyaltsen or, in abbreviated form, Paṇchen Losang Chögyen, the pre-incarnation of the author of our text. Subsequent occurrences of this epithet are directly rendered as Paṇchen Losang Chökyi Gyaltsen.
59. Gyalwang Tamché Khyenpa Chenpo, "great all-knowing powerful conqueror," refers to Ngawang Losang Gyatso, the Fifth Dalai Lama, who recognized the author as the reincarnation of Paṇchen Losang Chökyi Gyaltsen. Subsequent occurrences of this epithet are directly rendered as Ngawang Losang Gyatso, the Fifth Dalai Lama.
60. The *Words of Mañjuśrī* (*'Jam dpal zhal lung*) is one of the eight great lamrim texts.
61. The greater and smaller expositions refer to Tsongkhapa's *Great Exposition on the Stages of the Path to Enlightenment* and *Middle-Length Exposition on the Stages of the Path to Enlightenment.*
62. This enigmatic statement is found at the beginning of Tsongkhapa's *Great Exposition*, 2. To view this statement in context, see Tsong-kha-pa, *Great Treatise*, 1:36.
63. Here the *Stages of the Path* refers specifically to Tsongkhapa's *Great Exposition on the Stages of the Path to Enlightenment*, often referred to simply as *Lamrim Chenmo* (*Lam rim chen mo*).
64. Here the *Stages of the Teachings* refers specifically to *An Explanation of the Stages of the Path for Engaging in the Sugata's Precious Teachings*, often referred to simply as *Tenrim Chenmo* (*Bstan rim chen mo*), by Drolungpa Lodrö Jungné (Gro lung pa Blo gros 'byung gnas), who lived in the late eleventh and early twelfth centuries. This is a major commentary on the basic tenrim text in just twenty verses written by his teacher, the famous translator Ngok Lotsāwa Loden Sherab (Rnog lo tsā ba Blo ldan shes rab, 1059–1109). In the colophon of his *Great Exposition*, Tsongkhapa stated that he took as the basis for his composition the arrangement of the stages of the path of Ngok Lotsāwa and his spiritual son Drolungpa. The latest master in the line of reincarnations of Ngok Lotsāwa, known today as Dagyab Rinpoche, was born in 1940 and recognized at the age of four by the Fourteenth Dalai Lama.
65. *A Precious Garland of the Supreme Path* was composed by the founder of the Dakpo Kagyü tradition, Gampopa Sönam Rinchen (Sgam po pa bsod nam rin chen, 1079–1153), who is also commonly referred to as Dakpo Lhajé (Dwags po lha rje), "physician from Dakpo." Named after the region Gampo where he founded his monastery, Gampopa is credited with establishing the monastic order of the Kagyü school and combining the Kadam lamrim teachings with the mahāmudrā and tantric teachings he received from Milarepa. For English translation of this work, see Karthar Rinpoche, *Instructions of Gampopa*.
66. Naktso Lotsāwa Tsultrim Gyalwa (Nag 'tsho lo tsā ba Tshul khrims rgyal ba) was part of a mission that traveled to India to invite Atiśa to Tibet. He is credited with around one hundred translations in the Kangyur (the part of the Tibetan Buddhist canon that contains translations of the Buddha's words) and Tengyur (the part of the Tibetan Buddhist canon that contains translations of the Indian treatises), and he authored an extensive biography of Atiśa. Derived from the Sanskrit *loka-cakṣu* ("eye of the world"), *lotsāwa* is a Tibetan title for translators who translate Sanskrit Buddhist texts into Tibetan. Bear in mind that it was a long-standing tradition to transliterate Sanskrit *ca* with the Tibetan syllable *tsa*. Yangchen Gawai Lodrö, *Deciphering the Terms in the Great Exposition*, 56.
67. Naktso Lotsāwa Tsultrim Gyalwa, *Praise of Atiśa in Eighty Verses*, 340.
68. Somapuri (also Somapura) Mahāvihāra in Bangladesh was among the best-known

Buddhist vihāras in the Indian Subcontinent and is one of the most important archaeological sites in the country. The *Blaze of Reasoning* (Tengyur D 3856) is Bhāviveka's autocommentary on his *Heart of the Middle Way* (Tengyur D 3855).

69. Vikramaśīla was one of the most important centers of learning in India during the Pala Empire. Founded between the late eighth and early ninth centuries by King Dharmapāla, this great Buddhist monastery served as a central institution of learning before it was plundered and destroyed, along with the other nearby Buddhist universities of Nālandā and Odantapuri, at the end of the twelfth century.
70. Naktso Lotsāwa Tsultrim Gyalwa, *Praise of Atiśa in Eighty Verses*, 336.
71. Two of the four greatnesses of the lamrim teaching are mentioned here. The other two are the greatness of easily understanding the Conqueror's intent and the greatness of naturally ceasing serious misdeeds. For more details, see Tsong-kha-pa, *Great Treatise*, vol. 1, chap. 2.
72. Within the cycle of contaminated existence, the rebirths of gods, demigods, or humans are considered upper rebirths, while the rebirths as animals, hungry ghosts, or hell beings are considered lower rebirths. These are temporary states of existence that are projected by karma and afflictions. High rebirths (*abhyudaya*, *mngon mtho*) refer to the three types of rebirths in the upper realms.
73. *Beatitude* (*niḥśreyasa*, *nges legs*), literally "definite goodness," is a state of irreversible abandonment of suffering and its causes and includes liberation and omniscience. *Liberation* refers to one's individual liberation from suffering and its causes, while *omniscience* refers to buddhahood, in which one has become fully enlightened in order to work for the welfare of all sentient beings.
74. Consistent with the way the previous point is explained, the *Great Exposition* provides the explanation in relation to persons with *medium* capacity with a qualification: every Dharma taught based on the vehicles of hearers and solitary realizers is subsumed *under the actual Dharma of persons with medium capacity or* under the Dharma in common with that of persons with medium capacity. Tsongkhapa, *Great Exposition*, 77. To view this statement in context, see Tsong-kha-pa, *Great Treatise*, 1:130. For the etymologies of the terms *hearer* and *solitary realizer*, see notes 129 and 130.
75. The goal of the Mahāyāna is the attainment of buddhahood so that one can guide all sentient beings to liberation and enlightenment. In the Pāramitāyāna, or Perfection Vehicle, one focuses on the practice of the *pāramitās*—that is, the perfections of generosity, ethics, and so on. It is said that one takes three countless eons to achieve buddhahood through this vehicle. The other great vehicle is the Mantrayāna, a.k.a. the Vajrayāna or Tantra Vehicle, which can bring about buddhahood in a period as short as a single lifetime, provided the practitioner is highly qualified.
76. Bodhicitta (*byang chub kyi sems*) is the mind aspiring to attain full enlightenment for the benefit of all living beings. As soon as one generates uncontrived bodhicitta, one enters the Mahāyāna path. Such a spontaneous achievement must be preceded by repeated training in which one generates bodhicitta with effort through deliberate reflection on the reasons for wanting to attain enlightenment for the sake of all sentient beings. See chapters 11 and 12 for details on how to generate bodhicitta.
77. The Sanskrit word *saṃsāra* refers to cyclic existence in which one appropriates contaminated physical and mental aggregates under the power of karma and afflictions.
78. The two vehicles here refer to the Hīnayāna vehicles of hearers and solitary realizers. For the etymologies of the terms *hearer* and *solitary realizer*, see notes 129 and 130.

79. *Kṣitigarbha's Ten Wheels Sūtra*, Kangyur D 239, 179b7–180a1.
80. Tsongkhapa, *Great Exposition*, 80–81. To view this statement in context, see Tsong-kha-pa, *Great Treatise*, 1:134–35. Śāntideva, *Engaging in Bodhisattva Deeds*, 1.24, Tengyur D 3871, 3a3.
81. Characterized by intense suffering, a lower rebirth does not contain optimal conditions for spiritual development.
82. It is said that the practice of highest yoga tantra, the highest of the four classes of tantra, enables a highly qualified trainee to attain buddhahood in a single lifetime of this degenerate age. The four classes of tantra are those of action (*kriyā*), performance (*caryā*), yoga (*yoga*), and highest yoga (*anuttarayoga*).
83. Uncontrived renunciation and bodhicitta are the entrances to the Hīnayāna and the Mahāyāna, respectively. When one first trains in renunciation, one has to deliberately reflect on reasons in order to generate the wish to become free from saṃsāra. Through repeated cultivation, one will reach a point where effort is no longer required and renunciation is produced spontaneously. Similarly, through repeated familiarization with the causes of bodhicitta, one will be able to generate in an uncontrived manner the wish to attain full enlightenment for the benefit of all sentient beings.
84. The preparatory practices or *ngöndro* (*sngon 'gro*) described here in this chapter are presented in relation to the first meditation session of relying on the spiritual guide. They are to be implemented similarly in the subsequent meditation sessions, or at least the first session of each day.
85. Based on the instructions contained in the *Swift Path*, Dakpo Jampal Lhundrup Gyatso (1845–1919) composed a rite for conveniently performing the six preparatory practices entitled *A Necklace for the Fortunate*. This rite has become the standard procedure for implementing the preparatory practices in the Geluk tradition. His reincarnation, commonly known today as Dagpo Rinpoche, was born in 1932 and identified by the Thirteenth Dalai Lama when he was only one year old. For a full translation of this rite, see Pabongka, *Liberation in the Palm of Your Hand*, appendix 4.
86. The four kings are Vaiśravaṇa, Dhṛtarāṣṭra, Virūḍhaka, and Virūpākṣa. They are explicitly mentioned in the visualization of the merit field in the fourth preparatory practice explained below. As a result of prayers made during the time of the previous buddha Kāśyapa, the four kings were reborn in the time of Buddha Śākyamuni and received teachings from him. Apart from upholding the Dharma in their own realms, they survey the four directions and protect all who uphold the Buddha's teachings.
87. A *torma* (*bali*, *gtor ma*) is a ritual cake usually made of substances like barley flour and butter.
88. Sprinkling water on mud floors is a way to settle dust.
89. Unlike an offering maṇḍala (*mchod pa'i maṇḍala*) in which one makes offerings by placing precious substances in their respective positions to represent Mount Meru, the four continents, the sun, and other features of a world system, an accomplishment maṇḍala (*sgrub pa'i maṇḍala*) is such that, after eliminating interferers and purifying it into emptiness, one generates it into an inestimable mansion, invites the merit field, and places it on an altar. Chen Nga Lodrö Gyaltsen, *The Ultimate Profound Path*, 32–33.
90. Composed of the five substances from the cow—dung, urine, milk, curd, and butter—that have not fallen to the ground, ready-to-use *bachung* (*pañcagavya*, *ba byung*, "cow-arisen") pills may be obtained from Tibetan tantric colleges.
91. To draw a swastika in a "Dharma-turning" (*chos skor*) manner means to draw a

right-turning or clockwise swastika 卐. Contrast this with a "Bön-turning" (*bon skor*) swastika, which is left-turning or counterclockwise. Bön is considered the indigenous religious tradition of Tibet, and some of its current practices are mirror images of Tibetan Buddhist ones.

92. The Sanskrit word *svastika* (*bkra shis*) connotes auspiciousness or a lucky object.
93. *Artemisia* (*spra ba*) refers to the medicinal mugwort plant.
94. In the vajra posture, one crosses one's legs such that the left foot rests on the right thigh and the right foot on the left thigh.
95. According to the explanations of tantra, the body of a human of our Jambūdvīpa continent contains 72,000 channels through which energy winds (*prāṇa*) flow. The main channels are the right, left, and central channels.
96. For an enumeration of the seven essentials of the body, leave out the eighth feature of breathing naturally in the above list of eight attributes.
97. Losang Chökyi Gyaltsen, verse 14abc, *Highway of the Conquerors*, 2b2–3. To expel the stale winds over nine rounds, breathe in through your right nostril and out through the left three times, then breathe in through your left nostril and out through the right three times, and finally breathe in through both nostrils and out through both nostrils three times. For the Fourteenth Dalai Lama's commentary, see Tenzin Gyatso and Berzin, *The Gelug/Kagyü Tradition of Mahamudra*, 131.
98. This is a phrase that leads up to the statement of the Sanskrit title at the beginning of a Tibetan translation of a Sanskrit scripture. Stating the Sanskrit title at the beginning fulfills several purposes. Besides indicating that the translation has an authentic source in an Indian composition, the Sanskrit title leaves imprints of Sanskrit in the minds of those who study the text and blesses their mindstream. Chökyi Gyaltsen, *Ocean of Sport of the Fortunate Nāga King*, 1:35. Note that the author Chökyi Gyaltsen (1469–1544), commonly referred to as Jetsun Chökyi Gyaltsen, was an abbot of Sera Monastery and a prolific writer whose textbooks are used especially in the monastic colleges of Sera Jé and Ganden Jangtsé; he is a different person from Paṇchen Losang Chökyi Gyaltsen (1570–1662).
99. In his *Sincere Queries on the Salient Points of Spiritual Practice*, Tsongkhapa posed a number of questions to the eminent meditation practitioners of Tibet. Years later, Losang Chökyi Gyaltsen was requested to provide answers to these pertinent questions related to practice. Having studied and examined Tsongkhapa's writings, Losang Chökyi Gyaltsen composed the *Melodious Speech of Losang's Assertions* to address the queries. In response to the question about what the first step of meditation is, Losang Chökyi Gyaltsen replies based on his understanding of the intent of the "peerless lama"—that is, Tsongkhapa—that the first step of meditation is to check one's motivation. Losang Chökyi Gyaltsen, *Melodious Speech*, 4b4.
100. The eight worldly concerns are the preoccupations with gain and loss, reputation and infamy, comfort and discomfort, and praise and criticism.
101. *General Rituals for All Maṇḍalas Tantra*, Kangyur D 806, 145b4.
102. Even good rebirths within the upper realms of saṃsāra do not transcend the suffering nature of saṃsāra.
103. The *extreme of pacification* is individual liberation secured mainly out of concern for one's own welfare rather than omniscience secured to liberate other sentient beings from saṃsāra and lead them to enlightenment.
104. The Sanskrit word *karma* means "action." Besides generating the mental factor of

intention itself, one also creates physical and verbal actions induced by intention, so karma can be physical, verbal, or mental.

105. An arhat is one who has abandoned the afflictive obstructions and will never again take rebirth in saṃsāra by the power of karma and afflictions. The two types of arhats are the hearer and solitary realizer arhats.
106. Refer to chapters 11 and 12 for detailed instructions on how to generate bodhicitta.
107. *Conqueror* (*jina*) is an epithet of the Buddha, referring to him being victorious over the four *māras*, or demons. The four māras are those of the lord of death, afflictions, the son of the gods, and the aggregates.
108. The Buddha's round and symmetrical crown protrusion (*gtsug tor*, *uṣṇīṣa*) is one of the thirty-two signs of a buddha's body.
109. *Nectar* (*bdud rtsi*) translates the Sanskrit word *amṛta*, which means "deathless." Thus, etymologically speaking, "nectar" connotes the elixir of immortality.
110. A buddha's body is adorned with the thirty-two signs, such as the crown protrusion, and eighty exemplifying marks, such as copper-colored nails. A sign (*lakṣaṇa*, *mtshan*) signifies that a buddha is a holy being, while an exemplifying mark (*vyañjana*, *dpe byad*) helps the trainees to understand the pure excellent qualities in a buddha. Chökyi Gyaltsen, *Ocean of Sport of the Fortunate Nāga King*, 2:502. For a full listing of these signs and exemplifying marks as well as their causes, see appendix 2.
111. Here "deities" translates *yid dam* (also spelled *yi dam*), the tutelary deities to whom one has made firm mental commitment.
112. Heroes (*vīra*, *dpa' bo*) and heroines (*vīrā*, *dpa' mo*) are beings with tantric realizations who render assistance to practitioners and serve the Dharma.
113. Ḍākas (*mkha' 'gro*) and ḍākinīs (*mkha' 'gro ma*), "sky-goers," are realized yogis and yoginīs, often interchangeably referred to as heroes and heroines.
114. According to the cosmology described in the Abhidharma, there are four major human continents facing the four sides of the square-shaped Mount Meru, which is situated in the center of the world system. The oceans surrounding these four continents are the four oceans. For diagrams illustrating the structure of such a world system, see Sadakata, *Buddhist Cosmology*, 27–29.
115. Nāgārjuna, *Letter to a Friend*, verse 67, Tengyur D 4182, 43b6–7.
116. Āryadeva, *Four Hundred Verses*, 7.1, Tengyur D 3846, 8a4.
117. See chapters 6 and 9 for detailed instructions on how to meditate on the sufferings of the three lower rebirths and the general and specific sufferings of saṃsāra.
118. See chapter 4 for detailed instructions on how to meditate on the precious human rebirth.
119. See chapters 3 and 7 for detailed instructions on how to rely on the spiritual guide and go to the Three Jewels for refuge.
120. In the extensive way of refuge, which consists of four phases of recitation and visualization, one adds "I go for refuge to my teachers" to the usual refuge formula "I go for refuge to the Buddha, I go for refuge to the Dharma, I go for refuge to the Saṅgha." In the brief way of refuge that will be explained later, there is just a single phase wherein one goes for refuge to the Three Jewels collectively.
121. The visualization of five-colored nectar and light rays features prominently in tantric meditations. The five colors correspond to the five wisdoms (*pañcajñānāni*, *ye shes lnga*): mirror-like wisdom (*ādarśanajñāna*, *me long lta bu'i ye shes*); wisdom of equality (*samatājñāna*, *mnyam nyid ye shes*); wisdom of individual investigation (*pratyavekṣaṇājñāna*, *so rtog ye shes*); wisdom of accomplishing activities

(*kṛtyānuṣṭhānajñāna, bya sgrub ye shes*); and wisdom of dharmadhātu (*dharmadhātujñāna, chos dbyings ye shes*). See Lobsang Jampa, *Guhyasamāja Practice in the Ārya Nāgārjuna System*, 1:283.

122. Another way of interpreting this formula is to recite "I go for refuge to the Buddha" and think that the Buddha embodies all buddhas, such as Guhyasamāja, Heruka, Vajrabhairava, and so on mentioned in the visualization.

123. It is said that about one thousand founding buddhas will come in this present good eon (*bhadrakalpa, bskal pa bzang po*). Four have come so far: Krakucchanda, Kanakamuni, Kāśyapa, and Śākyamuni. Maitreya, who has appeared as a bodhisattva in the retinue of Śākyamuni along with other bodhisattvas such as Mañjuśrī and Avalokiteśvara, will come as the buddha of the future era after the teachings of Śākyamuni are no longer practiced. These buddhas are described in the *Good Eon Sūtra* (Kangyur D 94). See English translation at 84000.co (Toh 94).

124. The names of the Thirty-Five Buddhas are listed in the purification practice known as the *Confession of Downfalls* (*Ltung bshags*), or more extensively, the *Confession of Bodhisattva Downfalls* (*Byang chub ltung bshags*). This confession practice is extracted from *Ascertaining the Vinaya: Questions of Upāli Sūtra* (Kangyur D 68). See English translation at 84000.co (Toh 68), 1.43–46.

125. *Tathāgata*, "thus gone" (*de bzhin bshegs pa*), is an epithet for a buddha. Among the many interpretations of the etymology of this term, one account states that, because buddhas possess excellent qualities such as generosity and their minds are freed from faults of desire, they have lovingkindness that goes to anyone in whatever way that is beneficial, and so they are *thus gone*. Subhūticandra, *Wish-Granting Cow*, Tengyur D 4300, 255b7–256a1.

126. Hīnayāna, which is smaller in scope in that its goal is individual liberation rather than the welfare of all sentient beings, forms the foundation of the Mahāyāna and is thus referred to as the common, or shared, vehicle.

127. *Caityas* and *stūpas*, both rendered as *mchod rtan* in Tibetan, refer to Buddhist monuments or reliquaries containing holy objects such as the relics of a buddha or a holy being. As representations of the enlightened mind, they are objects venerated by devotees.

128. *King of Meditative Stabilizations Sūtra*, Kangyur D 127, 66a6. See English translation at 84000.co (Toh 127), 18.34–35.

129. A hearer (*śrāvaka, nyan thos*), whose goal is individual liberation, hears the Buddha's teachings and causes others to hear them.

130. A solitary realizer (*pratyekabuddha, rang sangs rgyas*) chooses to be reborn in his last life in a place where there is no buddha and eventually attains individual liberation without the help of a teacher in that life.

131. This is the first half of the commonly recited verse of refuge and bodhicitta, phonetically rendered as *sangyé chö dang tsok kyi chok nam la / jangchup bardu dakni kyab suchi*.

132. This is the second half of the commonly recited verse of refuge and bodhicitta: *dakgi jinsok gyi pé sönam kyi / drola phenchir sangyé drup par shok*.

133. The four means of gathering disciples are giving, agreeable speech, helpful activity, and consistent conduct. For an explanation on what the practice entails, see chapter 14.

134. The cultivation of divine identity (*nga rgyal*, literally "pride") is a practice belonging to tantric deity yoga. It involves meditating on emptiness and identifying oneself with

the attributes of a fully enlightened deity so as to overcome the conception of oneself as ordinary.

135. The section on calm abiding comes in chapter 15.

136. The four immeasurables are so called because, by cultivating them through observing *immeasurable* sentient beings, one accrues *immeasurable* collections of merit and wisdom, and as a result achieves the *immeasurable* excellent qualities of buddhahood.

137. Guru yoga is a practice in which one identifies one's spiritual guides as inseparable in nature from all the buddhas and meditates in order to transform one's body, speech, and mind into that of a fully enlightened being.

138. According to presentation of the Sūtra Vehicle, buddhahood is a result of the collection of merit and wisdom accrued over three countless eons. See Vasubandhu, *Treasury of Knowledge*, 3.93d, Tengyur D 4089, 10b1. Contrary to its literal meaning, "countless" (*asaṃkhyeya, grangs med*) refers to the astronomical but finite number 10^{59}. According to the presentation of the Tantra Vehicle, a qualified practitioner can complete these collections far more quickly. Practicing the three lower tantras enables one to attain buddhahood in a single lifetime. However, in order to attain enlightenment within such a short lifetime *of this degenerate age* to which we now belong, one has to rely on highest yoga tantra. See Tenzin Gyatso, *The Great Exposition of Secret Mantra*, 1:54.

139. According to the Abhidharma, a world system undergoes the cycles of dissolution, nothingness, creation, and abidance. During the cycle of abidance, the lifespan of human beings in this Jambūdvīpa continent where we reside decreases from an initial "infinity" and fluctuates repeatedly between ten and 80,000 years. The lifespan at this point has diminished to about a hundred years and will continue to decrease. This period is characterized by the five degenerations (*pañcakaṣāya, snyigs ma lnga*), which are the degenerations of lifespan, afflictions, sentient beings, time, and view. See Sadakata, *Buddhist Cosmology*, 102–8.

140. Tsongkhapa, *Great Exposition*, 135. To view this statement in context, see Tsong-kha-pa, *Great Treatise*, 1:201. In general, there are four kinds of fields (*kṣetra, zhing*) with respect to which one creates merit. These are the fields of living beings, suffering, benefit, and excellent qualities. Vasubandhu, *Treasury of Knowledge*, 4.117ab, Tengyur D 4089, 15b1.

141. Mokchokpa Rinchen Tsöndrü (Rmog lcog pa Rin chen brtson 'grus) (1110–70) is an early master of the Shangpa Kagyü lineage.

142. In general, *Lama Chöpa* (*Guru Pūjā*) can refer to any liturgy dedicated to the practice of making offerings to the spiritual guide. In this context, the term refers specifically to the *Lama Chöpa* composed by Paṇchen Losang Chökyi Gyaltsen, the previous incarnation of Paṇchen Losang Yeshé. The formal title of this work is *Indivisible Bliss and Emptiness: An Offering to the Spiritual Guide* (*Bla mchod bde stong dbyer med ma*). The practice is usually performed in Geluk Buddhist centers along with the *circle of tsok* (*gaṇacakra, tshogs kyi 'khor lo*) offerings on the tenth and twenty-fifth days of the Tibetan month. This text is referred to in his *Collected Works* as the *Rite of Making Offerings to the Spiritual Guide*.

143. "The system of this explicit instruction" refers to the system of the *Easy Path*, in which the central figure has the aspect of Buddha Śākyamuni. Paṇchen Losang Yeshé mentioned in the colophon that he composed the *Swift Path* as a supplement to the *Easy Path* composed by Paṇchen Losang Chökyi Gyaltsen, so it is natural for him to state the system of the *Easy Path* here. However, prior to doing so, he offers an alternative

system of visualization based on the system of *Lama Chöpa*, also composed by his predecessor, in which the central figure has the aspect of Tsongkhapa.

144. The "three principles" (*de nyid gsum*) here are three types of concentrations taught in the *Concentration Continuation*. For more information, see Tenzin Gyatso, *The Great Exposition of Secret Mantra*, 2:149.
145. See appendix 2 for a listing of the thirty-two signs and eighty exemplifying marks.
146. These eight great close spiritual sons (*nye ba'i sras chen brgyad*) are the great bodhisattvas Avalokiteśvara, Kṣitigarbha, Mañjuśrī, Samantabhadra, Maitreya, Vajrapāṇi, Ākāśagarbha, and Sarvanīvaraṇaviṣkambhin. Note that Ākāśagarbha is also known as Khagarbha, Gaganagarbha, or Gaganagañja.
147. The sixteen elders (*sthavira*, *gnas brtan*) are arhat disciples of the Buddha who promised to remain in this world in order to help preserve the Dharma for the benefit of sentient beings.
148. While there is no mention here of heroes, heroines, ḍākas, and ḍākinīs before the Dharma protectors and guardians, *Lama Chöpa* states that the hearers are encircled by heroes, heroines, ḍākas, and ḍākinīs, who are in turn encircled by the Dharma protectors and guardians. The supplication prayer stated later in this chapter also mentions ḍākas and ḍākinīs before the Dharma protectors.
149. Dhṛtarāṣṭra is the guardian in the east. Gandharvas are a type of nonhumans who subsist on odors.
150. Virūḍhaka is the guardian in the south. Kumbhāṇḍas are a type of nonhumans with an animal head and a human body.
151. Virūpākṣa is the guardian in the west. Nāgas are snake-like beings.
152. Vaiśravaṇa is the guardian in the north. Yakṣas are a type of nonhumans who can be mischievous and malevolent. When it is said that these kings dwell in the east, south, west, and north, respectively, these directions should be understood as the central figure's front, right, back, and left, respectively.
153. This detail here deviates from the *Easy Path*, which states that his right hand presses the ground.
154. Vajradhara is a tantric form taken on by Buddha Śākyamuni when he taught the tantras. Tilopa, Nāropa, Ḍombhipa, and Atiśa are examples of masters of the blessed practice lineage, as mentioned in the verses of homage below.
155. Maitreya, Asaṅga, Vasubandhu, Vimuktisena, Paramasena, Vinītasena, Kīrtisena, Haribhadra, Kuśalī the Elder, Kuśalī the Younger, and Suvarṇadvīpa are examples of masters of the vast deeds lineage, as mentioned in the verses of homage below.
156. Nāgārjuna, Candrakīrti, and Vidyākokila the Elder are examples of masters of the profound view lineage, as mentioned in the verses of homage below.
157. In general, Dharma protectors are of two types, mundane and supramundane. By specifying that the Dharma protectors are wisdom beings (*ye shes pa*) in this context, one understands that the supramundane ones are intended here.
158. Here, the wisdom beings (*ye shes pa*) refer to the actual figures invited to come and absorb into the commitment beings, who are the figures one has previously visualized.
159. This series of invocation verses can be found in a consecration rite composed by Ngawang Losang Gyatso, the Fifth Dalai Lama, entitled *Brilliance of a Hundred Thousand Auspiciousnesses*, 283–84.
160. This practice of offering ablution is presented in *A Necklace for the Fortunate*. After the bath, one dries and anoints the members of the merit field and then offers them

clothing and ornaments, before inviting them to return to their previous seats. See Pabongka, *Liberation in the Palm of Your Hand*, 704–6.

161. A buddha land is a pure land established from the roots of virtues of a buddha.
162. This position in the list of lineage masters is usually occupied by Vairocana, also known as Śāntarakṣita; *Kīrtisena (Grags pa'i sde) seems to be an alternate name for him. Some texts list *grags pa'i dpal* (*Yaśaśrī) at this juncture.
163. The "Ārya father" mentioned in the first line is Nāgārjuna. His spiritual sons include masters such as Āryadeva and Candrakīrti. An ārya is a person who has directly realized selflessness or emptiness.
164. The Land of Snows is Tibet.
165. This verse constitutes the famous four-line request to Tsongkhapa known as the *miktséma*, a name derived from the first and third syllables of the first line (*mikmé tsewai terchen chenresik*). Tsongkhapa had offered a four-line praise to his teacher Rendawa (Red mda' ba), who changed a few words of the verse and gave it back to him, saying that the praise was actually more fitting for Tsongkhapa himself. See Jinpa, *Tsongkhapa*, 196. For an explanation of the practice of the *miktséma* prayer and its various versions, see Jinpa et al., *Stages of the Path and the Oral Transmission*, 16–19. The nine verses beginning from this one are dedicated to the Geluk lineage masters, with the ninth verse directed at the author's direct teacher.
166. This verse is dedicated to Gelek Palsang, commonly known as Khedrup Jé.
167. This verse is dedicated to Baso Chökyi Gyaltsen.
168. This verse is dedicated to Drupchen Chökyi Dorjé.
169. Losang Döndrup, the predecessor of Paṇchen Losang Chökyi Gyaltsen, is commonly referred to as Ensapa (Dben sa pa).
170. This verse is dedicated to Paṇchen Losang Chökyi Gyaltsen, the predecessor of the author.
171. When performing this practice, insert the request verses of the subsequent lineage masters leading up to that of your own teacher.
172. The twelve verses constituting the seven-limbed practice cited in this section constitute the first twelve verses of the *King of Prayers of Excellent Deeds* (*Bhadracaryāpraṇidhānarāja*), commonly referred to as the *King of Prayers*. See English translation at 84000.co (Toh 44), 56.72–83. While existing independently as Kangyur D 1095 with an additional concluding verse, the *King of Prayers of Excellent Deeds* can also be found at the end of the forty-fifth and final chapter, known as the *Stem Array* (*Gaṇḍavyūha*), of *A Multitude of Buddhas Sūtra* (*Buddhāvataṃsakasūtra*), Kangyur D 44, 358b7–362a4. Note that *A Multitude of Buddhas Sūtra* is popularly known as the *Flower Ornament Sūtra*, in accordance with how the sūtra is titled in Chinese Buddhism.
173. One focuses one's attention on all buddhas, those in all ten directions—the four cardinal and four intermediate directions, above, and below—and all times, past, present, and future.
174. Joined together by a leather strap, these little cymbals (*ting shag/shags*) produce a clear and lasting ringing sound when their two thick plates are held horizontally and struck against each other.
175. Stiffened incense (*spos reng*) is, for example, incense sticks, as opposed to loose incense powder.
176. *Akaru* (*a ka ru*) is a resinous heartwood known as the agarwood, of which *Aquilaria*

malaccensis is the major source. *Duruka* (*du ru ka*), also called *olibanum*, is a resin from trees of the genus *Boswellia* and is commonly known as *frankincense*.

177. According to the cosmology presented in the Abhidharma, the universe is said to consist of a billion world systems, each of which is complete with a Mount Meru, four human continents, and other features of a world system.
178. Maṇḍalas are representations of the universe. A sand maṇḍala, which is primarily a two-dimensional form of the maṇḍala, is constructed from colored sand.
179. The practice of confession of misdeeds is explained more extensively in chapter 8.
180. The three types of vows are the prātimokṣa vows, bodhisattva vows, and tantric vows. For information on these vows, see notes 437 and 441.
181. The four powers of purification are the power of the support, the power of repudiation, the power of applying the antidote, and the power of turning away from misdeed. See pages 150–51.
182. The *General Confession* (*Spyi bshags*), also called *Bla ma rdor 'dzin ma* in Tibetan after its opening words, is the prayer beginning with "O gurus, vajra holders . . ." It is usually recited after having performed the practice of *Confession of Downfalls* (*Ltung bshags*). See Krung go bod brgyud, *Collection of Rituals of the Geluk Order*, 1:108–9.
183. The *Confession of Bodhisattva Downfalls* (*Byang chub ltung bshags*) is commonly referred to by the abbreviation *Confession of Downfalls* (*Ltung bshags*). See Krung go bod brgyud, *Collection of Rituals of the Geluk Order*, 1:103–7.
184. Situated on the western slopes of Mount Ödé Gungyal ('Od lde gung rgyal), Ölga Chölung ('Ol dga' chos lung) is a retreat commanding an impressive panoramic view of the vast Ölga (also Ölkha) Valley. Together with eight carefully selected disciples, Tsongkhapa undertook an intensive retreat there. He performed purification practices for months and received visions of various deities. In one of these extraordinary visions, a sword of light extending from Mañjuśrī's heart touched his own heart, and a stream of silver nectar flowed along the blade into him, filling his body and mind with bliss. See Jinpa, *Tsongkhapa*, 118–33.
185. Among the Thirty-Five Buddhas is a buddha referred to in the same way, King Who Is the Lord of Nāgas (Klu dbang gyi rgyal po).
186. Reading *gsum gyis rang bzhin* for *gsum gyi rang bzhin* in accordance with Tsongkhapa, *Great Exposition*, 51.
187. This declaration occurs in the *General Confession*.
188. After King Prasenajit of Kośala offered a splendid meal to the Buddha and his disciples, the Buddha asked the king whether he should assign the reward from the offering in the king's name or in the name of the person who had earned more merit than the king. Feeling smug after the offering, he requested the Buddha to assign the reward from the offering in the name of the person who had earned more merit than him. To his surprise, the Buddha assigned the reward in the name of a beggar dwelling among the spectators. This episode is recounted in the *Chapters on Vinaya*, Kangyur D 1, Vinaya *kha*, 165b3–166a1. See English translation at 84000.co (Toh 1–6), 9.99–102. See also Rotman, *Divine Stories*, 1:168.
189. Tsongkhapa, *Destiny Fulfilled*, 76. The related lines read:

    To create powerful merit with little effort,
    rejoicing in virtue is praised as best.
    In particular, regarding previous virtues you have accrued,

if you cultivate, free of conceit, great joy in your past virtues,
these previous virtues will increase even more.

190. Śāntideva, *Compendium of Trainings in Verse*, verse 15, Tengyur D 3939, 2b1–2.
191. The five types of persons are: (1) buddhas, (2) bodhisattvas, (3) solitary realizers, (4) hearers still in training and those of no more learning, and (5) other living beings. See Sopa and Patt, *Steps on the Path to Enlightenment*, 1:202.
192. Turning the wheel of Dharma does not involve any physical action of turning a wheel. Rather, it refers to the buddhas teaching the Dharma that they have realized and in turn causing trainees to generate the realizations of the Dharma.
193. Gendun Drupa, *Pulverizing the Armies of Māras*, 7a5–7b1. This passage occurs in the context of describing how the Buddha remained silent without teaching after he had just attained buddhahood. Only after having been requested by gods such as Brahmā did he give his first teaching on the four truths. See Frye, *The Sutra of the Wise and the Foolish*, chap. 1.
194. The Tibetan text misattributed the following citation to the *Questions of Sāgaramati Sūtra*.
195. *Teaching of Akṣayamati Sūtra*, Kangyur D 175, 107a1–2. See English translation at 84000.co (Toh 175), 1.101.
196. See note 90.
197. The two selves are the self of persons and the self of phenomena. To apprehend signs of the two selves is to conceive persons and phenomena other than persons as truly existent. For proofs of the selflessness of persons and the selflessness of phenomena, see chapter 16.
198. Recall your kind root teacher, whom you visualized in the fourth limb of the seven-limbed practice above. See page 67. As you make the following request, visualize that a second figure of Guru Munīndra emerges from Guru Munīndra and comes to reside above your crown.
199. Recall the previous description of the merit field. The five figures are Guru Munīndra in the center, Maitreya on his right, Mañjuśrī on his left, Vajradhara above him, and your kind root teacher in front of him.
200. The wisdom being (*ye shes sems dpa'*) is part of the three-tiered being (*sems dpa' gsum brtsegs*), in which the commitment being (*dam tshig sems dpa'*) has at his heart the wisdom being, who in turn has at his heart the concentration being (*ting nge 'dzin sems dpa'*). The concentration being, not mentioned here, usually takes the form of a seed syllable.
201. *Thub dbang rdo rje 'chang.*
202. The bodies of a buddha can be divided into the form body (*rūpakāya, gzugs sku*) and the dharma body (*dharmakāya, chos sku*). The form body is subdivided into the complete enjoyment body (*saṃbhogakāya, long sku*) and the emanation body (*nirmāṇakāya, sprul sku*). The dharma body is subdivided into the nature body (*svābhāvikakāya, ngo bo nyid sku*) and the wisdom body (*jñānakāya, ye shes kyi sku*).
203. The words set in italics in this passage indicate the realization pertaining to the first meditation topic of relying on the spiritual master. In the subsequent sessions pertaining to other topics, substitute them with the respective realizations of those topics.
204. Originally listed as the fourth benefit in the Tibetan text, this point has been shifted down to correspond with the order of the explanations below.
205. Nāgārjuna, *Five Stages*, 3.45, Tengyur D 1802, 53b4.

206. The Tibetan text misattributed the following citation to the *Words of Mañjuśrī*.
207. Reading *de mnyes* for *de gnyis* in the last line. Buddhaśrījñānapāda, *Oral Teaching Called Meditation on the Reality of the Two Stages*, Tengyur D 1853, 15b3.
208. Potowa Rinchen Sal, *Root Text of the Blue Manual*, 1. Sometimes attributed to Geshé Dölpa, this work is Geshé Dölpa's versified compilation of advice given by his teacher Potowa. Geshé Dölpa, named after his home region Döl, was also known by the names Rok Sherab Gyatso (Rog Shes rab rgya mtsho) and Dölpa Marshurwa (Dol pa Dmar zhur ba). For a complete English translation, see Roesler et al., *Stages of the Buddha's Teachings*, 37–117.
209. Appearing in a biography of Sakya Paṇḍita, this verse occurs in the context of recounting what Sakya Paṇḍita had taught. Yarlungpa Drakpa Gyaltsen, *Praise of the Dharma Lord Sakya Paṇḍita Kunga Gyaltsen*, 82.
210. The *Stem Array* (*Gaṇḍavyūha*), the final section of *A Multitude of Buddhas Sūtra* (*Buddhāvataṃsakasūtra*), narrates the encounters of the merchant's son Sudhana with many teachers in his quest for enlightenment, before he finally meets the bodhisattva Samantabhadra. See English translation at 84000.co (Toh 44), 53.23.
211. cf. *Saṃpuṭa Tantra*, Kangyur D 381, 108a2: *gang gi phyir rdzogs pa'i sangs rgyas dang byang chub sems dpa'i bsod nams gang zhig slob dpon gyi ba spu'i khung bu'i rtse mo la mthong ba de'i phyir byang chub sems dpas slob dpon la sangs rgyas kyis mchod pa byed pa mthong ngo*: "Thus, since whatever merit is possessed by perfectly awakened ones and bodhisattvas can be seen in the tips of the master's pores, the bodhisattvas witness buddhas worshiping the master." For a rendering based on the Sanskrit, see 84000.co (Toh 381), 5.121.
212. Aśvaghoṣa, *Fifty Verses on the Spiritual Guide*, Tengyur D 3721, 10a7–10b1.
213. Ratnākaraśānti, *Commentary on the Difficult Points of the Kṛṣṇayamāri Tantra*, Tengyur D 1919, 160b7.
214. *Lord of Secrets* (*guhyakādhipatiḥ, gsang ba'i bdag po*) is an epithet of Vajrapāṇi.
215. *Vajrapāṇi Initiation Tantra*, Kangyur D 496, 141b1–3.
216. The Tibetan text misattributed the following citation to the *Union with All the Buddhas Tantra* (Kangyur D 366).
217. *Ornament of Vajra Essence Tantra*, Kangyur D 451, 54b4.
218. Tsongkhapa, *Fulfilling the Disciples' Hopes*, 229.
219. *Ornament of Vajra Essence Tantra*, Kangyur D 451, 55a3–4.
220. The five actions of immediate retribution (*pañcānantarīyāṇi, mtshams med lnga*)—any of which can cause one to fall into a hell realm in the immediate next life—are killing one's father, killing one's mother, killing an arhat, causing a schism in the Saṅgha, and maliciously shedding the blood of a buddha.
221. Examples of abandoning the Dharma were provided on page 59.
222. The four defeats (*pārājika, pham pa*) of a fully ordained monastic are transgressions incurred by killing a human being, stealing an object that is of significant value, engaging in sexual conduct, and lying by claiming to have attained superior human qualities.
223. *Guhyasamāja Tantra*, 5.4–5ab, Kangyur D 442, 97a7–97b1.
224. Citation not identified.
225. Unrelenting Torment, or Avīci, is the lowest of the eight hot hells. See page 130.
226. *Vajrapāṇi Initiation Tantra*, Kangyur D 496, 141b3–4.
227. The three trainings are the trainings in ethics, meditative concentration, and wisdom. See chapters 10, 15, and 16 for details on how to cultivate them.
228. Potowa, *Blue Manual*, 32.

229. Thokmé Sangpo, *Thirty-Seven Practices of Bodhisattvas*, verse 5. Thokmé Sangpo is often called "child of the conquerors" (*rgyal sras*), which is another way of referring to a bodhisattva. Subsequent occurrences of this expression are directly rendered as "bodhisattva."
230. *Māras* refer to demons, either literally or figuratively. The four māras are those of the lord of death, afflictions, the son of the gods, and the aggregates.
231. *Foundations of Mindfulness*, Kangyur D 287, Sūtra *ra*, 206b1. See English translation at 84000.co (Toh 287), 4.B.-1190.
232. Citation not identified.
233. *Collection of Aphorisms*, 25.1 and 25.9, Kangyur D 326, 231b1–2 and 231b6–7.
234. Citation not identified.
235. *Vajra Tent Tantra*, Kangyur D 419, 65b1–2.
236. There are different explanations on how long the Buddha's teachings will remain in the world. By one account, the Buddha's teachings will last 5,000 years following the Buddha's passing. During the last period of 500 years, known as *period of merely holding signs* (*rtag tsam 'dzin pa'i dus*), while displaying shaved heads and donning robes, monastics lack scriptural understanding and spiritual realizations, and do not bear any vows at all. Tsalpa Kunga Dorjé, *Red Annals*, 199.
237. Citation not identified.
238. Citation not identified.
239. Cited in Aśvaghoṣa, *Fifty Verses on the Spiritual Guide*, Tengyur D 3721, 10b7.
240. Jayulwa Shönu Ö (Bya yul ba Gzhon nu 'od, 1075–1138) was an important teacher of the Kadam tradition. He was a student of Chen Ngawa Tsultrim Bar and a teacher of the Kagyü master Gampopa Sönam Rinchen (Sgam po pa Bsod nams rin chen).
241. The supporting and supported maṇḍalas refer to the inestimable mansion and the deities residing within it.
242. Chökyi Lodrö (Chos kyi blo gros) was the Dharma name given to Marpa (Mar pa) when he was twelve years old. *Tön*, in Martön (Mar ston), is the abbreviation of *tönpa*, which means "teacher."
243. Defying his parents, Marpa's son Darma Dodé went to attend a feast. On his way home, he fell from a horse and was badly injured. He first ejected his consciousness into the carcass of a pigeon and afterward into the corpse of a brahman boy who later became a monastic. After Darma Dodé's body was cremated, Marpa sang a song to his wife in which he proclaimed, "We have six sons who remain, but there is no hope that they will be holders of the teachings." For the full story, see Tsang Nyön Heruka, *The Life of Marpa the Translator*, 156–81.
244. *Meeting of Father and Son Sūtra*, Kangyur D 60, 33a7–33b1, 33b3, and 33b4.
245. Sunakṣatra (Legs pa'i skar ma) was a monk in the order of Buddha Śākyamuni for twenty years. Although he was very learned in the three scriptural baskets, he had no faith in the Buddha and held wrong views. *Passing into Great Nirvāṇa Sūtra*, Kangyur D 119, 185b6–193b5.
246. For the sake of being able to understand the hidden meanings of the Perfection of Wisdom sūtras, Asaṅga meditated on Maitreya with great effort but achieved no sign of accomplishment even after twelve years of practice. Despondent, he left his cave only to encounter a female dog infested with maggots. When he was motivated by strong compassion trying to save the dog as well as the maggots, the dog vanished and he beheld Maitreya. For a detailed account, see Tsonawa, *Indian Buddhist Pandits*, 27–29.
247. Nāropa was not able to find Tilopa in the western region of India and so he traveled

to Phulla Vihāra in eastern India. One day, an emaciated man came into the monastery, carrying several live fish in one end of his loincloth. After obtaining fire from the monks, he started to roast the fish. When Nāropa tried to stop him from cooking the fish alive, the man, who turned out to be Tilopa, blew upon the roasted fish. Shimmering as they came to life, the fish swam away when released into water. Kunga Gyaltsen, *A Hundred Thousand Syllables of Cakrasaṃvara Luipa*, 408–9.

248. Kusāli was a prince of Magadha. After receiving monastic vows, he became known as the novice monk Tailor (dge tshul Tshem bu pa). One day, he was traveling with the adept Kṛṣṇācārya and came to the River Ganges, where a leper woman was waiting to cross it. She asked Kṛṣṇācārya to carry her on his back, but he was so repulsed by her condition that he turned her down. Moved by compassion, Kusāli took on the task. Halfway across the river, the leper woman transformed into Vajravārāhī, one of the forms of Vajrayoginī, and took him to Khecara Pure Land. Pema Trinlé, *Clarifying Mirror*, 776–77.
249. When Vajraghaṇṭapa first met the swineherd girl in Oḍḍiyāna, he rejected her because of her extreme unattractiveness, but he later recognized her as his guru. See Dowman, *Masters of Mahāmudrā*, 273.
250. Sudhana's encounter with King Anala is described in the *Stem Array*. See English translation at 84000.co (Toh 44), chap. 20.
251. *Bodhisattvas' Grounds*, Tengyur D 4037, 186a4–5. To view this explanation in context, see Asaṅga, *The Bodhisattva Path to Unsurpassed Enlightenment*, 584.
252. Songtsen Gampo (Srong btsan sgam po), the thirty-third Tibetan king, is traditionally credited with the introduction of Buddhism to Tibet.
253. Tölung (Stod lung) is a district near Lhasa in central Tibet.
254. Denbak (Dan 'bag) is the name of a village below Drepung Monastery in Tibet.
255. One of the features of Avalokiteśvara is that he is ornamented at his crown by Amitābha, his guru.
256. An unadorned arhat is one who has attained liberation based on intelligence and has not attained any actual *dhyāna*.
257. In one of the Buddha's past lives as a king in Magadha, he requested the Dharma from a brahman, who agreed to teach him on the condition that he pierce his flesh and insert a thousand lamps in his own body. Having accepted the condition with delight, the king allowed his body to be burned with lamps. The king rejoiced after receiving the teaching from the brahman, but Indra, the lord of the gods, expressed disbelief at the king's proclamation that he harbored no thought of regret while his body was pierced and trembling with agony. By uttering the words of truth that his wounds may be healed if he did not engender the slightest regret for undergoing the immense physical suffering, the king's body became whole again. In another life, he inserted a thousand iron spikes into his body for the sake of receiving a Dharma teaching, and by similarly uttering the words of truth, his wounds were completely healed. See Frye, *The Sutra of the Wise and the Foolish*, 2–6.
258. Āryaśūra's *Garland of Birth Stories* does not contain a description of such an episode, though there is a story of the Buddha's past life as Viśvantara (Pāli: Vessantara), in which he gave away his two children and wife, who were eventually returned to him. The *Buddhavaṃsa* in the Pāli canon also tells the story of a past buddha called Maṅgala, who, when he was a bodhisattva, gave his two children to the yakṣa Kharadāṭhika, a flesh-eating demon, who devoured them in his very presence.
259. As it was well known that Suvarṇadvīpa Dharmakīrti had the most complete instructions on bodhicitta, Atiśa set out for Sumatra with 125 disciples on a thirteen-month

journey, during which they faced extraordinary challenges. When he set out to return to India after twelve years, Suvarṇadvīpa predicted that he would one day go to a snowy land in the north. Sumatra was known in ancient times by the Sanskrit name Suvarṇadvīpa ("Golden Isle"), on account of the gold deposits in the island's highlands. Note that the master Suvarṇadvīpa Dharmakīrti who was born in the tenth century is a different master from the renowned logician Dharmakīrti who lived a few centuries earlier. For the full story of Atiśa's voyage to Sumatra, see Jinpa, *Mind Training*, chap. 3.

260. Nāgārjuna, *Five Stages*, 4.2, Tengyur D 1802, 53b7–54a1. Ācārya, a title given to qualified spiritual teachers, refers to a person who knows and teaches the ācāra, or rules of conduct.
261. Potowa, *Blue Manual*, 3.
262. Potowa, *Blue Manual*, 3.
263. Potowa, *Blue Manual*, 3.
264. It was common in earlier times for a guru to provide resources such as lodging, bedding, clothing, and food to a disciple who leaves home to learn from him.
265. *Verses of the Nāga King Bherī*, Kangyur D 325, 205b3–4.
266. The three scriptural baskets (*tripitaka*, *sde snod gsum*) are broad categories classifying the Buddha's teachings according to their main subject matters. They are the scriptural baskets of higher knowledge (Abhidharma), discourses (Sūtra), and discipline (Vinaya).
267. Sakya Paṇḍita Kunga Gyaltsen, *Profound Path of Guru Yoga*, 96–97.
268. Setsun Wangchuk Shönu (Se btsun Dbang phyug gzhon nu) was one of Dromtönpa's first teachers. Dromtönpa first met him at the age of nineteen, almost twenty years before he met Atiśa.
269. Without stating the concluding passage completely, the Tibetan text indicates that the practitioner should apply a format similar to that of the previous topics. In this and subsequent instances, the concluding passage is spelled out in full for the convenience of readers.
270. This is the prayer mentioned in chapter 2. See note 172.
271. Not to be mistaken for the adoption of specific bodily postures, or *asanas*, Buddhist *yoga* mainly refers to mental training of the union of calm abiding and special insight.
272. See chapter 2, pages 51–83.
273. *Verse Summary on the Perfection of Wisdom*, 32.2ab, Kangyur D 13, 19b2. To view these lines in context, see Conze, *The Perfection of Wisdom in Eight Thousand Lines & Its Verse Summary*, 71.
274. Nāgārjuna, *Letter to a Friend*, verses 63–64, Tengyur D 4182, 43b4–5.
275. The four are fully ordained monks and nuns and male and female lay followers.
276. The major limbs (*aṅga*, *yan lag*) are the head, arms, and legs, while the minor limbs (*pratyaṅga*, *nying lag*) are the nose, ears, fingers, and toes.
277. Mahāmati, *Distinct Words*, Tengyur D 4190, 96b4.
278. The locations of saṃsāra may be considered as consisting of the three realms: the desire realm, form realm, and formless realm. The form realm consists of four *dhyānas* or concentrations, which are divided into a total of seventeen levels, with three levels in each of first three *dhyānas* and eight levels in the fourth *dhyāna*. Great Fruit (*mahāphala*, *'bras bu chen po*) is the third of the eight levels of the fourth *dhyāna*. These beings without discrimination are reborn there as a result of cultivating the meditative stabilization without discrimination (*asaṃjñāsamāpatti*, *'du shes med pa'i*

snyoms 'jug). They have a slight discrimination that they have been born there at the beginning of their lifetime and have the discrimination that they are about to die near the end of their lifetime. Otherwise they spend their lives in a meditative state devoid of discrimination. See Lati and Denma Lochö, *Meditative States*, 44.

279. Aśvaghoṣa, *Discussion of the Eight States Deprived of Liberty,* Tengyur D 4167, 177a7.
280. These versified lines are a paraphrase of Asaṅga, *Hearers' Grounds*, Tengyur D 4036, 3b4.
281. The "subduing Dharma" (*chos 'dul ba*) here refers to all three scriptural baskets (*tripiṭaka, sde snod gsum*). See Tsongkhapa, *Great Exposition*, 69, or in translation, Tsong-kha-pa, *Great Treatise,* 1:119.
282. These versified lines are a paraphrase of Asaṅga, *Hearers' Grounds*, Tengyur D 4036, 4a5–6.
283. "Field" (*kṣetra, zhing*) here refers to the subject in relation to whom one cultivates a practice. For example, when making offerings, the field is the recipient of one's offerings.
284. Brahmā is one of main gods of the first *dhyāna* within the form realm.
285. "Item" here refers to the article with which one engages in practice.
286. "Basis" here refers to the practitioner, who may uphold various types of ethical disciplines, such as lay vows, novice vows, full ordination vows, bodhisattva vows, and so on.
287. A "world system of endurance" (*sahālokadhātu, 'jig rten gyi khams mi mjed*) refers to a world system where sentient beings endure attachment, hatred, ignorance, and the bondage of afflictions. *White Lotus of Compassion Sūtra*, Kangyur D 112, 208a4–5.
288. These three continents are the other continents apart from the southern continent Jambūdvīpa. They are the eastern continent Pūrvavideha, the western continent Aparagodānīya, and the northern continent Uttarakuru.
289. *Saṃvarodaya Tantra*, 2.6–7ab, Kangyur D 373, 266a1–2.
290. Our human continent, Jambūdvīpa, is a land of karma (*karmabhūmi, las kyi sa pa*), where the karma created is powerful and can ripen in the same life.
291. Sukhāvatī, the Blissful pure land, where sentient beings experience neither physical pain nor mental suffering and the causes for their happiness are limitless, is the buddha land of Amitābha, as described in the *Display of Sukhāvatī Sūtra*, Kangyur D 115. See English translation at 84000.co (Toh 115).
292. The three types of vows are the prātimokṣa vows, bodhisattva vows, and tantric vows.
293. This sentence is a wondrously succinct summary of the sūtra explanation in which the Buddha offered more than twenty sets of combinations comparing the probabilities of pairs of rebirths: "The number of beings who are reborn from the *hell* realm into the *human* realm is like the atoms on the tip of my fingernail, whereas the number of beings who are reborn from the *hell* realm into the *animal* realm is like the atoms of the ground; the number of beings who are reborn from the *hell* realm into the *human* realm is like the atoms on the tip of my fingernail, whereas the number of beings who are reborn from the *hell* realm into the *hungry ghost* realm is like the atoms of the ground; the number of beings who are reborn from the *hell* realm into the *human* realm is like the atoms on the tip of my fingernail, whereas the number of beings who are reborn from the *hell* realm into the *hell* realm is like the atoms of the ground . . ." *Chapters on Vinaya*, Kangyur D 1, Vinaya *ka*, 87b2–89b2.
294. Āryadeva, *Four Hundred Verses*, 7.6, Tengyur D 3846, 8a7.
295. This explanation cannot be located in the *Teaching to Venerable Nanda on Entry into the Womb*, Kangyur D 58. See English translation at 84000.co (Toh 58). There is, how-

ever, an explanation of the rarity of the human rebirth sans analogies in the *Teaching to Nanda on Dwelling in the Womb*, Kangyur D 57, 227a6–7. For an indication of the possible mislabeling of these two texts, see note 308. The difficulty of obtaining a precious human rebirth is compared to the unlikelihood that a single white mustard seed would pass through the eye of an upright needle when someone tosses some white mustard seeds at it in *Nanda's Going Forth Sūtra*, Kangyur D 328, 257a1–2. See English translation at 84000.co (Toh 328), 1.17.

296. The *Connected Discourses* (*Saṃyukta-āgama, Yang dag par ldan pa'i lung*) corresponds roughly to the Saṃyutta Nikāya in the Pāli canon.
297. This explanation occurs in the *First Sutta on the Yoke with a Hole* (*Paṭhamachiggaḷa-yugasutta*, SN 56.47). See Bodhi, *Connected Discourses*, 1871. A similar example is used to illustrate the difficulty of obtaining a precious human rebirth in *Nanda's Going Forth Sūtra*, Kangyur D 328, 256b5–7. See English translation at 84000.co (Toh 328), 1.14.
298. The Nyang River (Nyang chu) is a tributary of the Yarlung Tsangpo River in Tibet.
299. See the advice given on page 105 at the end of chapter 3: "Do not read many other texts. Endowed with mindfulness and introspection, restrain the doors of your sense faculties. Consume food in appropriate quantities. Strive in yoga without lying down, and when you do lie down, practice accordingly. Strive in the yogas of washing and of eating."
300. See chapter 2, pages 51–83.
301. The following section describes the nine-round meditation on death. The three sets of three points have been numbered to facilitate easy identification.
302. *Collection of Aphorisms*, Kangyur D 326, 210a1. This verse is not in the extant Sanskrit edition but appears in the Tibetan translation between 1.24 and 1.25.
303. The vajra body is an indestructible body that is not subject to death and disintegration.
304. *Collection of Aphorisms* 1.25, Kangyur D 326, 210a1–2.
305. The Tibetan text misattributed the following citation to the *Collection of Aphorisms.*
306. Aśvaghoṣa, *Dispelling Sorrow*, Tengyur D 4177, 33b2–3.
307. Śāntideva, *Engaging in Bodhisattva Deeds*, 2.39, Tengyur D 3871, 5b2.
308. This explanation cannot be located in the *Teaching to Venerable Nanda on Entry into the Womb*, Kangyur D 58. See English translation at 84000.co (Toh 58). In fact, this explanation occurs in the *Teaching to Nanda on Dwelling in the Womb*, Kangyur D 57, 222a7–223b2. Based on the comparison of the titles and contents, it seems that the Tibetan compilers of the Ratnakūṭa switched the titles of the two texts, which were translated from Chinese. See Kritzer, "Tibetan Texts of Garbhāvakrāntisūtra."
309. Vasubandhu, *Treasury of Knowledge*, 3.78a, Tengyur D 4089, 9b7. According to Indian cosmology, Kuru is the northern continent among the four continents in our world system.
310. The inhabitants of the eastern continent, Videha, have a general lifespan of 250 years, while those of the western continent, Godānīya, have a general lifespan of 500 years. Among the four continents, only the inhabitants of Kuru are exempt from untimely death. Vasubandhu, *Treasury of Knowledge*, 3.78b and 3.85a, Tengyur D 4089, 9b7 and 10a3–4.
311. The lifespan in Jambūdvīpa, "Jambu Continent," is not fixed because it is ten years at the end of the eon and immeasurable in the beginning, with many periods of increase and decrease between. See Vasubandhu, *Treasury of Knowledge*, 3.91–92, Tengyur D 4089, 10a7–10b1. See also Sadakata, *Buddhist Cosmology*, 103–4.

312. Vasubandhu, *Treasury of Knowledge*, 3.78cd, Tengyur D 4089, 9b7.
313. *Collection of Aphorisms* 1.7–10, Kangyur D 326, 209a4–7.
314. The last verse could not be identified, even though the Tibetan text attributes it to the *Collection of Aphorisms*.
315. Nāgārjuna, *Precious Garland*, 3.78ab, Tengyur D 4158, 117b1.
316. *Tsen* (*btsan*) is the name of a class of evil spirits.
317. *Mātṛ* (*ma mo*) is the name of a class of female spirits.
318. The tantric medical system expounds that the four elements—earth, water, fire, and wind—within a person's body must be in a state of balance in order to maintain health.
319. In the *Sutta on the Seven Suns* (*Sattasūriyasutta*, AN 7.66), on the occasion of explaining that conditioned phenomena are impermanent, unstable, and unreliable, the Buddha describes a time when an increasing number of suns will appear. Eventually seven suns will appear, whereby the earth and Mount Meru will burn and blaze, and neither ash nor soot will remain. See Bodhi, *Numerical Discourses*, 1071–73.
320. Nāgārjuna, *Letter to a Friend*, verse 57, Tengyur D 4182, 43a7–43b1.
321. Nāgārjuna, *Precious Garland*, 4.17cd, Tengyur D 4158, 118b7–119a1.
322. According to Abhidharma system of calculation, one *yojana* (*dpag tshad*) is equal to 4,000 armspans, which translates to roughly 4.5 miles or 7.2 kilometers. See Vasubandhu, *Treasury of Knowledge*, 3.87–88a, Tengyur D 4089, 10a4–5. For a discussion of ancient Indian units of measurements, see Sadakata, *Buddhist Cosmology*, 185–87.
323. The mountains resemble the faces of animals, such as lice, goats, and sheep, that one has killed in the past.
324. According to the Abhidharma, a world system undergoes cycles of dissolution, nothingness, creation, and abidance. A cycle consisting of the four phases is presented beginning with the phase of dissolution, as is the Indian custom of calculating the month from the full moon. During the phase of dissolution, the world undergoes warming with the appearance of an increasing number of suns. Starting from the hells, the desire realm is progressively incinerated. Eventually, even the first level of the form realm is also destroyed by fire. See Sadakata, *Buddhist Cosmology*, 99–105.
325. *Gośīrṣa* ("ox head") sandalwood is named after the shape or name of the mountain where it grows. Reddish in color, this medicinal wood purportedly has the finest fragrance of all sandalwood. For a Buddhist story illustrating its great value and cooling properties, see McHugh, *Sandalwood and Carrion*, 203–9.
326. Nāgārjuna, *Letter to a Friend*, verse 87, Tengyur D 4182, 44b5–6.
327. The number 162 million has been emended to 1.62 trillion in accordance with the *Sūtra on Lifespans*, Kangyur D 307, 141b4. See English translation at 84000.co (Toh 307), 1.44. For the calculations leading to this figure, see Sadakata, *Buddhist Cosmology*, 59.
328. For the meaning of major and minor limbs, see note 276.
329. The trunk of a silk-cotton tree (*śāmali*, *shal ma li*) or *Ceiba pentandra* bears numerous conical thorns. *Kapok* is a name used in English-speaking countries for both the tree and the cotton-like fluff obtained from its seed pods. Its light and strong fiber has historically been used to fill mattresses, pillows, and dolls.
330. Asaṅga, *Grounds of Yogic Practitioners*, Tengyur D 4035, 38b3–4.
331. On his way home after having gathered jewels from an island in the ocean, Śroṇa Koṭikarṇa (Gro bzhin skyes rna ba bye ba ri) woke up one morning to find that the merchants' caravan had left without him. Setting off on his donkey cart, he eventually became lost and ended up setting out on foot alone. He arrived at a city of hungry

ghosts who resembled scorched wooden pillars, with stomachs like mountains and mouths like pinholes. After safely leaving that city, he encountered yet another city of thousands of hungry ghosts. Continuing his way, he saw a man who experienced divine pleasures with four nymphs in the night, but as soon as the sun rose he was ripped apart by four dogs until sunset. On another occasion he saw a man who experienced divine pleasures with a nymph in the night, but as soon as the sun rose a giant centipede wrapped around his body and started to eat him from the top of his head. As he continued his way, he encountered a beautiful woman, well dressed and attractively ornamented. Four hungry ghosts were bound to the corner posts of her bed. When Śroṇa Koṭikarṇa tossed food to them, it turned into dung beetles, balls of iron, and the hungry ghosts' own flesh and bloody pus. For the complete story, see Rotman, *Divine Stories*, vol. 1, chap. 1.

332. After returning from having taught the Dharma to the nāgas, Saṅgharakṣita (Dge 'dun srungs) woke up one morning to find that the merchants' boat had left without him. Setting off alone by foot, he came across a monastery where the monks were properly dressed and serene in their comportment. Soon after a gong was sounded, the monastery vanished and their alms bowls turned into iron hammers, with which they broke each other's skulls as they cried out in pain. This continued until night turned to day, and the monastery appeared again. At a second monastery, the monks' food and drink turned into molten iron, with which they doused each other's bodies. At a third monastery, the monastery caught fire and the monks' bodies were burned. When he set out once again, he saw beings with the forms of pillars, walls, trees, leaves, flowers, fruits, ropes, brooms, mortars, cups, and pots. He also saw beings, cut in half at the waist and held together with string, walking about. For the complete story, see Rotman, *Divine Stories,* vol. 2, chap. 23.

333. Prātimokṣa infractions (*duṣkṛta, nyes byas*) and prātimokṣa individual confessions (*pratideśanīya, sor bzhag*) are two classes of the vows of a fully ordained monk.

334. Rather than the root text *Engaging in Bodhisattva Deeds* itself, the information provided in this sentence seems to be based on commentarial literature elaborating on the root text such as verse 6.1, which is cited on page 186.

335. For an explanation of the four powers of purification, see pages 150–51.

336. Nāgārjuna, *Letter to a Friend*, verse 91, Tengyur D 4182, 45a1.

337. A human month is equivalent to a day for the hungry ghosts. See Vasubandhu, *Treasury of Knowledge*, 3.83d, Tengyur D 4089, 10a3.

338. 500 hungry ghost years = 500 x 12 x 30 hungry ghost days = 500 x 12 x 30 human months = 500 x 30 human years = 15,000 human years. For the sūtra source of this explanation, see the *Sūtra on Lifespans*, Kangyur D 307, 139b1–2. See English translation at 84000.co (Toh 307), 1.5.

339. "Month" (*zla ba*) has been emended to "day" (*nyin zhag*) in accordance with the cited *Foundations of Mindfulness*, Kangyur D 287, Sūtra *ya*, 288b1. See English translation at 84000.co (Toh 287), 2.1289.

340. 500 hungry ghost years = 500 x 12 x 30 hungry ghost days = 500 x 12 x 30 x 10 human years = 1,800,000 human years.

341. Mentioned frequently in Indian mythology, the garuḍa is a predatory bird that hunts nāgas. To render this point more accessible to the modern mind, we may imagine snakes that experience the terror of raptors swooping down on them and seizing them with razor-sharp claws.

342. Vasubandhu, *Treasury of Knowledge*, 3.83c, Tengyur D 4089, 10a2–3.

343. The *Easy Path* only provides the visualization of the refuge objects, the request, and the refuge formula, which are all cited near the end of this chapter, before the explanation of the benefits of going for refuge.
344. Losang Chökyi Gyaltsen, *Melodious Speech of Losang's Assertions*, 6a1–2. As explained in note 99, in this text Losang Chökyi Gyaltsen is providing responses based on Tsongkhapa's assertions, and so here "you who knows all" refers to Tsongkhapa.
345. Candrakīrti, *Seventy Verses on Refuge*, Tengyur D 3971, 251a1–2.
346. See appendix 2.
347. See appendix 3.
348. Reading *'di ni* for *'di'i* in accordance with Tsongkhapa, *Great Exposition*, 125.
349. Annotated in accordance with Sopa, *Steps on the Path*, 1:431.
350. These opening words belong to the *Recollection of the Buddha*, Kangyur D 279. This brief sūtra is listed in the Kangyur alongside two very brief sūtras, *Recollection of the Dharma* (Kangyur D 280) and *Recollection of the Saṅgha* (Kangyur D 281). The combination of these three sūtras is commonly known as the *Recollection of the Three Jewels* (*Dkon mchog rje dran*), though there is no such independent entry in the Dergé Kangyur catalogue.
351. Since the Buddha and the ārya Saṅgha are persons, increasing merit in relation to them is subsumed under the increase of merit in terms of persons.
352. One must have gone for refuge in order to be qualified to take the prātimokṣa vows, bodhisattva vows, or tantric vows.
353. For the complete story of Sūkarika, see Rotman, *Divine Stories*, vol. 1, chap. 14. An account of this story occurs in the *Narrative of a Sow Sūtra*, Kangyur D 345. See English translation at 84000.co (Toh 345).
354. Our Tibetan text specifies his brother's name as *'Byor ldan*, as opposed to *Shing gi rna cha can* (Dārukarṇin) mentioned in the *Chapters on Vinaya*.
355. This episode is recounted in the *Chapters on Vinaya*, Kangyur D 1, Vinaya *ka*, 307b4–309a1. See English translation at 84000.co (Toh 1–6), 2.242–58. For the complete story of Pūrṇa, see Rotman, *Divine Stories*, vol. 1, chap. 2.
356. Tīrthikas (*mu stegs pa*) are non-Buddhists who propound wrong views.
357. In terms of prescriptive guidelines, one should respect Buddha images, Dharma writings, and Saṅgha members as if they are the Three Jewels themselves. What do these guidelines entail? Defining them by negation, it is explained that one should not disparage images of tathāgatas, treat the scriptures as merchandise, revile monks and nuns, and so on. For details on how to observe the various guidelines, see Tsong-kha-pa, *Great Treatise*, 1:194–96.
358. *Dge tshul kyun te.*
359. See Frye, *The Sutra of the Wise and the Foolish*, chap. 52.
360. This is a common refrain appearing many times in the Kangyur, for example, in *A Hundred Karma Tales*, Kangyur D 340, 10a2–3. See English translation at 84000.co (Toh 340), 1.125.
361. One-day vows (*upavāsa*, *bsnyen gnas*) consist of eight vows, including abstinence from sexual activity for that day.
362. Annotated in accordance with Tsongkhapa, *Great Exposition*, 150. For English translation, see Tsong-kha-pa, *Great Treatise*, 1:222.
363. The text makes no mention of the execution. In relation to this point, the *Great Exposition* reports that the *Compendium of Determinations* states that the instigator causing others to commit sexual misconduct incurs the misdeed of sexual misconduct as well,

but the autocommentary of *Treasury of Knowledge* explains that such instigation does not itself constitute the actual karmic path of sexual misconduct. See Tsongkhapa, *Great Exposition*, 150–51. For English translation, see Tsong-kha-pa, *Great Treatise*, 1:222.

364. Tsongkhapa specifies that the content delivered is unpleasant. Tsongkhapa, *Great Exposition*, 152. For a detailed explanation, see Tsong-kha-pa, *Great Treatise*, 1:223.
365. See note 140 for the four types of fields.
366. The social context in India when Buddhist teachings were first given centuries ago was one in which women were denied many opportunities afforded to men. The Buddha did not discount women's capacity to develop themselves spiritually or otherwise and he did not view them as naturally inferior. In fact, Buddhism teaches that all sentient beings equally have the potential to achieve highest enlightenment and that there is no place for discrimination of any form in this regard.
367. Potowa, *Blue Manual*, 32.
368. Tsongkhapa, *Concise Exposition*, 82.
369. For example, one can arrange an image of the Buddha, a copy of a sūtra, and a stūpa to represent the enlightened body, speech, and mind respectively.
370. The three spheres of an action are its agent, object, and action. For example, the three spheres of killing are the killer, the victim, and the killing itself.
371. An example of this practice is the recitation of the names of the Thirty-Five Buddhas in the practice of the *Confession of Downfalls*.
372. The mind having gone astray in relation to the Dharma refers to the mind of someone who knows the words of the Dharma but fails to put the Dharma into practice, whereby their mind becomes incorrigible no matter how the Dharma is explained to them.
373. This verse is one of the sayings attributed to a king in the *Minor Points of the Vinaya*, Kangyur D 6, Vinaya *da*, 19b7–20a1. It is loosely parallel to a verse in *A Hundred Verses*:

    He who takes vows and then returns them,
    a woman who sees three men, and
    a jackal that escapes from a trap—
    know that these three are cunning.

    Vararuci, *A Hundred Verses*, Tengyur D 4332, 124b5. See Hahn, "Vararuci's Gāthāśataka," 423–24. In this verse, a person who simply gives the appearance of being a spiritual practitioner is depicted as being as reprehensible as a promiscuous person or a sly animal.
374. The Kadam lineage master Shawo Gangpa Pema Jangchup (Sha bo sgang pa Padma byang chub, 1067–1131) was a disciple of Langri Thangpa Dorjé Senge (Glang ri thang pa Rdo rje seng ge), who composed the well-known *Eight Verses of Mind Training* (*Blo sbyong tshigs brgyad ma*).
375. *Cha la kha phyir blta'i shes pa.*
376. Tsongkhapa, *Great Exposition*, 22. To view this statement in context, see Tsong-kha-pa, *Great Treatise*, 1:61.
377. Tsongkhapa, *Middle-Length Exposition*, 53. To view this statement in context in English, see Tsongkhapa, *Middle-Length Treatise*, 88.
378. Tsongkhapa, *Cakrasaṃvara Prayer*, 174.
379. For the meaning of *mental abidings*, see note 532.

380. The five supernatural powers (*abhijñā, mngon shes*) are the supernatural powers of (1) magical powers (*ṛddhi*), which can shake the earth, emanate one into many, etc., (2) divine ear (*divyaśrotra*), which can hear the sounds in all world systems, (3) knowing others' minds (*paracittajñāna*), which knows others' attachment, aversion, and so forth, (4) recollecting former lives (*pūrvanivāsānusmṛti*), which knows the past lives of oneself and others, and (5) divine eye (*divyacakṣu*), which can see distant forms.
381. The five sciences (*vidyāsthāna, rig gnas*) are the fields of study of arts and crafts (*śilpakarmasthāna*), medicine (*cikitsā*), language (*śabda*), logic (*hetu*), and spirituality (*adhyātma*).
382. The eight great feats (*mahāsiddhi, dngos grub chen po*) are the feats of the sword, the pill, the eye medicine, swift-footedness, the elixir, sky travel, invisibility, and underground travel.
383. See chapter 2, pages 51–83.
384. Nāgārjuna, *Letter to a Friend*, verse 66, Tengyur D 4182, 43b6.
385. Sometimes attributed to Ārya Kātyāyana, this stanza relates to a story recounted in *Classifications of Karma*, Kangyur D 338, 289b2–290a6. One day, while going on his alms round in Magadha, Ārya Mahāmaudgalyāyana encounters a householder cradling a child in his lap, eating a fish, and throwing the bones at a black dog. Maudgalyāyana, who was foremost in psychic power among the disciples of the Buddha, saw that the fish was actually the father of the householder in a past life. He used to fish at the pond behind his house, and due to attachment to his son, was reborn among the fishes in the pond. The dog was actually the mother of the householder in a past life. Due to attachment to her son, she was reborn as his dog. On one occasion, the householder caught his wife sleeping with another man and killed him out of anger. Out of his attachment to the householder's wife, the adulterer was reborn as her child. So as to induce disillusionment with respect to saṃsāra, Maudgalyāyana taught about these confounding relations by uttering the following verse:

    He eats his father's flesh,
    tosses the bones and scraps at his mother,
    and tends to his wife's baby—
    obscured by ignorance and attachment.

386. Attachment (*rāga, 'dod chags*) is often confused for love (*maitrī, byams pa*), which Buddhism encourages us to actively cultivate for all sentient beings. Exaggerating good qualities and projecting nonexistent attributes onto people and things, attachment is characterized by selfishness and sets us up for endless disappointment and frustration. For the differences between love and attachment, see Rabten, *The Mind and Its Functions*, 140–41.
387. *Questions of Subāhu Tantra*, Kangyur D 805, 122a2–3.
388. *Play in Full Sūtra*, 16.23, Kangyur D 95, 119a5–6. See English translation at 84000.co (Toh 95), 16.29.
389. Āryaśūra, *Compendium of the Perfections*, 5.27, Tengyur D 3944, 229b5–6.
390. As the king of gods, Śakra, also known as Indra, is worshiped for being a great warrior and protector.
391. A wheel-turning king (*cakravartin*) is a powerful sovereign who rules over one or more human continents. Several types of wheel-turning kings are explained in the context of the benefits of cultivating love in chapter 11, page 193.
392. Nāgārjuna, *Letter to a Friend*, verse 69, Tengyur D 4182, 43b7–44a1.

393. Situated above the desire realm, the Brahmā realms (Brahmāloka) are the levels of the first *dhyāna* of the form realm. In order to take rebirth there, one has to overcome the attachment of the desire realm.
394. Nāgārjuna, *Letter to a Friend*, verse 74, Tengyur D 4182, 44a3–4.
395. This verse was previously cited in chapter 2, page 57.
396. Nāgārjuna, *Letter to a Friend*, verse 67, Tengyur D 4182, 43b6–7.
397. Aśvaghoṣa, *Dispelling Sorrow*, Tengyur D 4177, 34a4–6.
398. *Classifications of Vinaya*, Kangyur D 3, 119a2. A similar verse appears in the *Collection of Aphorisms*, 1.22, Kangyur D 326, 209b6.
399. The Tibetan text misattributed the following citation to *Engaging in Bodhisattva Deeds*.
400. Āryaśūra, *Garland of Birth Stories*, 19.1, Tengyur D 4150, 62b5.
401. The first line is not cited in the Tibetan text and is filled in for completeness.
402. Śāntideva, *Engaging in Bodhisattva Deeds*, 8.32–33, Tengyur D 3871, 24b3–4.
403. Given the Mahāyāna context of the lamrim, one practices the medium scope with the attainment of buddhahood in mind.
404. "Establishing appropriated aggregates" means to take rebirth in saṃsāra under the influence of karma and afflictions. Subsequent occurrences of this expression are rendered as "taking rebirth."
405. "Charred" (*bsregs pa*) is probably a reference to the dark environment in the womb. At a certain point in its development, the fetus experiences five unmistaken perceptions, one of which is that of darkness. *Teaching to Venerable Nanda on Entry into the Womb*, Kangyur D 58, 244a6. See English translation at 84000.co (Toh 58), 1.55. In Buddhism, the bodies of both men and women are considered impure, filled with substances such as blood, pus, phlegm, excrement, and urine.
406. The many illnesses that afflict the body can be divided into 101 bile diseases, 101 wind diseases, 101 phlegm diseases, and 101 diseases that arise from a combination of wind, bile, and phlegm. *Teaching to Venerable Nanda on Entry into the Womb*, Kangyur D 58, 246b2–5. See English translation at 84000.co (Toh 58), 1.62–64.
407. "Interferers" (*vighna*, *gegs*) are nonhumans who create obstacles to the practice of virtue.
408. There are many types of microorganisms (*krimi/kṛmi*, *srin bu*, "worms") that feed on the various parts of the body. *Teaching to Venerable Nanda on Entry into the Womb*, Kangyur D 58, 244b7–246a1. See English translation at 84000.co (Toh 58), 1.58.
409. Nāgārjuna, *Letter to a Friend*, verses 103–4, Tengyur D 4182, 45b1–3.
410. *Play in Full Sūtra*, 13.89, Kangyur D 95, 88b7. See English translation at 84000.co (Toh 95), 13.98.
411. *Demigod* is the translation of *asura*, which is rendered in Tibetan as *lha ma yin*, "not-gods." For a discussion about the name *asura*, see Sadakata, *Buddhist Cosmology*, 55.
412. For the meaning of major and minor limbs, see note 276.
413. Nāgārjuna, *Letter to a Friend*, verses 99–100, Tengyur D 4182, 45a6–7.
414. *Foundations of Mindfulness*, Kangyur D 287, *ra*, 73b3. See English translation at 84000.co (Toh 287), 4.A.153.
415. In the classification of the three realms of saṃsāra as the desire realm, form realm, and formless realm, the "higher realms" (*khams gong ma*) refer to the form and formless realms. Rebirth in the higher realms should be distinguished from upper rebirths (*bde 'gro*), which also include the rebirths of humans and desire-realm gods.

416. This explanation was not located in Candragomin, *Praise of Confession*, Tengyur D 1159.
417. There are three kinds of suffering: the suffering of suffering (*duḥkhaduḥkhatā, sdug bsngal gyi sdug bsngal*), the suffering of change (*vipariṇāmaduḥkhatā, 'gyur ba'i sdug bsngal*), and conditioned suffering (*saṃskāraduḥkhatā, 'du byed kyi sdug bsngal*). The suffering of suffering is manifest pain. The suffering of change is contaminated happiness, which will change to pain. Conditioned suffering is one's pervasive susceptibility to suffering from having taken rebirth under the power of karma and afflictions.
418. See chapter 2, pages 51–83.
419. The three trainings are the trainings in ethics, meditative concentration, and wisdom. The author explains the training in wisdom and the training in ethics in this chapter but makes no mention of the training in meditative concentration. To understand the trainings in meditative concentration and wisdom in detail, see chapters 15 and 16, where the perfections of meditative concentration and wisdom are explained. It seems the explanation in this chapter emphasizes the training in ethics from among the three trainings; at the end of the chapter, one requests blessings to "uphold pure ethics untainted by faults."
420. *Neutral* (*lung ma bstan*) in this context refers to being neither virtuous nor nonvirtuous by nature.
421. To apprehend something *as a self* means to apprehend it *as inherently existent*.
422. Dharmakīrti, *Commentary on Validity*, 2.213ab, Tengyur D 4210, 115b5. The view of the transitory collection (*satkākadṛṣṭi, 'jig tshogs la lta ba*) is a type of conception of self of persons. While observing the I that is imputed in dependence on the aggregates in one's own continuum, it apprehends that I as truly existent. For commentary by the Seventh Karmapa, see Karmapa Chödrak Gyatso, *Establishing Validity*, verse 214cd.
423. Dharmakīrti, *Commentary on Validity*, 2.217cd–220ab, Tengyur D 4210, 115b7–116a2. For commentary by the Seventh Karmapa, see Karmapa Chödrak Gyatso, *Establishing Validity*, verses 219–21.
424. Candrakīrti, *Entering the Middle Way*, 1.3ab, Tengyur D 3861, 201a3.
425. *What Is Treasured by a Fully Ordained Monk Sūtra*, Kangyur D 302, 126b1–2.
426. *King of Meditative Stabilizations Sūtra*, 35.3–4, Kangyur D 127, 128a6–7. See English translation at 84000.co (Toh 127), 36.23–24.
427. Reaching up to a possible height of more than thirty meters, the *tala* tree (*borassus flabellifer*) is known also as the Palmyra palm. A Vinaya version of this story describes the monk as being reborn as a nāga with seven heads, from which emerge *ela* plants (*shing e la*) infested with hundreds of species of insects; swarms of bees hover around and land on the heads, from which fetid pus and blood drip. *Minor Points of the Vinaya*, Kangyur D 6, Vinaya *tha*, 280a7–282a7.
428. *Classifications of Vinaya*, Kangyur D 3, 21b3–4.
429. There are four doors to transgressions: (1) ignorance, (2) disrespect, (3) heedlessness, and (4) unchecked afflictions. The other three are explained below.
430. In the Tibetan Buddhist tradition, a novice monk (*śramaṇera, dge tshul*) or novice nun (*śrāmaṇerī/śrāmaṇerikā, dge tshul ma*) observes ten vows (sometimes enumerated as thirty-six) in accordance with the Mūlasarvāstivāda monastic system.
431. Nāgārjuna, *Mūlasarvāstivādin Śrāmaṇera*, Tengyur D 4127. Commonly known as *Fifty Verses on the Śrāmaṇera,* this text is sometimes attributed to Saṅghabhadra. Kamalaśīla composed a commentary on it entitled *Notes Concerning the Fifty Verses on the Śrāmaṇera* (Tengyur D 4128).

432. Śākyaprabha, *Mūlasarvāstivādin Śrāmaṇera*, Tengyur D 4124. This treatise is also called *Three Hundred Verses on the Śrāmaṇera*. The alternate names—expressed in terms of number of verses—provide a convenient way to distinguish between the two texts of Nāgārjuna and Śākyaprabha that are both entitled *Mūlasarvāstivādin Śrāmaṇera*.
433. In the Tibetan Buddhist tradition, a fully ordained monk (*bhikṣu*, *dge slong*) observes 253 vows in accordance with the Mūlasarvāstivāda monastic system, whereas a fully ordained nun (*bhikṣuṇī*, *dge slong ma*) observes 364 vows.
434. Perhaps the author is referring to *Several Important Topics such as the Precepts of a Fully Ordained Monk*.
435. Perhaps the author is referring to the explanations *Golden Victorious Elimination of Errors* and *Clear Lamp*.
436. These are the vase, secret, wisdom, and word initiations.
437. The bodhisattva vows, which stipulate the avoidance of the eighteen root downfalls and forty-six infractions, are the basis for taking the tantric vows, which stipulate the avoidance of the fourteen root downfalls and eight gross infractions.
438. Candragomin, *Twenty Verses on the Bodhisattva Vows*, Tengyur D 408.
439. "Teacher" here refers specifically to the Buddha.
440. Shame (*hrī*, *ngo tsha shes pa*) and embarrassment (*apatrāpya*, *khrel yod pa*) are two mental factors belonging to the category of eleven virtuous mental factors presented in Asaṅga's *Compendium of Knowledge*. In the case of shame, when one is about to engage in misconduct, one avoids it by thinking, "This is not something I should do," whereas in the case of embarrassment, one avoids it by thinking, "Since others will scorn me, this is not suitable." See Hopkins, *Meditation on Emptiness*, 250.
441. Prātimokṣa (*so sor thar pa*, "individual liberation") vows are of eight types: the vows of fully ordained monks and nuns, probationary nuns, novice monks and nuns, and male and female lay people and one-day vows. Vasubandhu, *Treasury of Knowledge*, 4.14a, Tengyur D 4089, 11a7.
442. The two vehicles here refer to the Hīnayāna vehicles of hearers (*śrāvaka*) and solitary realizers (*pratyekabuddha*).
443. Āryaśūra, *Compendium of the Perfections*, 6.65, Tengyur D 3944, 234b6–7.
444. Potowa, *Blue Manual*, 15.
445. In this section, *impartiality* (*sems snyoms pa*) should be understood as referring to the equanimity that is free from the bias of attachment and aversion. Note that the use of *impartiality* here excludes other meanings of equanimity (*btang snyoms*), such as that of the neutral feeling free from happiness and suffering, and that of desisting from unnecessary application of the antidotes to laxity and excitement.
446. See chapter 2, pages 51–83.
447. As in the *Easy Path*, our author also omits the explicit mention of the exceptional resolve here. The way to produce the exceptional resolve, which constitutes the sixth point in the sevenfold cause-and-effect instruction, is explained below, after the explanation on how to generate compassion.
448. The Tibetan text quotes only the first line of the verse. Tsongkhapa, *Supplication to the Lineage Masters of Glorious Guhyasamāja*, 1b3–4.
449. *Prophecy Concerning the Girl Candrottarā Sūtra*, Kangyur D 191, 231b4–5.
450. Reading *chas* for *'chi*.
451. Śāntideva, *Engaging in Bodhisattva Deeds*, 2.34 and 2.36, Tengyur D 3871, 5a6–7.
452. The Tibetan text attributed the following verse to *Lam rim blo bzlog bzhi pa*, which

largely matches what seems to be an informal title (*Skyes bu gsum gyi lam rim blo zlog bzhi*) mentioned at the end of the lamrim text *Countering the Four Attitudes of the Three Types of Beings* (*Skyes bu gsum gyi blo ldog bzhi bstan pa*) composed by the Kagyü master Phakmo Drupa Dorjé Gyalpo, but the verse cannot be located within the text.

453. Kharek Gomchung Wangchuk Lodrö, *Seventy Exhortations*, 5a6–5b1.
454. Śāntideva, *Engaging in Bodhisattva Deeds*, 6.1, Tengyur D 3871, 14b3.
455. Candrakīrti, *Entering the Middle Way*, 3.6, Tengyur D 3861, 203a5–6.
456. See page 159.
457. The fourth line of the verse was not quoted in the Tibetan text and has been added for completeness. Dharmakīrti, *Commentary on Validity*, 2.35, Tengyur D 4210, 108b7. For commentary by the Seventh Karmapa, see Karmapa Chödrak Gyatso, *Establishing Validity*, verse 37.
458. A substantial cause (*nyer len*) is a cause that produces an effect that is its substantial continuum. For example, when a sprout grows from a seed that has been watered, both the seed and water are considered causes of the sprout, but the seed is the substantial cause whereas the water is a cooperative condition (*lhan cig byed rkyen*).
459. Losang Chökyi Gyaltsen, *Melodious Speech of Losang's Assertions*, 3b3–4. The quote referenced in the last line is the statement from Dharmakīrti's *Commentary on Validity* cited above.
460. While her husband was away for a prolonged business trip, Utpalavarṇā (Pāli: Uppalavanna) found out that she was pregnant. Accusing her of infidelity, her mother-in-law chased her away. Later, Utpalavarṇā gave birth to a son but he was stolen by an evil merchant. She was taken in by a robber chief, with whom she bore a daughter. One day, she injured her daughter by mistake and, fearing the robber's wrath, fled from him. Years later, her son independently married Utpalavarṇā and her daughter. Then one day, Utpalavarṇā discovered a scar on her co-wife's head that identified the young woman as her own daughter. See Murcott, *First Buddhist Women*, 82.
461. This verse was cited in chapter 9, page 159, to illustrate the uncertainty of saṃsāra.
462. In another version of this story, the man whom the son murdered is reborn as his child. See note 385.
463. This argument uses the proof technique *reductio ad absurdum*, "reducing to an absurdity." See chapter 16 for other applications of this technique.
464. Just as a mother is the source of children, so these points are the foundation giving rise to later realizations.
465. Contaminated happiness is superficial pleasure that is occasioned by karma and afflictions, whereas uncontaminated happiness is true well-being free from the influence of karma and afflictions.
466. The continents mentioned in this section are the four major human continents surrounding Mount Meru in a world system as described in the Abhidharma.
467. In a previous life of the Buddha, he was King Maitrībala ("Power of Love"). With his own blood he satisfied five starving yakṣas, who in a later life became the first five disciples of the Buddha. See Frye, *The Sutra of the Wise and the Foolish*, chap. 13. See also Khoroche, *Once the Buddha Was a Monkey*, chap. 8.
468. *Smyug ram pa* emended to *Smyug rum pa*. Nyuk Rumpa Tsöndrü Gyaltsen (Smyug rum pa Brtson 'grus rgyal mtshan, 1042–1109) was a student of Chen Ngawa Tsultrim Bar. Nyuk Rumpa in turn was a teacher of Gampopa Sönam Rinchen.
469. *King of Meditative Stabilizations Sūtra*, 32.277, Kangyur D 127, 115b6. See English translation at 84000.co (Toh 127), 33.293.

470. Nāgārjuna, *Precious Garland*, 3.84ab–85, Tengyur D 4158, 117b4–5. The order of the lines cited here is slightly different from that in Dergé edition. Two lines are filled in so as to complete the listing of the eight benefits.
471. Nāgārjuna, *Precious Garland*, 3.83, Tengyur D 4158, 117b3–4.
472. Recall the description of animals' sufferings in chapter 6, pages 134–35, as it has been omitted here.
473. Śāntideva, *Engaging in Bodhisattva Deeds*, 8.120, Tengyur D 3871, 28a5.
474. Śāntideva, *Engaging in Bodhisattva Deeds*, 8.129–31, Tengyur D 3871, 28b3–4.
475. The legend of Maitrakanyaka is the thirty-sixth story in the *Avadānaśataka*, a collection of one hundred stories of deeds and their results. For the full translation of the Sanskrit narrative, see Appleton, "The Fourth Decade of the *Avadānaśataka*," 12–18.
476. See Tsong-kha-pa, *Great Treatise*, 2:61–68.
477. Śāntideva, *Engaging in Bodhisattva Deeds*, 3.22–23, Tengyur D 3871, 7b2–3.
478. Śāntideva, *Engaging in Bodhisattva Deeds*, 3.25–26, Tengyur D 3871, 7b3–5.
479. Śāntideva, *Engaging in Bodhisattva Deeds*, 1.9, Tengyur D 3871, 2a5–2b1.
480. The four white dharmas are: (1) never lying to your guru even at the cost of your life, (2) inspiring sentient beings to follow the Mahāyāna path, (3) respecting a bodhisattva just as you would a buddha, and (4) being honest with all beings.
481. See chapter 2, pages 51–83.
482. This is the first of the three kinds of generosity—(1) generosity of Dharma, (2) generosity of fearlessness, and (3) material generosity. The other two are explained below.
483. Nāgārjuna, *Precious Garland*, 1.5c, Tengyur D 4158, 107a4. Nāgārjuna explains that faith and wisdom are the means for attaining high rebirths and beatitude; wisdom is principal while faith acts as its prerequisite.
484. *A Bodhisattva's Accomplishment of the Four Prātimokṣa Qualities Sūtra*, Kangyur D 248, 54a1.
485. Giving blindly can lead to harm, for example, giving money to an alcoholic who is trying to buy alcohol. Therefore a good understanding of the goals and suitability of gifts is essential in order for oneself and others to derive maximum benefit from one's practice of generosity.
486. Śāntideva, *Engaging in Bodhisattva Deeds*, 3.11cd, Tengyur D 3871, 7a3.
487. Āryaśūra, *Garland of Birth Stories*, 3.23a, Tengyur D 4150, 11b6.
488. Atiśa, *Opening the Jewel Casket*, in *Collected Works*, 1:608. Curiously, the citation cannot be located in Atiśa's text with the same title (D 3930) in the Dergé Tengyur. What does it mean to bury your wealth as a hidden treasure? At the time of death you cannot take any of your material wealth with you, but you can arrange for it to be "delivered" to your future lives by giving it away while you are alive. This is because the merit created from practicing generosity in this life will act as the cause for you to enjoy wealth again in your future lives. It is as if you are burying a treasure—which you are certain to lose otherwise—so that you can retrieve it afterward.
489. A master from South India bearing the Indian names Kamalaśrī and Kamalaśīla, Phadampa Sangyé (Pha dam pa sangs rgyas) appears in many of the lineages of the *chö* (*gcod*) practice where the practitioner severs selfishness and other afflictions.
490. Phadampa Sangyé, *Hundred Admonitions to the People of Dingri*, 476. For the complete English translation, see Kapstein et al., *Sources of Tibetan Tradition*, 235–42.
491. Tsongkhapa, *Great Exposition*, 327. To view this statement in context, see Tsong-kha-pa, *Great Treatise*, 2:115.

492. This is the first of the three kinds of ethics—(1) the ethics of refraining from misdeeds, (2) the ethics of gathering virtue, and (3) the ethics of acting for the welfare of sentient beings. The other two are mentioned below.
493. *Classifications of Vinaya*, Kangyur D 3, 22b2.
494. This is the first of the three kinds of patience—(1) the patience of not retaliating, (2) the patience of accepting suffering, and (3) the patience of certitude about reality. The other two are mentioned below.
495. Śāntideva, *Engaging in Bodhisattva Deeds*, 6.72, Tengyur D 3871, 17b1.
496. Śāntideva, *Engaging in Bodhisattva Deeds*, 6.21, Tengyur D 3871, 15a7–15b1.
497. The twelve branches of scripture (*dvādaśakadharmapravacana, gsung rab kyi yan lag bcu gnyis*) are: (1) discourses (*sūtra, mdo sde*), (2) mixtures of prose and verse (*geya, dbyangs su bsnyad pa*), (3) prophecies (*vyākaraṇa, lung du bstan pa*), (4) poetic works (*gāthā, tshigs su bcad pa*), (5) aphorisms (*udāna, mched du brjod pa*), (6) descriptions of the occasion of teachings (*nidāna, gleng gzhi*), (7) narratives (*avadāna, rtogs pa brjod pa*), (8) stories about past lives of disciples (*itivṛttaka, de lta bu byung ba*), (9) the Buddha's accounts of his own former lives (*jātaka, skyes pa'i rabs*), (10) extensive sayings (*vaipulya, shin tu rgyas pa'i sde*), (11) marvels (*adbhutadharma, rmad du byung ba*), and (12) established instructions (*upadeśa, gtan la dbab pa*).
498. This is the first of the three kinds of joyous effort—(1) armor-like joyous effort, (2) the joyous effort of gathering virtue, and (3) the joyous effort of acting for the welfare of sentient beings. The other two are mentioned below.
499. Śāntideva, *Engaging in Bodhisattva Deeds*, 7.27ab, Tengyur D 3871, 21a4.
500. Śāntideva, *Engaging in Bodhisattva Deeds*, 7.30, Tengyur D 3871, 21a6. The second line was omitted in the Tibetan.
501. Nāgārjuna, *Precious Garland*, 5.86–87, Tengyur D 4158, 125a7–125b1. Annotated in accordance with Gyaltsab Darma Rinchen, *Illuminating the Essential Meanings of the Precious Garland of Madhyamaka*, 303.
502. Refer to chapter 15 for a detailed explanation of how to cultivate calm abiding.
503. Refer to chapter 16 for a detailed explanation of how to cultivate special insight.
504. The "way things exist" refers to the emptiness of true existence.
505. Maitreya, *Ornament for the Mahāyāna Sūtras*, 16.72, Tengyur D 4024, 24b6–7.
506. For Asaṅga's explanation on the means of gathering disciples, see Asaṅga, *The Bodhisattva Path to Unsurpassed Enlightenment*, chap. 15.
507. Maitreya, *Ornament for the Mahāyāna Sūtras*, 13.7, Tengyur D 4024, 17b7–18a1.
508. Refer to the earlier explanation of the eight attributes of posture under the section "Sitting upon a comfortable seat in the eightfold posture or any convenient posture and cultivating refuge, bodhicitta, and the four immeasurables." See pages 53–54.
509. The strategy underpinning this instruction is that one's initial priority should be the achievement of stability rather than that of clarity, as explained below. Even if the appearance of the object is partially clear (*cha phyed tsam gsal ba*), one focuses on it until stability is attained, instead of striving to attain total clarity from the outset. According to the Geluk tradition, this appearance, known technically as an object universal (*arthasāmānya, don spyi*), is a conceptual appearance of an object that appears as the object despite not being the object. For an explanation of the object universal and its role in concept formation, see Dreyfus, *Recognizing Reality*, chap. 14.
510. For the meaning of mental abidings, see note 532.
511. *Gsal sing nge ba.*

512. Saraha, *Songs from the Treasury of Dohā Verses*, Tengyur D 2224, 73a4. The *dohā* first emerged as a poetic form of religious expression consisting primarily of rhymed couplets, a genre that came to be designated *dohā*, the name of the meter most frequently employed.
513. *Ngar ldan*.
514. *Zhum pa*.
515. Candragomin, *Praise of Confession*, Tengyur D 1159, 205b5.
516. Losang Chökyi Gyaltsen, verse 18cd–19, *Highway of the Conquerors*, 2b6–3a1. For the Dalai Lama's commentary, see Tenzin Gyatso and Berzin, *Gelug/Kagyü Tradition*, 137–38. For Losang Chökyi Gyaltsen's autocommentary, see Jinpa et al., *Stages of the Path and the Oral Transmission*, 661, and also Jackson, *Mind Seeing Mind*, 507–8.
517. Losang Chökyi Gyaltsen, verse 27, *Highway of the Conquerors*, 3b1. For the Dalai Lama's commentary, see Tenzin Gyatso and Berzin, *Gelug/Kagyü Tradition*, 141–42.
518. Tsongkhapa, *Middle-Length Exposition*, 196. To view this statement in context, see Tsongkhapa, *The Middle-Length Treatise*, 299.
519. Asaṅga, *Compendium of Knowledge*, Tengyur D 4049, 48b3.
520. Maitreya, *Distinguishing the Middle from the Extremes*, 4.3cd, Tengyur D 4021, 43a3–4.
521. Maitreya, *Distinguishing the Middle from the Extremes*, 4.4, Tengyur D 4021, 43a4.
522. *Rmugs pa*.
523. *Gti mug*.
524. *Clarity* (*gsal cha*) involves clarity of both the object and the mind apprehending the object, while *limpidity* (*dwangs cha*) is clarity of the mind. See Gedün Lodrö, *Walking through Walls*, 177.
525. "Wind" (*prāṇa*, *rlung*) here is the internal energy winds flowing in the body that serve as mounts for consciousnesses.
526. The red and white drops are substances one obtains from one's mother and father, respectively, at the time of conception.
527. *Nam mkha' sgo 'byed kyi dbyings rig bsre ba*. The adjective "door-opening" seems to refer to space's property of being devoid of obstruction, which opens up infinite opportunities for unrestricted movement.
528. One of the five winds explained in tantric medical treatises, the white upward-moving wind (*gyen rgyu*) is based in the center of the chest and is mainly responsible for speech and the swallowing of food and saliva.
529. One of the five winds explained in tantric medical treatises, the yellow downward-voiding wind (*thur sel*) is based in the lower abdomen and functions to stop and start urination, defecation, and menstruation.
530. A popular subject of syllogisms in the debate courtyards of Tibetan monasteries, a vase (*bum pa*) by definition has a bulbous belly. Thus one holds the two winds together in this meditation as if they form a sphere at one's navel.
531. To get an idea of how excitement causes instability, imagine a person holding a cup filled to the brim with oil too tightly, as a result of which his hands shake and the oil spills. See Sopa and Blumenthal, *Steps on the Path*, 4:89.
532. The nine mental abidings (*sems gnas dgu*) are explained in Maitreya's *Ornament for the Mahāyāna Sūtras* as well as Asaṅga's *Hearers' Grounds*. These are: (1) setting the mind, (2) continuous setting, (3) resetting, (4) close setting, (5) disciplining, (6) pacifying, (7) thorough pacifying, (8) making one-pointed, and (9) setting in equipoise. For details on how to attain calm abiding through these nine stages, see Gedün Lodrö, *Walking through Walls*, chap. 8.

533. The bases of selflessness are divided into persons (*pudgala*, *gang zag*) and phenomena (*dharma*, *chos*). *Phenomena* takes on a restricted connotation in this twofold division, as it refers only to phenomena other than persons, such as pots and pillars, even though persons such as humans and animals are technically phenomena too. In the most general context, a phenomenon can be anything that is existent. That which is nonexistent, such as a moon made of green cheese, is not considered a phenomenon.
534. The reasoning presented in this chapter is the reasoning of absence of being one or many (*gcig du bral*). For other reasonings, such as the diamond slivers (*rdo rje gzegs ma*) and dependent arising (*rten 'brel*), see Hopkins, *Meditation on Emptiness*, 127–96.
535. *Ngar 'dzin.*
536. The five aggregates—of forms, feelings, discriminations, compositional factors, and consciousnesses—are a way of enumerating the physical and nonphysical components that make up a person. Since the five aggregates are equivalent to the body and mind, it seems the purpose of this explanation excerpted from the *Easy Path* is to encourage analysis of the components of the person from different points of view, a technical one in terms of the five aggregates and an intuitive one in terms of the body and mind.
537. "Self-instituting" (*tshugs thub tu grub pa*) implies true existence. For convenience of expression and ease of understanding, subsequent occurrences of the term are rendered as "independently existent."
538. It cannot be overemphasized throughout this investigation that, in order to prevent egregious confusion that will derail any attempt on your part to understand emptiness correctly, great care must be taken to distinguish between the conventionally existent I and the I that is the object of negation. A child observes a mirage, which exists, and believes there is water, which does not exist. Similarly, the self-grasping mind observes the conventionally existent I, which exists, and apprehends it as an inherently existent I, which does not exist. For more advice on how to identify the truly existent I, see Lobsang Jampa, *The Easy Path*, 244–46.
539. The object of the mode of apprehension (*'dzin stang kyi yul*) is the object the consciousness is understanding. For example, the object of the mode of apprehension of the thought apprehending a vase is the vase, and the object of the mode of apprehension of the conception of a pizza as truly existent is the truly existent pizza. See Lati Rinbochay, *Mind in Tibetan Buddhism*, 100.
540. It is not that the existence of the I is negated in general; rather, a *particular mode* of existence of the I is negated. The I does exist conventionally, but the I *that exists independently* does not exist at all. In the Consequence school (Prāsaṅgika, Thal 'gyur ba), the division of the Middle Way school (Madhyamaka, Dbu ma pa) founded by Buddhapālita and developed by Candrakīrti, the following expressions referring to such a nonexistent mode of existence are hypothetically synonymous: existing independently (*tshugs thub tu grub pa*), existing from its own side (*rang ngos nas grub pa*), existing truly (*bden par grub pa*), existing by way of its own character (*rang gi mtshan nyid kyis grub pa*), and existing inherently (*rang bzhin gyis grub pa*). For more information on this object of negation, see Hopkins, *Meditation on Emptiness*, 36.
541. When applying the reasoning of absence of being one or many to the I, one analyzes whether the I is identical to or different from the aggregates.
542. To be truly one means to be objectively one—that is, to be the same in every way.
543. Candrakīrti, *Entering the Middle Way*, 6.127ab, Tengyur D 3861, 210b1–2.
544. This is the first of many arguments in this section that use the *reductio ad absurdum* method for proving the falsity of a premise by showing that its logical consequence is absurd or contradictory. For example, to prove that there is no smallest positive

rational number, one could state the consequence, "If the smallest positive rational number *x* were to exist, then by dividing it by two, we would get a smaller one." This contradicts the premise that *x* is the smallest positive rational number and proves that there is no smallest positive rational number. In this case, since the position that the truly existent I is identical to the five aggregates leads to absurd consequence that the I would have five different continua, we have to conclude that it is untenable that the truly existent I is identical to the five aggregates.

545. The five aggregates—or simply put, the body and mind—are indeed impermanent phenomena that arise and transform moment by moment. However, an independently existent I could not have production and disintegration. See the arguments below.
546. Nāgārjuna, *Fundamental Verses on the Middle Way*, 18.1ab, Tengyur D 3824, 10b6.
547. So, the I of past lives, the I of this life, and the I of future lives would be different in an unrelated manner, but this position leads to absurd consequences as pointed out in the response below.
548. Candrakīrti, *Entering the Middle Way*, 6.61cd, Tengyur D 3861, 207a4.
549. Inherently existent things exist independently and cannot be related to each other, whereas previous and later instants of the I are causally related.
550. For a relationship of the appropriator and the appropriated to exist, there must be two distinct items. A single item cannot be both the appropriator and its appropriated item. Thus, if the I and the five aggregates would be established as identical in every sense, then there is effectively just a single item under consideration.
551. Nāgārjuna, *Fundamental Verses on the Middle Way*, 27.5cd, Tengyur D 3824, 18a1.
552. Since neither of these possibilities is tenable, the self and the aggregates cannot be a partless whole. Hence, the I as apprehended by self-grasping cannot be truly identical to the five aggregates.
553. Dharmakīrti, *Commentary on Validity*, 2.84, Tengyur D 4210, 110b5–6. For commentary by the Seventh Karmapa, see Karmapa Chödrak Gyatso, *Establishing Validity*, verse 86.
554. This is an ancillary reasoning to show that partless particles do not exist. A well-known argument used by the Mind Only school (Cittamātra, Sems tsam pa), it refutes the partless particles asserted by the Great Exposition school (Vaibhāṣika, Bye brag smra ba) and the Sūtra school (Sautrāntika, Mdo sde pa).
555. To present this very simply, we could say that if the side of the central particle facing the eastern particle does not face the western particle, then the central particle would have two parts, one facing the eastern particle but not the western particle and one facing the western particle but not the eastern particle.
556. If different particles were to occupy the same spatial location, gross objects composed of particles would be impossible. If a central particle is surrounded at the same time by six other particles in the six directions, then it must have at least six parts. However, if the central particle shares the same location with the other six particles, then the cluster of particles would have the size of a single particle. Therefore, no gross cluster would be visible.
557. The Tibetan text misattributed the following citation to the *Thirty Verses*.
558. Vasubandhu, *Twenty Verses*, verse 12, Tengyur D 4056, 3b3.
559. "Truly many" connotes multiple entities that are different in a truly existent manner.
560. These are the three aggregates of feelings, discriminations, and compositional factors.
561. Borrowing the example mentioned in the synopsis at the beginning of this book, if a plus sign existed from its own side upon +, then after removing those two intersecting

lines, there would have to be something remaining that you could identify as the plus sign. However, nothing whatsoever remains after removing those two intersecting lines.

562. Nāgārjuna, *Fundamental Verses on the Middle Way*, 27.7, Tengyur D 3824, 18a2.
563. *Meditative equipoise* (*samāhita, mnyam bzhag*) refers to the formal meditation period during which one's mind is single-pointedly focused on emptiness.
564. Having arisen from meditative equipoise, one enters the phase of post-equipoise (*anuprāpta, rjes thob,* "subsequent attainment"). When people and objects appear truly existent to one's mind, as a result of having ascertained the emptiness of true existence during meditative equipoise, one is aware that these phenomena cannot exist the way they appear and cultivates the realization that they are like magical illusions.
565. Compounded phenomena (*saṃskṛta, 'dus byas*), being composed by causes and conditions, are impermanent phenomena.
566. Uncompounded phenomena (*asaṃskṛta, 'dus ma byas*) are permanent phenomena in the sense that they do not change moment to moment.
567. A nonassociated compositional factor (*viprayuktasaṃskāra, ldan min 'du byed*) is a compounded phenomenon that is neither matter nor consciousness. Examples are time, number, collection, and person. For an explanation of the term and its divisions, see Hopkins, *Meditation on Emptiness*, 268–71.
568. This explanation is excerpted from the *Easy Path*. Note that the five limbs usually refer to the head, arms, and legs. Here, "five limbs" is a convenient way of referring to the components that make up a body, and so the expression includes also the torso.
569. That is, if such a consciousness were to exist as a truly existent consciousness.
570. To exist inherently as one entails being identical in every way.
571. This statement from *Entering the Middle Way* was previously cited in the context of establishing the selflessness of persons on page 238.
572. Nāgārjuna, *Precious Garland*, 1.99, Tengyur D 4158, 110b3. Because forms themselves are merely designations, space, which is the absence of obstructive form, is also merely a designation. Forms do not exist inherently, because the elements do not exist inherently. The designated does not exist inherently, and therefore even mere designations do not exist inherently. Gyaltsab Darma Rinchen, *Illuminating the Essential Meanings of the Precious Garland of Madhyamaka*, 232.
573. Note that if something were to exist from its own side—i.e., independently—it would have to be truly existent.
574. The special insight discussed in this chapter is specifically the special insight observing emptiness. Full-fledged special insight can also be cultivated in relation to other objects of observation, such as impermanence.
575. To be fettered by grasping at signs is to grasp at phenomena as truly existent. For example, when practicing generosity by giving money to a beggar, one may erroneously grasp at oneself as a truly existent giver, at the money as a truly existent gift, and at the beggar as a truly existent recipient.
576. One trains in space-like emptiness and illusion-like emptiness by cultivating the understanding of emptiness during the two phases of meditative equipoise and post-equipoise as explained on page 249.
577. *Myong khrid.*
578. Gyaltsab Darma Rinchen, *Ornament of the Essence*, 473–82.
579. Haribhadra, *Commentary on the Ornament for Clear Realizations*, Tengyur D 3793.

This commentary has come to be referred to as *Clear Meaning*, or *Sphuṭārtha*, based on its usual Tibetan name, *'Grel pa don gsal.*

580. An example of a creamy delicacy (*ldag pa shin tu gya nom pa*) is choice yogurt.
581. A cubit is the distance from the elbow to the tips of the fingers.
582. Reading *sogs pas* for *sogs pa* in accordance with Tsongkhapa, *Golden Rosary of Eloquence*, 359. Tsongkhapa gives shoes as an example of that which is given.
583. "Higher beings" (*skye bo bla ma*) are one's preceptors, abbots, teachers, parents, and the like. Tsongkhapa, *Golden Rosary of Eloquence,* 359.
584. The *nyagrodha* tree is commonly known as the banyan tree.
585. The five wrong livelihoods are flattery, hinting, bribery, extortion, and hypocrisy.
586. The knots here probably refer to knot-like lumps that are sometimes seen in those who suffer from varicose veins.
587. Assuming that the "smaller ankle bone" refers to the bony bump on the inner side of the ankle, this description implies that the bony bump on the outer side of the Buddha's ankle is prominent.
588. *Bimba* refers to the ivy gourd (*Coccinia grandis*), a tropical vine whose fruits turn a scarlet color when ripe.
589. The Dharma that subdues afflictions is the Abhidharma scriptural basket. The Dharma that subdues downfalls is the Vinaya scriptural basket.
590. The nine entanglements (*nava saṃyojanāni, kun tu sbyor ba dgu*) are: (1) attachment, (2) anger, (3) pride, (4) ignorance, (5) doubt, (6) the view of the transitory collection, view of extremes, and wrong view (counted as one entanglement), (7) the conception of bad view as supreme and conception of bad ethics and modes of conduct as supreme (counted as one entanglement), (8) jealousy, and (9) miserliness.
591. The Vedic practice of relying on the five fires (*pañcāgni*) involves an ascetic performing penance while being surrounded by fires in the four cardinal directions and the midday sun above.
592. The sixty-two bad views, presented in the *Encompassing Net Sūtra* (Kangyur D 352), are sixty-two views propounded by certain non-Buddhists concerning the past, present, and future. For the English translation of its Pāli counterpart (*Brahmajāla Sutta,* DN 1), see Walshe, *Long Discourses*, chap. 1.
593. Thokmé Sangpo, *Jewel Garland*, 252–55.
594. Vasubandhu, *Explanation of the Ornament for the Mahāyāna Sūtras*, Tengyur D 4026, 182b2–183b5.
595. Those who hold the three lineages are the practitioners of the three vehicles—namely, the two Hīnayāna vehicles of hearers and solitary realizers and the Mahāyāna.
596. Airāvaṇa (Sa srungs kyi bu, "Son of the Earth Guardian") is the mount of the god Indra.

Bibliography

Reference information for the canonical scriptures is based on the *sde dge par phud* edition of the Kangyur (*bka' 'gyur*), Delhi: Delhi Karmapae Choedhey, Gyalwae Sungrab Partun Khang, 1976–79, and the *sde dge* edition of the Tengyur (*bstan 'gyur*), Delhi: Delhi Karmapae Choedhey, Gyalwae Sungrab Partun Khang, 1982–85. Sūtras and tantras are listed alphabetically by their English titles. All other works are listed alphabetically by author or editor.

Sūtras and Tantras

Ascertaining the Vinaya: Questions of Upāli Sūtra. Vinayaviniścaya-upālipariprcchāsūtra. 'Dul ba rnam par gtan la dbab pa nye bar 'khor gyis zhus pa zhes bya ba theg pa chen po'i mdo. Kangyur D 68, Ratnakūṭa *ca*. English translation by UCSB Buddhist Studies Translation Group, *Ascertaining the Vinaya: Upāli's Questions* (ver 1.1.1). 84000.co, 2021.

A Bodhisattva's Accomplishment of the Four Prātimokṣa Qualities Sūtra. Bodhisattvaprātimokṣacatuṣkanirhārasūtra. Byang chub sems dpa'i so sor thar pa chos bzhi sgrub pa zhes bya ba theg pa chen po'i mdo. Kangyur D 248, Sūtra *za*.

Chapters on Vinaya. Vinayavastu. 'Dul ba gzhi. Kangyur D 1, Vinaya *ka* and *kha*. English translation of one chapter by the Bhaiṣajyavastu Translation Team, *"The Chapter on Medicines" from The Chapters on Monastic Discipline* (ver 1.0.10). 84000.co, 2021.

Classifications of Karma. Karmavibhaṅga. Las rnam par 'byed pa. Kangyur D 338, Sūtra *sa*.

Classifications of Vinaya. Vinayavibhaṅga. 'Dul ba rnam par 'byed pa. Kangyur D 3, Vinaya *ca*.

Collection of Aphorisms. Udānavarga. Ched du brjod pa'i tshoms. Kangyur D 326, Sūtra *sa*. Sanskrit edition by Bernhard, *Udānavarga*.

Concentration Continuation. Dhyānottarapaṭalakrama. Bsam gtan gyi phyi ma rim par phye ba. Kangyur D 808, Tantra *wa*.

Display of Sukhāvatī Sūtra. Sukhāvatīvyūhasūtra. 'Phags pa bde ba can gyi bkod pa zhes bya ba theg pa chen po'i mdo. Kangyur D 115, Sūtra *ja*. English translation by Sakya Pandita Translation Group, *The Display of the Pure Land of Sukhāvatī* (ver 2.20.8). 84000.co, 2011.

Encompassing Net Sūtra. Brahmajālasūtra. Tshangs pa'i dra ba'i mdo. Kangyur D 352, Sūtra *aḥ*.

Foundations of Mindfulness. Saddharmasmṛtyupasthāna. Dam pa'i chos dran pa nye bar gzhag pa. Kangyur D 287, Sūtra *ya* and *ra*. English translation by Dharmachakra Translation Committee, *The Application of Mindfulness of the Sacred Dharma* (ver 1.0.11). 84000.co, 2021.

General Rituals for All Maṇḍalas Tantra. Sarvamaṇḍalasāmānyavidhiguhyatantra. Dkyil 'khor thams cad kyi spyi'i cho ga gsang ba'i rgyud. Kangyur D 806, Tantra *wa*.

Good Eon Sūtra. Bhadrakalpikasūtra. 'Phags pa bskal pa bzang po pa zhes bya ba theg pa chen po'i mdo. Kangyur D 94, Sūtra *ka*. English translation by Dharmachakra Translation Committee, *The Good Eon* (ver 1.1.2). 84000.co, 2022.

Guhyasamāja Tantra. De bzhin gshegs pa thams cad kyi sku gsung thugs kyi gsang chen gsang ba 'dus pa zhes bya ba brtag pa'i rgyal po chen po. Kangyur D 442, Tantra *ca*. Sanskrit edition by Bhattacharyya, *Guhyasamāja Tantra or Tathāgataguhyaka*.

Hevajra Tantra. Kye'i rdo rje zhes bya ba rgyud kyi rgyal po. Kangyur D 417, Tantra *nga*.

A Hundred Karma Tales. Karmaśataka. Las brgya tham pa. Kangyur D 340, Sūtra *ha*. English translation by Lozang Jamspal and Kaia Tara Fischer, *The Hundred Deeds* (ver 1.3.22). 84000.co, 2020.

Kālacakra Tantra. Mchog gi dang po'i sangs rgyas las phyung ba rgyud kyi rgyal po dpal dus kyi 'khor lo zhes bya ba. Kangyur D 362, Tantra *ka*.

King of Meditative Stabilizations Sūtra. Samādhirājasūtra. 'Phags pa chos thams cad kyi rang bzhin mnyam pa nyid rnam par spros pa ting nge 'dzin gyi rgyal po zhes bya ba theg pa chen po'i mdo. Kangyur D 127, Sūtra *da*. English translation by Peter Alan Roberts, *The King of Samādhis Sūtra* (ver 1.45.18). 84000.co, 2018. Sanskrit edition by Dutt, *Gilgit Manuscripts Vol. II*, parts II and III.

King of Prayers of Excellent Deeds. Bhadracaryāpraṇidhānarāja. 'Phags pa bzang po spyod pa'i smon lam gyi rgyal po. Kangyur D 1095, Dhāraṇī *waṃ*. See also *A Multitude of Buddhas Sūtra*, Kangyur D 44.

Kṣitigarbha's Ten Wheels Sūtra. Daśacakrakṣitigarbhasūtra. 'Dus pa chen po las sa'i snying po'i 'khor lo bcu pa zhes bya ba theg pa chen po'i mdo. Kangyur D 239, Sūtra *zha*.

Meeting of Father and Son Sūtra. Pitāputrasamāgamanasūtra. 'Phags pa yab dang sras mjal ba zhes bya ba theg pa chen po'i mdo. Kangyur D 60, Ratnakūṭa *nga*.

Minor Points of the Vinaya. Vinayakṣudrakavastu. 'Dul ba phran tshegs kyi gzhi. Kangyur D 6, Vinaya *da* and *tha*.

A Multitude of Buddhas Sūtra. Buddhāvataṃsakasūtra. Sangs rgyas phal po che zhes bya ba shin tu rgyas pa chen po'i mdo. Kangyur D 44, Avataṃsaka *a*. English translation of its forty-fifth chapter, the *Stem Array* (*Gaṇḍavyūha, Sdong po bkod pa / Sdong po brgyan pa*), by Peter Alan Roberts, *The Stem Array* (ver 1.03). 84000.co, 2021. Sanskrit edition by Vaidya, *Gaṇḍavyūha Sūtram*. The *King of Prayers of Excellent Deeds* is located at the end of the *Stem Array*.

Nanda's Going Forth Sūtra. Nanda-pravrajyāsutra. Dga' bo rab tu byung ba'i mdo. Kangyur D 328, Sūtra *sa*. English translation by Alexander Csoma de Kőrös Translation Group, *The Sūtra of Nanda's Going Forth* (ver 1.0.9). 84000.co, 2022.

Narrative of a Sow Sūtra. Sūkarikāvadānanāmasutra. Phag mo'i rtogs pa brjod pa zhes bya ba'i mdo. Kangyur D 345, Sūtra *aṃ*. English translation by Bodhinidhi Translation Group, *The Magnificent Account About a Sow* (ver 1.0.7). 84000.co, 2022.

Ornament of Vajra Essence Tantra. Vajrahṛdayālaṃkāratantra. Dpal rdo rje snying po rgyan gyi rgyud ces bya ba. Kangyur D 451, Tantra *cha*.

*Passing into Great Nirvāṇa Sūtra. *Mahāparinirvāṇasūtra. 'Phags pa yongs su mya ngan las 'das pa chen po'i mdo.* Kangyur D 119, Sūtra *ta*.

Play in Full Sūtra. Lalitavistarasūtra. 'Phags pa rgya cher rol pa zhes bya ba theg pa chen po'i mdo. Kangyur D 95, Sūtra *kha*. English translation by Dharmachakra Translation Committee, *The Play in Full* (ver 4.48.3). 84000.co, 2013. Sanskrit edition by Vaidya, *Lalita-vistarah*.

Prophecy Concerning the Girl Candrottarā Sūtra. Candrottarādārikāvyākaraṇasūtra. 'Phags pa bu mo zla mchog lung bstan pa zhes bya ba theg pa chen po'i mdo. Kangyur D 191, Sūtra *tsa*.

Questions of Sāgaramati Sūtra. Sāgaramatiparipṛcchāsūtra. 'Phags pa blo gros rgya mtshos zhus pa zhes bya ba theg pa chen po'i mdo. Kangyur D 152, Sūtra *pha*. English translation by Dharmachakra Translation Committee, *The Questions of Sāgaramati* (ver 1.5.8). 84000.co, 2020."

Questions of Subāhu Tantra. Subāhuparipṛcchātantra. 'Phags pa dpung bzang gis zhus pa zhes bya ba'i rgyud. Kangyur D 805, Tantra *wa*.

Recollection of the Buddha. Buddhānusmṛti. 'Phags pa sangs rgyas rjes su dran pa. Kangyur D 279, Sūtra *ya*, 54b6–55a7.

Recollection of the Dharma. Dharmānusmṛti. Chos rjes su dran pa. Kangyur D 280, Sūtra *ya*, 55a7–55b4.

Recollection of the Saṅgha. Saṅghānusmṛti. Dge 'dun rjes su dran pa. Kangyur D 281, Sūtra *ya*, 55b4–55b6.

Saṃpuṭa Tantra. Yang dag par sbyor ba zhes bya ba'i rgyud chen po. Kangyur D 381, Tantra *ga*. English translation by Dharmachakra Translation Committee, *Emergence from Sampuṭa* (ver 1.11.14). 84000.co, 2020.

Saṃvarodaya Tantra. Śrī-mahāsaṃvarodaya-tantra-rāja-nāma. Dpal bde mchog 'byung ba zhes bya ba'i rgyud kyi rgyal po chen po. Kangyur D 373, Tantra *kha*. Sanskrit edition by Tsuda, *Saṁvarodaya-tantra*.

Sublime Golden Light Sūtra. Suvarṇaprabhāsottamasūtra. 'Phags pa gser 'od dam pa mdo sde'i dbang po'i rgyal po zhes bya ba theg pa chen po'i mdo. Kangyur D 556, Tantra *pa.*

Sūtra Gathering All Fragments. Sarvavaidalyasaṃgrahasūtra. Rnam par 'thag pa thams cad bsdus pa'i mdo. Kangyur D 337, Sūtra *dza.*

Sūtra on Lifespans. Āyuṣparyantasūtra. Tshe'i mtha'i mdo. Kangyur D 307, Sūtra *sa.* English translation by Bruno Galasek with Lama Kunga Thartse Rinpoche, *The Sūtra on the Limits of Life* (ver 1.0.17). 84000.co, 2021.

Teaching of Akṣayamati Sūtra. Akṣayamatinirdeśasūtra. 'Phags pa blo gros mi zad pas bstan pa zhes bya ba theg pa chen po'i mdo. Kangyur D 175, Sūtra *ma.* English translation by Jens Braarvig and David Welsh, *The Teaching of Akṣayamati* (ver 1.0.13). 84000.co, 2020.

Teaching on the Tathāgata's Inconceivable Secrets Sūtra. Tathāgata-acintyaguhya-nirdeśasūtra. 'Phags pa de bzhin gshegs pa'i gsang ba bsam gyis mi khyab pa bstan pa zhes bya ba theg pa chen po'i mdo. Kangyur D 47, Ratnakūṭa *ka.*

Teaching to Nanda on Dwelling in the Womb. Ānandagarbhāvakrāntinirdeśa. 'Phags pa dga' bo la mngal na gnas pa bstan pa zhes bya ba theg pa chen po'i mdo. Kangyur D 57, Ratnakūṭa *ga.*

Teaching to Venerable Nanda on Entry into the Womb. Āāyuṣmannandagarbhā-vakrāntinirdeśa. 'Phags pa tshe dang ldan pa dga' bo la mngal du 'jug pa bstan pa zhes bya ba theg pa chen po'i mdo. Kangyur D 58, Ratnakūṭa *ga.* English translation by Robert Kritzer, *The Teaching to Venerable Nanda on Entry into the Womb* (ver 1.1.1). 84000.co, 2021.

Union with All the Buddhas Tantra. Sarvabuddhasamāyogatantra. Dpal sangs rgyas thams cad dang mnyam par sbyor ba mkha' 'gro ma sgyu ma bde ba'i mchog ces bya ba'i rgyud phyi ma. Kangyur D 366, Tantra *ka.*

Unraveling the Intent Sūtra. Saṃdhinirmocanasūtra. 'Phags pa dgongs pa nges par 'grel pa zhes bya ba theg pa chen po'i mdo. Kangyur D 106, Sūtra *ca.* English translation by Buddhavacana Translation Group, *Unraveling the Intent* (ver 1.0.9). 84000.co, 2020.

Vajra Tent Tantra. Vajrapañjaratantra. Mkha' 'gro ma rdo rje gur zhes bya ba'i rgyud kyi rgyal po chen po'i brtag pa. Kangyur D 419, Tantra *nga.*

Vajrapāṇi Initiation Tantra. Vajrapāṇyabhiṣekamahātantra. Lag na rdo rje dbang bskur ba'i rgyud chen po. Kangyur D 496, Tantra *da.*

Verse Summary on the Perfection of Wisdom. Ārya-prajñāpāramitā-sañcayagāthā. 'Phags pa shes rab kyi pha rol tu phyin pa sdud pa tshigs su bcad pa. Kangyur D 13, Prajñāpāramitā (*shes phyin sna tshogs*) *ka.* Sanskrit edition by Yuyama, *Prajñā-pāramitā-ratna-guṇa-saṃcaya-gāthā.*

Verses of the Nāga King Bherī. Nāgarājabherīgāthā. Klu'i rgyal po rnga sgra'i tshigs su bcad pa. Kangyur D 325, Sūtra *sa.*

What Is Treasured by a Fully Ordained Monk Sūtra. Bhikṣuprarejusūtra. Dge slong la rab tu gces pa'i mdo. Kangyur D 302, Sūtra *sa.*

White Lotus of Compassion Sūtra. Karuṇāpuṇḍarīkasūtra. 'Phags pa snying rje pad ma dkar po zhes bya ba theg pa chen po'i mdo. Kangyur D 112, Sūtra *cha.*

Indian Treatises

Āryadeva. *Four Hundred Verses. Catuḥśatakaśāstra. Bstan bcos bzhi brgya pa zhes bya ba'i tshig le'ur byas pa.* Tengyur D 3846, Madhyamaka *tsha.*

Āryaśūra. *Compendium of the Perfections. Pāramitāsamāsa. Pha rol tu phyin pa bsdus pa zhes bya ba.* Tengyur D 3944, Madhyamaka *khi.* Sanskrit edition by Meadows, *Ārya-śūra's Compendium of the Perfections.*

———. *Garland of Birth Stories. Jātakamāla. Skyes pa'i rabs kyi rgyud.* Tengyur D 4150, Jātaka *hu.* Sanskrit edition by Vaidya, *Jātakamālā.*

Asaṅga. *Bodhisattvas' Grounds. *Bodhisattvabhūmi. Rnal 'byor spyod pa'i sa las byang chub sems dpa'i sa.* Tengyur D 4037, Cittamātra *wi.* Sanskrit edition by Dutt, *Bodhisattvabhūmiḥ.*

———. *Compendium of Knowledge. Abhidharmasamuccaya. Chos mngon pa kun las btus pa.* Tengyur D 4049, Cittamātra *ri.* Sanskrit edition by Pradhan, *Abhidharmasamuccaya of Asaṅga.*

———. *Grounds of Yogic Practitioners. Yogācārabhūmi-bhūmivastu. Rnal 'byor spyod pa'i sa las dngos gzhi sa mang po.* Tengyur D 4035, Cittamātra *tshi.*

———. *Hearers' Grounds. Śrāvakabhūmi. Rnal 'byor spyod pa'i sa las nyan thos kyi sa.* Tengyur D 4036, Cittamātra *dzi.* Sanskrit edition by Śrāvakabhūmi Study Group, *Śrāvakabhūmi.*

Aśvaghoṣa. *Discussion of the Eight States Deprived of Leisure. Aṣṭākṣaṇakathā. Mi khom pa brgyad kyi gtam.* Tengyur D 4167, Lekha *ge.*

———. *Dispelling Sorrow. Śokavinodana. Mya ngan bsal ba.* Tengyur D 4177, Lekha *nge.*

———. *Fifty Verses on the Spiritual Guide. Gurupañcāśikā. Bla ma lnga bcu pa.* Tengyur D 3721, Tantra *tshu.*

Atiśa. *Lamp for the Path to Enlightenment. Bodhipathapradīpa. Byang chub lam gyi sgron ma.* Tengyur D 3947, Madhyamaka *khi.*

———. *Opening the Jewel Casket: Instructions on the Middle. Ratnakaraṇḍodghāṭa-nāma-madhyamakopadeśa. Dbu ma'i man ngag rin po che'i za ma tog kha phye ba.* Tengyur D 3930, Madhyamaka *ki.* Also in *Collected Works,* 1:594–609. Beijing: Krung go'i bod rig pa dpe skrun khang, 2006.

Bhāviveka. *Blaze of Reasoning. Tarkajvālā. Dbu ma'i snying po'i 'grel pa rtog ge 'bar ba.* Tengyur D 3856, Madhyamaka *dza,* 40b7–329b4.

———. *Heart of the Middle Way. Madhyamakahṛdaya. Dbu ma'i snying po'i tshig le'ur byas pa.* Tengyur D 3855, Madhyamaka *dza,* 1b1–40b7.

Buddhaśrījñānapāda. *Oral Teaching Called Meditation on the Reality of the Two Stages. Dvikramatattvabhāvanānāmamukhāgama. Rim pa gnyis pa'i de kho na nyid bsgom pa zhes bya ba'i zhal gyi lung.* Tengyur D 1853, Tantra *di.*

Candragomin. *Praise of Confession. Deśanāstava. Bshags pa'i bstod pa.* Tengyur D 1159, Stotragaṇa *ka.*

———. *Twenty Verses on the Bodhisattva Vows. Bodhisattvasaṃvaraviṃśaka. Byang chub sems dpa'i sdom pa nyi shu pa.* Tengyur D 4081, Cittamātra *hi.*

Candrakīrti. *Entering the Middle Way. Madhyamakāvatāra. Dbu ma la 'jug pa.* Tengyur D 3861, Madhyamaka *'a.* Sanskrit edition by La Vallée Poussin, *Madhyamakāvatāra, par Candrakīrti.*

———. *Seventy Verses on Refuge. Triśaraṇasaptati. Gsum la skyabs su 'gro ba bdun cu pa.* Tengyur D 3971, Madhyamaka *gi.*

Dharmakīrti. *Commentary on Validity. Pramāṇavārttika. Tshad ma rnam 'grel gyi tshig le'ur byas pa.* Tengyur D 4210, Pramāṇa *ce.* Sanskrit edition by Miyasaka, "Pramāṇavārttika-kārikā."

Haribhadra. *Commentary on the Ornament for Clear Realizations. Abhisamayālaṃkāravṛtti. Mngon par rtogs pa'i rgyan gyi 'grel pa.* Tengyur D 3793, Prajñāpāramitā *ja.* Sanskrit edition by Amano, *Abhisamayālaṃkāra-kārikā-sāstra-vivṛti.*

Kamalaśīla. *Notes Concerning the Fifty Verses on the Śrāmaṇera. Śramaṇapañcāśatkārikāpadābhismaraṇa. Dge sbyong gi kā ri kā lnga bcu pa'i tshig gi brjed byang du byas pa.* Tengyur D 4128, Vinaya *su.*

Mahāmati. *Distinct Words: An Extensive Explanation of the Letter to a Friend. Vyaktapadāsuhṛllekhaṭīkā. Bshes pa'i spring yig gi rgya cher bshad pa tshig gsal ba.* Tengyur D 4190, Lekha *nge.*

Maitreya. *Distinguishing the Middle from the Extremes. Madhyāntavibhāga. Dbus dang mtha' rnam par 'byed pa'i tshig le'ur byas pa.* Tengyur D 4021, Cittamātra *phi.* Sanskrit edition by Pandeya, *Madhyānta-vibhāga-śāstra.*

———. *Ornament for Clear Realizations. Abhisamayālaṃkāra. Shes rab phyi pha rol tu phyin pa'i man ngag gi bstan bcos mngon par rtogs pa'i rgyan zhes bya ba'i tshig le'ur byas pa.* Tengyur D 3786, Prajñāpāramitā *ka.* Sanskrit edition by Stcherbatsky and Obermiller, *Abhisamayālaṅkāra-Prajñāpāramitā-Upadeśa-Śāstra.*

———. *Ornament for the Mahāyāna Sūtras. Mahāyānasūtrālaṃkāra. Theg pa chen po'i mdo sde rgyan gyi tshig le'ur byas pa.* Tengyur D 4020, Cittamātra *phi.* Sanskrit edition by Bagchi, *Mahāyānasūtrālaṅkāra of Asaṅga.*

———. *Sublime Continuum. Uttaratantra. Rgyud bla ma.* Tengyur D 4024, Cittamātra *phi.*

Nāgārjuna. *Five Stages. Pañcakrama. Rim pa lnga pa.* Tengyur D 1802, Tantra *ngi.* Sanskrit edition by Tripathi, *Piṇḍīkramaḥ Pañcakramaś ca.*

———. *Fundamental Verses on the Middle Way. Mūlamadhyamakakārikā. Dbu ma rtsa ba'i tshig le'ur byas pa shes rab ces bya ba*. Tengyur D 3824, Madhyamaka *tsa*. Sanskrit edition by Ye, *Mūlamadhyamakakārikā*.

———. *Letter to a Friend. Suhṛllekha. Bshes pa'i spring yig.* Tengyur D 4182, Lekha *nge*. Sanskrit edition by Padma Tendzin, *Suhṛllekha*.

———. *Mūlasarvāstivādin Śrāmaṇera / Fifty Verses on the Śrāmaṇera. Mūlasarvāstivādiśrāmaṇerakārikā. 'Phags pa gzhi thams cad yod par smra ba'i dge tshul gyi tshig le'ur byas ba / Dge tshul kā ri kā lnga bcu pa.* Tengyur D 4127, Vinaya *su*.

———. *Precious Garland. Ratnāvalī. Rgyal po la gtam bya ba rin po che'i phreng ba.* Tengyur D 4158, Lekha *ge*. Sanskrit edition by Hahn, *Nāgārjuna's Ratnāvalī*.

Ratnākaraśānti. *Commentary on the Difficult Points of the Kṛṣṇayamāri Tantra. Kṛṣṇayamārimahātantrarājapañjikā. Dpal gshin rje dgra nag po'i rgyud kyi rgyal po chen po'i dka' 'grel rin po che'i sgron ma.* Tengyur D 1919, Tantra *bi*.

Śākyaprabha. *Mūlasarvāstivādin Śrāmaṇera / Three Hundred Verses on the Śrāmaṇera's Precepts. Mūlasarvāstivādiśrāmaṇerakārikā. 'Phags pa gzhi thams cad yod par smra ba'i dge tshul gyi tshig le'u byas pa / Dge tshul gyi bslab bya sum brgya pa.* Tengyur D 4124, Vinaya *shu*.

Śāntideva. *Compendium of Trainings in Verse. Śikṣāsamuccayakārikā. Bslab pa kun las btus pa'i tshig le'u byas pa.* Tengyur D 3939, Madhyamaka *khi*. Sanskrit edition by Vaidya, *Śikṣā-samuccaya*.

———. *Engaging in Bodhisattva Deeds. Bodhicaryāvatāra. Byang chub sems dpa'i spyod la 'jug pa.* Tengyur D 3871, Madhyamaka *la*. Sanskrit edition by Bhattacharya, *Bodhicaryāvatāra*.

Saraha. *Songs from the Treasury of Dohā Verses. Dohakoṣagīti. Do ha mdzod kyi glu.* Tengyur D 2224, Tantra *wi*.

Subhūticandra. *Wish-Granting Cow: A Commentary on Amarakoṣa. Amarakoṣaṭīkākāmadhenu. 'Chi ba med pa'i mdzod kyi rgya cher 'grel pa 'dod 'jo'i ba mo zhes bya ba.* Tengyur D 4300, Śabdavidyā *se*.

Vararuci. *A Hundred Verses. Śatagāthā. Tshigs su bcad pa brgya pa.* Tengyur D 4332, Nītiśāstra *ngo*.

Vasubandhu. *Explanation of the Ornament for the Mahāyāna Sūtras. Sūtrālaṃkārabhāṣya. Mdo sde'i rgyan gyi bshad pa.* Tengyur D 4026, Cittamātra *phi*.

———. *Thirty Verses. Triṃśikā. Sum cu pa'i tshig le'ur byas pa.* Tengyur D 4055, Cittamātra *shi*. Sanskrit edition by Lévi, *Vijñaptimātratāsiddhi*.

———. *Treasury of Knowledge. Abhidharmakośakārikā. Chos mngon pa'i mdzod kyi tshig le'ur byas pa.* Tengyur D 4089, Abhidharma *ku*. Sanskrit edition by Pradhan, *Abhidharm-koshabhāṣya of Vasubandhu*.

———. *Twenty Verses. Viṃśikā/Viṃśatikā/Vijñaptimātratāsiddhi. Nyi shu pa'i tshig le'ur byas pa.* Tengyur D 4056, Cittamātra *shi*. Sanskrit edition by Lévi, *Vijñaptimātratāsiddhi*.

Other Works

Amano, Hirofusa, ed. *Abhisamayālaṃkāra-kārikā-sāstra-vivṛti: Haribhadra's Commentary on the Abhisamaya-alamkāra-kārikā-śāstra Edited for the First Time from a Sanskrit Manuscript.* Kyoto: Heirakuji shoten, 2000.

Appleton, Naomi. "The Fourth Decade of the *Avadānaśataka*." *Asian Literature and Translation* 2.5 (2014): 1–35.

Asaṅga, Ārya. *The Bodhisattva Path to Unsurpassed Enlightenment: A Complete Translation of the Bodhisattvabhūmi.* Translated by Artemus B. Engle. Boulder, CO: Snow Lion, 2016.

Bagchi, S., ed. *Mahāyānasūtrālaṅkāra of Asaṅga.* Darbhanga: Mithila Institute of Post-Graduate Studies and Research in Sanskrit Learning, 1970.

Bernhard, Franz, ed. *Udānavarga.* Göttingen: Vandenhoeck & Ruprecht, 1965.

Bhattacharya, Vidhushekhara, ed. *Bodhicaryāvatāra.* Calcutta: Asiatic Society, 1960.

Bhattacharyya, Benoytosh, ed. *Guhyasamāja Tantra or Tathāgataguhyaka.* Baroda: Oriental Institute, 1967.

Bodhi, Bhikkhu. *The Connected Discourses of the Buddha: A Translation of the Saṃyutta Nikāya.* Boston: Wisdom Publications, 2000.

———. *The Numerical Discourses of the Buddha: A Translation of the Aṅguttara Nikāya.* Boston: Wisdom Publications, 2012.

Chen Nga Lodrö Gyaltsen (Spyan snga Blo gros rgyal mtshan). *The Ultimate Profound Path: Oral Tradition of the Instruction on the Middle Way View Free from Extremes. Mtha' bral dbu ma'i lta khrid kyi snyan brgyud zab lam mthar thug.* In *Collected Works,* 5:28–54. Lhasa: Ser gtsug nang bstan dpe rnying 'tshol bsdu phyogs sgrig khang, 2011.

Chökyi Gyaltsen, Jetsun (Rje btsun Chos kyi rgyal mtshan). *Ocean of Sport of the Fortunate Nāga King,* 2 vols. *Shes rab kyi pha rol tu phyin pa'i man ngag gi bstan bcos mngon par rtogs pa'i rgyan'grel pa dang bces pa'i rgya cher bshad pa legs bshad gser gyi phreng ba and rnam bshad snying po'i rgyan.* Mundgod, India: Library of Ganden Jangtse Monastery, 1999.

Conze, Edward. *The Perfection of Wisdom in Eight Thousand Lines & Its Verse Summary.* Delhi: Sri Satguru Publications, 1994.

Dakpo Jampal Lhundrup Gyatso (Dwags po 'Jam dpal lhun grub rgya mtsho). *A Necklace for the Fortunate: A Convenient Recitation Rite for Performing the Preparatory Practices according to the Swift Path to Omniscience, An Explicit Instruction on the Stages of the Path to Enlightenment. Byang chub lam gyi rim pa'i dmar khrid myur lam gyi sngon 'gro'i ngag 'don gyi rim pa khyer bde bklag chog bskal bzang mgrin rgyan.* In Krung go bod brgyud, *Collection of Rituals of the Geluk Order,* 1:133–58.

Dakpo Ngawang Drakpa (Dwags po Ngag dbang grags pa). *Essence of Excellent*

Discourses. Legs gsung nying khu. In Yongzin Lingtsang Labrang, *Commentaries on the Stages of the Path to Enlightenment*, 3:1–55.

Dowman, Keith. *Masters of Mahāmudrā: Songs and Histories of the Eighty-Four Buddhist Siddhas*. Albany: State University of New York Press, 1985.

Dreyfus, Georges B. J. *Recognizing Reality: Dharmakīrti's Philosophy and Its Tibetan Interpretations*. Albany: State University of New York Press, 1997.

Drolungpa Lodrö Jungné (Gro lung pa Blo gros 'byung gnas). *An Explanation of the Stages of the Path for Engaging in the Sugata's Precious Teachings. Bde bar gshegs pa'i bstan pa rin po che la 'jug pa'i lam gyi rim pa rnam par bshad pa*. Mundgod: Khri byang bla brang dpe mdzod, 2001.

Dutt, Nalinaksha, ed. *Bodhisattvabhūmiḥ*. Patna: K. P. Jayaswal Research Institute, 1966.

———, ed. *Gilgit Manuscripts Vol. II*, part II. Calcutta: J. C. Sarkhel, 1953.

———, ed. *Gilgit Manuscripts Vol. II*, part III. Calcutta: J. C. Sarkhel, 1954.

Edgerton, Franklin. *Buddhist Hybrid Sanskrit Grammar and Dictionary*. New Haven, CT: Yale University Press, 1953.

Frye, Stanley. *The Sutra of the Wise and the Foolish*. Dharamsala, India: Library of Tibetan Works and Archives, 2006.

Gampopa Sönam Rinchen (Sgam po pa Bsod nam rin chen). *A Precious Garland of the Supreme Path. Lam mchog rin po che'i phreng ba*. In *Collected Works of the Succession of Gampo Abbots* (*Sgam po'i gdan rabs rim byon gyi gsung 'bum*), 4:244–64. Beijing: Krung go'i bod rig pa dpe skrun khang, 2013.

Gedün Lodrö, Geshe. *Walking through Walls: A Presentation of Tibetan Meditation*. Translated by Jeffrey Hopkins. Ithaca, NY: Snow Lion Publications, 1992.

Gendun Drupa (Dge 'dun grub pa), the First Dalai Lama. *Pulverizing the Armies of Maras: A Praise of the Bhagavān Munīndra. Thub dbang rnam thar la bstod pa bdud dpung phye ma 'thag pa*. In *Collected Works*, 5:377–92. Gangtok: Dodrup Lama Sangye, 1978–81.

Gyaltsab Darma Rinchen (Rgyal tshab Dar ma rin chen). *Illuminating the Essential Meanings of the Precious Garland of Madhyamaka. Dbu ma rin chen 'phreng ba'i snying po'i don gsal bar byed pa*. In *Collected Works*, vol. *ka*, 199–308. Mundgod, India: Drepung Loseling Pethub Khangtsen Education Society, 2019.

———. *Ornament of the Essence. Shes rab kyi pha rol tu phyin pa'i man ngag gi bstan bcos mngon par rtogs pa'i rgyan gyi rtsa ba 'grel pa dang bces pa'i rnam bshad snying po'i rgyan*. In *Collected Works*, vol. *kha*. Mundgod, India: Drepung Loseling Pethub Khangtsen Education Society, 2019.

Hahn, Michael, ed. *Nāgārjuna's Ratnāvalī, Vol. 1: The Basic Texts (Sanskrit, Tibetan, Chinese)*. Bonn: Indica et Tibetica Verlag, 1983.

———. "Vararuci's Gāthāśataka (*Tshigs su bcad pa brgya pa*) and Its Indian Sources." *South Asian Classical Studies* 7 (2012): 367–458.

Hopkins, Jeffrey. *Meditation on Emptiness*. Boston: Wisdom Publications, 1996.

Jackson, David. "The bsTan rim ('Stages of the Doctrine') and Similar Graded Expositions of the Bodhisattvas Path." In *Tibetan Literature: Studies in Genre*, edited by José Ignacio Cabezon and Roger R. Jackson, 229–43. Ithaca, NY: Snow Lion Publications, 1996.

Jackson, Roger R. *Mind Seeing Mind: Mahāmudrā and the Geluk Tradition of Tibetan Buddhism*. Studies in Indian and Tibetan Buddhism. Boston: Wisdom Publications, 2019.

Jinpa, Thupten. *The Book of Kadam: The Core Texts*. The Library of Tibetan Classics 2. Boston: Wisdom Publications, 2008.

———. *Mind Training: The Great Collection*. The Library of Tibetan Classics 1. Boston: Wisdom Publications, 2006.

———. *Tsongkhapa: A Buddha in the Land of* Snows. Boulder, CO: Shambhala Publications, 2019.

Jinpa, Thupten, and Rosemary Patton with Dagpo Rinpoché. *Stages of the Path and the Oral Transmission: Selected Teachings of the Geluk School*. The Library of Tibetan Classics 6. Somerville, MA: Wisdom Publications, 2021.

Kapstein, Matthew T., Gray Tuttle, and Kurtis R. Schaeffer, eds. *Sources of Tibetan Tradition*. New York: Columbia University Press, 2013.

Karmapa Chödrak Gyatso. *Establishing Validity*. Translated by David Karma Choephel. Woodstock, NY: KTD Publications, 2016.

Karthar Rinpoche, Khenpo. *The Instructions of Gampopa: A Precious Garland of the Supreme Path*. Translated by Lama Yeshe Gyamtso. Ithaca, NY: Snow Lion, 1996.

Kharek Gomchung Wangchuk Lodrö (Kha reg sgom chung Dbang phyug blo gros) *Seventy Exhortations. Ang yig bdun cu ma*. Place of publication and publisher unknown. 1980.

Khoroche, Peter. *Once the Buddha Was a Monkey: Ārya Śūra's Jātakamālā*. Chicago: University of Chicago Press, 2006.

Kritzer, Robert. "Tibetan Texts of Garbhāvakrāntisūtra: Differences and Borrowings." *Annual Report of The International Research Institute for Advanced Buddhology at Soka University* 15 (2012): 131–45.

Krung go bod brgyud mtho rim nang bstan slob gling brgyud nang bstan zhib 'jug khang, ed. *Collection of Rituals of the Geluk Order*, vols. 1 and 2. Dge lugs pa'i chos spyod phyogs bsgrigs. Xining: Mtsho sngon mi rigs dpe skrun khang, 1995.

Kunga Gyaltsen (Kun dga' rgyal mtshan). *A Hundred Thousand Syllables of Cakrasaṃvara Luipa. Bde mchog lu hi pa'i 'bru 'bum*. In *Collected Works*, vol. 2. Beijing: Krung go'i bod rig pa dpe skrun khang, 2007.

La Vallée Poussin, Louis de, ed. *Madhyamakāvatāra, par Candrakīrti. Traduction Tibétaine Publiée par Louis de la Vallée Poussin*. St. Pétersbourg: Impr. de l'Académie impériale des sciences, 1912.

Lati Rinbochay. *Mind in Tibetan Buddhism*. Translated by Elizabeth Napper. Ithaca, NY: Snow Lion Publications, 1986.

Lati Rinbochay and Denma Lochö Rinbochay. *Meditative States in Tibetan Buddhism*. Translated by Leah Zahler and Jeffrey Hopkins. Boston: Wisdom Publications, 1997.

Lévi, Sylvain, ed. *Vijñaptimātratāsiddhi: Deux Traités de Vasubandhu: Viṁśatikā (La Vingtaine) Accompagnée D'une Explication en Prose et Triṁśikā (La Trentaine), avec le Commentaire de Sthiramati, 1re partie*. Paris: Librairie Ancienne Honoré Champion, 1925.

Lobsang Jampa, Gyumé Khensur. *Guhyasamāja Practice in the Ārya Nāgārjuna System*, vol. 1. Translated by Artemus B. Engle. Boulder, CO: Snow Lion Publications, 2019.

Lobsang Jampa, Gyumed Khensur. *The Easy Path: Illuminating the First Panchen Lama's Secret Instructions*. Edited by Lorne Ladner. Boston: Wisdom Publications, 2013.

Losang Chökyi Gyaltsen, Paṇchen (Paṇ chen Blo bzang chos kyi rgyal mtshan). *Easy Path to Omniscience: An Explicit Instruction on the Stages of the Path. Byang chub lam gyi rim pa'i dmar khrid thams cad mkhyen par bgrod pa'i bde lam*. In *Collected Works*, 4:367–432. New Delhi, India: Mongolian Lama Gurudeva, 1973.

———. *Highway of the Conquerors: A Root Text for the Precious Geluk Tradition of Mahāmudrā. Dge ldan bka' brgyud rin po che'i phyag chen rtsa ba rgyal ba'i gzhung lam*. In *Collected Works*, 4:83–94. New Delhi, India: Mongolian Lama Gurudeva, 1973.

———. *Melodious Speech of Losang's Assertions: Responses to Sincere Queries. Dri ba lhag bsam rab dkar gyi dris lan blo bzang bzhad pa'i sgra dbyangs*. In *Collected Works*, 4:539–60. New Delhi, India: Mongolian Lama Gurudeva, 1973.

———. *Rite of Making Offerings to the Spiritual Guide. Bla ma mchod pa'i cho ga*. In *Collected Works*, 1:779–830. New Delhi, India: Mongolian Lama Gurudeva, 1973.

———. *Several Important Topics Such as the Precepts of a Fully Ordained Monk. Dge slong gi bslab bya sogs nye bar mkho ba 'ga 'zhig*. In *Collected Works*, 4:431–56. New Delhi, India: Mongolian Lama Gurudeva, 1973.

Losang Yeshé, Paṇchen (Paṇ chen Blo bzang ye shes). *Swift Path to Omniscience: An Explicit Instruction on the Stages of the Path. Byang chub lam gyi rim pa'i dmar khrid thams cad mkhyen par bgrod pa'i nyur lam*. In Yongzin Lingtsang Labrang, *Commentaries on the Stages of the Path to Enlightenment*, 3:357–486.

McHugh, James. *Sandalwood and Carrion: Smell in Indian Religion and Culture*. New York: Oxford University Press, 2012.

Meadows, Carol. *Ārya-śūra's Compendium of the Perfections: Text, Translation, and Analysis of the Pāramitāsamāsa*. Bonn: Indica et Tibetica Verlag, 1986.

Miyasaka, Yūsho, ed. "Pramāṇavārttika-kārikā: (Sanskrit and Tibetan)." *Acta Indologica* 2 (1972): 1–206.

Murcott, Susan. *First Buddhist Women: Poems and Stories of Awakening*. Berkeley: Parallax Press, 2002.

Naktso Lotsāwa Tsultrim Gyalwa (Nag 'tsho lo tsā ba Tshul khrims rgyal ba). *Praise of Atiśa in Eighty Verses. Jo bo rje'i bstod pa brgyad cu.* In *Compendium of Essential Mind Training Instructions* (*Blo sbyong nyer mkho phyogs bsgrigs*), 331–41. Lanzhou: Kan su'u mi rigs dpe skrun khang, 2003.

Ngawang Kunga Sönam / Jamgön Anyé Shab (Ngag dbang kun dga' bsod nams / 'Jam mgon a myes zhabs). *A Brief and Clear Source of Delight for All: A Good Explanation of the Historical Background of Glorious Atiśa's Kadam Followers. Jo bo rje dpal ldan a ti sha'i rjes 'brang bka' gdams kyi byung tshul legs par bshad pa nyung gsal kun dga'.* In *Collected Works*, vol. *cha*. Kathmandu: Sa skya rgyal yongs gsung rab slob gnyer khang, 2000.

Ngawang Losang Gyatso (Ngag dbang blo bzang rgya mtsho), the Fifth Dalai Lama. *Brilliance of a Hundred Thousand Auspiciousnesses. Rab tu gnas pa'i cho ga bkra shis 'bum phrag gsar dngom.* In *Collected Works*, 27:275–99. Beijing: Krung go'i bod rig pa dpe skrun khang, 2009.

———. *Clear Lamp: A Little Benefit for Intelligent Ones Who Delight in Prātimokṣa Ethics. So thar gyi tshul khrims la dga' ba'i dpyod ldan tshogs la phan byed nyung ngu rnam gsal sgron ma.* In *Collected Works*, 17:364–85. Beijing: Krung go'i bod rig pa dpe skrun khang, 2009.

———. *Golden Victorious Elimination of Errors: The Rite that Benefits Monastics, Who Are the Root of the Teachings, and Lay People along with Decisive Analysis. Bstan pa'i rtsa ba rab byung dang khyim pa la phan gdags pa'i cho ga mtha' dpyod dang bcas pa 'khrul spong rnam rgyal gser mdog.* In *Collected Works*, 17:1–363. New Delhi, India: Mongolian Lama Gurudeva, 1973.

———. *Words of Mañjuśrī. 'Jam dpal zhal lung.* In Yongzin Lingtsang Labrang, *Commentaries on the Stages of the Path to Enlightenment*, 3:143–304.

Pabongka Rinpoche. *Liberation in the Palm of Your Hand: A Concise Discourse on the Path to Enlightenment*. Translated by Michael Richards. Boston: Wisdom Publications, 2006.

Padma Tendzin, ed. *Suhṛllekha of Ācārya Nāgārjuna and Vyaktapadāṭīkā of Ācārya Mahāmati. Sanskrit restoration and critically edited Tibetan text.* Sarnath, Varanasi: Central Institute of Higher Tibetan Studies, 2002.

Pandeya, Ram Chandra, ed. *Madhyānta-vibhāga-śāstra, containing the Kārikā-s of Maitreya, Bhāṣya of Vasubandhu, and Ṭīkā by Sthiramati*. Delhi: Motilal Banarsidass, 1972.

Pema Trinlé (Padma phrin las). *Clarifying Mirror: A Convenient Practice of the Eleven Yogas of Nāro Khecarī. Nā ro mkha' spyod kyi rnal 'byor bcu gcig gi nyams len nag 'gros gsal ba'i me long.* In *Khecarī Manual of the Glorious Sakya Tradi-*

tion (*Dpal sa skya'i mkha' spyod be'u bum*), 2:705–85. Dergé, Kham: Rdzong sar khams bye lnga rig nang bstan slob gling, n.d.

Phabongkha Dechen Nyingpo (Pha bong kha Bde chen snying po). *Liberation in the Palm of Your Hand. Rnam grol lag bcangs.* Lhasa: Ser gtsug nang bstan dpe rnying 'tshol bsdu phyogs sgrig khang, 2009. For English translation, see Pabongka, *Liberation.*

———. *Opening the Door to the Excellent Path. Lam bzang sgo 'byed.* Bylakuppe, India: Sera Mey Library, 2009.

Phadampa Sangyé (Pha dam pa sangs rgyas). *Hundred Admonitions to the People of Dingri. Rje btsun dam pa sangs rgyas kyi zhal gdams ding ri brgya rtsa ma.* In *Compendium of Essential Mind Training Instructions* (*Blo sbyong nyer mkho phyogs bsgrigs*), 470–77. Lanzhou: Kan su'u mi rigs dpe skrun khang, 2003.

Phakmo Drupa Dorjé Gyalpo (Phag mo gru pa Rdo rje rgyal po). *Countering the Four Attitudes of the Three Types of Beings. Skyes bu gsum gyi blo ldog bzhi bstan pa.* In *Collected Works*, vol. *ja*, 1a–11b. Kathmandu: Khenpo Shedrub Tenzin and Lama Thinley Namgyal, 2003.

Potowa Rinchen Sal Choklé Namgyal (Po to ba Rin chen gsal Phyogs las rnam rgyal). *Root Text of the Blue Manual: Potowa's Instructions. Po to ba'i man ngag be'u bum sngon po'i rtsa ba.* In *Collection of Texts Showing the Stages for Embarking on the Teachings* (*Bstan pa la 'jug pa'i rim pa ston pa'i gzhung gces btus*), 1–41. New Delhi, India: Bod kyi gtsug lag zhib 'jug khang, 2009.

Pradhan, Prahlad, ed. *Abhidharmasamuccaya of Asaṅga.* Santiniketan, India: Visva Bharati, 1950.

———, ed. *Abhidharm-koshabhāṣya of Vasubandhu.* Patna: K. P. Jayaswal Research Institute, 1967.

Rabten, Geshe. *The Mind and Its Functions.* Translated by Stephen Batchelor. Le Mont-Pèlerin, Switzerland: Editions Rabten Choeling, 1992.

Roesler, Ulrike, Ken Holmes, and David P. Jackson, trans. *Stages of the Buddha's Teachings: Three Key Texts.* The Library of Tibetan Classics 10. Boston: Wisdom Publications, 2015.

Rotman, Andy. *Divine Stories: Divyāvadāna*, vol. 1. Boston: Wisdom Publications, 2008.

———. *Divine Stories: Divyāvadāna*, vol. 2. Somerville, MA: Wisdom Publications, 2017.

Sadakata, Akira. *Buddhist Cosmology: Philosophy and Origins.* Tokyo: Kōsei Publishing Company, 2004.

Sakya Paṇḍita Kunga Gyaltsen (Sa skya Paṇḍita Kun dga' rgyal mtshan). *Profound Path of Guru Yoga. Lam zab mob la ma'i rnal 'byor.* In *Collected Works*, 2:92–108. Beijing: Krung go'i bod rig pa dpe skrun khang, 2007.

Sönam Gyatso (Bsod nams rgya mtsho), the Third Dalai Lama. *Essence of Refined*

Gold. Gser gyi yang zhun. In Yongzin Lingtsang Labrang, *Commentaries on the Stages of the Path to Enlightenment*, 3:59–81.

Sopa, Geshe Lhundub, and Jeffrey Hopkins. *Cutting Through Appearances.* Ithaca, NY: Snow Lion Publications, 1989.

Sopa, Geshe Lhundub, with David Patt. *Steps on the Path to Enlightenment*, vol. 1. Boston: Wisdom Publications, 2004.

Sopa, Geshe Lhundub, with James Blumenthal. *Steps on the Path to Enlightenment*, vol. 4. Somerville, MA: Wisdom Publications, 2016.

Śrāvakabhūmi Study Group, ed. *Śrāvakabhūmi: Revised Sanskrit Text and Japanese Translation, The First Chapter*. Tokyo: Sankibō Busshōrin, 1998.

Stcherbatsky, Th., and E. Obermiller, ed. *Abhisamayālaṅkāra-Prajñāpāramitā-Upadeśa-Śāstra: The Work of Bodhisattva Maitreya*. Delhi: Sri Satguru Publications, 2016.

Tenzin Gyatso, H. H. the Dalai Lama. *The Great Exposition of Secret Mantra*, vol. 1. Translated by Jeffrey Hopkins. Boulder, CO: Snow Lion, 2016.

———. *The Great Exposition of Secret Mantra*, vol. 2. Translated by Jeffrey Hopkins. Boulder, CO: Snow Lion, 2017.

———. *Path to Bliss: A Practical Guide to Stages of Meditation*. Translated by Geshe Thupten Jinpa. Ithaca, NY: Snow Lion Publications, 1991.

Tenzin Gyatso, H. H. the Dalai Lama, and Alexander Berzin. *The Gelug/Kagyü Tradition of Mahamudra*. Ithaca, NY: Snow Lion Publications, 1997.

Thokmé Sangpo (Thogs med bzang po). *Jewel Garland: A Commentary on the Ornament for the Mahāyāna Sūtras. Theg pa chen po mdo sde'i rgyan gyi 'grel pa rin po che'i phreng ba.* Varanasi: Vajra Vidya Institute Library, 2014.

———. *Thirty-Seven Practices of Bodhisattvas. Rgyal sras lag len so bdun ma.* Sarnath, Varanasi: Central Institute of Higher Tibetan Studies, 1988.

Tripathi, Ram Shankar, ed. *Piṇḍīkramaḥ Pañcakramaś ca*. Sarnath, Varanasi: Central Institute of Higher Tibetan Studies, 2001.

Tsalpa Kunga Dorjé (Tshal pa Kun dga' rdo rjes). *Red Annals. Deb ther dmar po.* Beijing: Mi rigs dpe skrun khang, 1981.

Tsang Nyön Heruka. *The Life of Marpa the Translator: Seeing Accomplishes All.* Translated by the Nālandā Translation Committee. Boston: Shambhala Publications, 1982.

Tsonawa, Losang Norbu. *Indian Buddhist Pandits from "The Jewel Garland of Buddhist History."* Dharamsala: Library of Tibetan Works and Archives, 1985.

Tsong-kha-pa. *The Great Treatise on the Stages of the Path to Enlightenment*, 3 vols. Translated by the Lamrim Chenmo Translation Committee. Ithaca, NY: Snow Lion Publications, 2000–2004.

Tsongkhapa. *The Middle-Length Treatise on the Stages of the Path to Enlightenment.* Translated by Philip Quarcoo. Somerville, MA: Wisdom Publications, 2021.

Tsongkhapa Losang Drakpa (Tsong kha pa Blo bzang grags pa). *Cakrasaṃvara*

Prayer. *Bde mchog smon lam*. In Krung go bod brgyud, *Collection of Rituals of the Geluk Order*, 2:173–79.

———. *Concise Exposition on the Stages of the Path to Enlightenment / Song of Spiritual Experience*. *Lam rim bsdus don / Nyams mgur*. In *Collected Works*, vol. *kha*, 81–85. Mundgod, India: Drepung Loseling Pethub Khangtsen Education Society, 2019.

———. *Destiny Fulfilled*. *Rtogs brjod mdun legs ma / Rtogs brjod 'dun legs ma*. In *Collected Works*, vol. *kha*, 76–81. Mundgod, India: Drepung Loseling Pethub Khangtsen Education Society, 2019.

———. *Fulfilling the Disciples' Hopes: Explanation of the Fifty Verses on the Spiritual Guide*. *Bla ma lnga bcu pa'i rnam bshad slob ma'i re ba kun skong*. In *Collected Works*, vol. *ka*, 213–54. Mundgod, India: Drepung Loseling Pethub Khangtsen Education Society, 2019.

———. *Golden Rosary of Eloquence*. *Bstan bcos mngon rtogs rgyan 'grel pa dang bcas pa'i rgya cher bshad pa legs bshad gser gyi phreng ba*. In *Collected Works*, vol. *tsha*. Mundgod, India: Drepung Loseling Pethub Khangtsen Education Society, 2019.

———. *Greater Exposition on the Stages of the Path to Enlightenment*. *Byang chub lam rim che ba*. In *Collected Works*, vol. *pa*. Mundgod, India: Drepung Loseling Pethub Khangtsen Education Society, 2019.

———. *Middle-Length Exposition on the Stages of the Path to Enlightenment*. *Byang chub lam rim 'bring ba*. In *Collected Works*, vol. *pha*. Mundgod, India: Drepung Loseling Pethub Khangtsen Education Society, 2019.

———. *Opening the Door to the Supreme Path*. *Lam rim gsol 'debs lam mchog sgo 'byed / Byang chub lam gyi rim pa'i brgyud pa rnams la gsol ba 'debs pa'i rim pa*. In *Collected Works*, vol. *kha*, 1–4. Mundgod, India: Drepung Loseling Pethub Khangtsen Education Society, 2019.

———. *Sincere Queries on the Salient Points of Spiritual Practice*. *Dge sbyor gyi gnad kyi dri ba snyan bskul lhag bsam rab dkar*. In *Collected Works*, vol. *kha*, 107–26. Mundgod, India: Drepung Loseling Pethub Khangtsen Education Society, 2019.

———. *Supplication to the Lineage Masters of Glorious Guhyasamāja and Self-Generation Recitation According to the Tradition of Tashi Lhunpo Monastery*. *Dpal gsang ba 'dus pa'i bla brgyud gsol 'debs dang bdag bskyed ngag 'don bkra shis lhun po rgyud pa grwa tshang gi 'don rgyun la rje thams cad mkhyen pas zhus dag mdzad pa*. In the *Collected Ritual Texts of Namgyal Monastery* (*Rnam par rgyal ba'i grwa tshang phan bde legs bshad gling 'dus sde'i zhal 'don phyogs gcig tu sdebs pa*), vol. *kha*. Dharamsala, India: Rnam rgyal grwa tshang gi chos spyod, 1977.

———. *Three Principal Aspects of the Path*. *Lam gyi gtso bo rnam gsum*. In *Collected Works*, vol. *kha*, 286–87. Mundgod, India: Drepung Loseling Pethub Khangtsen Education Society, 2019.

Tsuda, Shiníchi, ed. *The Saṁvarodaya-tantra: Selected Chapters*. Tokyo: Hokuseido Press, 1974.

Vaidya, P. L., ed. *Gaṇḍavyūha Sūtram*. Darbhanga: Mithila Institute of Post-Graduate Studies and Research in Sanskrit Learning, 1960.

———, ed. *Jātakamālā*. Darbhanga: Mithila Institute of Post-Graduate Studies and Research in Sanskrit Learning, 1959.

———, ed. *Lalita-vistarah*. Darbhanga: Mithila Institute of Post-Graduate Studies and Research in Sanskrit Learning, 1958.

———, ed. *Śikṣā-samuccaya*. Darbhanga: Mithila Institute of Post-Graduate Studies and Research in Sanskrit Learning, 1960.

Vetturini, Gianpaolo. *The bKa' gdams pa School of Tibetan Buddhism*. PhD diss., SOAS, University of London, 2007.

Walshe, Maurice. *The Long Discourses of the Buddha: A Translation of the Dīgha Nikāya*. Boston: Wisdom Publications, 1995.

Yangchen Gawai Lodrö (Dbyangs can dga' ba'i blo gros). *A Brief Essential Explanation Deciphering the Terms in the Great Exposition of the Stages of the Path to Enlightenment. Byang chub lam gyi rim pa chen po las byung ba'i brda bkrol nyer mkho bsdus pa*. In *Collected Works*, 1: 46–110. Lanzhou: Kan su'u mi rigs dpe skrun khang, 2011.

Yarlungpa Drakpa Gyaltsen (Yar klung pa Grags pa rgyal mtshan). *Praise of the Dharma Lord Sakya Paṇḍita Kunga Gyaltsen. Chos kyi rje sa skya paṇḍita kun dga' rgyal mtshan dpal bzang po la bstod pa*. In *Path and Result of the Sakya Tradition* (*Sa skya'i lam 'bras*), 1:73–86. Dergé Dzongsar: Rdzong sar lnga rig slob gling, 2007.

Ye, Shaoyong, ed. *Mūlamadhyamakakārikā: Dbu ma rtsa ba'i tshig le'ur byas pa shes rab ces bya ba; Zhonglun song; Fanzanghan hejiao, daodu, yizhu*. Shanghai: Zhongxi shuju, 2011.

Yongzin Lingtsang Labrang, ed. *Commentaries on the Stages of the Path to Enlightenment*, vol. 3. *Byang chub lam gyi rim pa'i khrid yig*, vol. 3. Mundgod, India: Yongzin Lingtsang Labrang, 2012.

Yuyama, Akira. *Prajñā-pāramitā-ratna-guṇa-saṃcaya-gāthā (Sanskrit Recension A): Edited with an Introduction, Bibliographical Notes and a Tibetan Version from Tunhuang*. London: Cambridge University Press, 1976.

Index

C

E

Q

R

About the Authors

THE AUTHOR OF *Swift Path*, Paṇchen Losang Yeshé, is commonly known as the Second Paṇchen Lama. In 1668, at the age of four, he was recognized as the reincarnation of the famous teacher Losang Chökyi Gyaltsen by the Fifth Dalai Lama and enthroned at Tashi Lhunpo Monastery in Shigatsé. Years later, he conferred ordination vows on the Sixth Dalai Lama and subsequently the Seventh Dalai Lama. By the time he passed way in 1737 at the age of about seventy-four, he had written on a vast range of subjects, including biographies, poetry, lamrim explanations, tantric commentaries, and supplication prayers, which are available in his collected works.

SZEGEE TOH holds an honors degree in mathematics from the National University of Singapore. She graduated from the FPMT (Foundation for the Preservation of the Mahayana Tradition) Masters Program in Buddhist philosophy in 2004. Since then she has served variously as interpreter and teaching assistant in the Masters Programs held in Istituto Lama Tzong Khapa, Italy, and Nalanda Monastery, France. Several of her text translations are used in the FPMT study programs.

What to Read Next from Wisdom Publications

Liberation in the Palm of Your Hand
A Concise Discourse on the Path to Enlightenment
Pabongka Rinpoche
Edited by Trijang Rinpoche
Translated by Michael Richards

"The richest and most enjoyable volume from the lamrim tradition . . . published to date."—*Golden Drum*

The Middle-Length Treatise on the Stages of the Path to Enlightenment
Tsongkhapa
Translated by Philip Quarcoo

Tsongkhapa (1357–1419), author of the well-known *Great Treatise on the Stages of the Path to Enlightenment* and guru to the First Dalai Lama, is renowned as perhaps Tibet's greatest scholar-saint. A dozen years after writing his *Great Treatise*, he wrote the *Middle-Length Treatise on the Stages of the Path to Enlightenment*, presented here in its first complete English translation.

Steps on the Path to Enlightenment (5 vols.)
A Commentary on Tsongkhapa's Lamrim Chenmo
Geshe Lhundub Sopa

"An indispensable companion to Tsongkhapa's elegant and elaborate Great Exposition on the Stages of the Path."—*Buddhadharma*

Practicing the Path
A Commentary on the Lamrim Chenmo
Yangsi Rinpoche
Foreword by Geshe Lhundub Sopa
Preface by Lama Zopa Rinpoche

"It brings this great classical tradition into the very palms of our hands." —Jose Ignacio Cabezón, XIVth Dalai Lama Professor of Tibetan Buddhism and Cultural Studies, University of California, Santa Barbara

The Easy Path
Illuminating the First Panchen Lama's Secret Instructions
Gyumed Khensur Lobsang Jampa
Edited by Lorne Ladner

"A marvel."—Janice Willis, author of *Dreaming Me: Black, Baptist, and Buddhist*

Wisdom Energy
Basic Buddhist Teachings
Lama Thubten Yeshe and Lama Zopa Rinpoche

"This is a superb book that presents basic Buddhist teachings with great lucidity and clarity."—*Resource Magazine*

Stages of the Path and the Oral Transmission
Selected Teachings of the Geluk School
Translated by Thupten Jinpa

"Because so many of its doctrinal works have been translated into English, it is often assumed that the Geluk tradition is concerned above all with scholastic philosophy. However, like all Tibetan traditions, the Geluk has a rich canon of devotional works, meditation manuals, and practical instructions for the vision of reality. The most famous of those works are collected in this remarkable volume, works composed by some of the greatest masters and saints of the Land of Snows."—Donald Lopez, Arthur E. Link Distinguished University Professor of Buddhist and Tibetan Studies, University of Michigan

About Wisdom Publications

Wisdom Publications is the leading publisher of classic and contemporary Buddhist books and practical works on mindfulness. To learn more about us or to explore our other books, please visit our website at wisdomexperience.org or contact us at the address below.

Wisdom Publications
199 Elm Street
Somerville, MA 02144 USA

We are a 501(c)(3) organization, and donations in support of our mission are tax deductible.

Wisdom Publications is affiliated with the Foundation for the Preservation of the Mahayana Tradition (FPMT).